hurchill, Jeremy.
onda VFR750 & 700
-fours owners workshop
c199.
994
3305000...3034
GI   02/14/96

D0817163

Santa Clara County
LIBRARY

Renewals:
(800) 471-0991
www.santaclaracountylib.org

Honda VFR750 & 700 V-Fours Owners Workshop Manual

by Jeremy Churchill and Mark Coombs

Models covered:

Honda VFR750F. 748cc. US 1986, and 1990 through 1994
Honda VFR750F. 748cc. UK 1986 through 1994
Honda VFR700F & FII. 699cc. US 1986 and 1987

ABCDE
FGHIJ
KLMNO
PQRST

Haynes Publishing
Sparkford Nr Yeovil
Somerset BA22 7JJ England

Haynes North America, Inc
861 Lawrence Drive
Newbury Park
California 91320 USA

Acknowledgments

Our thanks to Andy Stokes and P.R. Taylor & Sons of Chippenham who supplied the VFR750F-L, to Paul Branson Motorcycles of Yeovil who supplied the VFR750F-H, and to Bridge Motorcycle World of Exeter who supplied the VFR750F-R model. We would also like to thank NGK Spark Plugs (UK) Ltd for supplying the color spark plug condition photos and the Avon Rubber Company for supplying information on tire fitting.

© Haynes North America, Inc. 1995

With permission from J.H. Haynes & Co. Ltd.

A book in the Haynes Owners Workshop Manual Series

Printed by J. H. Haynes & Co. Ltd., Sparkford, Nr Yeovil, Somerset BA22 7JJ, England

---

All rights reserved. No part of this book may be reproduced or transmitted in any form or by any means, electronic or mechanical, including photocopying, recording or by any information storage or retrieval system, without permission in writing from the copyright holder.

ISBN 1 56392 101 4

Library of Congress Catalog Card Number 95-75235

British Library Cataloguing in Publication Data
A catalogue record for this book is available from the British Library

---

We take great pride in the accuracy of information given in this manual, but motorcycle manufacturers make alterations and design changes during the production run of a particular motorcycle of which they do not inform us. No liability can be accepted by the authors or publishers for loss, damage or injury caused by any errors in, or omissions from, the information given.

94-280

Contents

Right side view of the 1987 Honda VFR750F-H

Right front view of the 1988 Honda VFR750F-J

Right front view of the 1990 Honda VFR750F-L

Right front view of the 1994 Honda VFR750F-R

About this manual

Its purpose

The purpose of this manual is to help you get the best value from your motorcycle. It can do so in several ways. It can help you decide what work must be done, even if you choose to have it done by a dealer service department or a repair shop; it provides information and procedures for routine maintenance and servicing; and it offers diagnostic and repair procedures to follow when trouble occurs.

We hope you use the manual to tackle the work yourself. For many simpler jobs, doing it yourself may be quicker than arranging an appointment to get the vehicle into a shop and making the trips to leave it and pick it up. More importantly, a lot of money can be saved by avoiding the expense the shop must pass on to you to cover its labor and overhead costs. An added benefit is the sense of satisfaction and accomplishment that you feel after doing the job yourself.

Using the manual

The manual is divided into Chapters. Each Chapter is divided into numbered Sections, which are headed in bold type between horizontal lines. Each Section consists of consecutively numbered paragraphs or steps.

At the beginning of each numbered Section you will be referred to any illustrations which apply to the procedures in that Section. The reference numbers used in illustration captions pinpoint the pertinent Section and the Step within that Section. That is, illustration 3.2 means the illustration refers to Section 3 and Step (or paragraph) 2 within that Section.

Procedures, once described in the text, are not normally repeated. When it's necessary to refer to another Chapter, the reference will be given as Chapter and Section number. Cross references given without use of the word `Chapter' apply to Sections and/or paragraphs in the same Chapter. For example, `see Section 8' means in the same Chapter.

References to the left or right side of the vehicle assume you are sitting on the seat, facing forward.

Motorcycle manufacturers continually make changes to specifications and recommendations, and these, when notified, are incorporated into our manuals at the earliest opportunity.

Even though we have prepared this manual with extreme care, neither the publisher nor the authors can accept responsibility for any errors in, or omissions from, the information given.

NOTE

A **Note** provides information necessary to properly complete a procedure or information which will make the procedure easier to understand.

CAUTION

A **Caution** provides a special procedure or special steps which must be taken while completing the procedure where the Caution is found. Not heeding a Caution can result in damage to the assembly being worked on.

WARNING

A **Warning** provides a special procedure or special steps which must be taken while completing the procedure where the Warning is found. Not heeding a Warning can result in personal injury.

Introduction to the Honda VFR700 & 750 V-Fours

The Honda VFR750F (and VFR700F) is a high-performance sport/touring motorcycle.

The engine is a liquid-cooled, 90° Vee-four with double overhead camshafts and four valves per cylinder. The only significant change to the engine unit occurred in 1990 when revised cylinder heads and valve gear were fitted.

Fuel is delivered through four Keihin CV carburetors.

The front suspension is by a pair of oil-damped, coil spring, telescopic fork legs. The forks on early (1986 through 1989) models are equipped with a mechanical anti-dive system.

The rear suspension uses Honda's Pro-Link design, which employs a shock absorber/spring unit mounted ahead of the swingarm. The suspension provides a progressive damping effect. On early (1986 through 1989) models, the swingarm is of the conventional type, and on later (1990-on) models the swingarm is of the single-sided Pro-arm type.

The front brake uses dual discs and the rear brake use a single disc.

Identification numbers

The frame serial number is stamped into the right side of the steering head, and is also stamped on the identification plate attached to the right side of the frame. The engine number is stamped into the right upper side of the crankcase, directly above the clutch unit. Both of these numbers should be recorded and kept in a safe place so they can be furnished to law enforcement officials in the event of a theft.

The frame serial number, engine serial number and carburetor identification number should also be kept in a handy place (such as with your driver's license) so they are always available when purchasing or ordering parts for your machine.

Identifying codes

The procedures in this manual identify each model by its code letter. The model code (e.g. VFR750FL) is printed on the color code label, stuck to the rear fender (mudguard) under the seat. The model code and production year can also be determined from the engine and frame serial numbers as follows:

Model code is printed on the color code label located on the rear fender (mudguard)

Frame number is stamped on the right side of the steering head

Frame number can also be found on the identification plate on the right side of the frame

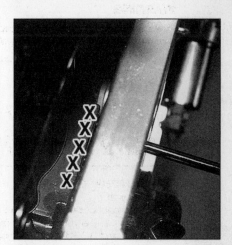

Engine number is stamped on the right side of the crankcase

California models

700 models	Engine number	Frame number
VFR700F-G (1986)	RC26E-2000008 to 2004359	RC261-GM000000 to GM001036
VFR700FII-G (1986)	RC26E-2000237 to 2001470	RC263-GM000001 to GM000500
VFR700FII-H (1987)	RC26E-2100002 to 2102665	RC263-HA105346 to HA105615/RC263-HM100001 to HM100490

750 models		
VFR750F-G (1986)	RC24E-2000519 on	RC241-GM000002 on
VFR750F-L (1990)	RC36E-2006122 to 2010154	RC361-LM000011 to LM000227
VFR750F-M (1991)	RC36E-2100001 to 2104645	RC361-MM100001 to MM100403
VFR750F-N (1992)	RC36E-2201399 to 2202943	RC361-NM200006 to NM200186
VFR750F-P (1993)	RC36E-2300001 on	RC361-PM300001 on
VFR750F-R (1994)	RC36E-2400001 on	RC361-RM400001 on

US models (except California)

700 models	Engine number	Frame number
VFR700F-G (1986)	RC26E-2000004 to 2004121	RC260-GM000000 to GM001826
VFR700FII-G (1986)	RC26E-2000065 to 2001875	RC262-GM000001 to GM001000
VFR700FII-H (1987)	RC26E-2100001 to 2101798	RC262-HA105001 to HA105395/RC262-HM100001 to HM101781

750 models	Engine number	Frame number
VFR750F-G (1986)	RC24E-2000485 on	RC240-GM000008 on
VFR750F-L (1990)	RC36E-2006112 to 2010294	RC360-LM000009 to LM000788
VFR750F-M (1991)	RC36E-2100001 to 2104057	RC360-MM100001 to MM101581
VFR750F-N (1992)	RC36E-2201394 to 2208553	RC360-NM200008 to NM200817
VFR750F-P (1993)	RC36E-2300006 on	RC360-PM300001 on
VFR750F-R (1994)	RC36E-2400068 on	RC360-RM400003 on

UK models

	Engine number	Frame number
VFR750F-G (1986)	RC24E-2000101 to 2013035	RC24-2000068 to 2009621
VFR750F-H (1987)	RC24E-2100065 to 2104493	RC24-2100061 to 2104084
VFR750F-J (1988)	RC24E-2202367 on	RC24-2202353 on
VFR750F-K (1989)	RC24E-2300001 on	RC24-2300001 on
VFR750F-L (1990)	RC36E-2000085 to 2013323	RC36-2000067 to 2010938
VFR750F-M (1991)	RC36E-2101280 to 2112012	RC36-2101254 to 2108971
VFR750F-N (1992)	RC36E-2200020 to 2208633	RC36-2200020 to 2206995
VFR750F-P (1993)	RC36E-2300001 on	RC36-2300001 on
VFR750F-R (1994)	RC36E-2400024 on	RC36-2400015 on

Buying parts

Once you have found all the identification numbers, record them for reference when buying parts. Since the manufacturers change specifications, parts and vendors (companies that manufacture various components on the machine), providing the ID numbers is the only way to be reasonably sure that you are buying the correct parts.

Whenever possible, take the worn part to the dealer so direct comparison with the new component can be made. Along the trail from the manufacturer to the parts shelf, there are numerous places that the part can end up with the wrong number or be listed incorrectly.

The two places to purchase new parts for your motorcycle - the accessory store and the franchised dealer - differ in the type of parts they carry. While dealers can obtain virtually every part for your motorcycle, the accessory dealer is usually limited to normal high wear items such as shock absorbers, tune-up parts, various engine gaskets, cables, chains, brake parts, etc. Rarely will an accessory outlet have major suspension components, cylinders, transmission gears, or cases.

Used parts can be obtained for roughly half the price of new ones, but you can't always be sure of what you're getting. Once again, take your worn part to the wrecking yard (breaker) for direct comparison.

Whether buying new, used or rebuilt parts, the best course is to deal directly with someone who specializes in parts for your particular make.

General specifications

Wheelbase
    G through K models .... 1480 mm (58.3 in)
    L model onward .... 1470 mm (57.9 in)
Overall length
    G through K models .... 2175 mm (85.6 in)
    L through P models .... 2180 mm (85.8 in)
    R models .... 2100 mm (82.7 in)
Overall width
    G through K models .... 730 mm (28.7 in)
    L through P models .... 700 mm (27.6 in)
    R models .... 720 mm (28.3 in)
Overall height
    G and H models .... 1170 mm (46.1 in)
    J model onward... 1185 mm (46.7 in)
Seat height... 800 mm (31.5 in)
Ground clearance
    G through K models .... 135 mm (5.3 in)
    L model onwards.. 130 mm (5.1 in)
Weight (with oil and full fuel tank)
    G and H models .... 222 kg (489 lb)
    J and K models .... 226 kg (498 lb)
    L through P models .... 240 kg (529 lb)
    R models .... 236 kg (520 lb)

Maintenance techniques, tools and working facilities

Basic maintenance techniques

There are a number of techniques involved in maintenance and repair that will be referred to throughout this manual. Application of these techniques will enable the amateur mechanic to be more efficient, better organized and capable of performing the various tasks properly, which will ensure that the repair job is thorough and complete.

Fastening systems

Fasteners, basically, are nuts, bolts and screws used to hold two or more parts together. There are a few things to keep in mind when working with fasteners. Almost all of them use a locking device of some type (either a lock washer, locknut, locking tab or thread adhesive). All threaded fasteners should be clean, straight, have undamaged threads and undamaged corners on the hex head where the wrench fits. Develop the habit of replacing all damaged nuts and bolts with new ones.

Rusted nuts and bolts should be treated with a penetrating oil to ease removal and prevent breakage. Some mechanics use turpentine in a spout type oil can, which works quite well. After applying the rust penetrant, let it -work for a few minutes before trying to loosen the nut or bolt. Badly rusted fasteners may have to be chiseled off or removed with a special nut breaker, available at tool stores.

If a bolt or stud breaks off in an assembly, it can be drilled out and removed with a special tool called an E-Z out (or screw extractor). Most dealer service departments and motorcycle repair shops can perform this task, as well as others (such as the repair of threaded holes that have been stripped out).

Flat washers and lock washers, when removed from an assembly, should always be replaced exactly as removed. Replace any damaged washers with new ones. Always use a flat washer between a lock washer and any soft metal surface (such as aluminum), thin sheet metal or plastic. Special locknuts can only be used once or twice before they lose their locking ability and must be replaced.

Tightening sequences and procedures

When threaded fasteners are tightened, they are often tightened to a specific torque value (torque is basically a twisting force). Over-tightening the fastener can weaken it and cause it to break, while under-tightening can cause it to eventually come loose. Each bolt, depending on the material it's made of, the diameter of its shank and the material it is threaded into, has a specific torque value, which is noted in the Specifications. Be sure to follow the torque recommendations closely.

Fasteners laid out in a pattern (i.e. cylinder head bolts, engine case bolts, etc.) must be loosened or tightened in a sequence to avoid warping the component. Initially, the bolts/nuts should go on finger tight only. Next, they should be tightened one full turn each, in a criss-cross or diagonal pattern. After each one has been tightened one full turn, return to the first one tightened and tighten them all one half turn, following the same pattern. Finally, tighten each of them one quarter turn at a time until each fastener has been tightened to the proper torque. To loosen and remove the fasteners the procedure would be reversed.

Disassembly sequence

Component disassembly should be done with care and purpose to help ensure that the parts go back together properly during reassembly. Always keep track of the sequence in which parts are removed. Take note of special characteristics or marks on parts that can be installed more than one way (such as a grooved thrust washer on a shaft). It's a good idea to lay the disassembled parts out on a clean surface in the order that they were removed. It may also be helpful to make sketches or take instant photos of components before removal.

When removing fasteners from a component, keep track of their locations. Sometimes threading a bolt back in a part, or putting the washers and nut back on a stud, can prevent mix-ups later. If nuts and bolts can't be returned to their original locations, they should be kept in a compartmented box or a series of small boxes. A cupcake or muffin tin is ideal for this purpose, since each cavity can hold the bolts and nuts from a particular area (i.e. engine case bolts, valve cover bolts, engine mount bolts, etc.). A pan of this type is especially helpful when working on assemblies with very small parts (such as the carburetors and the valve train). The cavities can be marked with paint or tape to identify the contents.

Whenever wiring looms, harnesses or connectors are separated, it's a good idea to identify the two halves with numbered pieces of masking tape so they can be easily reconnected.

Gasket sealing surfaces

Throughout any motorcycle, gaskets are used to seal the mating surfaces between components and keep lubricants, fluids, vacuum or pressure contained in an assembly.

Many times these gaskets are coated with a liquid or paste type gasket sealing compound before assembly. Age, heat and pressure can sometimes cause the two parts to stick together so tightly that they are very difficult to separate. In most cases, the part can be loosened by striking it with a soft-faced hammer near the mating surfaces. A regular hammer can be used if a block of wood is placed between the hammer and the part. Do not hammer on cast parts or parts that could be easily damaged. With any particularly stubborn part, always recheck to make sure that every fastener has been removed.

Avoid using a screwdriver or bar to pry apart components, as they can easily mar the gasket sealing surfaces of the parts (which must remain smooth). If prying is absolutely necessary, use a piece of wood, but keep in mind that extra clean-up will be necessary if the wood splinters.

After the parts are separated, the old gasket must be carefully scraped off and the gasket surfaces cleaned. Stubborn gasket material can be soaked with a gasket remover (available in aerosol cans) to soften it so it can be easily scraped off. A scraper can be fashioned from a piece of copper tubing by flattening and sharpening one end. Copper is recommended because it is usually softer than the surfaces to be scraped, which reduces the chance of gouging the part. Some gaskets can be removed with a wire brush, but regardless of the method used, the mating surfaces must be left clean and smooth. If for some reason the gasket surface is gouged, then a gasket sealer thick enough to fill scratches will have to be used during reassembly of the components. For most applications, a non-drying (or semi-drying) gasket sealer is best.

Hose removal tips

Hose removal precautions closely parallel gasket removal precautions. Avoid scratching or gouging the surface that the hose mates against or the connection may leak. Because of various chemical reactions, the rubber in hoses can bond itself to the metal spigot that the hose fits over. To remove a hose, first loosen the hose clamps that secure it to the spigot. Then, with slip joint pliers, grab the hose at the clamp and rotate it around the spigot. Work it back and forth until it is completely free, then pull it off (silicone or other lubricants will ease removal if they can be applied between the hose and the outside of the spigot). Apply the same lubricant to the inside of the hose and the outside of the spigot to simplify installation.

If a hose clamp is broken or damaged, do not reuse it. Also, do not reuse hoses that are cracked, split or torn.

Spark plug gap adjusting tool

Feeler gauge set

Control cable pressure luber

Hand impact screwdriver and bits

Tools

A selection of good tools is a basic requirement for anyone who plans to maintain and repair a motorcycle. For the owner who has few tools, if any, the initial investment might seem high, but when compared to the spiraling costs of routine maintenance and repair, it is a wise one.

To help the owner decide which tools are needed to perform the tasks detailed in this manual, the following tool lists are offered: Maintenance and minor repair, Repair and overhaul and Special. The newcomer to practical mechanics should start off with the Maintenance and minor repair tool kit, which is adequate for the simpler jobs. Then, as confidence and experience grow, the owner can tackle more difficult tasks, buying additional tools as they are needed. Eventually the basic kit will be built into the Repair and overhaul tool set. Over a period of time, the experienced do-it-yourselfer will assemble a tool set complete enough for most repair and overhaul procedures and will add tools from the Special category when it is felt that the expense is justified by the frequency of use.

Maintenance and minor repair tool kit

The tools in this list should be considered the minimum required for performance of routine maintenance, servicing and minor repair work. We recommend the purchase of combination wrenches (box end and open end combined in one wrench); while more expensive than

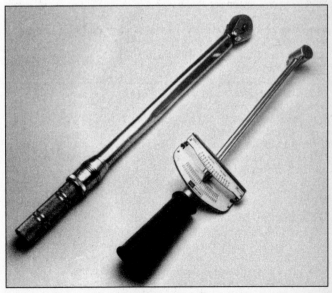

Torque wrenches (left - click; right - beam type)

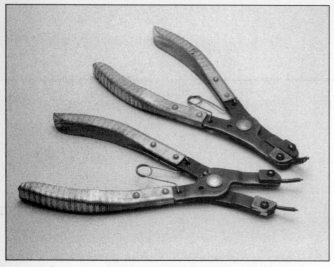

Snap-ring pliers (top - external; bottom - internal)

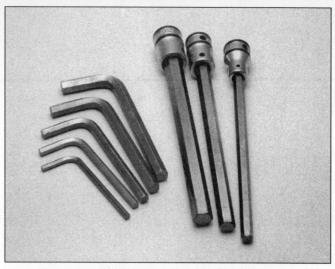

Allen wrenches (left), and Allen head sockets (right)

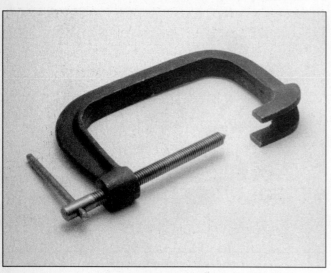

Valve spring compressor

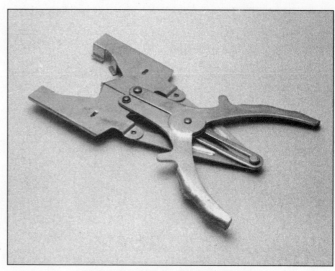

Piston ring removal/installation tool

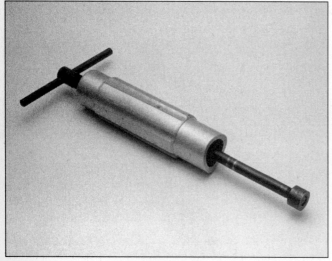

Piston pin puller

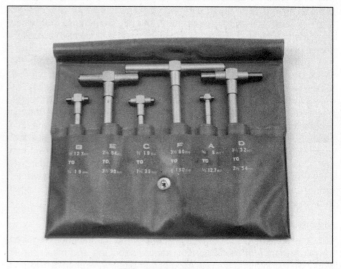

Telescoping gauges

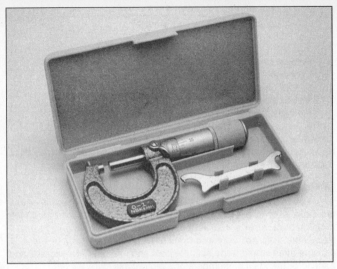

0-to-1 inch micrometer

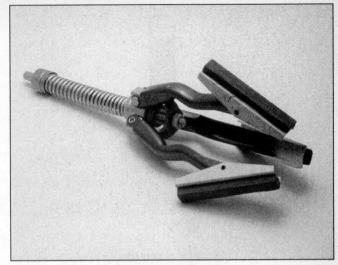

Cylinder surfacing hone

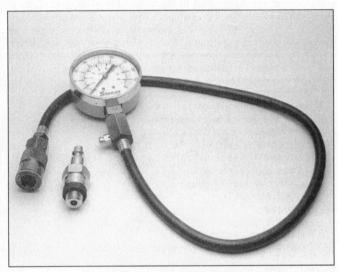

Cylinder compression gauge

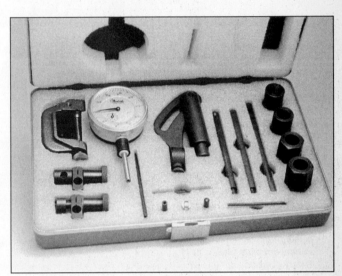

Dial indicator set

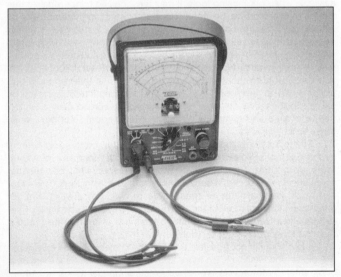

Multimeter (volt/ohm/ammeter)

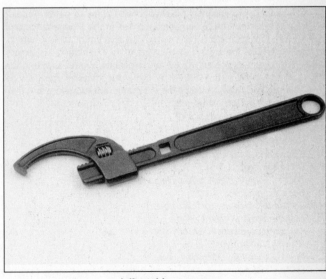

Adjustable spanner

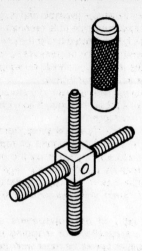

Alternator rotor puller

open-ended ones, they offer the advantages of both types of wrench.

Combination wrench set (6 mm to 22 mm)
Adjustable wrench - 8 in
Spark plug socket (with rubber insert)
Spark plug gap adjusting tool
Feeler gauge set
Standard screwdriver (5/16 in x 6 in)
Phillips screwdriver (No. 2 x 6 in)
Allen (hex) wrench set (4 mm to 12 mm)
Combination (slip-joint) pliers - 6 in
Hacksaw and assortment of blades
Tire pressure gauge
Control cable pressure luber
Grease gun
Oil can
Fine emery cloth
Wire brush
Hand impact screwdriver and bits
Funnel (medium size)
Safety goggles
Drain pan
Work light with extension cord

Repair and overhaul tool set

These tools are essential for anyone who plans to perform major repairs and are intended to supplement those in the Maintenance and minor repair tool kit. Included is a comprehensive set of sockets which, though expensive, are invaluable because of their versatility (especially when various extensions and drives are available). We recommend the 3/8 inch drive over the 1/2 inch drive for general motorcycle maintenance and repair (ideally, the mechanic would have a 3/8 inch drive set and a 1/2 inch drive set).

Alternator rotor removal tool
Socket set(s)
Reversible ratchet
Extension - 6 in
Universal joint
Torque wrench (same size drive as sockets)
Ball pein hammer - 8 oz
Soft-faced hammer (plastic/rubber)
Standard screwdriver (1/4 in x 6 in)
Standard screwdriver (stubby - 5/16 in)
Phillips screwdriver (No. 3 x 8 in)
Phillips screwdriver (stubby - No. 2)
Pliers - locking
Pliers - lineman's

Pliers - needle nose
Pliers - snap-ring (internal and external)
Cold chisel - 1/2 in
Scriber
Scraper (made from flattened copper tubing)
Center punch
Pin punches (1/16, 1/8, 3/16 in)
Steel rule/straightedge - 12 in
Pin-type spanner wrench
A selection of files
Wire brush (large)

Note: Another tool which is often useful is an electric drill with a chuck capacity of 3/8 inch (and a set of good quality drill bits).

Special tools

The tools in this list include those which are not used regularly, are expensive to buy, or which need to be used in accordance with their manufacturer's instructions. Unless these tools will be used frequently, it is not very economical to purchase many of them. A consideration would be to split the cost and use between yourself and a friend or friends (i.e. members of a motorcycle club).

This list primarily contains tools and instruments widely available to the public, as well as some special tools produced by the vehicle manufacturer for distribution to dealer service departments. As a result, references to the manufacturer's special tools are occasionally included in the text of this manual. Generally, an alternative method of doing the job without the special tool is offered. However, sometimes there is no alternative to their use. Where this is the case, and the tool can't be purchased or borrowed, the work should be turned over to the dealer service department or a motorcycle repair shop.

Paddock stand (for models not fitted with a centerstand)
Valve spring compressor
Piston ring removal and installation tool
Piston pin puller
Telescoping gauges
Micrometer(s) and/or dial/Vernier calipers
Cylinder surfacing hone
Cylinder compression gauge
Dial indicator set
Multimeter
Adjustable spanner
Manometer or vacuum gauge set
Small air compressor with blow gun and tire chuck

Buying tools

For the do-it-yourselfer who is just starting to get involved in motorcycle maintenance and repair, there are a number of options available when purchasing tools. If maintenance and minor repair is the extent of the work to be done, the purchase of individual tools is satisfactory. If, on the other hand, extensive work is planned, it would be a good idea to purchase a modest tool set from one of the large retail chain stores. A set can usually be bought at a substantial savings over the individual tool prices (and they often come with a tool box). As additional tools are needed, add-on sets, individual tools and a larger tool box can be purchased to expand the tool selection. Building a tool set gradually allows the cost of the tools to be spread over a longer period of time and gives the mechanic the freedom to choose only those tools that will actually be used.

Tool stores and motorcycle dealers will often be the only source of some of the special tools that are needed, but regardless of where tools are bought, try to avoid cheap ones (especially when buying screwdrivers and sockets) because they won't last very long. There are plenty of tools around at reasonable prices, but always aim to purchase items which meet the relevant national safety standards. The expense involved in replacing cheap tools will eventually be greater than the initial cost of quality tools.

It is obviously not possible to cover the subject of tools fully here. For those who wish to learn more about tools and their use, there is a book entitled *Motorcycle Workshop Practice Manual* (Book no. 1454) available from the publishers of this manual. It also provides an introduction to basic workshop practice which will be of interest to a home mechanic working on any type of motorcycle.

Care and maintenance of tools

Good tools are expensive, so it makes sense to treat them with respect. Keep them clean and in usable condition and store them properly when not in use. Always wipe off any dirt, grease or metal chips before putting them away. Never leave tools lying around in the work area.

Some tools, such as screwdrivers, pliers, wrenches and sockets, can be hung on a panel mounted on the garage or workshop wall, while others should be kept in a tool box or tray. Measuring instruments, gauges, meters, etc. must be carefully stored where they can't be damaged by weather or impact from other tools.

When tools are used with care and stored properly, they will last a very long time. Even with the best of care, tools will wear out if used frequently. When a tool is damaged or worn out, replace it; subsequent jobs will be safer and more enjoyable if you do.

Working facilities

Not to be overlooked when discussing tools is the workshop. If anything more than routine maintenance is to be carried out, some sort of suitable work area is essential.

It is understood, and appreciated, that many home mechanics do not have a good workshop or garage available and end up removing an engine or doing major repairs outside (it is recommended, however, that the overhaul or repair be completed under the cover of a roof).

A clean, flat workbench or table of comfortable working height is an absolute necessity. The workbench should be equipped with a vise that has a jaw opening of at least four inches.

As mentioned previously, some clean, dry storage space is also required for tools, as well as the lubricants, fluids, cleaning solvents, etc. which soon become necessary.

Sometimes waste oil and fluids, drained from the engine or cooling system during normal maintenance or repairs, present a disposal problem. To avoid pouring them on the ground or into a sewage system, simply pour the used fluids into large containers, seal them with caps and take them to an authorized disposal site or service station. Plastic jugs (such as old antifreeze containers) are ideal for this purpose.

Always keep a supply of old newspapers and clean rags available. Old towels are excellent for mopping up spills. Many mechanics use rolls of paper towels for most work because they are readily available and disposable. To help keep the area under the motorcycle clean, a large cardboard box can be cut open and flattened to protect the garage or shop floor.

Whenever working over a painted surface (such as the fuel tank) cover it with an old blanket or bedspread to protect the finish.

Safety first

Professional mechanics are trained in safe working procedures. However enthusiastic you may be about getting on with the job at hand, take the time to ensure that your safety is not put at risk. A moment's lack of attention can result in an accident, as can failure to observe simple precautions.

There will always be new ways of having accidents, and the following is not a comprehensive list of all dangers; it is intended rather to make you aware of the risks and to encourage a safe approach to all work you carry out on your bike.

Essential DOs and DON'Ts

DON'T start the engine without first ascertaining that the transmission is in neutral.

DON'T suddenly remove the pressure cap from a hot cooling system - cover it with a cloth and release the pressure gradually first, or you may get scalded by escaping coolant.

DON'T attempt to drain oil until you are sure it has cooled sufficiently to avoid scalding you.

DON'T grasp any part of the engine or exhaust system without first ascertaining that it is cool enough not to burn you.

DON'T allow brake fluid or antifreeze to contact the machine's paint work or plastic components.

DON'T siphon toxic liquids such as fuel, hydraulic fluid or antifreeze by mouth, or allow them to remain on your skin.

DON'T inhale dust - it may be injurious to health (see *Asbestos* heading).

DON'T allow any spilled oil or grease to remain on the floor - wipe it up right away, before someone slips on it.

DON'T use ill fitting wrenches or other tools which may slip and cause injury.

DON'T attempt to lift a heavy component which may be beyond your capability - get assistance.

DON'T rush to finish a job or take unverified short cuts.

DON'T allow children or animals in or around an unattended vehicle.

DON'T inflate a tire to a pressure above the recommended maximum. Apart from over stressing the carcase and wheel rim, in extreme cases the tire may blow off forcibly.

DO ensure that the machine is supported securely at all times. This is especially important when the machine is blocked up to aid wheel or fork removal.

DO take care when attempting to loosen a stubborn nut or bolt. It is generally better to pull on a wrench, rather than push, so that if you slip, you fall away from the machine rather than onto it.

DO wear eye protection when using power tools such as drill, sander, bench grinder etc.

DO use a barrier cream on your hands prior to undertaking dirty jobs - it will protect your skin from infection as well as making the dirt easier to remove afterwards; but make sure your hands aren't left slippery. Note that long-term contact with used engine oil can be a health

hazard.

DO keep loose clothing (cuffs, ties etc. and long hair) well out of the way of moving mechanical parts.

DO remove rings, wristwatch etc., before working on the vehicle - especially the electrical system.

DO keep your work area tidy - it is only too easy to fall over articles left lying around.

DO exercise caution when compressing springs for removal or installation. Ensure that the tension is applied and released in a controlled manner, using suitable tools which preclude the possibility of the spring escaping violently.

DO ensure that any lifting tackle used has a safe working load rating adequate for the job.

DO get someone to check periodically that all is well, when working alone on the vehicle.

DO carry out work in a logical sequence and check that everything is correctly assembled and tightened afterwards.

DO remember that your vehicle's safety affects that of yourself and others. If in doubt on any point, get professional advice.

IF, in spite of following these precautions, you are unfortunate enough to injure yourself, seek medical attention as soon as possible.

Asbestos

Certain friction, insulating, sealing and other products - such as brake pads, clutch linings, gaskets, etc. - contain asbestos. *Extreme care must be taken to avoid inhalation of dust from such products since it is hazardous to health*. If in doubt, assume that they *do* contain asbestos.

Fire

Remember at all times that gasoline (petrol) is highly flammable. Never smoke or have any kind of naked flame around, when working on the vehicle. But the risk does not end there - a spark caused by an electrical short-circuit, by two metal surfaces contacting each other, by careless use of tools, or even by static electricity built up in your body under certain conditions, can ignite gasoline (petrol) vapor, which in a confined space is highly explosive. Never use gasoline (petrol) as a cleaning solvent. Use an approved safety solvent.

Always disconnect the battery ground (earth) terminal before working on any part of the fuel or electrical system, and never risk spilling fuel on to a hot engine or exhaust.

It is recommended that a fire extinguisher of a type suitable for fuel and electrical fires is kept handy in the garage or workplace at all times. Never try to extinguish a fuel or electrical fire with water.

Fumes

Certain fumes are highly toxic and can quickly cause unconsciousness and even death if inhaled to any extent. Gasoline (petrol) vapor comes into this category, as do the vapors from certain solvents such as trichloroethylene. Any draining or pouring of such volatile fluids should be done in a well ventilated area.

When using cleaning fluids and solvents, read the instructions carefully. Never use materials from unmarked containers - they may give off poisonous vapors.

Never run the engine of a motor vehicle in an enclosed space such as a garage. Exhaust fumes contain carbon monoxide which is extremely poisonous; if you need to run the engine, always do so in the open air or at least have the rear of the vehicle outside the workplace.

The battery

Never cause a spark, or allow a naked light near the vehicle's battery. It will normally be giving off a certain amount of hydrogen gas, which is highly explosive.

Always disconnect the battery ground (earth) terminal before working on the fuel or electrical systems (except where noted).

If possible, loosen the filler plugs or cover when charging the battery from an external source. Do not charge at an excessive rate or the battery may burst.

Take care when topping up, cleaning or carrying the battery. The acid electrolyte, even when diluted, is very corrosive and should not be allowed to contact the eyes or skin. Always wear rubber gloves and goggles or a face shield. If you ever need to prepare electrolyte yourself, always add the acid slowly to the water; never add the water to the acid.

Electricity

When using an electric power tool, inspection light etc., always ensure that the appliance is correctly connected to its plug and that, where necessary, it is properly grounded (earthed). Do not use such appliances in damp conditions and, again, beware of creating a spark or applying excessive heat in the vicinity of fuel or fuel vapor. Also ensure that the appliances meet national safety standards.

A severe electric shock can result from touching certain parts of the electrical system, such as the spark plug wires (HT leads), when the engine is running or being cranked, particularly if components are damp or the insulation is defective. Where an electronic ignition system is used, the secondary (HT) voltage is much higher and could prove fatal.

Motorcycle chemicals and lubricants

A number of chemicals and lubricants are available for use in motorcycle maintenance and repair. They include a wide variety of products ranging from cleaning solvents and degreasers to lubricants and protective sprays for rubber, plastic and vinyl.

Contact point/spark plug cleaner is a solvent used to clean oily film and dirt from points, grime from electrical connectors and oil deposits from spark plugs. It is oil free and leaves no residue. It can also be used to remove gum and varnish from carburetor jets and other orifices.

Carburetor cleaner is similar to contact point/spark plug cleaner but it usually has a stronger solvent and may leave a slight oily reside. It is not recommended for cleaning electrical components or connections.

Brake system cleaner is used to remove grease or brake fluid from brake system components (where clean surfaces are absolutely necessary and petroleum-based solvents cannot be used); it also leaves no residue.

Silicone-based lubricants are used to protect rubber parts such as hoses and grommets, and are used as lubricants for hinges and locks.

Multi-purpose grease is an all purpose lubricant used wherever grease is more practical than a liquid lubricant such as oil. Some multi-purpose grease is cKolored white and specially formulated to be more resistant to water than ordinary grease.

Gear oil (sometimes called gear lube) is a specially designed oil used in transmissions and final drive units, a s well as other areas where high friction, high temperature lubrication is required. It is available in a number of viscosities (weights) for various applications.

Motor oil, of course, is the lubricant specially formulated for use in the engine. It normally contains a wide variety of additives to prevent corrosion and reduce foaming and wear. Motor oil comes in various weights (viscosity ratings) of from 5 to 80. The recommended weight of the oil depends on the seasonal temperature and the demands on the engine. Light oil is used in cold climates and under light load conditions; heavy oil is used in hot climates and where high loads are encountered. Multi-viscosity oils are designed to have characteristics of both light and heavy oils and are available in a number of weights from 5W-20 to 20W-50.

Gas (petrol) additives perform several functions, depending on their chemical makeup. They usually contain solvents that help dissolve gum and varnish that build up on carburetor and intake parts. They also serve to break down carbon deposits that form on the inside surfaces of the combustion chambers. Some additives contain upper cylinder lubricants for valves and piston rings.

Brake fluid is a specially formulated hydraulic fluid that can withstand the heat and pressure encountered in brake systems. Care must be taken that this fluid does not come in contact with painted surfaces or plastics. An opened container should always be resealed to prevent contamination by water or dirt.

Chain lubricants are formulated especially for use on motorcycle final drive chains. A good chain lube should adhere well and have good penetrating qualities to be effective as a lubricant inside the chain and on the side plates, pins and rollers. Most chain lubes are either the foaming type or quick drying type and are usually marketed as sprays.

Degreasers are heavy duty solvents used to remove grease and grime that may accumulate on engine and frame components. They can be sprayed or brushed on and, depending on the type, are rinsed with either water or solvent.

Solvents are used alone or in combination with degreasers to clean parts and assemblies during repair and overhaul. The home mechanic should use only solvents that are non-flammable and that do not produce irritating fumes.

Gasket sealing compounds may be used in conjunction with gaskets, to improve their sealing capabilities, or alone, to seal metal-to-metal joints. Many gasket sealers can withstand extreme heat, some are impervious to gasoline and lubricants, while others are capable of filling and sealing large cavities. Depending on the intended use, gasket sealers either dry hard or stay relatively soft and pliable. They are usually applied by hand, with a brush, or are sprayed on the gasket sealing surfaces.

Thread cement is an adhesive locking compound that prevents threaded fasteners from loosening because of vibration. It is available in a variety of types for different applications.

Moisture dispersants are usually sprays that can be used to dry out electrical components such as the fuse block and wiring connectors. Some types can also be used as treatment for rubber and as a lubricant for hinges, cables and locks.

Waxes and polishes are used to help protect painted and plated surfaces from the weather. Different types of paint may require the use of different types of wax polish. Some polishes utilize a chemical or abrasive cleaner to help remove the top layer of oxidized (dull) paint on older vehicles. In recent years, many non-wax polishes (that contain a wide variety of chemicals such as polymers and silicones) have been introduced. These non-wax polishes are usually easier to apply and last longer than conventional waxes and polishes.

Troubleshooting

Contents

Engine doesn't start or is difficult to start

1   Starter motor doesn't rotate

1   Engine kill switch Off.
2   Fuse blown. Check fuse block (Chapter 9).
3   Battery voltage low. Check and recharge battery (Chapter 9).
4   Starter motor defective. Make sure the wiring to the starter is secure. Make sure the starter relay clicks when the start button is pushed. If the relay clicks, then the fault is in the wiring or motor.
5   Starter relay faulty. Check it according to the procedure in Chapter 9.
6   Starter button not contacting. The contacts could be wet, corroded or dirty. Disassemble and clean the switch (Chapter 9).
7   Wiring open or shorted. Check all wiring connections and harnesses to make sure that they are dry, tight and not corroded. Also check for broken or frayed wires that can cause a short to ground (earth) (see wiring diagram, Chapter 9).
8   Ignition switch defective. Check the switch according to the procedure in Chapter 9. Replace the switch with a new one if it is defective.
9   Engine kill switch defective. Check for wet, dirty or corroded contacts. Clean or replace the switch as necessary (Chapter 9).
10   Faulty neutral/sidestand/clutch switch(es) (as appropriate). Check the wiring to each switch and the switch itself according to the procedures in Chapter 9.

2   Starter motor rotates but engine does not turn over

1   Starter motor clutch defective. Inspect and repair or replace (Chapter 2).
2   Damaged idler or starter gears. Inspect and replace the damaged parts (Chapter 2).

3   Starter works but engine won't turn over (seized)

Seized engine caused by one or more internally damaged components. Failure due to wear, abuse or lack of lubrication. Damage can include seized valves, followers, camshafts, pistons, crankshaft, connecting rod bearings, or transmission gears or bearings. Refer to Chapter 2 for engine disassembly.

4   No fuel flow

1   No fuel in tank.
2   Fuel pump faulty (see Chapter 9).
3   Tank cap air vent obstructed (not California models). Usually caused by dirt or water. Remove it and clean the cap vent hole.
4   Fuel filter clogged. Remove the tap and clean it and the filter and check the in-line filter (Chapter 1).
5   Fuel line clogged. Pull the fuel line loose and carefully blow through it.
6   Inlet needle valve clogged. For all of the valves to be clogged, either a very bad batch of fuel with an unusual additive has been used, or some other foreign material has entered the tank. Many times after a machine has been stored for many months without running, the fuel turns to a varnish-like liquid and forms deposits on the inlet needle valves and jets. The carburetors should be removed and overhauled if draining the float bowls doesn't solve the problem.

5   Engine flooded

1   Float height too high. Check as described in Chapter 4.

2   Inlet needle valve worn or stuck open. A piece of dirt, rust or other debris can cause the inlet needle to seat improperly, causing excess fuel to be admitted to the float bowl. In this case, the float chamber should be cleaned and the needle and seat inspected. If the needle and seat are worn, then the leaking will persist and the parts should be replaced with new ones (Chapter 4).
3   Starting technique incorrect. Under normal circumstances (i.e., if all the carburetor functions are sound) the machine should start with little or no throttle. When the engine is cold, the choke should be operated and the engine started without opening the throttle. When the engine is at operating temperature, only a very slight amount of throttle should be necessary. If the engine is flooded, turn the fuel tap off and hold the throttle open while cranking the engine. This will allow additional air to reach the cylinders. Remember to turn the fuel tap back on after the engine starts.

6   No spark or weak spark

1   Ignition switch Off.
2   Engine kill switch turned to the Off position.
3   Battery voltage low. Check and recharge battery as necessary (Chapter 9).
4   Spark plug dirty, defective or worn out. Locate reason for fouled plug(s) using spark plug condition chart and follow the plug maintenance procedures in Chapter 1.
5   Spark plug cap or secondary (HT) wiring faulty. Check condition. Replace either or both components if cracks or deterioration are evident (Chapter 5).
6   Spark plug cap not making good contact. Make sure that the plug cap fits snugly over the plug end.
7   Spark unit defective. Check the unit, referring to Chapter 5 for details.
8   Pulse generator defective. Check the unit, referring to Chapter 5 for details.
9   Ignition coil(s) defective. Check the coils, referring to Chapter 5.
10   Ignition or kill switch shorted. This is usually caused by water, corrosion, damage or excessive wear. The switches can be disassembled and cleaned with electrical contact cleaner. If cleaning does not help, replace the switches (Chapter 9).
11   Wiring shorted or broken between:

   a) *Ignition switch and engine kill switch (or blown fuse)*
   b) *Spark unit and engine kill switch*
   c) *Spark unit and ignition coil*
   d) *Ignition coil and plug*
   e) *Spark unit and pulse generator*

Make sure that all wiring connections are clean, dry and tight. Look for chafed and broken wires (Chapters 5 and 9).

7   Compression low

1   Spark plug loose. Remove the plug and inspect the threads. Reinstall and tighten to the specified torque (Chapter 1).
2   Cylinder head not sufficiently tightened down. If the cylinder head is suspected of being loose, then there's a chance that the gasket or head is damaged if the problem has persisted for any length of time. The head bolts should be tightened to the proper torque in the correct sequence (Chapter 2).
3   Improper valve clearance. This means that the valve is not closing completely and compression pressure is leaking past the valve. Check and adjust the valve clearances (Chapter 1).
4   Cylinder and/or piston worn. Excessive wear will cause compression pressure to leak past the rings. This is usually accompanied by worn rings as well. A top end overhaul is necessary (Chapter 2).
5   Piston rings worn, weak, broken, or sticking. Broken or sticking piston rings usually indicate a lubrication or carburation problem that

causes excess carbon deposits or seizures to form on the pistons and rings. Top end overhaul is necessary (Chapter 2).
6 Piston ring-to-groove clearance excessive. This is caused by excessive wear of the piston ring lands. Piston replacement is necessary (Chapter 2).
7 Cylinder head gasket damaged. If the head is allowed to become loose, or if excessive carbon build-up on the piston crown and combustion chamber causes extremely high compression, the head gasket may leak. Retorquing the head is not always sufficient to restore the seal, so gasket replacement is necessary (Chapter 2).
8 Cylinder head warped. This is caused by overheating or improperly tightened head bolts. Machine shop resurfacing or head replacement is necessary (Chapter 2).
9 Valve spring broken or weak. Caused by component failure or wear; the spring(s) must be replaced (Chapter 2).
10 Valve not seating properly. This is caused by a bent valve (from over-revving or improper valve adjustment), burned valve or seat (improper carburation) or an accumulation of carbon deposits on the seat (from carburation or lubrication problems). The valves must be cleaned and/or replaced and the seats serviced if possible (Chapter 2).

8 Stalls after starting

1 Improper choke action. Make sure the choke rod is getting a full stroke and staying in the out position.
2 Ignition malfunction. See Chapter 5.
3 Carburetor malfunction. See Chapter 4.
4 Fuel contaminated. The fuel can be contaminated with either dirt or water, or can change chemically if the machine is allowed to sit for several months or more. Drain the tank and float bowls (Chapter 4).
5 Intake air leak. Check for loose carburetor-to-intake manifold connections, loose or missing vacuum gauge access port cap or screw, or loose carburetor top (Chapter 4).
6 Engine idle speed incorrect. Turn throttle stop screw until the engine idles at the specified rpm (Chapters 1 and 4).

9 Rough idle

1 Ignition malfunction. See Chapter 5.
2 Idle speed incorrect. See Chapter 1.
3 Carburetors not synchronized. Adjust carburetors with vacuum gauge or manometer set as described in Chapter 1.
4 Carburetor malfunction. See Chapter 4.
5 Fuel contaminated. The fuel can be contaminated with either dirt or water, or can change chemically if the machine is allowed to sit for several months or more. Drain the tank and float bowls (Chapter 4).
6 Intake air leak. Check for loose carburetor-to-intake manifold connections, loose or missing vacuum gauge access port cap or screw, or loose carburetor top (Chapter 4).
7 Air cleaner clogged. Service or replace air filter element (Chapter 1).

Poor running at low speed

10 Spark weak

1 Battery voltage low. Check and recharge battery (Chapter 9).
2 Spark plug fouled, defective or worn out. Refer to Chapter 1 for spark plug maintenance.
3 Spark plug cap or high tension wiring defective. Refer to Chapters 1 and 5 for details on the ignition system.
4 Spark plug cap not making contact.
5 Incorrect spark plug. Wrong type, heat range or cap configuration. Check and install correct plugs listed in Chapter 1. A cold plug

or one with a recessed firing electrode will not operate at low speeds without fouling.
6 Spark unit defective. See Chapter 5.
7 Pulse generator defective. See Chapter 5.
8 Ignition coil(s) defective. See Chapter 5.

11 Fuel/air mixture incorrect

1 Pilot screw(s) out of adjustment (Chapter 4).
2 Pilot jet or air passage clogged. Remove and overhaul the carburetors (Chapter 4).
3 Air bleed holes clogged. Remove carburetor and blow out all passages (Chapter 4).
4 Air cleaner clogged, poorly sealed or missing (Chapter 1).
5 Air cleaner housing poorly sealed. Look for cracks, holes or loose clamps and replace or repair defective parts.
6 Fuel level too high or too low. Check the float height (Chapter 4).
7 Fuel tank air vent obstructed (not California models). Make sure that the air vent passage in the filler cap is open.
8 Carburetor intake manifolds loose. Check for cracks, breaks, tears or loose clamps or bolts. Repair or replace the rubber boots.

12 Compression low

1 Spark plug loose. Remove the plug and inspect the threads. Reinstall and tighten to the specified torque (Chapter 1).
2 Cylinder head not sufficiently tightened down. If the cylinder head is suspected of being loose, then there's a chance that the gasket and head are damaged if the problem has persisted for any length of time. The head bolts should be tightened to the proper torque in the correct sequence (Chapter 2).
3 Improper valve clearance. This means that the valve is not closing completely and compression pressure is leaking past the valve. Check and adjust the valve clearances (Chapter 1).
4 Cylinder and/or piston worn. Excessive wear will cause compression pressure to leak past the rings. This is usually accompanied by worn rings as well. A top end overhaul is necessary (Chapter 2).
5 Piston rings worn, weak, broken, or sticking. Broken or sticking piston rings usually indicate a lubrication or carburation problem that causes excess carbon deposits or seizures to form on the pistons and rings. Top end overhaul is necessary (Chapter 2).
6 Piston ring-to-groove clearance excessive. This is caused by excessive wear of the piston ring lands. Piston replacement is necessary (Chapter 2).
7 Cylinder head gasket damaged. If the head is allowed to become loose, or if excessive carbon build-up on the piston crown and combustion chamber causes extremely high compression, the head gasket may leak. Retorquing the head is not always sufficient to restore the seal, so gasket replacement is necessary (Chapter 2).
8 Cylinder head warped. This is caused by overheating or improperly tightened head bolts. Machine shop resurfacing or head replacement is necessary (Chapter 2).
9 Valve spring broken or weak. Caused by component failure or wear; the spring(s) must be replaced (Chapter 2).
10 Valve not seating properly. This is caused by a bent valve (from over-revving or improper valve adjustment), burned valve or seat (improper carburation) or an accumulation of carbon deposits on the seat (from carburation, lubrication problems). The valves must be cleaned and/or replaced and the seats serviced if possible (Chapter 2).

13 Poor acceleration

1 Carburetors leaking or dirty. Overhaul the carburetors (Chapter 4).
2 Timing not advancing. The pulse generator or the spark unit may

be defective. If so, they must be replaced with new ones, as they can't be repaired.

3   Carburetors not synchronized. Adjust them with a vacuum gauge set or manometer (Chapter 1).

4   Engine oil viscosity too high. Using a heavier oil than that recommended in Chapter 1 can damage the oil pump or lubrication system and cause drag on the engine.

5   Brakes dragging. Usually caused by debris which has entered the brake piston seals, or from a warped disc or bent axle. Repair as necessary (Chapter 7).

Poor running or no power at high speed

14 Firing incorrect

1   Air filter restricted. Clean or replace filter (Chapter 1).

2   Spark plug fouled, defective or worn out. See Chapter 1 for spark plug maintenance.

3   Spark plug cap or secondary (HT) wiring defective. See Chapters 1 and 5 for details of the ignition system.

4   Spark plug cap not in good contact. See Chapter 5.

5   Incorrect spark plug. Wrong type, heat range or cap configuration. Check and install correct plugs listed in Chapter 1. A cold plug or one with a recessed firing electrode will not operate at low speeds without fouling.

6   Spark unit defective. See Chapter 5.

7   Ignition coil(s) defective. See Chapter 5.

15 Fuel/air mixture incorrect

1   Main jet clogged. Dirt, water or other contaminants can clog the main jets. Clean the fuel tap filter, the float bowl area, and the jets and carburetor orifices (Chapter 4).

2   Main jet wrong size. The standard jetting is for sea level atmospheric pressure and oxygen content.

3   Throttle shaft-to-carburetor body clearance excessive. Refer to Chapter 4 for inspection and part replacement procedures.

4   Air bleed holes clogged. Remove and overhaul carburetors (Chapter 4).

5   Air cleaner clogged, poorly sealed, or missing (Chapter 1).

6   Air cleaner housing poorly sealed. Look for cracks, holes or loose clamps, and replace or repair defective parts.

7   Fuel level too high or too low. Check the float height (Chapter 4).

8   Fuel tank air vent obstructed (not California models). Make sure the air vent passage in the filler cap is open.

9   Carburetor intake manifolds loose. Check for cracks, breaks, tears or loose clamps or bolts. Repair or replace the rubbers (Chapter 4).

10   Fuel tap/in-line filter clogged. Remove the tap and clean it and the filter and check the in-line filter (Chapter 1).

11   Fuel line clogged. Pull the fuel line loose and carefully blow through it.

16 Compression low

1   Spark plug loose. Remove the plug and inspect the threads. Reinstall and tighten to the specified torque (Chapter 1).

2   Cylinder head not sufficiently tightened down. If the cylinder head is suspected of being loose, then there's a chance that the gasket and head are damaged if the problem has persisted for any length of time. The head bolts should be tightened to the proper torque in the correct sequence (Chapter 2).

3   Improper valve clearance. This means that the valve is not closing completely and compression pressure is leaking past the valve. Check and adjust the valve clearances (Chapter 1).

4   Cylinder and/or piston worn. Excessive wear will cause compression pressure to leak past the rings. This is usually accompanied by worn rings as well. A top end overhaul is necessary (Chapter 2).

5   Piston rings worn, weak, broken, or sticking. Broken or sticking piston rings usually indicate a lubrication or carburation problem that causes excess carbon deposits or seizures to form on the pistons and rings. Top end overhaul is necessary (Chapter 2).

6   Piston ring-to-groove clearance excessive. This is caused by excessive wear of the piston ring lands. Piston replacement is necessary (Chapter 2).

7   Cylinder head gasket damaged. If the head is allowed to become loose, or if excessive carbon build-up on the piston crown and combustion chamber causes extremely high compression, the head gasket may leak. Retorquing the head is not always sufficient to restore the seal, so gasket replacement is necessary (Chapter 2).

8   Cylinder head warped. This is caused by overheating or improperly tightened head bolts. Machine shop resurfacing or head replacement is necessary (Chapter 2).

9   Valve spring broken or weak. Caused by component failure or wear; the spring(s) must be replaced (Chapter 2).

10   Valve not seating properly. This is caused by a bent valve (from over-revving or improper valve adjustment), burned valve or seat (improper carburation) or an accumulation of carbon deposits on the seat (from carburation or lubrication problems). The valves must be cleaned and/or replaced and the seats serviced if possible (Chapter 2).

17 Knocking or pinging

1   Carbon build-up in combustion chamber. Use of a fuel additive that will dissolve the adhesive bonding the carbon particles to the crown and chamber is the easiest way to remove the build-up. Otherwise, the cylinder head will have to be removed and decarbonized (Chapter 2).

2   Incorrect or poor quality fuel. Old or improper grades of fuel can cause detonation. This causes the piston to rattle, thus the knocking or pinging sound. Drain old fuel and always use the recommended fuel grade.

3   Spark plug heat range incorrect. Uncontrolled detonation indicates the plug heat range is too hot. The plug in effect becomes a glow plug, raising cylinder temperatures. Install the proper heat range plug (Chapter 1).

4   Improper air/fuel mixture. This will cause the cylinder to run hot, which leads to detonation. Clogged jets or an air leak can cause this imbalance. See Chapter 4.

18 Miscellaneous causes

1   Throttle valve doesn't open fully. Adjust the cable slack (Chapter 1).

2   Clutch slipping. May be caused by loose or worn clutch components. Refer to Chapter 2 for clutch overhaul procedures.

3   Timing not advancing.

4   Engine oil viscosity too high. Using a heavier oil than the one recommended in Chapter 1 can damage the oil pump or lubrication system and cause drag on the engine.

5   Brakes dragging. Usually caused by debris which has entered the brake piston seals, or from a warped disc or bent axle. Repair as necessary.

Overheating

19 Engine overheats

1   Coolant level low. Check and add coolant (Chapter 1).

2   Leak in cooling system. Check cooling system hoses and radiator

for leaks and other damage. Repair or replace parts as necessary (Chapter 3).

3   Thermostat sticking open or closed. Check and replace as described in Chapter 3.

4   Faulty radiator cap. Remove the cap and have it checked at a service station.

5   Coolant passages clogged. Have the entire system drained and flushed, then refill with fresh coolant.

6   Water pump defective. Remove the pump and check the components (Chapter 3).

7   Clogged radiator fins. Clean them by blowing compressed air through the fins from the backside.

20   Firing incorrect

1   Spark plugs fouled, defective or worn out. See Chapter 1 for spark plug maintenance.

2   Incorrect spark plugs.

3   Faulty ignition coil(s) (Chapter 5).

21   Fuel/air mixture incorrect

1   Main jet clogged. Dirt, water and other contaminants can clog the main jets. Clean the fuel tap filter/in-line filter, the float bowl area and the jets and carburetor orifices (Chapter 4).

2   Main jet wrong size. The standard jetting is for sea level atmospheric pressure and oxygen content.

3   Air cleaner clogged, poorly sealed or missing (Chapter 1).

4   Air cleaner housing poorly sealed. Look for cracks, holes or loose clamps and replace or repair.

5   Fuel level too low. Check float height(s) (Chapter 4).

6   Fuel tank air vent obstructed (not California models). Make sure that the air vent passage in the filler cap is open.

7   Carburetor intake manifolds loose. Check for cracks, breaks, tears or loose clamps or bolts. Repair or replace the rubber joints (Chapter 4).

22   Compression too high

1   Carbon build-up in combustion chamber. Use of a fuel additive that will dissolve the adhesive bonding the carbon particles to the piston crown and chamber is the easiest way to remove the build-up. Otherwise, the cylinder head will have to be removed and decarbonized (Chapter 2).

2   Improperly machined head surface or installation of incorrect gasket during engine assembly.

23   Engine load excessive

1   Clutch slipping. Can be caused by damaged, loose or worn clutch components. Refer to Chapter 2 for overhaul procedures.

2   Engine oil level too high. The addition of too much oil will cause pressurization of the crankcase and inefficient engine operation. Check Specifications and drain to proper level (Chapter 1).

3   Engine oil viscosity too high. Using a heavier oil than the one recommended in Chapter 1 can damage the oil pump or lubrication system as well as cause drag on the engine.

4   Brakes dragging. Usually caused by debris which has entered the brake piston seals, or from a warped disc or bent axle. Repair as necessary.

24   Lubrication inadequate

1   Engine oil level too low. Friction caused by intermittent lack of lubrication or from oil that is overworked can cause overheating. The oil provides a definite cooling function in the engine. Check the oil level (Chapter 1).

2   Poor quality engine oil or incorrect viscosity or type. Oil is rated not only according to viscosity but also according to type. Some oils are not rated high enough for use in this engine. Check the Specifications section and change to the correct oil (Chapter 1).

25   Miscellaneous causes

Modification to exhaust system. Most aftermarket exhaust systems cause the engine to run leaner, which makes it run hotter. When installing an accessory exhaust system, always rejet the carburetors.

Clutch problems

26   Clutch slipping

1   Clutch master cylinder reservoir fluid level too high. Check level (Chapter 1).

2   Friction plates worn or warped. Overhaul the clutch assembly (Chapter 2).

3   Steel plates worn or warped (Chapter 2).

4   Clutch spring(s) broken or weak. Old or heat-damaged (from slipping clutch) springs should be replaced with new ones (Chapter 2).

5   Clutch pushrod bent. Check and, if necessary, replace (Chapter 2).

6   Clutch center or drum unevenly worn. This causes improper engagement of the plates. Replace the damaged or worn parts (Chapter 2).

27   Clutch not disengaging completely

1   Clutch master cylinder reservoir fluid level too low. Top up and bleed the hydraulic system (Chapters 1 and 2).

2   Clutch plates warped or damaged. This will cause clutch drag, which in turn will cause the machine to creep. Overhaul the clutch assembly (Chapter 2).

3   Clutch spring tension uneven. Usually caused by a sagged or broken spring. Check and replace the spring (Chapter 2).

4   Engine oil deteriorated. Old, thin, worn out oil will not provide proper lubrication for the discs, causing the clutch to drag. Replace the oil and filter (Chapter 1).

5   Engine oil viscosity too high. Using a heavier oil than recommended in Chapter 1 can cause the plates to stick together, putting a drag on the engine. Change to the correct weight oil (Chapter 1).

6   Clutch drum seized on shaft. Lack of lubrication, severe wear or damage can cause the drum to seize on the shaft. Overhaul of the clutch, and perhaps transmission, may be necessary to repair the damage (Chapter 2).

7   Clutch pushrod bent. Check and, if necessary, replace (Chapter 2).

8   Loose clutch center nut. Causes drum and center misalignment putting a drag on the engine. Engagement adjustment continually varies. Overhaul the clutch assembly (Chapter 2).

Gear shifting problems

28   Doesn't go into gear or lever doesn't return

1   Clutch not disengaging. See Section 27.

2   Shift fork(s) bent or seized. Often caused by dropping the

machine or from lack of lubrication. Overhaul the transmission (Chapter 2).

3   Gear(s) stuck on shaft. Most often caused by a lack of lubrication or excessive wear in transmission bearings and bushings. Overhaul the transmission (Chapter 2).

4   Shift drum binding. Caused by lubrication failure or excessive wear. Replace the drum and bearing (Chapter 2).

5   Shift lever return spring weak or broken (Chapter 2).

6   Shift lever broken. Splines stripped out of lever or shaft, caused by allowing the lever to get loose or from dropping the machine. Replace necessary parts (Chapter 2).

7   Shift mechanism stopper arm broken or worn. Full engagement and rotary movement of shift drum results. Replace the arm (Chapter 2).

8   Stopper arm spring broken. Allows arm to float, causing sporadic shift operation. Replace spring (Chapter 2).

29   Jumps out of gear

1   Shift fork(s) worn. Overhaul the transmission (Chapter 2).

2   Gear groove(s) worn. Overhaul the transmission (Chapter 2).

3   Gear dogs or dog slots worn or damaged. The gears should be inspected and replaced. No attempt should be made to service the worn parts.

30   Overshifts

1   Stopper arm spring weak or broken (Chapter 2).

2   Gearshift shaft return spring post broken or distorted (Chapter 2).

Abnormal engine noise

31   Knocking or pinging

1   Carbon build-up in combustion chamber. Use of a fuel additive that will dissolve the adhesive bonding the carbon particles to the piston crown and chamber is the easiest way to remove the build-up. Otherwise, the cylinder head will have to be removed and decarbonized (Chapter 2).

2   Incorrect or poor quality fuel. Old or improper fuel can cause detonation. This causes the pistons to rattle, thus the knocking or pinging sound. Drain the old fuel and always use the recommended grade fuel (Chapter 4).

3   Spark plug heat range incorrect. Uncontrolled detonation indicates that the plug heat range is too hot. The plug in effect becomes a glow plug, raising cylinder temperatures. Install the proper heat range plug (Chapter 1).

4   Improper air/fuel mixture. This will cause the cylinders to run hot and lead to detonation. Clogged jets or an air leak can cause this imbalance. See Chapter 4.

32   Piston slap or rattling

1   Cylinder-to-piston clearance excessive. Caused by improper assembly. Inspect and overhaul top end parts (Chapter 2).

2   Connecting rod bent. Caused by over-revving, trying to start a badly flooded engine or from ingesting a foreign object into the combustion chamber. Replace the damaged parts (Chapter 2).

3   Piston pin or piston pin bore worn or seized from wear or lack of lubrication. Replace damaged parts (Chapter 2).

4   Piston ring(s) worn, broken or sticking. Overhaul the top end (Chapter 2).

5   Piston seizure damage. Usually from lack of lubrication or overheating. Replace the pistons and bore the cylinders, as necessary (Chapter 2).

6   Connecting rod upper or lower end clearance excessive. Caused by excessive wear or lack of lubrication. Replace worn parts.

33   Valve noise

1   Incorrect valve clearances. Adjust the clearances by referring to Chapter 1.

2   Valve spring broken or weak. Check and replace weak valve springs (Chapter 2).

3   Camshaft or cylinder head worn or damaged. Lack of lubrication at high rpm is usually the cause of damage. Insufficient oil or failure to change the oil at the recommended intervals are the chief causes. Since there are no replaceable bearings in the head, the head/bearing caps itself will have to be replaced if there is excessive wear or damage (Chapter 2).

34   Other noise

1   Cylinder head gasket leaking.

2   Exhaust pipe leaking at cylinder head connection. Caused by improper fit of pipe(s) or loose exhaust flange. All exhaust fasteners should be tightened evenly and carefully. Failure to do this will lead to a leak.

3   Crankshaft runout excessive. Caused by a bent crankshaft (from over-revving) or damage from an upper cylinder component failure. Can also be attributed to dropping the machine on either of the crankshaft ends.

4   Engine mounting bolts loose. Tighten all engine mount bolts (Chapter 2).

5   Crankshaft bearings worn (Chapter 2).

6   Camshaft drive gears worn (Chapter 2).

Abnormal driveline noise

35   Clutch noise

1   Clutch drum/friction plate clearance excessive (Chapter 2).

2   Loose or damaged clutch pressure plate and/or bolts (Chapter 2).

36   Transmission noise

1   Bearings worn. Also includes the possibility that the shafts are worn. Overhaul the transmission (Chapter 2).

2   Gears worn or chipped (Chapter 2).

3   Metal chips jammed in gear teeth. Probably pieces from a broken clutch, gear or shift mechanism that were picked up by the gears. This will cause early bearing failure (Chapter 2).

4   Engine oil level too low. Causes a howl from transmission. Also affects engine power and clutch operation (Chapter 1).

37   Final drive noise

1   Chain not adjusted properly (Chapter 1).

2   Engine sprocket or rear sprocket loose. Tighten fasteners (Chapters 2 and 6).

3   Sprocket(s) worn. Replace sprocket(s) (Chapter 6).

4   Rear sprocket warped. Replace (Chapter 6).

5   Wheel coupling worn. Replace coupling (Chapter 6).

Abnormal frame and suspension noise

38 Front end noise

1   Low fluid level or improper viscosity oil in forks. This can sound like spurting and is usually accompanied by irregular fork action (Chapter 6).
2   Spring weak or broken. Makes a clicking or scraping sound. Fork oil, when drained, will have a lot of metal particles in it (Chapter 6).
3   Steering head bearings loose or damaged. Clicks when braking. Check and adjust or replace as necessary (Chapters 1 and 6).
4   Fork clamps loose. Make sure all fork clamp pinch bolts are tight (Chapter 6).
5   Fork tube bent. Good possibility if machine has been dropped. Replace tube with a new one (Chapter 6).
6   Front axle or axle clamp bolt loose. Tighten them to the specified torque (Chapter 6).

39 Shock absorber noise

1   Fluid level incorrect. Indicates a leak caused by defective seal. Shock will be covered with oil. Replace shock (Chapter 6).
2   Defective shock absorber with internal damage. This is in the body of the shock and can't be remedied. The shock must be replaced with a new one (Chapter 6).
3   Bent or damaged shock body. Replace the shock with a new one (Chapter 6).

40 Brake noise

1   Squeal caused by pad shim not installed or positioned correctly (Chapter 7).
2   Squeal caused by dust on brake pads. Usually found in combination with glazed pads. Clean using brake cleaning solvent (Chapter 7).
3   Contamination of brake pads. Oil, brake fluid or dirt causing brake to chatter or squeal. Clean or replace pads (Chapter 7).
4   Pads glazed. Caused by excessive heat from prolonged use or from contamination. Do not use sandpaper, emery cloth, carborundum cloth or any other abrasive to roughen the pad surfaces as abrasives will stay in the pad material and damage the disc. A very fine flat file can be used, but pad replacement is suggested as a cure (Chapter 7).
5   Disc warped. Can cause a chattering, clicking or intermittent squeal. Usually accompanied by a pulsating lever and uneven braking. Replace the disc (Chapter 7).
6   Loose or worn wheel bearings. Check and replace as needed (Chapter 7).

Oil pressure indicator light comes on

41 Engine lubrication system

1   Engine oil pump defective (Chapter 2).
2   Engine oil level low. Inspect for leak or other problem causing low oil level and add recommended oil (Chapters 1 and 2).
3   Engine oil viscosity too low. Very old, thin oil or an improper weight of oil used in the engine. Change to correct oil (Chapter 1).
4   Camshaft or journals worn. Excessive wear causing drop in oil pressure. Replace cam and/or cylinder head. Abnormal wear could be caused by oil starvation at high rpm from low oil level or improper weight of type of oil (Chapter 1).
5   Crankshaft and/or bearings worn. Same problems as Step 4. Check and replace crankshaft and/or bearings (Chapter 2).

42 Electrical system

1   Oil pressure switch defective. Check the switch according to the procedure in Chapter 9. Replace it if it is defective.
2   Oil pressure indicator light circuit defective. Check for pinched, shorted, disconnected or damaged wiring (Chapter 9).

Excessive exhaust smoke

43 White smoke

1   Piston oil ring worn. The ring may be broken or damaged, causing oil from the crankcase to be pulled past the piston into the combustion chamber. Replace the rings with new ones (Chapter 2).
2   Cylinders worn, cracked, or scored. Caused by overheating or oil starvation. The cylinders will have to be rebored and new pistons installed.
3   Valve oil seal damaged or worn. Replace oil seals with new ones (Chapter 2).
4   Valve guide worn. Perform a complete valve job (Chapter 2).
5   Engine oil level too high, which causes the oil to be forced past the rings. Drain oil to the proper level (Chapter 1).
6   Head gasket broken between oil return and cylinder. Causes oil to be pulled into the combustion chamber. Replace the head gasket and check the head for warpage (Chapter 2).
7   Abnormal crankcase pressurization, which forces oil past the rings. Clogged breather or hoses usually the cause (Chapter 3).

44 Black smoke

1   Air cleaner clogged. Clean or replace the element (Chapter 1).
2   Main jet too large or loose. Compare the jet size to the Specifications (Chapter 4).
3   Choke stuck, causing fuel to be pulled through choke circuit (Chapter 4).
4   Fuel level too high. Check and adjust the float height(s) as necessary (Chapter 4).
5   Inlet needle held off needle seat. Clean the float bowls and fuel line and replace the needles and seats if necessary (Chapter 4).

45 Brown smoke

1   Main jet too small or clogged. Lean condition caused by wrong size main jet or by a restricted orifice. Clean float bowl and jets and compare jet size to Specifications (Chapter 4).
2   Fuel flow insufficient. Fuel inlet needle valve stuck closed due to chemical reaction with old fuel. Float height incorrect. Restricted fuel line. Clean line and float bowl and adjust floats if necessary.
3   Carburetor intake manifolds loose (Chapter 4).
4   Air cleaner poorly sealed or not installed (Chapter 1).

Poor handling or stability

46 Handlebar hard to turn

1   Steering stem nut too tight (Chapter 6).
2   Bearings damaged. Roughness can be felt as the bars are turned from side-to-side. Replace bearings and races (Chapter 6).
3   Races dented or worn. Denting results from wear in only one position (e.g., straight-ahead), from a collision or hitting a pothole or from dropping the machine. Replace races and bearings (Chapter 6).

4   Steering stem lubrication inadequate. Causes are grease getting hard from age or being washed out by high pressure car washes. Disassemble steering head and repack bearings (Chapter 6).
5   Steering stem bent. Caused by a collision, hitting a pothole or by dropping the machine. Replace damaged part. Don't try to straighten the steering stem (Chapter 6).
6   Front tire air pressure too low (Chapter 1).

47   Handlebar shakes or vibrates excessively

1   Tires worn or out of balance (Chapter 7).
2   Swingarm bearings worn. Replace worn bearings by referring to Chapter 6.
3   Rim(s) warped or damaged. Inspect wheels for runout (Chapter 7).
4   Wheel bearings worn. Worn front or rear wheel bearings can cause poor tracking. Worn front bearings will cause wobble (Chapter 7).
5   Handlebar clamp bolts loose (Chapter 6).
6   Steering stem or fork clamps loose. Tighten them to the specified torque (Chapter 6).
7   Engine mounting bolts loose. Will cause excessive vibration with increased engine rpm (Chapter 2).

48   Handlebar pulls to one side

1   Frame bent. Definitely suspect this if the machine has been dropped. May or may not be accompanied by cracking near the bend. Replace the frame (Chapter 6).
2   Wheel out of alignment. Caused by improper location of axle spacers or from bent steering stem or frame (Chapter 6).
3   Swingarm bent or twisted. Caused by age (metal fatigue) or impact damage. Replace the arm (Chapter 6).
4   Steering stem bent. Caused by impact damage or by dropping the motorcycle. Replace the steering stem (Chapter 6).
5   Fork leg bent. Disassemble the forks and replace the damaged parts (Chapter 6).
6   Fork oil level uneven. Check and add or drain as necessary (Chapter 6).

49   Poor shock absorbing qualities

1   Too hard:
 a) *Fork oil level excessive (Chapter 6).*
 b) *Fork oil viscosity too high. Use a lighter oil (see the Specifications in Chapter 6).*
 c) *Fork tube bent. Causes a harsh, sticking feeling (Chapter 6).*
 d) *Shock shaft or body bent or damaged (Chapter 6).*
 e) *Fork internal damage (Chapter 6).*
 f) *Shock internal damage.*
 g) *Tire pressure too high (Chapter 1).*
2   Too soft:
 a) *Fork or shock oil insufficient and/or leaking (Chapter 6).*
 b) *Fork oil level too low (Chapter 6).*
 c) *Fork oil viscosity too light (Chapter 6).*
 d) *Fork springs weak or broken (Chapter 6).*
 e) *Shock internal damage or leakage (Chapter 6).*

Braking problems

50   Brakes are spongy, don't hold

1   Air in brake line. Caused by inattention to master cylinder fluid level or by leakage. Locate problem and bleed brakes (Chapter 7).

2   Pad or disc worn (Chapters 1 and 7).
3   Brake fluid leak. See paragraph 1.
4   Contaminated pads. Caused by contamination with oil, grease, brake fluid, etc. Clean or replace pads. Clean disc thoroughly with brake cleaner (Chapter 7).
5   Brake fluid deteriorated. Fluid is old or contaminated. Drain system, replenish with new fluid and bleed the system (Chapter 7).
6   Master cylinder internal parts worn or damaged causing fluid to bypass (Chapter 7).
7   Master cylinder bore scratched by foreign material or broken spring. Repair or replace master cylinder (Chapter 7).
8   Disc warped. Replace disc (Chapter 7).

51   Brake lever or pedal pulsates

1   Disc warped. Replace disc (Chapter 7).
2   Axle bent. Replace axle (Chapter 7).
3   Brake caliper bolts loose (Chapter 7).
4   Brake caliper sliders damaged or sticking, causing caliper to bind. Lube the sliders or replace them if they are corroded or bent (Chapter 7).
5   Wheel warped or otherwise damaged (Chapter 7).
6   Wheel bearings damaged or worn (Chapter 7).

52   Brakes drag

1   Master cylinder piston seized. Caused by wear or damage to piston or cylinder bore (Chapter 7).
2   Lever balky or stuck. Check pivot and lubricate (Chapter 7).
3   Brake caliper binds. Caused by inadequate lubrication or damage to caliper sliders (Chapter 7).
4   Brake caliper piston seized in bore. Caused by wear or ingestion of dirt past deteriorated seal (Chapter 7).
5   Brake pad damaged. Pad material separated from backing plate. Usually caused by faulty manufacturing process or from contact with chemicals. Replace pads (Chapter 7).
6   Pads improperly installed (Chapter 7).
7   Rear brake pedal freeplay insufficient.

Electrical problems

53   Battery dead or weak

1   Battery faulty. Caused by sulfated plates which are shorted through sedimentation or low electrolyte level. Also, broken battery terminal making only occasional contact (Chapter 9).
2   Battery cables making poor contact (Chapter 9).
3   Load excessive. Caused by addition of high wattage lights or other electrical accessories.
4   Ignition switch defective. Switch either grounds (earths) internally or fails to shut off system. Replace the switch (Chapter 9).
5   Regulator/rectifier defective (Chapter 9).
6   Stator coil open or shorted (Chapter 9).
7   Wiring faulty. Wiring grounded (earthed) or connections loose in ignition, charging or lighting circuits (Chapter 9).

54   Battery overcharged

1   Regulator/rectifier defective. Overcharging is noticed when battery gets excessively warm or boils over (Chapter 9).
2   Battery defective. Replace battery with a new one (Chapter 9).
3   Battery amperage too low, wrong type or size. Install manufacturer's specified amp-hour battery to handle charging load (Chapter 9).

Chapter 1
Tune-up and routine maintenance

Note: *Refer to 'Identification numbers' at the beginning of this Manual to establish the model code of your motorcycle.*

Contents

Specifications

Engine

Cylinder identification
- No. 1 ... Left rear cylinder
- No. 2 ... Left front cylinder
- No. 3 ... Right rear cylinder
- No. 4 ... Right front cylinder

Spark plugs
- Type
  - G through K models
    - Standard ... NGK DPR9EA-9 or ND X27EPR-U9
    - Cold climates - below 5°C (41°F) ... NGK DPR8EA-9 or ND X24EPR-U9
  - L through P models
    - Standard ... NGK CR8EH9 or ND U24FER9
    - For extended high-speed riding ... NGK CR9EH9 or ND U27FER9
  - UK R models
    - Standard ... NGK CR8EH9 or ND U24FER9
    - For extended high-speed riding ... NGK CR9EH9 or ND U27FER9
  - US R models
    - Standard ... NGK CR9EH9 or ND U27FER9
    - Cold climates - below 5°C (41°F) ... NGK CR8EH9 or ND U24FER9
- Electrode gap (all models) ... 0.8 to 0.9 mm (0.031 to 0.035 in)

Valve clearances (COLD engine)
- G through K models
  - Intake ... 0.13 mm (0.005 in)
  - Exhaust ... 0.20 mm (0.007 in)
- L models onward
  - Intake ... 0.16 ± 0.03 mm (0.006 ± 0.001 in)
  - Exhaust ... 0.25 ± 0.03 mm (0.010 ± 0.001 in)

Engine idle speed
    California models .... 1200 ± 100 rpm
    US models (except California)
        G through K models.. 1200 ± 100 rpm
        L through P models .... 1000 ± 100 rpm
        R models.. 1100 ± 100 rpm
    UK models
        G through K models.. 1000 ± 100 rpm
        L through P models .... 1200 ± 100 rpm
        R models.. 1000 ± 100 rpm
Cylinder compression pressures .... 199 ± 28 psi (14.0 ± 2.0 Bars)
Carburetor synchronization
    Maximum vacuum difference between any two cylinders................. 20 mm Hg

Miscellaneous

Brake pad minimum thickness .... See text
Battery specific gravity 1.280
Freeplay adjustments
    Throttle grip.. 2 to 6 mm (0.08 to 0.24 in)
    Choke lever .... 2 to 3 mm (0.08 to 0.12 in)
    Drive chain... 15 to 25 mm (0.6 to 1.0 in)
Minimum tire tread depth*
    Front... 1.5 mm (0.06 in)
    Rear.. 2.0 mm (0.08 in)
Tire pressures (cold)
    Front... 36 psi (2.5 Bars)
    Rear.. 42 psi (2.9 Bars)

In the UK, tread depth must be at least 1 mm over 3/4 of the tread breadth all the way around the tire, with no bald patches.

Torque setting

	Nm	Ft-lbs
Engine oil pan drain plug	38	27
Oil filter (using Honda service tool)	12	9
Spark plugs		
G through K models	14	11
L models onward	12	9
Valve adjuster locknut (G through K models)	23	16

Recommended lubricants and fluids

Engine/transmission oil
    Type.. API grade SE, SF or SG
    Viscosity .... SAE 10W40
    Capacity (approximate)
        With filter change .... 3.1 liters (3.3 US qt, 5.4 Imp pts)
        Oil change only .... 3.0 liters (3.2 US qt, 5.2 Imp pts)
        After engine rebuild
            R models .... 3.8 liters (4.0 US qt, 6.6 Imp pts)
            All other models... 4.0 liters (4.3 US qt, 7.0 Imp pts)
Coolant
    Mixture type .... 50% distilled water, 50% corrosion inhibited ethylene glycol antifreeze
    Capacity
        Radiator and engine... 2.3 liters (2.4 US qt, 4.0 Imp pts)
        Coolant reservoir.. 0.33 liters (0.35 US qt, 0.6 Imp pts)
Brake fluid... DOT 4

Miscellaneous

Drive chain.. SAE 80 to 90W gear oil
Wheel bearings .... Medium weight, lithium-based multi-purpose grease
Swingarm pivot bearings .... Molybdenum disulfide grease
Suspension linkage bearings.. Molybdenum disulfide grease
Shock absorber mounting bearings .... Molybdenum disulfide grease
Cables and lever pivots .... Chain and cable lubricant or 10W40 motor oil
Sidestand/centerstand pivots... Medium-weight, lithium-based multi-purpose grease
Brake pedal/shift lever pivots .... Chain and cable lubricant or 10W40 motor oil
Throttle grip .... Multi-purpose grease or dry film lubricant

1 Honda VFR750/700 Routine maintenance intervals

Routine maintenance intervals

Note: *The pre-ride inspection outlined in the owner's manual covers the checks and maintenance that should be carried out on a daily basis. It's condensed and included here to remind you of its importance. Always perform the pre-ride inspection at every maintenance interval (in addition to the procedures listed). The intervals listed below are the shortest intervals recommended by the manufacturer for each particular operation during the model years covered in this manual. Your owner's manual may have different intervals for your model.*

Daily or pre-ride inspection

Check the engine oil level
Check the fuel level and inspect for leaks
Check the engine coolant level and look for leaks
Check the operation of both brakes - also check the
    fluid levels and look for leakage
Check the tires for damage, the presence of foreign
    objects and correct air pressure
Check the throttle for smooth operation
Check the operation of the clutch - make sure the
    freeplay is correct
Make sure the steering operates smoothly, without
    looseness or binding
Check for proper operation of the headlight, taillight,
    brake light, turn signals, indicator lights, speedometer
    and horn
Make sure the sidestand and centerstand return to their
    fully up positions and stay there under spring
    pressure
Make sure the engine kill switch works properly

After the initial 600 miles (1000 km)

Replace the engine oil and oil filter
Check and adjust the valve clearances
Check and adjust the idle speed
Check the brake fluid levels
Check the clutch operation
Check, adjust and lubricate the drive chain
Check the tightness of all fasteners
Check the steering head bearings

Every 600 miles (1000 km)

Check, adjust and lubricate the drive chain

Every 4000 miles (6000 km) or 6 months (whichever comes sooner)

Clean and adjust the spark plugs - G through P models*
Check and adjust the idle speed

Check the brake pads and discs
Check the brake fluid levels
Check the clutch fluid level
Check the battery
Lubricate the clutch and brake lever pivots
Lubricate the shift/brake lever pivots and the
    sidestand/centerstand pivots

On G through K models, this operation is specified only after the initial 4000 miles (6000 km). After this it only needs to be performed every 8000 miles (12,000 km).

Every 8000 miles (12,000 km) or 12 months (whichever comes sooner)

Replace the engine oil and filter
Replace the spark plugs - G through P models
Check and adjust the spark plugs - R models
Check and adjust the valve clearances - G through K
    models only
Check the fuel system hoses and tap filter
Check and adjust the throttle and choke cables
Check/adjust the carburetor synchronization
Check the condition of the EVAP and PAIR system
    hoses - California models only
Check the cooling system hoses
Check the drive chain slider
Check the condition of the exhaust system
Check and adjust the brake light switch
Check the condition of the wheels and tires
Check and adjust the headlight aim
Check the operation of the sidestand switch
Check the operation of the front and rear suspension
Check and adjust the steering head bearings
Check the tightness of all nuts, bolts and fasteners

Every 12,000 miles (18,000 km) or 18 months (whichever comes first)

Replace the air cleaner element
Change the brake fluid
Change the clutch fluid

Every 16,000 miles (24,000 km) or two years (whichever comes sooner)

Check and adjust the valve clearances - L models
    onward
Replace the spark plugs - R models

Every 24,000 miles (36,000 km) or two years (whichever comes sooner)

Check the cooling system and replace the coolant

3.3 Engine oil level must be between the marks (arrows) on the dipstick

3.7 The front brake fluid level must be above the LOWER mark on the reservoir body when the reservoir is level

3.9 Undo the two retaining screws then lift off the reservoir cover, diaphragm plate and diaphragm. The maximum level mark is cast onto the reservoir body (arrow)

2   Introduction to tune-up and routine maintenance

This Chapter covers in detail the checks and procedures necessary for the tune-up and routine maintenance of your motorcycle. Section 1 includes the routine maintenance schedule, which is designed to keep the machine in proper running condition and prevent possible problems. The remaining Sections contain detailed procedures for carrying out the items listed on the maintenance schedule, as well as additional maintenance information designed to increase reliability.

Since routine maintenance plays such an important role in the safe and efficient operation of your motorcycle, it is presented here as a comprehensive check list. For the rider who does all his/her own maintenance, these lists outline the procedures and checks that should be done on a routine basis.

Maintenance information is printed on decals attached to the motorcycle. If the information on the decals differs from that included here, use the information on the decal.

Deciding where to start or plug into the routine maintenance schedule depends on several factors. If you have a motorcycle whose warranty has recently expired, and if it has been maintained according to the warranty standards, you may want to pick-up routine maintenance as it coincides with the next mileage or calendar interval. If you have owned the machine for some time but have never performed any maintenance on it, then you may want to start at the nearest interval and include some additional procedures to ensure that nothing important is overlooked. If you have just had a major engine overhaul, then you may want to start the maintenance routine from the beginning. If you have a used machine and have no knowledge of its history or maintenance record, you may desire to combine all the checks into one large service initially and then settle into the maintenance schedule prescribed.

The Sections which outline the inspection and maintenance procedures are written as step-by-step comprehensive guides to the performance of the work. They explain in detail each of the routine inspections and maintenance procedures on the check list. References to additional information in applicable Chapters is also included and should not be overlooked.

Before beginning any maintenance or repair, the machine should be cleaned thoroughly, especially around the oil filter, spark plugs, cylinder head cover, side covers, carburetors, etc. Cleaning will help ensure that dirt does not contaminate the engine and will allow you to detect wear and damage that could otherwise easily go unnoticed.

3   Fluid levels - check

Engine oil

Refer to illustration 3.3

1   Start the engine and allow it to reach normal operating temperature. **Caution:** *Do not run the engine in an enclosed space such as a garage or shop.*

2   Stop the engine and allow the machine to sit undisturbed for 2 to 3 minutes. Place the motorcycle on its centerstand. Where no centerstand is fitted support the motorcycle in an upright position.

3   Unscrew the filler cap and dipstick from the right crankcase cover and wipe it clean. Insert the dipstick until its threads are resting on the crankcase cover, then remove it and check the oil level. **Note:** *Do not screw the dipstick into position.* The oil level should be between marks on the end of the dipstick **(see illustration)**.

4   If the level is below the lower (minimum) dipstick mark, the oil level should be topped up, using oil of the recommended grade and type, bringing the level up to the upper (maximum) mark on the dipstick. **Note:** *Do not overfill the engine.* Unscrew the filler cap from the cover and top up as necessary. When the oil level is correct screw the dipstick and filler cap into the cover.

Brake fluid

5   In order to ensure proper operation of the hydraulic disc brakes, the fluid level in the master cylinder reservoirs must be properly maintained.

Front brake

Refer to illustrations 3.7 and 3.9

6   With the motorcycle on the centerstand or supported in an upright position, turn the handlebars until the top of the master cylinder is as level as possible. If necessary, tilt the motorcycle to make it level.

7   Look closely at the inspection window in the master cylinder reservoir. Make sure that the fluid level, visible through the sightglass, is above the LOWER mark on the reservoir **(see illustration)**.

8   If the level is low, the fluid must be replenished. Before removing the master cylinder cover, cover the fuel tank to protect it from brake fluid spills (which will damage the paint) and remove all dust and dirt from the area around the cap.

9   Unscrew the retaining screws and lift off the cover, diaphragm plate and diaphragm. Using a good quality brake fluid of the recommended type, from a freshly opened container, top up the

3.11 Rear brake fluid reservoir markings; level is visible through reservoir body

3.19 Coolant reservoir level markings (H model shown); level is visible through reservoir

3.22 The clutch fluid level must be above the LOWER mark on the reservoir body when the reservoir is level

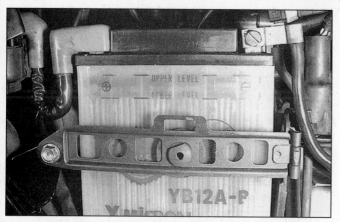

4.3 On G through K models ensure the electrolyte level is between the UPPER and LOWER level markings on the battery casing

reservoir to the upper level mark; this mark is in the form of a line, cast on the inside of the front face of the reservoir (see illustration).

10   When the fluid level is correct, clean and dry the diaphragm, fold it into its compressed state and install it in the reservoir followed by the diaphragm plate. Install the reservoir cover and securely tighten its retaining screws.

Rear brake

Refer to illustration 3.11

11   With the motorcycle on the centerstand, or supported in an upright position, check the level in the rear brake reservoir. On G through K models it will be necessary to remove the right side cover (see Chapter 8, if necessary) to gain access to the reservoir. On L models onward the reservoir markings are visible through the inspection hole in the right side cover. Make sure that the fluid level, visible through the translucent body of the reservoir, is between the UPPER and LOWER marks on the reservoir (see illustration).

12   If the level is low, the fluid must be replenished. Remove the right side cover (see Chapter 8) if not already removed, and wipe all dust and dirt from the area around the cap.

13   Unscrew the reservoir cap and remove the diaphragm plate and diaphragm. Using a good quality brake fluid of the recommended type, from a freshly opened container, top up the reservoir to the UPPER level mark.

14   When the fluid level is correct, clean and dry the diaphragm, fold it into its compressed state and install it in the reservoir followed by the diaphragm plate. Install the reservoir cap, tightening it securely, and install the right side cover.

Both brakes

15   Check the operation of both brakes before taking the machine on the road; if there is evidence of air in the system, it must be bled as described in Chapter 7.

16   If the brake fluid level was low, inspect the brake system for leaks.

Coolant level

Refer to illustration 3.19

17   Warm the engine up to normal operating temperature (see Step 1).

18   Stop the engine. On G through K models remove the left side cover, and on L models onward remove the right middle fairing panel (see Chapter 8, if necessary).

19   The coolant level should be between the UPPER and LOWER marks on the side of the coolant reservoir. The reservoir is made of translucent plastic so that the coolant level can be easily seen in relation to the marks (see illustration).

20   If the level is below the lower mark, remove the reservoir filler cap, and top up the level to the upper mark using a coolant mixture of the required strength. **Note:** *Use only the specified ingredients as given in the Specifications at the start of this Chapter.* If the coolant is significantly above the upper level mark at any time, the surplus coolant should be siphoned off to prevent it from being expelled out of the breather hose when the engine is running.

21   If the coolant level falls steadily, check the system for leaks as described in Section 19. If no leaks are found and the level still continues to fall, it is recommended that the machine be taken to a Honda service agent who will pressure test the system.

Clutch fluid

Refer to illustration 3.22

22   Refer to information given above for the front brake (see illustration).

---

4   Battery - check

G through K models

Refer to illustration 4.3

Caution: *Be extremely careful when handling or working around the battery. The electrolyte is very caustic and an explosive gas (hydrogen) is given off when the battery is charging.*

1   Remove the right side cover (see Chapter 8).

2   Remove the screws securing the battery cables to the battery terminals (remove the negative cable first, positive cable last). Undo the battery retaining clamp nut and remove the battery.

3   The electrolyte level is visible through the translucent battery case - it should be between the UPPER and LOWER level marks (see illustration).

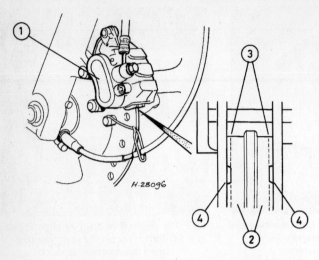

H.28096

5.1a **Front brake pad wear indicator groove details (typical)**

1   *Front brake caliper*
2   *Pads*
3   *Wear limit*
4   *Minimum thickness cutouts*

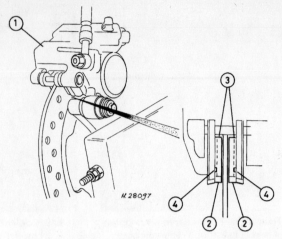

H.28097

5.1b **Rear brake pad wear indicator groove details (typical)**

1   *Rear brake caliper*
2   *Pads*
3   *Wear limit*
4   *Minimum thickness cutouts*

4   If the electrolyte is low, remove the cell caps and fill each cell to the upper level mark with distilled water. Do not use tap water (except in an emergency), and do not overfill. The cell holes are quite small, so it may help to use a plastic squeeze bottle with a small spout to add the water. If the level is within the marks on the case, additional water is not necessary.

5   Next, check the specific gravity of the electrolyte in each cell with a small hydrometer made especially for motorcycle batteries. These are available from most dealer parts departments or motorcycle accessory stores.

6   Remove the caps, draw some electrolyte from the first cell into the hydrometer and note the specific gravity. Compare the reading to the Specifications listed in this Chapter. **Note:** *Add 0.004 points to the reading for every 10°F above 68°F - subtract 0.004 points from the reading for every 10°F below 68°F. Return the electrolyte to the appropriate cell and repeat the check for the remaining cells. When the check is complete, rinse the hydrometer thoroughly with clean water.*

7   If the specific gravity of the electrolyte in each cell is as specified, the battery is in good condition and is apparently being charged by the machine's charging system.

8   If the specific gravity is low, the battery is not fully charged. This may be due to corroded battery terminals, a dirty battery case, a malfunctioning charging system, or loose or corroded wiring connections. On the other hand, it may be that the battery is worn out, especially if the machine is old, or that infrequent use of the motorcycle prevents normal charging from taking place.

9   Be sure to correct any problems and charge the battery if necessary. Refer to Chapter 9 for additional battery maintenance and charging procedures.

10   Install the battery cell caps, tightening them securely. Reconnect the cables to the battery, attaching the positive cable first and the negative cable last. Make sure to install the insulating boot over the positive terminal. Securely tighten the clamp nut and install the side cover. Be very careful not to pinch or otherwise restrict the battery vent tube, as the battery may build up enough internal pressure during normal charging system operation to explode.

L models onward

11   All later models are fitted with a sealed battery, and therefore require no maintenance. **Note:** *Do not attempt to remove the battery caps to check the electrolyte level or battery specific gravity. Removal will damage the caps, resulting in electrolyte leakage and battery damage.* All that should be done is to check that its terminals are clean

and tight and that the casing is not damaged or leaking. See Chapter 9 for further details.

All models

12   If the machine is not in regular use, disconnect the battery and give it a refresher charge every month to six weeks, as described in Chapter 9.

5   Brake pads - wear check

Refer to illustrations 5.1a and 5.1b

1   A quick check of the brake pads can be made without removing them from the caliper. The pad wear can be judged by looking at the thickness of the pad from the rear of the caliper (both front and rear) **(see illustrations)**.

2   If either pad has worn down to, or beyond the groove in the friction material, both pads must be replaced as a set. However, it is recommended that the pads be removed and a more detailed inspection be carried out as described in Chapter 7.

6   Brake system - general check

Refer to illustration 6.5

1   A routine general check of the brakes will ensure that any problems are discovered and remedied before the rider's safety is jeopardized.

2   Check the brake lever and pedal for loose connections, excessive play, bends, and other damage. Replace any damaged parts with new ones (see Chapter 7).

3   Make sure all brake fasteners are tight. Check the brake pads for wear (see Section 5) and make sure the fluid level in the reservoirs is correct (see Section 3). Look for leaks at the hose connections and check for cracks in the hoses. If the lever or pedal is spongy, bleed the brakes as described in Chapter 7.

4   Make sure the brake light operates when the front brake lever is pulled in. The front brake light switch is not adjustable. If it fails to operate properly, replace it with a new one (see Chapter 9).

5   Make sure the brake light is activated just before the rear brake pedal takes effect. If adjustment is necessary, hold the switch and turn the adjusting ring on the switch body until the brake light is activated when required **(see illustration)**. If the switch doesn't operate the brake lights, check it as described in Chapter 9.

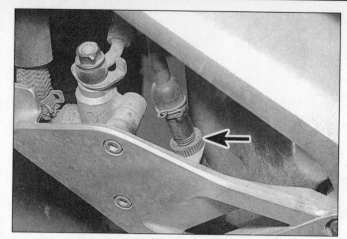

6.5 Adjust rear brake light switch by turning the adjusting ring (arrow)

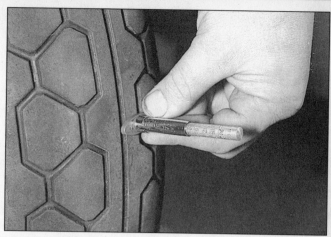

7.2 Checking tire tread depth with a depth gauge

7.4 Checking tire pressure with a pressure gauge

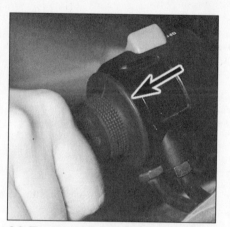

8.3 Throttle cable freeplay is measured in terms of twistgrip rotation at the grip flange (arrow) . . .

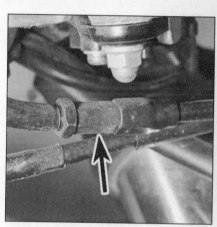

8.4 . . . and is adjusted using the upper cable adjuster (arrow)

7 Tires/wheels - general check

Refer to illustrations 7.2 and 7.4

1   Routine tire and wheel checks should be made with the realization that your safety depends to a great extent on their condition.

2   Check the tires carefully for cuts, tears, embedded nails or other sharp objects and excessive wear. Operation of the motorcycle with excessively worn tires is extremely hazardous, as traction and handling are directly affected. Measure the tread depth at the center of the tire and replace worn tires with new ones when the tread depth is less than specified **(see illustration)**.

3   Repair or replace punctured tires as soon as damage is noted. Do not try to patch a torn tire, as wheel balance and tire reliability may be impaired.

4   Check the tire pressures when the tires are **cold** and keep them properly inflated **(see illustration)**. Proper air pressure will increase tire life and provide maximum stability and ride comfort. Keep in mind that low tire pressures may cause the tire to slip on the rim or come off, while high tire pressures will cause abnormal tread wear and unsafe handling.

5   The cast wheels used on this machine are virtually maintenance free, but they should be kept clean and checked periodically for cracks and other damage. Never attempt to repair damaged cast wheels; they must be replaced with new ones.

6   Check the valve rubber for signs of damage or deterioration and have it replaced if necessary. Also, make sure the valve stem cap is in place and tight. If it is missing, install a new one made of metal or hard plastic.

8 Throttle and choke operation/grip freeplay - check and adjustment

Throttle cables

Refer to illustrations 8.3 and 8.4

1   Make sure the throttle grip rotates easily from fully closed to fully open with the front wheel turned at various angles. The grip should return automatically from fully open to fully closed when released.

2   If the throttle sticks, this is probably due to a cable fault. Remove the cables as described in Chapter 4 and lubricate them as described in Section 15. Install each cable, routing them so they take the smoothest route possible. If this fails to improve the operation of the throttle, the cables must be replaced. Note that in very rare cases the fault could lie in the carburetors rather than the cables, necessitating the removal of the carburetors and inspection of the throttle linkage (see Chapter 4).

3   With the throttle operating smoothly, check for a small amount of freeplay at the grip. The amount of freeplay in the throttle cables, measured in terms of twistgrip rotation, should be as given in this Chapter's Specifications **(see illustration)**. If adjustment is necessary, adjust idle speed first (see Section 17).

4   Slacken the locknut on the cable upper adjuster and rotate the adjuster until the correct amount of freeplay is obtained, then tighten the locknut **(see illustration)**. If it is not possible to obtain the correct freeplay with the upper adjuster, it will also be necessary to make adjustment at the lower adjuster, situated on the carburetors.

8.8 Check that the choke lever operates smoothly and easily

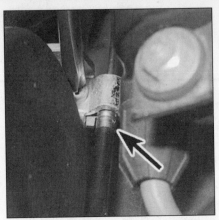

8.10 To adjust the choke cable, slacken the screw and reposition the outer cable (arrow) in the clamp

10.3 Checking drive chain slack (H model shown)

5   To gain access to the lower adjuster remove the left lower or middle fairing panel, as applicable (see Chapter 8). Screw the upper cable adjuster in to obtain the maximum possible freeplay, then slacken the lower adjuster locknut and set the cable freeplay using first the lower adjuster and then, if necessary, the upper adjuster. Once the freeplay is correct tighten the locknuts securely.

6   Check that the throttle twistgrip operates smoothly and snaps shut quickly when released. **Warning:** *Turn the handlebars all the way through their travel with the engine idling. Idle speed should not change. If it does, the cables may be routed incorrectly. Correct this condition before riding the bike* (see Chapter 4).

Choke cable

Refer to illustrations 8.8 and 8.10

7   Remove the fuel tank and air filter housing as described in Chapter 4. Note that on some models it will only be necessary to remove the air filter housing lid to gain access to the choke mechanism.

8   Operate the handlebar mounted lever whilst observing the movement of the carburetor choke mechanism **(see illustration)**. The mechanism should extend smoothly when the lever is pulled, and return home fully when the lever is returned.

9   If the choke mechanism does not operate smoothly this is probably due to a cable fault. Remove the cable as described in Chapter 4 and lubricate it as described in Section 15. Install the cable, routing it so it takes the smoothest route possible. If this fails to improve the operation of the choke, the cable must be replaced. Note that in very rare cases the fault could lie in the carburetors rather than the cable, necessitating the removal of the carburetors and inspection of the choke plungers as described in Chapter 4.

10   With the choke mechanism operating smoothly, check for a small amount of freeplay at the base of the choke lever. The amount of freeplay is measured in terms of lever travel, before the mechanism starts to operate. This should be as given in this Chapter's Specifications. To adjust the cable, slacken the choke cable clamping screw, situated on the carburetors, then move the lower end of the outer cable until the required amount of freeplay is obtained **(see illustration)**. Tighten the clamping screw securely.

11   Once the choke mechanism is correctly adjusted, install the air filter housing and fuel tank as described in Chapter 4.

9   Clutch - check

1   Hydraulic clutches require no checks or adjustment other than ensuring the fluid level is correct (see Section 3).

2   Inspect the fluid hose and connections for signs of cracking, deterioration or leaks. Replace the hose if it shows signs of damage or fluid leakage. If the clutch lever has a spongy feel, indicating that there is air in the system, bleed the clutch (see Chapter 2).

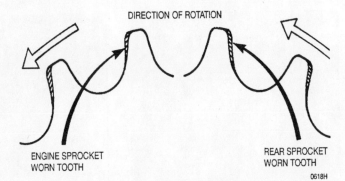

10.5 Check the sprockets in the areas indicated to see if they are worn excessively

10   Drive chain and sprockets - check, adjustment and lubrication

Check

Refer to illustrations 10.3 and 10.5

1   A neglected drive chain won't last long and can quickly damage the sprockets. Routine chain adjustment and lubrication isn't difficult and will ensure maximum chain and sprocket life.

2   To check the chain, shift the transmission into neutral and place the bike on its centerstand. Where no centerstand is fitted, support the bike in an upright position, ideally with the rear wheel clear of the ground. Make sure the ignition switch is off.

3   Push up on the bottom run of the chain and measure the slack midway between the two sprockets, then compare your measurements to the value listed in this Chapter's Specifications **(see illustration)**. **Warning:** *If the machine is ridden with more than 40 mm (1.6 in) of slack in the drive chain, the chain will contact the frame and swingarm, causing severe damage. As wear occurs, the chain will actually stretch, necessitating adjustment to take up some slack from the chain. In some cases where lubrication has been neglected, corrosion and galling may cause the links to bind and kink, which effectively shortens the chain's length. If the chain is tight between the sprockets, rusty or kinked, it's time to replace it with a new one.* **Note:** *Repeat the chain slack measurement along the length of the chain - ideally, every inch or so. If you find a tight area, mark it with felt pen or paint, and repeat the measurement after the bike has been ridden. If the chain's still tight in the same area, it may be damaged or worn. Because a tight or kinked chain can damage the transmission countershaft bearing, it's a good idea to replace it.*

4   Check the entire length of the chain for damaged rollers, loose

10.9a On G through K models, slacken each chain adjuster locknut . . .

10.9b . . . then rotate the adjuster nut as required to obtain the correct chain tension . . .

10.9c . . . using the marks on the plates (arrow) to ensure the rear wheel is kept in alignment

10.9d When the notch on the wheel axle washer aligns with the decal mark, the chain should be replaced

10.13 On L models onward, slacken the bearing holder clamp bolt . . .

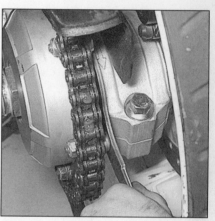

10.14 . . . then adjust the chain tension by rotating the bearing holder with a suitable pin spanner (C-spanner) (bike's tool kit spanner shown)

links and pins and replace it if damage is found. **Note:** *Never install a new chain on old sprockets, and never use the old chain if you install new sprockets - replace the chain and sprockets as a set.*

5   Remove the engine sprocket cover (see Chapter 6). Check the teeth on the engine sprocket and the rear wheel sprocket for wear **(see illustration)**.

6   Inspect the drive chain slider on the swingarm for excessive wear and replace it if necessary (see Chapter 6).

Adjustment

G through K models

Refer to illustrations 10.9a, 10.9b, 10.9c and 10.9d

7   Rotate the rear wheel until the chain is positioned with the tightest point at the center of its bottom run.

8   Slacken the rear axle nut and the locknut on each chain adjuster.

9   Turn the axle adjusting nuts on both sides of the swingarm until the proper chain tension is obtained (get the adjuster on the chain side close, then set the adjuster on the opposite side). Be sure to turn the adjusting nuts evenly to keep the rear wheel in alignment in accordance with the marks on the plates. If the adjusting nuts reach the end of their travel, the chain is excessively worn and should be replaced with a new one (see Chapter 6). The chain wear decals will also indicate the need for chain replacement when the notch on the wheel axle washer aligns with the 'replace chain' zone of the decal **(see illustrations)**.

10   When the chain has the correct amount of slack, make sure the notches on the axle washers correspond to the same relative marks on

each side of the swingarm. Tighten the axle nut to the torque listed in the Chapter 7 Specifications.

11   With the axle nut tightened, securely tighten the chain adjuster locknuts.

L models onward

Refer to illustrations 10.13 and 10.14

12   Rotate the rear wheel until the chain is positioned with the tightest point at the center of its bottom run.

13   Slacken the bearing holder clamp bolt on the swingarm **(see illustration)**.

14   Using a suitable pin spanner (C-spanner), such as the one supplied in the bike's tool kit, rotate the bearing holder clockwise or counterclockwise (anti-clockwise) (as applicable) until the proper chain tension is obtained **(see illustration)**. If it is not possible to adjust the chain correctly it is excessively worn and should be replaced with a new one (see Chapter 6). The chain wear decal on the chainguard will also indicate the need for chain replacement when the tip of the sprocket teeth align with the 'replace chain' zone of the decal.

15   When the chain has the correct amount of slack, tighten the bearing holder clamp bolt to the specified torque (see Chapter 6 Specifications).

Lubrication

Note: *If the chain is extremely dirty, it should be removed and cleaned before it's lubricated* (see Chapter 6).

16   For routine lubrication, the best time to lubricate the chain is after

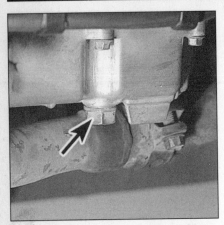

11.4 Engine oil drain plug (arrow) is situated on the base of the oil pan

11.5 If the oil filter is tight, use a strap wrench or chain wrench to loosen it

11.8a Apply a smear of engine oil to the filter sealing ring . . .

the motorcycle has been ridden. When the chain is warm, the lubricant will penetrate the joints between the side plates better than when cold. **Note:** *Honda specifies SAE 80 to SAE 90W gear oil only; do not use chain lube, which may contain solvents that could damage the O-rings.* Apply the oil to the area where the side plates overlap - not the middle of the rollers. Apply the oil to the top of the lower chain run, so centrifugal force will work the oil into the chain when the bike is moving. After applying the lubricant, let it soak in a few minutes before wiping off any excess.

11   Engine oil/filter - change

Refer to illustrations 11.4, 11.5, 11.8a and 11.8b

1   Consistent routine oil and filter changes are the single most important maintenance procedure you can perform on a motorcycle. The oil not only lubricates the internal parts of the engine, transmission and clutch, but it also acts as a coolant, a cleaner, a sealant, and a protectant. Because of these demands, the oil takes a terrific amount of abuse and should be replaced often with new oil of the recommended grade and type. Saving a little money on the difference in cost between a good oil and a cheap oil won't pay off if the engine is damaged.

2   Before changing the oil and filter, warm up the engine so the oil will drain easily. Be careful when draining the oil, as the exhaust pipes, the engine, and the oil itself can cause severe burns.

3   Put the motorcycle on the centerstand or support it in an upright position. Position a clean drain pan below the engine. Unscrew the oil filler cap to vent the crankcase and act as a reminder that there is no oil in the engine. Refer to Chapter 8 and remove the lower fairing panel(s).

4   Next, remove the drain plug from the oil pan and allow the oil to drain into the pan **(see illustration)**. Discard the sealing washer on the drain plug; it should be replaced whenever the plug is removed.

5   Make sure the drain pan is under the filter, then slacken the oil filter using a strap or chain wrench **(see illustration)**. **Warning:** *Take great care not to burn your hands on the exhaust system.* Unscrew the filter from the engine unit and empty its contents into the drain pan. If additional maintenance is planned for this time period, check or service another component while the oil is allowed to drain completely.

6   Clean the filter thread and housing on the crankcase with solvent or clean shop towels. Wipe any remaining oil off the filter sealing area of the crankcase.

7   Slip a new sealing washer over the drain plug. Fit the plug to the oil pan and tighten it to the specified torque setting. Avoid overtightening, as damage to the oil pan will result.

8   Apply a smear of clean oil to the sealing ring of the new filter and screw it into position on the engine. Tighten the filter firmly by hand **(see illustrations)**. If access to the special Honda oil filter tool can be gained, the filter should be tightened to the specified torque setting.

9   Before refilling the engine, check the old oil carefully. If the oil was drained into a clean pan, small pieces of metal or other material can be

11.8b . . . and screw the filter onto the engine

easily detected. If the oil is very metallic colored, then the engine is experiencing wear from break-in (new engine) or from insufficient lubrication. If there are flakes or chips of metal in the oil, then something is drastically wrong internally and the engine will have to be disassembled for inspection and repair.

10   If there are pieces of fiber-like material in the oil, the clutch is experiencing excessive wear and should be checked.

11   If inspection of the oil turns up nothing unusual, refill the crankcase to the proper level with the recommended type and amount of oil and install the filler cap. Start the engine and let it run for two or three minutes. Shut it off, wait a few minutes, then check the oil level. If necessary, add more oil to bring the level up to the upper mark. Check around the drain plug and filter for leaks. Refit the lower fairing panel(s).

12   The old oil drained from the engine cannot be re-used and should be disposed of properly. Check with your local refuse disposal company, disposal facility or environmental agency to see whether they will accept the used oil for recycling. Don't pour used oil into drains or onto the ground. After the oil has cooled, it can be drained into a suitable container (capped plastic jugs, topped bottles, milk cartons, etc.) for transport to one of these disposal sites.

12   Air filter element - change

Refer to illustrations 12.2, 12.3a, 12.3b and 12.7

1   Remove the fuel tank as described in Chapter 4.

2   Undo the retaining screws and remove the cover from the air filter housing **(see illustration)**.

12.2 Undo the retaining screws . . .

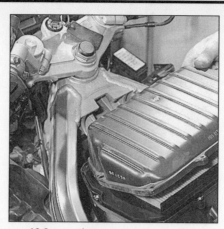
12.3a . . . then remove the air filter housing cover . . .

12.3b . . . and lift out the filter element

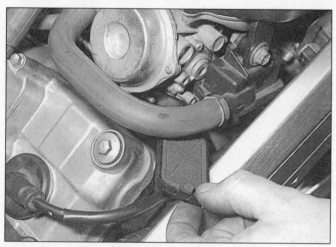
12.7 On L models onward also clean the air vent filter situated on the right side of the filter housing

3   Lift out the air filter element noting which way around it is fitted **(see illustrations)**.
4   Wipe out the housing with a clean rag.
5   Tap the element on a hard surface to shake out any dirt. If compressed air is available, use it to clean the element by blowing from the bottom of the element ups. If the element is extremely dirty or torn, replace the element with a new one.
6   Fit the element to the housing, making sure it is the correct way up with its TOP marking ups. Install the cover and securely tighten its retaining screws.
7   On L models onward, also clean the air vent filter situated in the small housing bolted to the right of the main filter housing. Depress the retaining tangs, unclip the base from the vent filter housing and remove the foam filter element **(see illustration)**. Wash the filter in a high flash point solvent, squeeze it dry, then soak it in clean SAE 80 to 90W gear oil. Squeeze excess oil out of the filter element, install the element in the housing and clip the base into position.
8   Install the fuel tank as described in Chapter 4.

13 Cylinder compression - check

1   Among other things, poor engine performance may be caused by leaking valves, incorrect valve clearances, a leaking head gasket, or worn pistons, rings and/or cylinder walls. A cylinder compression check will help pinpoint these conditions and can also indicate the presence of excessive carbon deposits in the cylinder heads.
2   The only tools required are a compression gauge and a spark

plug wrench. Depending on the outcome of the initial test, a squirt-type oil can may also be needed.
3   Start the engine and allow it to reach normal operating temperature, then stop it.
4   Place the motorcycle on the centerstand or support it in an upright position.
5   Remove the spark plugs as described in Section 14. **Caution:** *Work carefully - don't strip the spark plug hole threads and don't burn your hands on the hot cylinder heads.*
6   Disable the ignition by switching the kill switch to OFF.
7   On models where the starter will not operate with the kill switch off, refit the spark plugs to their caps and securely ground (earth) each plug on the engine unit. **Caution:** *If the plugs are not properly grounded, there is a risk of damaging the spark unit.* Prior to turning the engine over, cover the three remaining spark plug holes with rag to prevent the risk of igniting the fuel vapor.
8   Install the compression gauge in one of the spark plug holes and place a rag over the other three plug holes as a precaution against the risk of fire.
9   Hold the throttle wide open and crank the engine over a minimum of four or five revolutions (or until the gauge reading stops increasing) and observe the initial movement of the compression gauge needle as well as the final total gauge reading. Repeat the procedure for the other cylinders and compare the results to the value listed in this Chapter's Specifications.
10 If the compression in all four cylinders built up quickly and evenly to the specified amount, you can assume the engine upper end is in reasonably good mechanical condition. Worn or sticking piston rings and worn cylinders will produce very little initial movement of the gauge needle, but compression will tend to build up gradually as the engine spins over. Valve and valve seat leakage, or head gasket leakage, is indicated by low initial compression which does not tend to build up.
11 To further confirm your findings, add a small amount of engine oil to each cylinder by inserting the nozzle of a squirt-type oil can through the spark plug holes. The oil will tend to seal the piston rings if they are leaking. Repeat the test for the other cylinders.
12 If the compression increases significantly after the addition of the oil, the piston rings and/or cylinders are definitely worn. If the compression does not increase, the pressure is leaking past the valves or the head gasket. Leakage past the valves may be due to insufficient valve clearances, burned, warped or cracked valves or valve seats, or valves that are hanging up in the guides.
13 If the compression readings are considerably higher than specified, the combustion chambers are probably coated with excessive carbon deposits. It is possible (but not very likely) for carbon deposits to raise the compression enough to compensate for the effects of leakage past rings or valves. Use of a fuel additive that will dissolve the adhesive bonding the carbon particles to the crown and chamber is the easiest way to remove the build-up. Otherwise, the cylinder heads will have to be removed and decarbonized (Chapter 2).

14.3a Disconnect the spark plug caps . . .

14.3b . . . then unscrew the spark plugs . . .

14.3c . . . and remove them from the engine; spark plug removal tool shown is the one supplied in the bike's tool kit

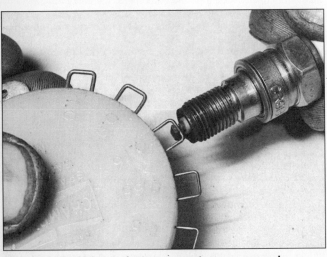

14.7a Using a wire type gauge to measure spark plug electrode gap

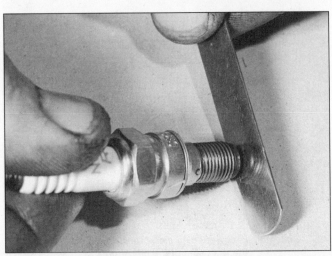

14.7b Using a feeler gauge to measure spark plug electrode gap

14 Spark plugs - check and replacement

Refer to illustrations 14.3a, 14.3b, 14.3c, 14.7a, 14.7b and 14.7c

Note: *Make sure your spark plug socket is the correct size before attempting to remove the plugs; a suitable one is supplied in the motorcycle's tool kit.*

1   On G through K models, the spark plugs have 12 mm threads and an 18 mm wrench hex. To gain access to the rear cylinder spark plugs remove the side covers (see Chapter 8), and to gain access to the front spark plugs undo the two lower radiator mounting bolts then pivot the radiator forwards and tie it to the fork legs.

2   On L models onward, the spark plugs have 10 mm threads and a 16 mm wrench hex. To gain access to the front cylinder spark plugs, remove the middle fairing panels (see Chapter 8); to improve access to the spark plug caps, undo the lower radiator mounting bolts and swing the radiator forwards. To gain access to the rear cylinder spark plugs, remove the seat (see Chapter 8), then remove the fuel tank rear mounting bolt. Raise the rear of the tank and hold it in position by inserting the U-shaped tool included in the motorcycle's tool kit through the tank and frame bolt holes.

3   On all models, disconnect the spark plug caps from the spark plugs. If available, use compressed air to blow any accumulated debris from around the spark plugs. Remove the plugs and lay them out in relation to their cylinder number; if any plug shows up a problem it will

then be easy to identify the troublesome cylinder **(see illustrations)**.

4   Inspect the electrodes for wear. Both the center and side electrodes should have square edges and the side electrode should be of uniform thickness. Look for excessive deposits and evidence of a cracked or chipped insulator around the center electrode. Compare your spark plugs to the color spark plug reading chart. Check the threads, the washer and the ceramic insulator body for cracks and other damage.

5   If the electrodes are not excessively worn, and if the deposits can be easily removed with a wire brush, the plugs can be re-gapped and re-used (if no cracks or chips are visible in the insulator). If in doubt concerning the condition of the plugs, replace them with new ones, as the expense is minimal.

6   Cleaning spark plugs by sandblasting is permitted, provided you clean the plugs with a high flash-point solvent afterwards.

7   Before installing new plugs, make sure they are the correct type and heat range. Check the gap between the electrodes, as they are not preset. For best results, use a wire-type gauge rather than a flat (feeler) gauge to check the gap. If the gap must be adjusted, bend the side electrode only and be very careful not to chip or crack the insulator nose **(see illustrations)**. Make sure the washer is in place before installing each plug.

8   Since the cylinder head is made of aluminum, which is soft and easily damaged, thread the plugs into the heads by hand. The plugs are recessed, so slip a short length of hose over the end of the plug to

Spark plug maintenance: Checking plug gap with feeler gauges

Altering the plug gap. Note use of correct tool

Spark plug conditions: A brown, tan or grey firing end is indicative of correct engine running conditions and the selection of the appropriate heat rating plug

White deposits have accumulated from excessive amounts of oil in the combustion chamber or through the use of low quality oil. Remove deposits or a hot spot may form

Black sooty deposits indicate an over-rich fuel/air mixture, or a malfunctioning ignition system. If no improvement is obtained, try one grade hotter plug

Wet, oily carbon deposits form an electrical leakage path along the insulator nose, resulting in a misfire. The cause may be a badly worn engine or a malfunctioning ignition system

A blistered white insulator or melted electrode indicates over-advanced ignition timing or a malfunctioning cooling system. If correction does not prove effective, try a colder grade plug

A worn spark plug not only wastes fuel but also overloads the whole ignition system because the increased gap requires higher voltage to initiate the spark. This condition can also affect air pollution

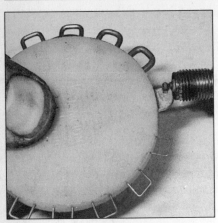

14.7c Electrode gap is adjusted by bending the side electrode

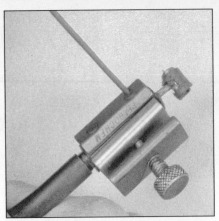

15.3 Lubricating a cable with a pressure lube adapter (make sure the tool seats around the inner cable)

16.4a On G through K models, position the crankshaft so the line next to the 'T' mark of No. 1 cylinder is aligned with the cover mark (arrow) . . .

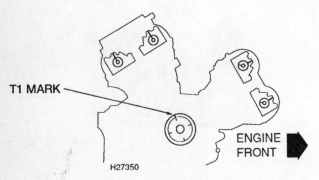

T1 MARK

ENGINE FRONT

H27350

16.4b . . . and check the marks on the camshaft ends are positioned as shown

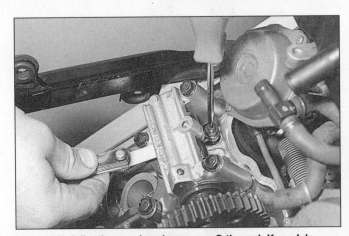

16.7 Adjusting a valve clearance - G through K models

use as a tool to thread it into place. The hose will grip the plug well enough to turn it, but will start to slip if the plug begins to cross-thread in the hole - this will prevent damaged threads and the resultant repair costs.

9   Once the plugs are finger-tight, the job can be finished with a socket. If a torque wrench is available, tighten the spark plugs to the specified torque listed in this Chapter's Specifications. If you do not have a torque wrench, tighten the plugs finger-tight (until the washers bottom on the cylinder head) then use a wrench to tighten them an additional 1/4 turn. Regardless of the method used, do not over-tighten them.

10   Reconnect the spark plug caps and reinstall all components removed for access.

15 Lubrication - general

Refer to illustration 15.3

1   Since the controls, cables and various other components of a motorcycle are exposed to the elements, they should be lubricated periodically to ensure safe and trouble-free operation.

2   The footpegs, clutch and brake lever, brake pedal, shift lever and side and centerstand pivots should be lubricated frequently. In order for the lubricant to be applied where it will do the most good, the component should be disassembled. However, if chain and cable lubricant is being used, it can be applied to the pivot joint gaps and will usually work its way into the areas where friction occurs. If motor oil or light grease is being used, apply it sparingly as it may attract dirt (which could cause the controls to bind or wear at an accelerated rate). **Note:** *One of the best lubricants for the control lever pivots is a dry-film*

lubricant (available from many sources by different names).

3   To lubricate the cables, disconnect the relevant cable at its upper end, then lubricate the cable with a pressure lube adapter **(see illustration)**. See Chapter 4 for the choke and throttle cable removal procedures.

4   The speedometer cable (where fitted) should be removed from its housing and lubricated with motor oil or cable lubricant. Do not lubricate the upper few inches of the cable as the lubricant may travel up into the speedometer head.

16 Valve clearances - check and adjustment

Note: *Refer to Specifications for cylinder identification information.*

1   The engine must be completely cool for this maintenance procedure, so let the machine sit overnight before beginning.

2   Remove the valve covers as described in Chapter 2.

3   Unscrew the center plug from the crankcase right cover. Proceed as described under the relevant sub-heading.

G through K models

Refer to illustrations 16.4a, 16.4b, 16.7, 16.9, 16.11 and 16.13

Note: *Adjustment of the valve clearances is greatly simplified if the Honda service tool 07GMA-ML70100 is available.*

4   Using a suitable socket, rotate the crankshaft clockwise until the 'T' mark of No. 1 cylinder is aligned with the index mark, in the form of a line on the casing **(see illustration)**. Now, check the position of the

16.9 Rotate the crankshaft through 180° so that the 'T' mark of No. 3 cylinder is aligned with the cover mark then check cylinder No. 3 valve clearances

16.11 Rotate the crankshaft through 270° so that the 'T' mark of No. 2 cylinder is aligned with the cover mark then check cylinder No. 2 valve clearances

16.13 Rotate the crankshaft through 180° so that the 'T' mark of No. 4 cylinder is aligned with the cover mark then check cylinder No. 4 valve clearances

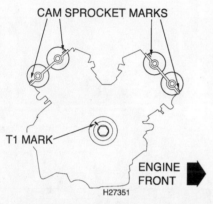

16.17 On L models onward, align the 'T' mark of No.1 cylinder with the cover mark and check that the camshaft gear straight lines are level with the cylinder head surfaces as shown

16.19 Measuring a valve clearance - L models onward

No. 1 cylinder cam lobes - they should be pointing away from the followers and the index marks on the right end of the camshafts should be positioned as shown in illustration 16.4b **(see illustration)**. If the lobes and marks are not correctly positioned, turn the crankshaft through 360° (one complete turn). Piston No. 1 is now at TDC compression. **Note:** *Turn the engine in the normal direction of rotation (clockwise), viewed from the right end of the engine.*

5   With the engine in this position, all four valves for cylinder No. 1 can be checked.

6   Insert a feeler gauge of the correct thickness (see Specifications) between each cam lobe and follower and check that it is a firm sliding fit. **Note:** *The intake and exhaust valve clearances are different.* If there is no drag, the clearance is too loose; if there is a heavy drag, the clearance is too tight.

7   If the clearance is incorrect, loosen the follower adjuster screw locknut with a suitable wrench and turn the adjuster screw in or out as needed **(see illustration)**.

8   Hold the adjuster screw (to prevent it turning) and tighten the locknut to the specified torque setting. Recheck the valve clearance to make sure it hasn't changed. Repeat the adjustment procedure as necessary until all four valves are correctly adjusted.

9   With No. 1 cylinder valves correctly adjusted, rotate the crankshaft 180° (half a turn) clockwise until the 'T' mark of No. 3 cylinder is aligned with the index mark on the casing. Piston No. 3 is now at TDC compression **(see illustration)**.

10   Check and, if necessary, adjust the four valves of No. 3 cylinder as described in Steps 6 to 8.

11   With No. 3 cylinder valves correctly adjusted, rotate the crankshaft 270° (three-quarters of a turn) clockwise until the 'T' mark of No. 2 cylinder is aligned with the index mark on the casing. Piston

No. 2 is now at TDC compression **(see illustration)**.

12   Check and, if necessary, adjust the four valves of No. 2 cylinder as described in Steps 6 to 8.

13   With No. 2 cylinder valves correctly adjusted, rotate the crankshaft 180° (half a turn) clockwise until the 'T' mark of No. 4 cylinder is aligned with the index mark on the casing. Piston No. 4 is now at TDC compression **(see illustration)**.

14   Check and, if necessary, adjust the four valves of No. 4 cylinder as described in Steps 6 to 8.

15   When all valve clearances are correctly set, install the valve covers as described in Chapter 2.

L models onward

Refer to illustrations 16.17, 16.19, 16.26a and 16.26b

16   Draw the valve positions on a piece of paper.

17   Using a suitable socket, rotate the crankshaft clockwise until the 'T' mark of No. 1 cylinder is aligned with the index mark, in the form of a cutout, on the casing. Now, check the position of the No. 1 cylinder cam lobes - they should be pointing away from the followers and the straight lines marked on each camshaft gear should be level with the cylinder head upper surface **(see illustration)**. If the lobes and marks are not correctly positioned, turn the crankshaft through 360° (one complete turn). Piston No. 1 is now at TDC compression. **Note:** *Turn the engine in the normal direction of rotation (clockwise), viewed from the right end of the engine.*

18   With the engine in this position, all four valves for cylinder No. 1 can be checked.

19   Insert a feeler gauge of the correct thickness (see Specifications) between each cam lobe and follower and check that it is a firm sliding fit **(see illustration)**. If it is not, use the feeler gauges to obtain the

16.26a Shim thickness is indicated by three numbers stamped on its surface; example shown 210 indicates that the shim is 2.100 mm thick

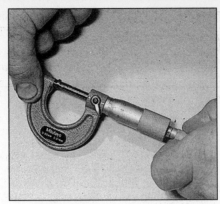

16.26b Measuring shim thickness

17.3a On early models the idle speed adjusting screw is mounted on the side of the carburetors . . .

exact clearance. **Note:** *The intake and exhaust valve clearances are different.*

20   Record the clearance of each valve next to its relevant location on the piece of paper.

21   With the four valves of No. 1 cylinder measured, rotate the crankshaft through 180° (half a turn) until the 'T' mark of No. 3 cylinder is aligned with the index mark on the casing. Piston No. 3 is now at TDC compression. Measure the clearances of the No. 3 cylinder valves and record them on the piece of paper.

22   With the four valves of No. 3 cylinder measured, rotate the crankshaft through 270° (three-quarters of a turn) until the 'T' mark of No. 2 cylinder is aligned with the index mark on the casing. Piston No. 2 is now at TDC compression. Measure the clearances of the No. 2 cylinder valves and record them on the piece of paper.

23   With the four valves of No. 2 cylinder measured, rotate the crankshaft through 180° (half a turn) until the 'T' mark of No. 4 cylinder is aligned with the index mark on the casing. Piston No. 4 is now at TDC compression. Measure the clearances of the No. 4 cylinder valves and record them on the piece of paper.

24   If any of the clearances need to be adjusted the relevant camshaft(s) must be removed as described in Chapter 2.

25   With the camshaft removed, using a magnet, lift the follower on the valve to be adjusted out of the cylinder head and remove the shim. Note that the shim is likely to stick to the inside of the follower so take great care not to lose it as the follower is removed. If more than one follower and shim is to be removed, make sure they are not interchanged.

26   The shim size should be stamped on its face, however, it is recommended that the shim is measured to check that it has not worn **(see illustrations)**. The size marking is in the form of a three figure number, e.g. 180 indicating that the shim is 1.800 mm thick. Where the number does not equal a shim thickness, it should be rounded up or down, e.g. 182 or 183 both indicate that the shim is 1.825 mm thick. Shims are available in 0.025 mm increments from 1.200 to 2.800 mm. The new shim thickness required can then be calculated as follows. **Note:** *Always aim to get the clearance at the mid-point of the specified range.*

27   If the valve clearance was less than specified, subtract the measured clearance from the specified clearance then deduct the result from the original shim thickness. For example:

Sample calculation - intake valve clearance too small
> *Clearance measured (A) - 0.08 mm*
> *Specified clearance (B) - 0.16 mm*
> *Difference (B - A) - 0.08 mm*
> *Shim thickness fitted - 2.475 mm*
> *Correct shim thickness required - 2.475 - 0.08 = 2.395 mm*

28   If the valve clearance was greater than specified, subtract the specified clearance from the measured clearance, and add the result to the thickness of the original shim. For example:

17.3b . . . and on later models it has an extension cable and is clipped to the frame

Sample calculation - exhaust valve clearance too large
> *Clearance measured (A) - 0.38 mm*
> *Specified clearance (B) - 0.25 mm*
> *Difference (A - B) - 0.13 mm*
> *Shim thickness fitted - 1.975 mm*
> *Correct shim thickness required - 1.975 + 0.13 = 2.105 mm*

29   Obtain the correct thickness shims from your Honda dealer.

30   Install the shim in position on top of the relevant valve, making sure it is correctly seated in the valve spring retainer.

31   Install the followers in their respective positions in the cylinder head, making sure each one squarely enters its bore.

32   Install the camshaft(s) as described in Chapter 2.

33   Rotate the crankshaft a few times, to settle all disturbed components, and recheck all valve clearances as described above. If necessary, repeat the adjustment procedure.

34   When all the valve clearances are correctly set, install the valve covers as described in Chapter 2.

17   Idle speed - check and adjustment

Refer to illustrations 17.3a and 17.3b

1   The idle speed should be checked and adjusted before and after the carburetors are synchronized and when it is obviously too high or too low. Before adjusting the idle speed, make sure the valve clearances and spark plug gaps are correct. Also, turn the handlebars back-and-forth and see if the idle speed changes as this is done. If it does, the throttle cables may not be adjusted correctly, or may be worn out. This is a dangerous condition that can cause loss of control

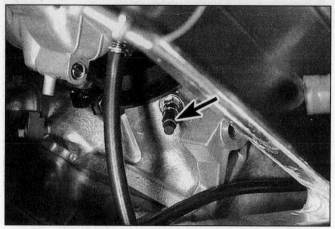

18.2 On R models adapters (arrow) are already screwed into the intake ports; simply remove the cap and connect the vacuum gauge

of the bike. Be sure to correct this problem before proceeding.

2   The engine should be at normal operating temperature (usually reached after 10 to 15 minutes of stop and go riding) and running. Place the motorcycle on the centerstand or support it securely and make sure the transmission is in Neutral.

3   Turn the idle speed screw, which is located on the left side of the machine, behind the lower/middle fairing panel (the screw can be reached from behind the fairing panel or through the ventilation hole in the fairing panel), until the idle speed listed in this Chapter's Specifications is obtained. Note that on early models the screw is mounted on the side of the carburetors and on later models it has an extension cable and is positioned away from the carburetors for easier access **(see illustrations)**.

4   Snap the throttle open and shut a few times, then recheck the idle speed. If necessary, repeat the adjustment procedure.

5   If a smooth, steady idle can't be achieved, the fuel/air mixture may be incorrect. Refer to Chapter 4 for additional carburetor information.

18 Carburetor synchronization - check and adjustment

Refer to illustration 18.2

Warning: *Gasoline (petrol) is extremely flammable, so take extra precautions when you work on any part of the fuel system. Don't smoke or allow open flames or bare light bulbs near the work area, and don't work in a garage where a natural gas-type appliance (such as a water heater or clothes dryer) is present. If you spill any fuel on your skin, rinse it off immediately with soap and water. When you perform any kind of work on the fuel system, wear safety glasses and have a fire extinguisher suitable for a Class B type fire (flammable liquids) on hand.*

1   Carburetor synchronization is simply the process of adjusting the carburetors so they pass the same amount of fuel/air mixture to each cylinder. This is done by measuring the vacuum produced in each cylinder. Carburetors that are out of synchronization will result in decreased fuel mileage, increased engine temperature, less than ideal throttle response and higher vibration levels.

2   To properly synchronize the carburetors, you will need some sort of vacuum gauge setup, preferably with a gauge for each cylinder, or a mercury manometer, which is a calibrated tube arrangement that utilizes columns of mercury to indicate engine vacuum. On G through P models, four adapters will also be required, one for each cylinder, to screw into the holes in the cylinder intake ports. On R models adapters are already screwed into the ports **(see illustration)**.

3   A manometer can be purchased from a motorcycle dealer or accessory shop and should have the necessary rubber hoses supplied with it for hooking into the vacuum hose fittings/adapters.

4   A vacuum gauge setup can also be purchased from a dealer or fabricated from commonly available hardware and automotive vacuum gauges.

5   The manometer is the more reliable and accurate instrument, and for that reason is preferred over the vacuum gauge setup; however, since the mercury used in the manometer is a liquid, and extremely toxic, extra precautions must be taken during use and storage of the instrument.

6   Because of the nature of the synchronization procedure and the need for special instruments, most owners leave the task to a dealer service department or a reputable motorcycle repair shop.

7   Start the engine and let it run until it reaches normal operating temperature, then shut it off.

8   Remove the left and right lower/middle panels (as applicable) as described in Chapter 8.

9   On G through P models, undo the screw from the side of each intake port and screw in the adapter; on R models remove the rubber caps from the intake port adapters. **Warning:** *Take great care not to burn your hand on the hot engine unit.*

10   Hook up the vacuum gauge set or the manometer according to the manufacturer's instructions. Make sure there are no leaks in the setup, as false readings will result.

11   Start the engine and make sure the idle speed is correct. If it isn't, adjust it (see Section 17). If the gauges are fitted with damping adjustment, set this so that the needle flutter is just eliminated but so that they can still respond to small changes in pressure.

12   The vacuum readings for all of the cylinders should be the same, or at least within the tolerance listed in this Chapter's Specifications. If the vacuum readings vary, adjust as necessary.

13   The carburetors are adjusted by the three screws situated in-between each carburetor, in the throttle linkage. The screws are accessible from underneath the carburetors. **Note:** *Do not press on the screws whilst adjusting them, otherwise a false reading will be obtained. When all the carburetors are synchronized, open and close the throttle quickly to settle the linkage, and recheck the gauge readings, re-adjusting if necessary.*

14   When the adjustment is complete, recheck the vacuum readings and idle speed, then stop the engine. Remove the vacuum gauge or manometer.

15   On G through P models, fit the screws to the intake ports and tighten them securely. On R models fit the rubber caps to the adapters making sure they are securely retained by their clips.

16   Install the fairing panels as described in Chapter 8.

19 Cooling system - check

Refer to illustrations 19.7a and 19.7b

Warning: *The engine must be cool before beginning this procedure.*

1   Check the coolant level as described in Section 3.

2   Remove the left and right lower/middle fairing panels (as applicable) as described in Chapter 8.

3   The entire cooling system should be checked for evidence of leakage. Examine each rubber coolant hose along its entire length. Look for cracks, abrasions and other damage. Squeeze each hose at various points. They should feel firm, yet pliable, and return to their original shape when released. If they are dried out or hard, replace them with new ones.

4   Check for evidence of leaks at each cooling system joint. Tighten the hose clips carefully to prevent future leaks.

5   Check the radiator for leaks and other damage. Leaks in the radiator leave telltale scale deposits or coolant stains on the outside of the core below the leak. If leaks are noted, remove the radiator (see Chapter 3) and have it repaired at a radiator shop or replace it with a new one. **Caution:** *Do not use a liquid leak stopping compound to try to repair leaks.*

6   Check the radiator fins for mud, dirt and insects, which may impede the flow of air through the radiator. If the fins are dirty, force water or low pressure compressed air through the fins from the

1

backside. If the fins are bent or distorted, straighten them carefully with a screwdriver.

7   Undo the retaining screw(s) and remove the inner panel from the right side of the upper fairing (see Chapter 8) to gain access to the radiator pressure cap **(see illustrations)**.

8   Remove the pressure cap by turning it counterclockwise (anti-clockwise) until it reaches a stop. If you hear a hissing sound (indicating there is still pressure in the system), wait until it stops. Now press down on the cap and continue turning it until it can be removed. Check the condition of the coolant in the system. If it is rust-colored or if accumulations of scale are visible, drain, flush and refill the system with new coolant (See Section 20). Check the cap seal for cracks and other damage. If in doubt about the pressure cap's condition, have it tested by a dealer service department or replace it with a new one. Install the cap by turning it clockwise until it reaches the first stop then push down on the cap and continue turning until it can turn no further.

9   Check the antifreeze content of the coolant with an antifreeze hydrometer. Sometimes coolant looks like it's in good condition, but might be too weak to offer adequate protection. If the hydrometer indicates a weak mixture, drain, flush and refill the system (see Section 20).

10   Start the engine and let it reach normal operating temperature, then check for leaks again. As the coolant temperature increases, the fan should come on automatically and the temperature should begin to drop. If it does not, refer to Chapter 3 and check the fan and fan circuit carefully.

11   If the coolant level is consistently low, and no evidence of leaks can be found, have the entire system pressure checked by a Honda dealer service department, motorcycle repair shop or service station.

12   Ensure the pressure cap is correctly installed then fit the fairing panels as described in Chapter 8.

20   Cooling system - draining, flushing and refilling

Warning: *Allow the engine to cool completely before performing this maintenance operation. Also, don't allow antifreeze to come into contact with your skin or the painted surfaces of the motorcycle. Rinse off spills immediately with plenty of water. Antifreeze is highly toxic if ingested. Never leave antifreeze lying around in an open container or in puddles on the floor; children and pets are attracted by its sweet smell and may drink it. Check with local authorities (councils) about disposing of antifreeze. Many communities have collection centers which will see that antifreeze is disposed of safely. Antifreeze is also combustible, so don't store it near open flames.*

Draining

Refer to illustrations 20.2 and 20.4

1   Undo the retaining screw(s) and remove the inner panel from the right side of the upper fairing to gain access to the radiator pressure cap.

2   Position a suitable container beneath the water pump, then

19.7a On G through K models remove the right inner panel . . .

remove the drain bolt and sealing washer from the pump cover **(see illustration). Note:** *On some models it may be necessary to remove the lower fairing panel to gain access to the water pump drain bolt* (see Chapter 8).

3   Remove the pressure cap by turning it counterclockwise (anti-clockwise) until it reaches a stop. If you hear a hissing sound (indicating there is still pressure in the system), wait until it stops. Now press down on the cap and continue turning the cap until it can be removed. As the cap is removed the flow of coolant will increase, be prepared for this.

4   Once the flow of coolant has stopped from the pump, position the container beneath the front of the engine and remove the drain bolts from the front of the front cylinder block **(see illustration)**.

5   Drain the coolant reservoir. Refer to Chapter 3 for reservoir removal procedure. Wash out the reservoir with water.

Flushing

6   Flush the system with clean tap water by inserting a garden hose in the radiator filler neck. Allow the water to run through the system until it is clear and flows cleanly out of all drain holes. If the radiator is extremely corroded, remove it by referring to Chapter 3 and have it cleaned at a radiator shop.

7   Clean the holes then install the drain bolts and sealing washers, tightening them securely.

8   Fill the cooling system with clean water mixed with a flushing compound. Make sure the flushing compound is compatible with aluminum components, and follow the manufacturer's instructions carefully.

9   Start the engine and allow it reach normal operating temperature. Let it run for about ten minutes.

10   Stop the engine. Let it cool for a while, then cover the pressure

19.7b . . . to gain access to the pressure cap

20.2 Location of cooling system drain bolt on the water pump cover . . .

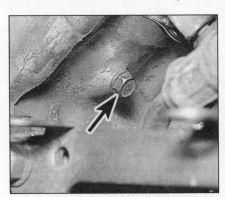

20.4 . . . and bolts on the front of the cylinder block (right side bolt arrowed)

20.14 Fill the cooling system using a funnel to avoid spilling coolant over the bodywork (H model shown)

23.4 Grasp the front wheel and try to pull it back and forth; if it moves, the steering head bearings are loose and in need of adjustment

cap with a heavy shop towel and turn it counterclockwise (anticlockwise) to the first stop, releasing any pressure that may be present in the system. Once the hissing stops, push down on the cap and remove it completely.

11   Drain the system once again.

12   Fill the system with clean water and repeat the procedure in Steps 9 to 11.

Refilling

Refer to illustration 20.14

13   Fit new sealing washers to the drain bolts and install them in the front of the cylinder block and pump cover, tightening each one securely.

14   Fill the system with the proper coolant mixture (see this Chapter's Specifications) **(see illustration)**.

15   When the system is full (all the way up to the top of the radiator filler neck), start the engine and allow it to idle for 2 to 3 minutes. Flick the throttle twistgrip part open 3 or 4 times, so that the engine speed rises to approximately 4000 - 5000 rpm, then stop the engine. This process will bleed any trapped air bubbles from the system.

16   Top up the coolant level to the base of the filler neck and install the pressure cap. Also top up the coolant reservoir to the UPPER level mark.

17   Start the engine and allow it to reach normal operating temperature, then shut it off.

18   Let the engine cool then remove the pressure cap as described in Step 10. Check that the coolant level is still up to the radiator filler neck. If it's low, add more of the specified mixture until it reaches the top of the filler neck. Reinstall the cap.

19   Check the coolant level in the reservoir and top up if necessary.

20   Check the system for leaks. If all is well, install the fairing panels (Chapter 8).

21   Do not dispose of the old coolant by pouring it down the drain. Instead pour it into a heavy plastic container, cap it tightly and take it into an authorized disposal site or service station - see Warning at the beginning of this Section.

21   Evaporative Emission Control (EVAP) system and Pulse Secondary Air Injection (PAIR) system (California models only) - check

1   These systems are installed on California models to conform to stringent emission control standards. The Evaporative emission (EVAP) system, routes fuel vapors from the fuel system into the engine to be burned, instead of letting them evaporate into the atmosphere. When the engine isn't running, vapors are stored in a carbon canister. The

Pulse secondary air (PAIR) system is explained in greater detail in Chapter 4.

2   To begin the inspection of the system, remove the side covers, seat, fuel tank and lower/middle fairing panels (see Chapters 4 and 8). Inspect the hoses from the fuel tank and carburetors to the canister (mounted underneath the bike) for cracking, kinks or other signs of deterioration. Details of the correct routing of all hoses is given on a label attached to the top of the rear fender (mudguard).

3   Label and disconnect the hoses, then remove the canister from the machine.

4   Inspect the canister for cracks or other signs of damage. Tip the canister so the nozzles point down. If fuel runs out of the canister, it is probably damaged internally, so it would be a good idea to replace it.

22   Exhaust system - check

1   Periodically check all of the exhaust system joints for leaks and loose fasteners. The lower fairing panels will have to be removed to do this properly (see Chapter 8). If tightening the fasteners fails to stop any leaks, replace the gaskets with new ones (a procedure which requires disassembly of the system). Refer to Chapter 4 for further information.

2   The exhaust pipe flange nuts at the cylinder heads are especially prone to loosening, which could cause damage to the head. Check them frequently and keep them tight.

23   Steering head bearings - check and adjustment

1   This vehicle is equipped with caged ball type steering head bearings which can become dented, rough or loose during normal use of the machine. In extreme cases, worn or loose steering head bearings can cause steering wobble - a condition that is potentially dangerous.

Check

Refer to illustration 23.4

2   To check the bearings, place the motorcycle on the centerstand and block the machine so the front wheel is in the air. Where no centerstand is fitted, support the motorcycle in an upright position so that its front wheel is clear of the ground.

3   Point the wheel straight-ahead and slowly move the handlebars from side-to-side. Dents or roughness in the bearing races will be felt and the bars will not move smoothly.

4   Next, grasp the forks and try to move them forward and backward **(see illustration)**. Any looseness in the steering head bearings will be

felt as front-to-rear movement of the fork legs. If play is felt in the bearings, adjust the steering head as follows.

Adjustment

5   Referring to Chapter 6 for further information, carefully pry off the snap-ring from the top of each fork tube.

6   Slacken each handlebar's clamp bolt. Slide the handlebars off of the fork tube and support them to prevent straining the hydraulic hose or the possible leakage of fluid from the master cylinders.

7   Slacken the top triple clamp bolts then pry off the cap from the steering stem top nut. Slacken and remove the nut and lift off the top triple clamp.

8   Bend the lockwasher tabs out of the slots in the locknut, then using a suitable C-wrench, slacken and remove the adjuster nut locknut.

9   Remove the lock washer and discard it; a new one must be fitted on reassembly.

10   Slacken the adjuster nut slightly until pressure is just released, then turn it slowly clockwise until resistance is just evident. The object is to set the adjuster nut so that the bearings are under a very light loading, just enough to remove any freeplay. **Caution:** *Take great care not to apply excessive pressure because this will cause premature failure of the bearings.*

11   With the bearings correctly adjusted, fit a new lock washer to the adjuster nut. Bend down two opposite lock washer tabs into the grooves of the adjuster nut.

12   Install the locknut and tighten it finger-tight only.

13   Hold the adjuster nut, to prevent it from moving, and tighten the locknut approximately 90° more until its slots align with the remaining lock washer tabs. Secure the locknut in position by bending up the lock washer tabs into its slots.

14   Fit the top triple clamp to the steering stem then install the stem top nut and tighten it and both the clamp bolts to their specified torque settings (see Chapter 6). Fit the cap.

15   Re-check the bearing adjustment as described above and re-adjust if necessary.

16   With the bearing adjustment correctly set, install the handlebars to the top of the fork tubes, ensuring that the lug on the bottom of each casting is correctly located with the cutout on the top triple clamp.

17   Fit the snap-rings to each fork tube making sure they are correctly located in their grooves. Tighten the handlebar clamp bolts to the specified torque whilst pushing each handlebar fully forwards (see Chapter 6).

24 Fasteners - check

1   Since vibration of the machine tends to loosen fasteners, all nuts, bolts, screws, etc. should be periodically checked for proper tightness.

2   Pay particular attention to the following:

Spark plugs
Engine oil drain plug
Gearshift lever
SAE, sidestand and centerstand
Engine mounting bolts
Shock absorber mounting bolts
Handlebar and triple clamp bolts
Rear suspension linkage bolts
Front axle and clamp bolts
Rear axle nut
Exhaust system bolts/nuts

3   If a torque wrench is available, use it along with the torque specifications at the beginning of this, or other, Chapters.

25 Fuel system - check and filter cleaning

Refer to illustration 25.6

Warning: *Gasoline (petrol) is extremely flammable, so take extra*

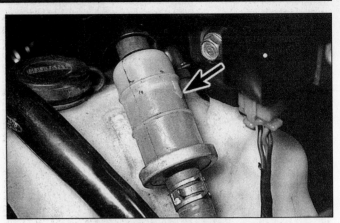

25.6 On installation ensure the fuel filter arrow (arrowed) is pointing towards the fuel pump

precautions when you work on any part of the fuel system. Don't smoke or allow open flames or bare light bulbs near the work area, and don't work in a garage where a natural gas-type appliance (such as a water heater or clothes dryer) is present. If you spill any fuel on your skin, rinse it off immediately with soap and water. When you perform any kind of work on the fuel system, wear safety glasses and have a fire extinguisher suitable for a Class B type fire (flammable liquids) on hand.

Check

1   Remove the fuel tank as described in Chapter 4.

2   Check the fuel tank, the tank breather hose (not California models), the fuel tap, the lines and the carburetors for leaks and evidence of damage.

3   If the carburetor gaskets are leaking, the carburetors should be disassembled and rebuilt by referring to Chapter 4.

4   If the fuel tap is leaking, tightening its retaining nuts/bolts may help but if leakage persists, the tap should be disassembled and repaired or replaced with a new one.

5   If the fuel lines are cracked or otherwise deteriorated, replace them with new ones.

Fuel filter

6   The fuel filter, fitted to the line between the fuel tap and fuel pump, should be inspected for signs of clogging. If there are any traces of debris visible through the translucent material of the filter, it must be replaced. The new filter must be installed with the arrow on its body pointing towards the outlet (fuel pump) side of the filter **(see illustration)**.

7   On L models onward, the fuel filter, which is attached to the fuel tap, may become clogged and should be removed and cleaned periodically. In order to clean the filter, the fuel tank must be drained and the fuel tap removed.

8   Remove the fuel tank (see Chapter 4). Drain the fuel into an approved fuel container.

9   Once the tank is emptied, unscrew the bolts and remove the tap and filter. Recover the O-ring from the tap.

10   Clean the filter with solvent and blow it dry with compressed air. If the filter is torn or otherwise damaged, replace the entire fuel tap with a new one. Check the O-ring and replace it if it is damaged or worn.

11   Install the O-ring, filter and fuel tap to the tank and securely tighten the retaining bolts. Install the tank (see Chapter 4) and refill with fuel. Check carefully for leaks around the tap.

26 Suspension - check

Refer to illustration 26.3

1   The suspension components must be maintained in top operating condition to ensure rider safety. Loose, worn or damaged suspension

26.3 Check above and below the fork seals (arrow) for signs of oil leakage

parts decrease the vehicle's stability and control.

2   While standing alongside the motorcycle, apply the front brake and push on the handlebars to compress the forks several times. See if they move up-and-down smoothly without binding. If binding is felt, the forks should be disassembled and inspected as described in Chapter 6.

3   Carefully inspect the area around the fork seals for any signs of fork oil leakage **(see illustration)**. If leakage is evident, the seals must be replaced as described in Chapter 6.

4   Check the tightness of all suspension nuts and bolts to be sure none have worked loose.

5   Inspect the rear shock for fluid leakage and tightness of the mounting nuts. If leakage is found, the shock should be replaced.

6   Set the bike on its centerstand or support it in an upright position so that its rear wheel is clear of the ground. Grab the swingarm on each side, just ahead of the axle. Rock the swingarm from side to side - there should be no discernible movement at the rear. If there's a little movement or a slight clicking can be heard, make sure the pivot shaft bolt(s)/adjuster nut are tight (see Chapter 6). If they are tight but movement is still noticeable, the swingarm will have to be removed and the bearings replaced as described in Chapter 6.

7   Inspect the tightness of the rear suspension nuts and bolts.

27 Brake and clutch fluid change

Note: *To prevent damage to the paint from spilled brake fluid, always cover the fuel tank when working on the master cylinder(s).*

1   The procedure is similar to that for the bleeding of the hydraulic system as described in Chapters 2 (clutch) or 7 (brakes), except that the fluid reservoir should be emptied, by siphoning, before starting and filled with fresh hydraulic fluid.

2   Working as described, open the bleeder valve and pump the lever/pedal gently. Be careful to keep the master cylinder reservoir topped up to above the LOWER level at all times or air may enter the system and greatly increase the length of the task. Continue pumping until new fluid can be seen emerging from the bleeder valve. **Note:** *Old hydraulic fluid is usually much darker in color than the new, making it easy to distinguish the two.*

3   When the new fluid is seen to be emerging, hold the lever/pedal and securely tighten the bleeder valve. Top up the reservoir level up to the UPPER level line and fit the diaphragm, plate and cover.

4   When the operation is complete, wash off all traces of spilt fluid and recheck the reservoir fluid level (see Section 3).

5   Check the operation of the clutch/brake before riding the motorcycle.

Notes

Chapter 2
Engine, clutch and transmission

Note: *Refer to Identification numbers at the beginning of this Manual to establish the model code of your motorcycle.*

Contents

Specifications

General

Capacity	
700 models	699 cc
750 models	748 cc
Bore	70.0 mm (2.76 in)
Stroke	
700 models	45.4 mm (1.79 in)
750 models	48.6 mm (1.91 in)
Compression ratio	
G and H models	10.5 to 1
J models onward	11.0 to 1

Camshafts

Intake cam lobe height
  California models
    G and H models
      Standard .... 31.406 to 31.566 mm (1.2365 to 1.2428 in)
      Service limit .... 31.37 mm (1.235 in)
    L models onward
      Standard .... 33.980 to 34.140 mm (1.3378 to 1.3441 in)
      Service limit .... 33.95 mm (1.3366 in)
  All other models
    G through K models
      Standard .... 31.406 to 31.566 mm (1.2365 to 1.2428 in)
      Service limit .... 31.37 mm (1.235 in)
    L models onward
      Standard .... 36.280 to 36.360 mm (1.4283 to 1.4315 in)
      Service limit .... 36.25 mm (1.427 in)
Exhaust cam lobe height
  California models
    G and H models
      Standard .... 31.460 to 31.620 mm (1.2386 to 1.2449 in)
      Service limit .... 31.41 mm (1.237 in)
    L through P models
      Standard .... 35.270 to 35.430 mm (1.3886 to 1.3949 in)
      Service limit .... 35.24 mm (1.3874 in)
    R models
      Standard .... 35.470 to 35.630 mm (1.3965 to 1.4028 in)
      Service limit .... 35.44 mm (1.3953 in)
  All other models
    G and H models
      Standard .... 31.460 to 31.620 mm (1.2386 to 1.2449 in)
      Service limit .... 31.41 mm (1.237 in)
    L through P models
      Standard .... 36.370 to 36.450 mm (1.4319 to 1.4350 in)
      Service limit .... 36.34 mm (1.431 in)
    R models
      Standard .... 36.070 to 36.230 mm (1.4201 to 1.4264 in)
      Service limit .... 36.04 mm (1.419 in)
Camshaft journal OD
  G through K models
    Standard .... 27.939 to 27.960 mm (1.1000 to 1.1008 in)
    Service limit .... 27.93 mm (1.100 in)
  L models onward
    Standard .... 24.949 to 24.970 mm (0.9822 to 0.9831 in)
    Service limit .... 24.94 mm (0.982 in)
Camshaft bearing cap ID
  G through K models
    Standard .... 28.000 to 28.021 mm (1.1024 to 1.1032 in)
    Service limit .... 28.03 mm (1.104 in)
  L models onward
    Standard .... 25.000 to 25.021 mm (0.9843 to 0.9851 in)
    Service limit .... Not available
Camshaft bearing oil clearance
  G through K models
    Standard .... 0.040 to 0.082 mm (0.0016 to 0.0032 in)
    Service limit .... 0.10 mm (0.004 in)
  L models onward
    Standard .... 0.020 to 0.062 mm (0.0008 to 0.0024 in)
    Service limit .... 0.10 mm (0.004 in)
Camshaft runout
  G through K models .... Less than 0.03 mm (0.001 in)
  L models onward .... Less than 0.05 mm (0.002 in)
Camshaft follower OD - L models onward
  Standard .... 25.978 to 25.993 mm (1.0228 to 1.0233 in)
  Service limit .... 25.968 mm (1.0224 in)

Cylinder head

Maximum warpage .... 0.10 mm (0.004 in)
Cylinder head follower bore ID - L models onward
  Standard .... 26.010 to 26.026 mm (1.0240 to 1.0246 in)
  Service limit .... 26.040 mm (1.0252 in)

Valves, guides and springs

Intake valve stem OD
  G and H models
    Standard .... 5.475 to 5.490 mm (0.2156 to 0.2161 in)
    Service limit .... 5.47 mm (0.215 in)
  J and K models
    Standard .... 4.975 to 4.990 mm (0.1959 to 0.1965 in)
    Service limit .... 4.965 mm (0.1955 in)
  L models onward
    Standard .... 4.475 to 4.490 mm (0.1762 to 0.1767 in)
    Service limit .... 4.465 mm (0.1758 in)

Exhaust valve stem OD
  G and H models
    Standard .... 5.455 to 5.470 mm (0.2148 to 0.2154 in)
    Service limit .... 5.45 mm (0.214 in)
  J and K models
    Standard .... 4.955 to 4.970 mm (0.1951 to 0.1957 in)
    Service limit .... 4.945 mm (0.1947 in)
  L models onward
    Standard .... 4.465 to 4.480 mm (0.1758 to 0.1764 in)
    Service limit .... 4.455 mm (0.1754 in)

Valve guide ID - intake and exhaust
  G and H models
    Standard .... 5.500 to 5.515 mm (0.2165 to 0.2171 in)
    Service limit .... 5.55 mm (0.219 in)
  J and K models
    Standard .... 5.000 to 5.012 mm (0.1969 to 0.1973 in)
    Service limit .... 5.080 mm (0.2000 in)
  L models onward
    Standard .... 4.500 to 4.512 mm (0.1772 to 0.1776 in)
    Service limit .... 4.562 mm (0.1796 in)

Valve stem-to-guide clearance
  G through K models
    Intake .... 0.010 to 0.037 mm (0.0004 to 0.0015 in)
    Exhaust .... 0.030 to 0.057 mm (0.0012 to 0.0022 in)
  L models onward .... Not available

Valve seat width
  G through K models
    Standard .... 1.0 to 1.3 mm (0.04 to 0.05 in)
    Service limit .... 1.5 mm (0.06 in)
  L models onward
    Standard .... 1.0 mm (0.04 in)
    Service limit .... 1.5 mm (0.06 in)

Inner valve spring free length
  G and H models
    Standard .... 32.8 mm (1.29 in)
    Service limit .... 31.3 mm (1.23 in)
  J and K models
    Standard .... 32.2 mm (1.27 in)
    Service limit .... 30.7 mm (1.21 in)
  L models onward
    Standard .... 34.2 mm (1.35 in)
    Service limit .... 32.5 mm (32.5 in)

Outer valve spring free length
  G and H models
    Standard .... 37.0 mm (1.46 in)
    Service limit .... 35.4 mm (1.39 in)
  J and K models
    Standard .... 37.4 mm (1.47 in)
    Service limit .... 35.8 mm (1.41 in)
  L models onward
    Standard .... 38.1 mm (1.50 in)
    Service limit .... 36.2 mm (1.43 in)

Clutch

Friction plate thickness
  Standard .... 2.92 to 3.08 mm (0.115 to 0.121 in)
  Service limit .... 2.50 mm (0.10 in)
Plain plate maximum warpage .... 0.3 mm (0.012 in)

Clutch (continued)

Clutch spring free length
    Standard.. 44.4 mm (1.75 in)
    Service limit... 41.2 mm (1.62 in)
Clutch drum center bush ID
    Standard.. 24.995 to 25.012 mm (0.9841 to 0.9847 in)
    Service limit... 25.08 mm (0.987 in)
Master cylinder bore ID
    Standard.. 14.000 to 14.043 mm (0.5512 to 0.5529 in)
    Service limit... 14.06 mm (0.553 in)
Master cylinder piston OD
    Standard.. 13.957 to 13.984 mm (0.5495 to 0.5506 in)
    Service limit... 13.94 mm (0.549 in)
Release cylinder bore ID
    Standard.. 35.700 to 35.762 mm (1.4055 to 1.4079 in)
    Service limit... 35.78 mm (1.409 in)
Release cylinder piston OD
    Standard.. 35.650 to 35.675 mm (1.4035 to 1.4045 in)
    Service limit... 35.63 mm (1.403 in)

Lubrication system

Oil pressure (at 5000 rpm) .... 71 to 85 psi (4.9 to 5.9 Bars) at 80°C (176°F)
Oil pump inner rotor tip-to-outer rotor clearance
    G through K models
        Standard .... 0.15 mm (0.006 in)
        Service limit... 0.20 mm (0.008 in)
    L models onward
        Standard .... 0.10 mm (0.004 in)
        Service limit... 0.15 mm (0.006 in)
Oil pump outer rotor-to-body clearance
    Standard.. 0.15 to 0.22 mm (0.006 to 0.009 in)
    Service limit... 0.35 mm (0.014 in)
Oil pump rotor endfloat
    Standard.. 0.02 to 0.07 mm (0.001 to 0.003 in)
    Service limit... 0.10 mm (0.004 in)

Starter motor clutch

Driven gear OD
    Standard.. 47.175 to 42.200 mm (1.8573 to 1.8583 in)
    Service limit... 47.16 mm (1.857 in)

Cylinder block

Cylinder bore ID
    Standard.. 70.000 to 70.015 mm (2.755 to 2.756 in)
    Service limit... 70.10 mm (2.759 in)
Maximum ovality (out-of-round) .... 0.10 mm (0.004 in)
Maximum taper... 0.10 mm (0.004 in)
Cylinder-to-piston clearance .... 0.010 to 0.045 mm (0.0004 to 0.0018 in)
Maximum gasket face warpage .... 0.10 mm (0.004 in)

Pistons

Piston OD (measured 10 mm up from base of skirt)
    Standard.. 69.970 to 69.990 mm (2.754 to 2.755 in)
    Service limit... 69.85 mm (2.750 in)
Piston pin bore OD
    Standard.. 17.002 to 17.008 mm (0.6694 to 0.6696 in)
    Service limit... 17.02 mm (0.670 in)
Piston pin OD
    Standard.. 16.994 to 17.000 mm (0.6691 to 0.6693 in)
    Service limit... 16.98 mm (0.669 in)
Piston-to-piston pin clearance .... 0.002 to 0.014 mm (0.0001 to 0.0005 in)

Piston rings

Top ring-to-groove clearance
    Standard.. 0.015 to 0.050 mm (0.0006 to 0.0019 in)
    Service limit... 0.10 mm (0.004 in)
Second (middle) ring-to-groove clearance
    Standard.. 0.015 to 0.045 mm (0.0006 to 0.0018 in)
    Service limit... 0.10 mm (0.004 in)

Top ring end gap
  G through K models
    Standard .... 0.20 to 0.40 mm (0.008 to 0.016 in)
    Service limit .... 0.55 mm (0.022 in)
  L models onward
    Standard .... 0.20 to 0.35 mm (0.008 to 0.014 in)
    Service limit... 0.5 mm (0.02 in)
Second ring end gap
  G through K models
    Standard .... 0.20 to 0.40 mm (0.008 to 0.016 in)
    Service limit... 0.55 mm (0.022 in)
  L models onward
    Standard .... 0.35 to 0.50 mm (0.014 to 0.020 in)
    Service limit... 0.7 mm (0.03 in)
Oil control ring side rail end gap
    Standard.. 0.2 to 0.8 mm (0.01 to 0.03 in)
    Service limit .... 1.0 mm (0.04 in)

Shift drum and forks

Shift fork end thickness
    Standard.. 6.43 to 6.50 mm (0.253 to 0.256 in)
    Service limit.. 6.40 mm (0.252 in)
Shift fork bore ID
    Standard.. 14.016 to 14.034 mm (0.5518 to 0.5525 in)
    Service limit.. 14.050 mm (0.553 in)
Shift fork shaft OD
    Standard.. 13.973 to 13.984 mm (0.5501 to 0.5506 in)
    Service limit.. 13.90 mm (0.547 in)

Connecting rods and bearings

Connecting rod side clearance
    Standard.. 0.10 to 0.30 mm (0.004 to 0.012 in)
    Service limit .... 0.4 mm (0.016 in)
Connecting rod piston pin bore ID
    Standard.. 17.016 to 17.034 mm (0.6699 to 0.6706 in)
    Service limit .... 17.04 mm (0.671 in)
Connecting rod crankpin bore ID
    Size group 1 .... 39.000 to 39.005 mm (1.5354 to 1.5356 in)
    Size group 2 .... 39.006 to 39.011 mm (1.5357 to 1.5359 in)
    Size group 3 .... 39.012 to 39.018 mm (1.5359 to 1.5361 in)
Crankshaft crankpin OD
    Size group A .... 35.995 to 36.000 mm (1.4171 to 1.4173 in)
    Size group B .... 35.989 to 35.994 mm (1.4169 to 1.4171 in)
    Size group C .... 35.982 to 35.988 mm (1.4166 to 1.4169 in)
Connecting rod bearing oil clearance
    Standard.. 0.030 to 0.052 mm (0.0012 to 0.0020 in)
    Service limit .... 0.08 mm (0.003 in)
Bearing insert thicknesses
    Blue .... 1.497 to 1.500 mm (0.0589 to 0.0590 in)
    Black .... 1.494 to 1.498 mm (0.0588 to 0.0590 in)
    Brown .... 1.491 to 1.494 mm (0.0587 to 0.0588 in)
    Green .... 1.487 to 1.491 mm (0.0585 to 0.0587 in)
    Yellow.. 1.485 to 1.488 mm (0.0585 to 0.0586 in)

Crankshaft and main bearings

Maximum crankshaft runout.. 0.05 mm (0.002 in)
Crankcase main bearing bore ID
    Size group A.. 37.000 to 37.005 mm (1.4567 to 1.4569 in)
    Size group B.. 37.006 to 37.011 mm (1.4569 to 1.4572 in)
    Size group C.. 37.012 to 37.018 mm (1.4572 to 1.4574 in)
Crankshaft journal OD
    Size group 1 .... 33.998 to 34.003 mm (1.3385 to 1.3387 in)
    Size group 2 .... 33.992 to 33.997 mm (1.3383 to 1.3385 in)
    Size group 3 .... 33.985 to 33.991 mm (1.3380 to 1.3382 in)
Main bearing oil clearance
    Standard.. 0.023 to 0.045 mm (0.0009 to 0.0018 in)
    Service limit .... 0.06 mm (0.002 in)
Bearing insert thicknesses
    Blue .... 1.500 to 1.503 mm (0.0591 to 0.0592 in)
    Black .... 1.497 to 1.501 mm (0.0589 to 0.0591 in)

2

Crankshaft and main bearings (continued)

Bearing insert thicknesses (continued)

Brown	1.494 to 1.497 mm (0.0587 to 0.0589 in)
Green	1.490 to 1.494 mm (0.0587 to 0.0588 in)
Yellow	1.488 to 1.491 mm (0.0586 to 0.0587 in)

Transmission shafts

Ratios

1st	2.8461 to 1 (37/13T)
2nd	2.0625 to 1 (33/16T)
3rd	1.6315 to 1 (31/19T)
4th	1.3333 to 1 (28/21T)
5th	1.1538 to 1 (30/26T)
6th	1.0357 to 1 (29/28T)

Gear ID

Mainshaft 5th and 6th gears

Standard	28.000 to 28.021 mm (1.1024 to 1.1032 in)
Service limit	28.04 mm (1.104 in)

Countershaft 2nd, 3rd and 4th gears

Standard	31.000 to 31.016 mm (1.2205 to 1.2211 in)
Service limit	31.04 mm (1.222 in)

Gear bushing OD

Mainshaft 5th and 6th gears

Standard	27.959 to 27.980 mm (1.1007 to 1.1016 in)
Service limit	27.94 mm (1.100 in)

Countershaft 3rd and 4th gears

Standard	30.950 to 30.975 mm (1.2185 to 1.2195 in)
Service limit	30.93 mm (1.218 in)

Countershaft 2nd gear

Standard	30.970 to 30.995 mm (1.2193 to 1.2203 in)
Service limit	30.95 mm (1.219 in)

Gear bushing ID

Mainshaft 5th and 6th gears

Standard	24.985 to 25.006 mm (0.9837 to 0.9845 in)
Service limit	25.03 mm (0.985 in)

Countershaft 2nd gear

Standard	28.000 to 28.021 mm (1.1024 to 1.1032 in)
Service limit	28.04 mm (1.104 in)

Countershaft 3rd and 4th gears

Standard	27.995 to 28.016 mm (1.1022 to 1.1029 in)
Service limit	28.04 mm (1.104 in)

Gear-to-bushing clearance

Mainshaft 5th and 6th gear	0.020 to 0.062 mm (0.0008 to 0.0024 in)
Countershaft 2nd gear	0.005 to 0.046 mm (0.0002 to 0.0019 in)
Countershaft 3rd and 4th gears	0.025 to 0.066 mm (0.0010 to 0.0026 in)

Mainshaft OD at 5th gear bushing point

Standard	24.959 to 24.980 mm (0.9826 to 0.9835 in)
Service limit	24.950 mm (0.982 in)

Countershaft OD at 2nd gear bushing point

Standard	27.967 to 27.980 mm (1.0904 to 1.1016 in)
Service limit	27.96 mm (1.101 in)

Shaft-to-bushing clearance

Mainshaft 5th and 6th gears	0.005 to 0.047 mm (0.0002 to 0.0019 in)
Countershaft 2nd gear	0.020 to 0.054 mm (0.0008 to 0.0021 in)
Countershaft 3rd and 4th gears	0.015 to 0.049 mm (0.0006 to 0.0019 in)

Torque settings

	Nm	Ft-lbs
Engine mounting bolts		
G through K models		
Lower mounting bolt	10	7
Lower mounting bolt nut	55	40
Lower mounting bolt locknut	55	40
10 mm mounting bolts	40	29
8 mm mounting bolts	28	20
L models onward		
Mounting adjuster	9	7
Adjuster locknut	55	40
Lower mounting bolt nut	55	40
All other mounting bolts	40	29

Torque settings

	Nm	Ft-lbs
Valve cover bolts	10	7
Camshaft bearing holder bolts	12	9
Camshaft follower spring nuts - H through K models	12	9
Camshaft drive gear bolts		
G through K models		
Upper bolts (gear to cylinder head)	37	26
Side bolt (gear to block/crankcase)	27	20
L models onward		
Upper bolts	10	7
Side bolt (gear to block/crankcase)	27	20
Cylinder head bolts		
G through K models		
9 mm bolts	37	26
6 mm bolts	12	9
L models onward		
9 mm bolts	45	33
6 mm bolts	12	9
Starter motor clutch		
Retaining bolt	90	65
Clutch body cover bolts		
G through K models	28	21
L models onward	40	29
Crankcase cover bolts	12	9
Clutch		
Center nut	90	65
Hydraulic hose banjo fitting bolts	35	25
Lever pivot bolt nut	6	4
Oil pan bolts	12	9
Oil pump		
Mounting bolts	12	9
Pump cover bolts	12	9
Pump driven sprocket bolt	18	13
Gearshift pedal clamp bolt	12	9
Sidestand mounting bolt	22	16
Shift cam bolt - J models onward	23	17
Alternator rotor bolt		
G through K models	90	65
L models onward	85	61
Crankcase bolts		
6 mm bolts	12	9
8 mm bolt	23	17
9 mm bolts	33	24
10 mm bolts	40	29
Connecting rod bearing cap nuts	34	25

1 General information

The engine/transmission unit is of liquid-cooled 90° Vee-four cylinder design. Its sixteen valves are operated by double overhead camshafts, gear-driven off the center of the crankshaft; there are four camshafts (two for each pair of cylinders). The engine/transmission unit is constructed in aluminum alloy with the crankcase being divided horizontally. The crankcase incorporates a wet sump, pressure fed lubrication system, and houses a chain-driven dual rotor oil pump.

The alternator and flywheel are situated on the left end of the crankshaft with the starter clutch mounted on the right end of the crankshaft. The water pump is mounted on the left side of the crankcase and is driven off the oil pump shaft.

The clutch is of the wet multi-plate type and is driven off the crankshaft by the starter motor clutch gear. The transmission is of the six-speed constant mesh type. Final drive to the rear wheel is by chain and sprockets, the drive sprocket being mounted on the end of the countershaft (output shaft).

2 Operations possible with the engine in the frame

The components and assemblies listed below can be removed without having to remove the engine/transmission assembly from the frame. If however, a number of areas require attention at the same time, removal of the engine is recommended.

Gearshift selector mechanism components
Starter motor
Starter motor clutch
Alternator
Clutch assembly
Oil pan, oil pump and relief valves
Valve cover
Camshafts
Camshaft drive gears
Front cylinder head - all models
Rear cylinder head - L models onward

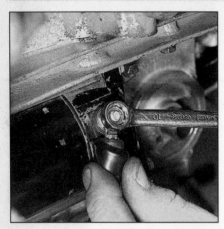

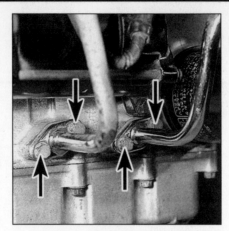

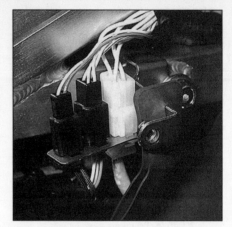

5.11 Undo the nut and disconnect the lead from the starter motor

5.12 Undo the bolts (arrows) and disconnect the oil cooler hoses from the front of the crankcase

5.13 Engine wiring connectors (R model shown)

3   Operations requiring engine removal

It is necessary to remove the engine/transmission assembly from the frame to enable the following components to be removed.
Rear cylinder head - G through K models
Transmission shafts
Shift drum and forks
Crankshaft and bearings
Piston/connecting rod assemblies and bearings

4   Major engine repair - general note

1   It is not always easy to determine when or if an engine should be completely overhauled, as a number of factors must be considered.
2   High mileage is not necessarily an indication that an overhaul is needed, while low mileage, on the other hand, does not preclude the need for an overhaul. Frequency of servicing is probably the single most important consideration. An engine that has regular and frequent oil and filter changes, as well as other required maintenance, will most likely give many miles of reliable service. Conversely, a neglected engine, or one which has not been broken in properly, may require an overhaul very early in its life.
3   Exhaust smoke and excessive oil consumption are both indications that piston rings and/or valve guides are in need of attention, although make sure that the fault is not due to oil leakage. Refer to Chapter 1 and perform a cylinder compression check to determine for certain the nature and extent of the work required.
4   If the engine is making obvious knocking or rumbling noises, the connecting rod and/or main bearings are probably at fault.
5   Loss of power, rough running, excessive valve train noise and high fuel consumption rates may also point to the need for an overhaul, especially if they are all present at the same time. If a complete tune-up does not remedy the situation, major mechanical work is the only solution.
6   An engine overhaul generally involves restoring the internal parts to the specifications of a new engine. During an overhaul the piston rings are replaced and the cylinder walls are bored and/or honed. If a rebore is done, then new pistons will also be required. The main and connecting rod bearings are usually replaced during a major overhaul. Generally the valve seats are serviced as well, since they are usually in less than perfect condition at this point. While the engine is being overhauled, other components such as the carburetors and the starter motor can also be rebuilt. The end result should be a like new engine that will give as many trouble-free miles as the original.
7   Before beginning the engine overhaul, read through the related procedures to familiarize yourself with the scope and requirements of the job. Overhauling an engine is not all that difficult, but it is time consuming. Plan on the motorcycle being tied up for a minimum of two weeks. Check on the availability of parts and make sure that any necessary special tools, equipment and supplies are obtained in advance.
8   Most work can be done with typical shop hand tools, although a number of precision measuring tools are required for inspecting parts to determine if they must be replaced. Often a dealer service department or motorcycle repair shop will handle the inspection of parts and offer advice concerning reconditioning and replacement. As a general rule, time is the primary cost of an overhaul so it does not pay to install worn or substandard parts.
9   As a final note, to ensure maximum life and minimum trouble from a rebuilt engine, everything must be assembled with care in a spotlessly clean environment.

5   Engine - removal and installation

Note: *Engine removal and installation should be carried out with the aid of an assistant; personal injury or damage could occur if the engine falls or is dropped. A hydraulic floor-type jack should be used to support and lower the engine to the floor if possible (they can be rented at low cost).*

Removal

G through K models

Refer to illustrations 5.11, 5.12, 5.13, 5.19a, 5.19b, 5.20, 5.21, 5.23a, 5.23b, 5.23c and 5.23d
1   Set the bike on its centerstand (where fitted). On models without a centerstand, support the motorcycle securely in an upright position so it can't be accidentally knocked over whilst the engine is removed.
2   If the machine is dirty, wash it thoroughly before starting any major dismantling work. This will make work much easier and rule out the possibility of caked on lumps of dirt falling into some vital component. Work can also be made easier by raising the machine to a suitable working height on a hydraulic ramp or a suitable platform.
3   Remove the lower fairing panels as described in Chapter 8.
4   Drain the engine oil and remove the oil filter as described in Chapter 1.
5   Remove the water pump as described in Chapter 3.
6   Disconnect both battery cables from the battery. **Warning:** *Always disconnect the battery negative lead first and reconnect it last to prevent a battery explosion.*
7   Remove the mufflers (silencers) as described in Chapter 4.
8   Remove the carburetors as described in Chapter 4 and plug the cylinder head intake openings with clean shop towels. Also remove the

5.19a Slacken and remove the retaining bolt and washer . . .

5.19b . . . then disengage the sprocket from the chain

5.20 Undo the coolant pipe retaining bolt and disconnect the ground (earth) lead (arrow)

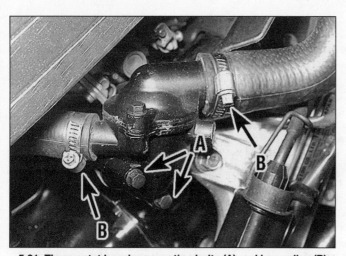

5.21 Thermostat housing mounting bolts (A) and hose clips (B)

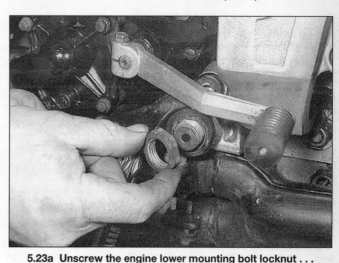

5.23a Unscrew the engine lower mounting bolt locknut . . .

2

carburetor heatshield.

9   Undo the radiator lower mounting bolt(s) and swing the radiator away from the engine unit. Tie the radiator to the fork legs so that it is positioned clear of the engine unit.

10   Disconnect the spark plug caps from the plugs.

11   Peel back the rubber cover then undo the nut and disconnect the lead from the starter motor (see illustration). Screw the nut back onto the starter motor terminal for safe-keeping and free the starter motor lead from its clips on the bottom of the engine unit.

12   Undo the bolts securing the oil cooler hose unions to the front of the engine unit (see illustration). Recover the O-ring from each union and position both hoses clear of the engine unit.

13   Trace the wiring back from the pulse generators and the alternator to their wiring connectors (see illustration). Disconnect the wiring connectors then work back along the wiring, releasing it from any retaining clips so that it is free to be removed with the engine unit. Similarly, disconnect the wires from the oil pressure switch and neutral switch.

14   Remove Nos. 2 and 4 cylinder ignition HT coils as described in Chapter 5.

15   Undo the clamp bolt and disconnect the gearshift lever pedal from the engine.

16   Undo the three bolts securing the clutch release cylinder to the sprocket cover.

17   Withdraw the clutch release cylinder and recover the gasket and locating dowels from the sprocket cover. Position the cylinder clear of the engine unit. Note: Do not operate the clutch lever whilst the release cylinder is disconnected from the engine. Wrap a stout elastic band

around the cylinder to prevent the piston being accidentally expelled.

18   Unscrew the remaining screws securing the sprocket cover to the engine unit. Remove the sprocket cover and gasket and recover the two cover locating dowels.

19   Have an assistant apply the rear brake, then slacken and remove the sprocket retaining bolt and washer. Slide the engine sprocket off the countershaft then separate the sprocket from the chain (see illustrations). Note that if the drive chain is tight it may be necessary to slacken the drive chain adjustment to allow the sprocket to be slid off the shaft (see Chapter 1).

20   Unscrew the bolt securing the metal coolant pipe to the left of the engine unit, noting the ground (earth) lead which is positioned underneath the bolt (see illustration). Remove the pipe and recover the sealing ring from its upper end.

21   Slacken their clips and disconnect the cooling system hoses from the thermostat housing. Disconnect the wiring connector from the coolant temperature sender, then undo the mounting bolts and remove the complete thermostat housing from the engine unit (see illustration). Recover the O-ring from behind the housing.

22   Position a jack and block of wood beneath the engine and raise the jack so that it is supporting the weight of the engine/transmission unit. Do not position the jack underneath the exhaust front pipes.

23   Unscrew the engine lower mounting bolt locknut and the mounting bolt and remove the sidestand bracket. From the opposite side, unscrew the engine lower mounting bolt nut and remove it along with the fairing mounting bracket. Pry out the trim plug from the center of the bolt head on the left side. Unscrew the engine lower mounting bolt and remove it, noting the washer which is positioned between the

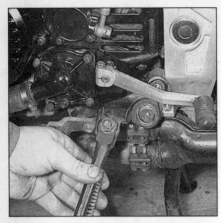

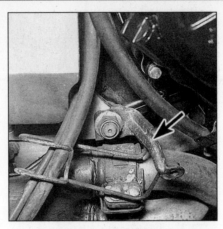

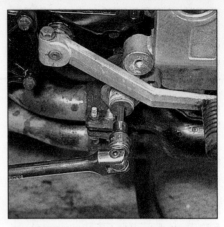

5.23b . . . then undo the bolt and remove the sidestand assembly

5.23c Unscrew the engine lower mounting bolt nut and recover the fairing mounting bracket (arrow) . . .

5.23d . . . then unscrew the bolt

5.28 On L models onward, undo the two bolts and free the speedometer drive from the sprocket cover

5.31a Undo the thermostat housing mounting bolt (arrow) . . .

5.31b . . . then slacken the hose clips and remove the thermostat housing assembly

bolt head and the engine **(see illustrations)**.

24   Slacken and remove the eight remaining engine unit mounting bolts (four on each side) and recover the spacers fitted to each of the 10 mm bolts; note the correct fitted location of each bolt and spacer **(see illustration 5.48)**.

25   Make a final check to make sure that all wires and hoses are disconnected.

26   Slowly and carefully lower the engine unit out of the frame. **Warning:** *The engine unit is heavy and may cause injury if it falls. Be sure it is securely supported. Have an assistant help you steady the engine as it is lowered out of position.*

27   With the aid of an assistant lift the engine unit off the jack and lower it carefully onto the work surface.

L models onward

Refer to illustrations 5.28, 5.31a, 5.31b, 5.33, 5.35a, 5.35b, 5.35c, 5.36, 5.38, 5.39, 5.41 and 5.42

Note: *A suitable peg wrench will be required to slacken and tighten the rear engine mounting adjuster locknuts. In the absence of the special Honda service tool (Part No. 07HMA-MR70200), it will be necessary to fabricate a suitable alternative before starting work.*

28   Carry out the operations described above in Steps 1 through 20, noting the following points.

a) *Remove the complete exhaust system (not just the mufflers/silencers) as described in Chapter 4.*

b) *It is not necessary to remove the ignition coils.*

c) *Prior to removing the sprocket cover, undo the bolts and free the speedometer drive from the sprocket cover* **(see illustration)**.

29   Disconnect the coolant reservoir overflow tube from the radiator neck. Undo the mounting bolt and remove the reservoir from the bike.

30   Remove the sidestand switch as described in Chapter 9.

31   Slacken the retaining clips and disconnect the three coolant hoses from the thermostat housing. Disconnect the wiring connector from the coolant temperature sender, then undo the mounting bolt and remove the thermostat housing assembly from the engine unit **(see illustrations)**.

32   Undo the two bolts and release the rubber cover from the rear cylinder head cover.

33   Unbolt the sidestand bracket from the frame and remove the sidestand from the bike **(see illustration)**. Where the bracket bolt(s) also act as centerstand bolt(s), screw them back into position to avoid placing any undue strain on the remaining bolts.

34   Position a jack and block of wood beneath the engine and raise the jack so that it is supporting the weight of the engine/transmission unit.

35   Unscrew the nut from the left end of the lower rear mounting bolt. Using the peg wrench, slacken the adjuster locknut on the right side of the bolt then, using a suitable Allen wrench, rotate the mounting bolt to unscrew the mounting adjuster. Withdraw the lower rear mounting bolt **(see illustrations)**.

36   Slacken and remove the upper, rear right mounting bolt. Slacken the adjuster locknut with the peg wrench then unscrew the adjuster **(see illustration)**.

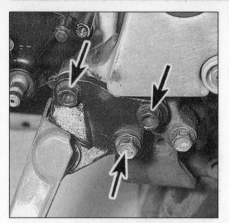

5.33 Undo the retaining bolts (arrows) and
remove the sidestand assembly

5.35a Engine unit mounting bolt
locations (arrows)

5.35b Slacken and remove the lower rear
mounting bolt nut . . .

5.35c . . . then withdraw the bolt from the
right side of the bike

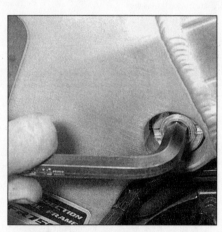

5.36 Slacken the locknut then unscrew
the adjuster with an Allen wrench

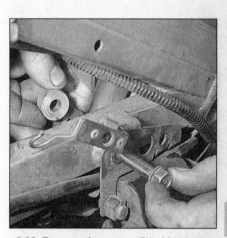

5.38 Recover the spacer fitted between
the engine and frame when removing the
left center mounting bolt

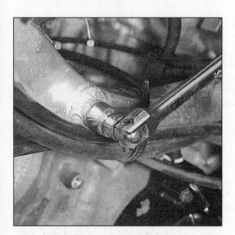

5.39 Removing the left front
mounting bolt

5.41 Lower the engine unit out of position
with a jack . . .

5.42 . . . then remove the jack and lower
the unit onto the work surface

37   Unscrew the upper, rear left mounting bolt.
38   Unscrew the right and left center mounting bolts, noting how the
bolts also retain the ignition HT coil mounting brackets. Recover the
spacer fitted between the engine and frame on the left side **(see
illustration)**.
39   Slacken and remove the left and right front mounting bolts **(see
illustration)**.
40   Make a final check to make sure that all wires and hoses are
disconnected.
41   Slowly and carefully lower the engine unit out of the frame **(see
illustration)**. **Warning:** *The engine unit is heavy and may cause injury if
it falls. Be sure it is securely supported. Have an assistant help you
steady the engine as it is lowered out of position.*
42   With the aid of an assistant lift the engine unit off the jack and
lower it carefully onto the work surface **(see illustration)**.

2

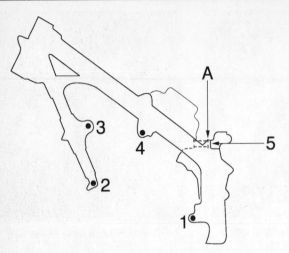

5.48 Engine mounting bolt locations - G through K models. Tighten the bolts in the specified order (see text) to make sure no clearance exists at point A

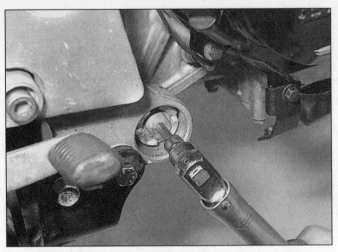

5.56a Tighten the lower rear mounting adjuster to the specified torque . . .

5.56b . . . then tighten the locknut to the specified torque using the special peg wrench

5.57 Fit the lower rear mounting bolt nut and tighten it to the specified torque . . .

5.58 . . . then go around and tighten the other bolts to their specified torque settings

Installation

G through K models

Refer to illustration 5.48

43   With the aid of an assistant place the engine unit on top of the jack and block of wood and carefully raise it into position in the frame.

44   Position the washer between the engine and frame on the left side, then slide the lower mounting bolt into position.

45   Install the remaining mounting bolts in their original locations and position the spacers (fitted to each of the 10 mm bolts) between the engine unit and frame.

46   With all mounting bolts in position, tighten the lower mounting bolt to the specified torque setting. Once the bolt is correctly tightened, tighten its nut to the specified torque.

47   Fit the sidestand bracket and tighten its mounting bolt to the specified torque. Install the lower engine mounting bolt locknut and tighten it to the specified torque setting.

48   With the lower mounting bolt correctly tightened, go around and tighten the remaining mounting bolts in the following sequence **(see illustration).**

a) *Upper rear bolts (position 5 in illustration).*
b) *Upper center bolts (position 4 in illustration).*
c) *Upper front bolts (position 3 in illustration).*
d) *Lower front bolts (position 2 in illustration).*

49   With all the bolts tightened, make sure that there is no clearance between the upper rear bolt spacers and the frame (position A in illustration 5.48).

50   The remainder of the installation procedure is a direct reversal of the removal sequence, noting the following points.

a) *Tighten all nuts and bolts to the specified torque settings (where given) and replace all gaskets and O-rings disturbed on removal.*
b) *Align the punch marks on the gearshift pedal and shaft when locating the pedal on the shaft splines.*
c) *Make sure all wiring is correctly routed and retained by all the relevant clips and ties.*
d) *Adjust the drive chain as described in Chapter 1.*
e) *Fill the engine oil and cooling systems as described in Chapter 1.*
f) *Prior to installing the lower fairing panels start the engine and check for signs of coolant/oil leakage.*

L models onward

Refer to illustrations 5.56a, 5.56b, 5.57, 5.58, 5.59 and 5.60

51   With the aid of an assistant place the engine unit on top of the jack and block of wood and carefully raise it into position in the frame.

52   Apply a thin coat of grease to the lower rear mounting bolt and insert the bolt. Tighten the mounting adjuster fully by hand, then engage the bolt head with the adjuster.

53   Install the front mounting bolts and tighten them lightly.

54   Position the spacer between the mounting and frame on the left

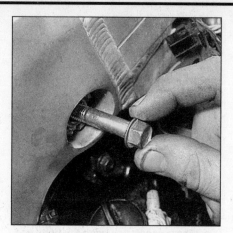

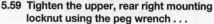

5.59 Tighten the upper, rear right mounting locknut using the peg wrench . . .

5.60 . . . then fit the mounting bolt

7.4 Removing a valve cover bolt

side and install the center mounting bolts. Ensure the ignition HT coil brackets are correctly fitted to the bolts, and lightly tighten them.

55   Install the upper, rear left bolt and lightly tighten it.

56   With all bolts except the upper, rear right bolt in position, tighten the lower rear mounting adjuster to the specified torque using a suitable Allen wrench fitted to the mounting bolt head. Hold the mounting bolt stationary and tighten the adjuster locknut to the specified torque with the peg wrench **(see illustrations)**.

57   Fit the lower rear mounting bolt nut and tighten it to the specified torque setting **(see illustration)**.

58   Work around the engine unit and tighten all the other mounting bolts to their specified torque settings **(see illustration)**.

59   Using an Allen wrench, tighten the upper, rear right mounting adjuster to the specified torque setting. Hold the adjuster stationary then tighten the adjuster locknut to the specified torque setting with the peg wrench **(see illustration)**.

60   Install the upper, rear right mounting bolt and tighten it to the specified torque setting **(see illustration)**.

61   The remainder of the installation procedure is a direct reversal of the removal sequence, noting the following points.

a) *Tighten all nuts and bolts to the specified torque settings (where given) and replace all gaskets and O-rings disturbed on removal.*

b) *Align the punch marks on the gearshift pedal and shaft when locating the pedal on the shaft splines.*

c) *Make sure all wiring is correctly routed and retained by all the relevant clips and ties.*

d) *Adjust the drive chain as described in Chapter 1.*

e) *Fill the engine oil and cooling systems as described in Chapter 1.*

f) *Prior to installing the lower fairing panels start the engine and check for signs of coolant/oil leakage.*

6   Engine disassembly and reassembly - general information

Note: *Refer to the `Maintenance techniques, tools and working facilities' in the Introductory pages of this manual for further information.*

Disassembly

1   Before disassembling the engine, the external surfaces of the unit should be thoroughly cleaned and degreased. This will prevent contamination of the engine internals, and will also make working a lot easier and cleaner. A high flash-point solvent, such as kerosene (paraffin) can be used, or better still, a proprietary engine degreaser. Use old paintbrushes and toothbrushes to work the solvent into the various recesses of the engine casings. Take care to exclude solvent or water from the electrical components and intake and exhaust ports. **Warning:** *The use of gasoline (petrol) as a cleaning agent should be*

avoided because of the risk of fire.

2   When clean and dry, arrange the unit on the workbench, leaving suitable clear area for working. Gather a selection of small containers and plastic bags so that parts can be grouped together in an easily identifiable manner. Some paper and a pen should be on hand to permit notes to be made and labels attached where necessary. A supply of clean shop towels is also required.

3   Before commencing work, read through the appropriate section so that some idea of the necessary procedure can be gained. When removing various engine components it should be noted that great force is seldom required, unless specified. In many cases, a component's reluctance to be removed is indicative of an incorrect approach or removal method. If in any doubt, re-check with the text.

4   When disassembling the engine, keep 'mated' parts together (including gears, cylinders, pistons, valves, etc. that have been in contact with each other during engine operation). These 'mated' parts must be re-used or replaced as an assembly. **Note:** *Do not interchange front and rear cylinder head components.*

5   Engine/transmission disassembly should be done in the following general order with reference to the appropriate Sections.

Remove the exhaust system - G through K models only (see Chapter 4)
Remove the camshafts
Remove the cylinder head
Remove the starter motor clutch
Remove the clutch
Remove the alternator rotor
Remove the external shift mechanism
Remove the starter motor (see Chapter 9)
Remove the oil pan
Remove the oil pump and associated components
Separate the crankcase halves
Remove the connecting rod/piston assemblies
Remove the crankshaft
Remove the transmission shafts/gears
Remove the shift cam/forks

Reassembly

6   Reassembly is accomplished by reversing the general disassembly sequence.

7   Valve cover - removal and installation

Note: *Either valve cover can be removed with the engine in the frame. If the engine has been removed, ignore the steps which do not apply.*

Removal

Front cylinder valve cover

Refer to illustration 7.4

7.8 Disconnecting the breather hose from the rear valve cover

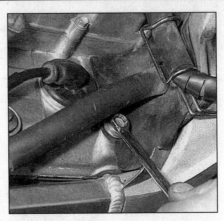

7.9a Where necessary, undo the bolts and free the rubber cover from the rear valve cover. . .

7.9b . . . and disconnect the hose from the fuel tank drain

7.10 Removing the rear cylinder valve cover

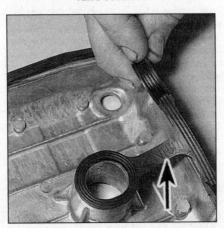

7.12 Fit the seal to the valve cover making sure its IN marking (arrow) is pointing towards the intake (carburetor) side of the cover

7.15 Fit the sealing washers making sure their UP marks are facing up

1   Remove the left and right lower (G and H models) or middle fairing panels (J models onward) as described in Chapter 8.

2   Slacken and remove the radiator lower mounting bolt(s) and recover the spacer from each mounting damper. Swing the radiator away from the valve cover and tie it to the fork legs. If necessary, access can be further improved by removing the radiator as described in Chapter 3.

3   Disconnect the spark plug caps from the plugs and position them clear of the cover.

4   Slacken and remove the four valve cover bolts along with their sealing washers **(see illustration)**.

5   Lift the valve cover away from the head and maneuver it out from between the frame tubes. Recover the valve cover rubber seal.

6   Examine the rubber seal for signs of damage or deterioration and replace if it is cracked or brittle. Also check the cover bolt seals for signs of damage and replace if necessary.

Rear cylinder valve cover

Refer to illustrations 7.8, 7.9a, 7.9b and 7.10

7   Remove the fuel tank as described in Chapter 4.

8   Slacken the retaining clips and remove the breather hose connecting the rear cover to the air cleaner housing **(see illustration)**.

9   Where necessary, undo the two bolts and free the rubber cover from the valve cover, then release the retaining clip and disconnect the hose from the fuel tank drain **(see illustrations)**.

10   Remove the valve cover as described above in Steps 3 through 6 **(see illustration)**.

Installation

Front cylinder valve cover

Refer to illustrations 7.12 and 7.15

11   Remove all traces of sealant from the cover groove and rubber seal.

12   Ensure the cover is clean and dry, then apply a small bead of sealant to the cover grooves. Noting that the cover must be fitted with its cast arrow pointing towards the front of the bike, fit the seal to the cover so that its IN marking is pointing towards the intake (carburetor) side of the head **(see illustration)**.

13   Make sure the seal is correctly located. The sealant will help to hold it in position as the cover is fitted.

14   Carefully install the cover on the cylinder head taking great care not to dislodge the seal. With the cover in position, lift it slightly and check that the seal is correctly located in both the cover outer groove and spark plug hole grooves.

15   Fit the sealing washers to the cylinder head cover making sure the 'UP' mark on each one is facing up **(see illustration)**.

16   Install the cover retaining bolts and tighten them to the specified torque setting.

17   The remainder of installation is the reverse of removal.

Rear cylinder head cover

18   Install the cover as described above noting that there is no arrow on the valve cover; the cover must be installed with its breather hose union facing towards the front of the bike.

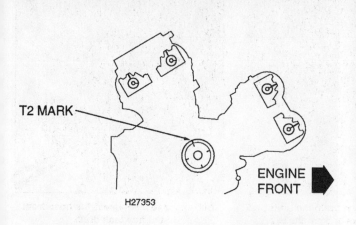

8.4a For the front camshafts on G through K models, align the 'T' of No. 2 cylinder and check that the camshaft marks are positioned as shown, indicating that No. 2 cylinder is at TDC on compression

8.4b With No. 2 cylinder at TDC, the rear cylinder camshaft markings (arrow) will be positioned as shown . . .

8.4c . . . and the front cylinder camshaft markings should be aligned with the holder marks (arrow)

8.6 Slacken the camshaft holder bolts as described in text

8.7 Remove the bolts and lift off the oil pipe which is fitted in the center of the holders

8 Camshaft and followers - removal, inspection and installation

Note: *This procedure can be carried out with the engine in the frame.*

Removal

1   Remove the front and rear valve covers as described in Section 7.
2   Remove all the spark plugs as described in Chapter 1 and proceed as described under the relevant sub-heading.

Front camshafts only - G through K models

Refer to illustrations 8.4a, 8.4b, 8.4c, 8.6, 8.7 and 8.8

3   Unscrew the center plug from the right crankcase cover.
4   Using a suitable socket, rotate the crankshaft clockwise until the 'T' mark of No. 2 cylinder is aligned with the index mark, in the form of a line, on the casing. Now check the position of the No. 2 cylinder cam lobes - they should be pointing away from the followers and the index marks on the right end of the camshafts should be positioned as shown in the accompanying illustrations **(see illustrations)**. If the lobes and marks are not correctly positioned, turn the crankshaft through 360° (one complete turn). Piston No. 2 is now at TDC compression. **Note:** *Turn the engine in the normal direction of rotation (clockwise), viewed from the right end of the engine.*

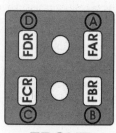

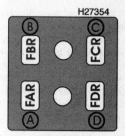

FRONT CYLINDERS

REAR CYLINDERS

8.8 Camshaft holder and cylinder head identification markings - G through K models

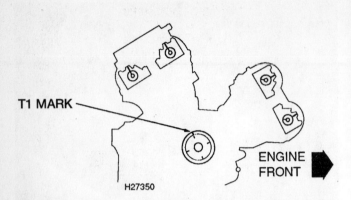

8.13a For the rear camshafts on G through K models, align the 'T' of No. 1 cylinder and check that the camshaft marks are positioned as shown, indicating that No. 1 cylinder is at TDC on compression

8.13b With No. 1 cylinder at TDC, the rear cylinder camshaft markings (arrow) should be aligned with the holder marks . . .

5   Slacken the follower adjuster screw locknuts and unscrew the adjusting screws until valve spring pressure is relieved from the front cylinder followers.
6   Working in a criss-cross pattern, gradually slacken the camshaft holder retaining bolts by half-a-turn at a time **(see illustration)**.
7   When all bolts are loose, unscrew the four center bolts and remove the oil pipe from the cylinder head **(see illustration)**. **Note:** *Take care not to drop the bolts down into the engine unit as they are removed. If a bolt is dropped, it must be recovered before the engine can be started - drain the engine oil and remove the oil pan to recover the bolt.*
8   Unscrew the remaining bolts and lift off the camshaft holders complete with camshafts. Recover the locating dowels from each holder. **Note:** *The camshafts and holders are not interchangeable. Both camshafts are marked 'FR' indicating that they belong to the front cylinders. The intake camshaft is marked 'IN' and the exhaust camshaft 'EX'. The holders are also marked for location* **(see illustration)**.
9   If the followers are to be removed, obtain a container which is divided into eight compartments, and label each compartment with the number of its corresponding valve in the cylinder head.
10   On G models, the followers are removed in pairs. Slacken and remove the follower holder bolts and remove the spring and retaining plate, noting their correct fitted positions. Remove the follower holder complete with followers, noting that it may be necessary to lever the plate away from the head to release the follower balljoints.
11   On H through K models, all four followers for each cylinder are retained by the same holder. Slacken and remove the follower holder nuts then lift off the spring and holder and recover the locating dowels. Slacken and remove the adjuster locknut from the follower and remove the follower by rotating the adjuster screw in a clockwise direction. To remove the adjuster screws from the cylinder head, place one of the camshaft holder dowels over the adjuster screw and fit the locknut. The adjuster screw can then be drawn out of the cylinder head by carefully tightening the locknut whilst retaining the adjuster screw.

Rear camshafts only - G through K models

Refer to illustrations 8.13a, 8.13b and 8.13c

12   Unscrew the center plug from the right crankcase cover.
13   Using a suitable socket, rotate the crankshaft clockwise until the 'T' mark of No. 1 cylinder is aligned with the index mark, in the form of a line, on the casing. Now, check the position of the No. 1 cylinder cam lobes - they should be pointing away from the followers and the index marks on the right end of the camshafts should be positioned as shown in the accompanying illustrations **(see illustrations)**. If the lobes and marks are not correctly positioned, turn the crankshaft through 360° (one complete turn). Piston No. 1 is now at TDC

compression. **Note:** *Turn the engine in the normal direction of rotation (clockwise), viewed from the right end of the engine.*
14   Remove the camshafts as described in Steps 5 through 8, noting that the camshafts are marked 'RR' (instead of 'FR') to indicate that they belong to the rear cylinders.
15   If necessary, remove the followers as described in Steps 9 through 11 (as applicable).

Front and rear camshafts - G through K models

Refer to illustration 8.17

16   Remove the front camshafts as described above in Steps 3 through 8.
17   Since both front and rear cylinder camshaft holders carry identical markings, great care must be taken to ensure the front and rear holders are not interchanged. To prevent this happening, use white paint or a suitable marker to highlight the F of each identification marking on the front holders, and the R of each marking on the rear holders **(see illustration)**.
18   Remove the rear camshafts as described in Steps 12 through 14.
19   If necessary, remove the followers as described in Steps 9 through 11 (as applicable). Keep the followers and associated components in two separate containers, one for the front cylinders and one for the rear, to avoid interchanging them.

8.13c . . . and the front cylinder camshaft markings will be positioned as shown (arrow)

8.17 Camshaft holder identification marking

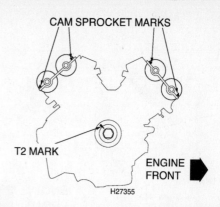

8.21 For the front camshafts on L models onward, align the 'T' of No. 2 cylinder and check that all the camshaft gear arrows are correctly aligned with the cylinder head upper surfaces, indicating that No. 2 cylinder is at TDC on compression

Front camshafts only - L models onward

Refer to illustrations 8.21, 8.23a, 8.23b and 8.26

20   Unscrew the center plug from the right crankcase cover.

21   Using a suitable socket, rotate the crankshaft clockwise until the 'T' mark of No. 2 cylinder is aligned with the index mark, in the form of a cutout in the cover. Now check the position of the No. 2 cylinder cam lobes - they should be pointing away from the followers and the arrows marked on each camshaft gear should be level with the cylinder head upper surface (see illustration). If the lobes and arrows are not correctly positioned, turn the crankshaft through 360° (one complete turn). Piston No. 2 is now at TDC compression. **Note:** *Turn the engine in the normal direction of rotation (clockwise), viewed from the right end of the engine.*

22   Starting with the exhaust camshaft, working in a criss-cross pattern, loosen the bearing holder bolts by half a turn at a time to gently relieve valve spring pressure on the holder. Whilst slackening the bolts make sure that the bearing holders are lifting squarely away from the cylinder head and are not sticking on the holder locating dowels. **Caution:** *If the bolts are carelessly loosened and the holders do not come squarely away from the head, they are likely to break. If this happens the complete cylinder head assembly must be replaced; the bearing holders are matched to the cylinder head and cannot be replaced separately.*

23   Once spring pressure is released from the holder, remove all the bolts then lift off the bearing holders and remove the camshaft. Recover the locating dowels. **Note:** *The camshafts and holders are not interchangeable. Both camshafts are marked 'FR' indicating that they belong to the front cylinders. The intake camshaft is marked 'IN' and the exhaust camshaft 'EX'. The holders and cylinder head are marked for location* (see illustrations).

24   Repeat the operations in Steps 22 and 23 and remove the intake camshaft.

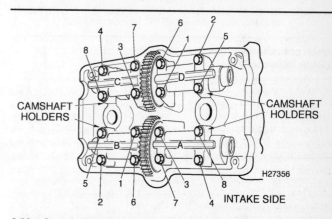

8.23a Camshaft bearing holder and head identification markings; numbers indicate bearing holder bolt tightening sequence

25   Obtain a container which is divided into eight compartments and label each compartment with the number of its corresponding valve in the cylinder head.

26   Using a magnet, lift each follower out of the cylinder head and store it in its corresponding compartment in the container. Note that the shim is likely to stick to the inside of the follower so take great care not to lose it as the follower is removed. Remove the shims and store each one with its respective follower (see illustration).

8.23b Identification markings are stamped on the holders and head (arrows)

8.26 Using a magnet to withdraw a follower

2

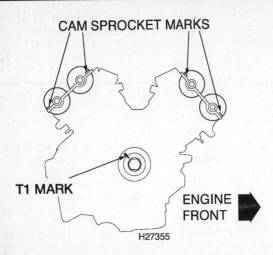

CAM SPROCKET MARKS

T1 MARK

ENGINE FRONT ➤

H27355

8.28 For the rear camshafts on L onwards models, align the 'T' of No. 1 cylinder and check that all the camshaft gear arrows are correctly aligned with the cylinder head upper surfaces, indicating that No. 1 cylinder is at TDC on compression

Rear camshafts only - L models onward

Refer to illustration 8.28

27   Unscrew the center plug from the right crankcase cover.

28   Using a suitable socket, rotate the crankshaft clockwise until the 'T' mark of No. 1 cylinder is aligned with the index mark, in the form of a cutout in the cover. Now, check the position of the No. 1 cylinder cam lobes - they should be pointing away from the followers and the straight lines marked on each camshaft gear should be level with the cylinder head upper surface **(see illustration)**. If the lobes and marks are not correctly positioned, turn the crankshaft through 360° (one complete turn). Piston No. 1 is now at TDC compression. **Note:** *Turn the engine in the normal direction of rotation (clockwise), viewed from the right end of the engine.*

29   Remove the camshafts as described in Steps 22 through 24, noting that the camshafts are marked 'RR' (instead of 'FR') to indicate that they belong to the rear cylinders.

30   If necessary, remove the followers as described in Steps 25 and 26.

Front and rear camshafts - L models onward

31   Remove the front camshafts as described in Steps 20 through 24.

32   Since both front and rear cylinder camshaft holders carry identical markings, great care must be taken to ensure the front and rear holders are not interchanged. To remove any possibility of this happening, mark the holders of the front cylinders using a dab of white paint or a suitable marker.

33   Remove the rear camshafts as described in Steps 27 through 29.

34   If necessary, remove the followers as described in Steps 25 and 26. Keep the followers and shims for the front and rear cylinders in two separate containers, one for the front cylinders and one for the rear.

Inspection

Note: *Before replacing the camshafts or the holders/cylinder head (as applicable) because of damage, check with local machine shops specializing in motorcycle engineering work. In the case of the camshafts, it may be possible for cam lobes to be welded, reground and hardened, at a cost far lower than that of a new camshaft. If the bearing surfaces are damaged, it may be possible for them to be bored out to accept bearing inserts. Due to the cost of new components it is recommended that all options be explored before condemning worn components as trash!*

G through K models

Refer to illustrations 8.35 and 8.37

35   Inspect the cam bearing surfaces of the holders and camshafts.

8.35 Check lobes for wear - here's a good example of damage which will require replacement (or repair) of the camshaft

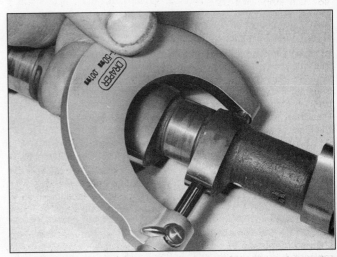

8.37 Measure the height of the camshaft lobes with a micrometer

Look for score marks, deep scratches and evidence of spalling (a pitted appearance). Check the camshaft lobes for heat discoloration (blue appearance), score marks, chipped areas, flat spots and spalling **(see illustration)**.

36   Camshaft runout can be checked by supporting each end of the camshaft on V-blocks, and measuring any runout using a dial gauge. If the runout exceeds the specified limit the camshaft must be replaced.

37   Measure the height of each lobe with a micrometer and compare the results to the lobe height service limit listed in this Chapter's Specifications **(see illustration)**. If damage is noted or wear is excessive, the camshaft must be replaced.

38   Measure the diameter of each of the camshaft bearing journals and compare the result to the service limit listed in this Chapter's Specifications. If damage is noted or wear is excessive, the camshaft must be replaced.

39   Measure the diameter of each holder journal and compare the measurements obtained with the service limit given in the Specifications at the start of this Chapter. If any journal is worn beyond the service limit, the holder must be repaired/replaced.

40   The camshaft bearing oil clearance can be calculated by subtracting the camshaft bearing journal diameter from the holder journal diameter.

41   Check the camshaft gear teeth for signs of damage such as chipped or missing teeth. If damage is found the camshaft must be replaced; it is not possible to remove the gear from the camshaft.

L models onward

42   Check the camshafts for wear as described above in Steps 35 to 37.

43   The camshaft bearing oil clearance should then be checked. There are two possible ways of checking this, the first method by direct measurement (see Steps 44 and 48) and the second by the use of a product known as Plastigage (see Steps 45 through 48).

44   If the first method is to be used, make sure the locating dowels are in position then fit the bearing holders to the head. Make sure the holders are correctly positioned (see Step 23). Working in a criss-cross pattern, tighten the retaining bolts evenly and progressively to the specified torque. Measure the diameter of each bearing holder journal and compare the measurements obtained with the service limit given in the Specifications at the start of this Chapter. If any journal is worn beyond the service limit, the cylinder head must be repaired/replaced. The camshaft bearing oil clearance can then be calculated by subtracting the camshaft bearing journal diameter from the bearing holder journal diameter.

45   If the second method is to be used, clean the camshafts, the bearing surfaces in the cylinder head and the bearing holders with a clean, lint-free cloth, then lay the cams in place in the cylinder head (see Step 23).

46   Cut strips of Plastigage and lay one piece on each bearing journal, parallel with the camshaft centerline. Make sure the bearing holder dowels are installed and fit the bearing holders in their proper positions (see note in Step 23). Ensuring the camshafts are not rotated at all, tighten the holder retaining bolts to the specified torque working in sequence as described in Steps 87 through 89.

47   Now unscrew the bolts as described in Steps 22 and 23 and carefully lift off the bearing holders, again making sure the camshafts are not rotated. To determine the oil clearance, compare the crushed Plastigage (at its widest point) on each journal to the scale printed on the Plastigage container.

48   Compare the results to this Chapter's Specifications. If the oil clearance is greater than specified, measure the diameter of the cam bearing journal with a micrometer. If the journal diameter is less than the specified limit, replace the camshaft with a new one and recheck the clearance. If the clearance is still too great, replace the cylinder head and bearing holders with new parts (see the Note at the start of this sub-section).

49   Check the camshaft gear teeth for signs of damage such as chipped or missing teeth. If damage is found the camshaft must be replaced; it is not possible to remove the gear from the camshaft.

50   Check each follower for wear by measuring its outside diameter; replace any follower which exceeds the service limit given in this Chapter's Specifications. Check for wear of the follower bores by measuring their inside diameters; if worn to or beyond the service limit, cylinder head replacement is required.

Installation

Front camshafts only - G through K models

51   On G models, apply a smear of clean engine oil to the follower balljoints to ease installation. Align both balljoints with their sockets in the cylinder head and tap each follower into position using a 10 mm socket as a drift. Clean the threads of the holder bolts and apply a few drops of locking compound to their threads. Install the spring and retaining plate, making sure they are correctly located, then fit the bolts and tighten them securely. Check that both followers pivot smoothly then repeat the procedure for the remaining followers.

52   On H through K models, if the follower adjuster screws were removed, fit the screws to the relevant follower, followed by the locknut. Apply a smear of engine oil to the screw pivot, then install the follower assembly in the cylinder head by gently tapping the adjuster screw into position using a 10 mm socket, fitted to the locknut, as a drift. If the adjuster screws were not removed simply screw the follower fully onto the adjuster screw by rotating the screw itself then fit the locknut. Fit the locating dowels to the studs and install the holder, making sure its 'EX' mark is facing towards the exhaust side of the

cylinder head. Locate each follower in its holder slot then fit the spring and tighten the retaining nuts to the specified torque setting.

53   Referring to Step 4, rotate the crankshaft clockwise until the 'T' mark of No. 2 cylinder is aligned with the index mark, in the form of a line, on the casing. Now, check the position of the index marks on the right end of the rear cylinder camshafts; they should be positioned as shown in illustrations 8.4a, 8.4b and 8.4c. If the marks are not correctly positioned, turn the crankshaft through 360° (one complete turn). **Note:** *Turn the engine in the normal direction of rotation (clockwise), viewed from the right end of the engine.*

54   Apply a smear of clean engine oil to the bearing surfaces of the camshafts and holders and assemble each camshaft with its relevant holders (see Step 8).

55   Check that all the followers are correctly engaged with their holders. To ensure the exhaust followers remain in position as the camshaft is installed, fit a spacer, such as a piece of rubber hose, between the follower and head.

56   Make sure the locating dowels are in position in the holders or cylinder head.

57   Align the index mark on the right end of each camshaft with the mark on the top of the holder.

58   Keeping the index marks aligned, install the camshaft and holder assemblies on the cylinder head, engaging the camshaft gears with the drive gear.

59   Locate each assembly on its dowels and fit the oil pipe to the top of the holders. Install the holder retaining bolts, tightening them by hand only until all bolts are contacting the holders.

60   Starting with the bolts which are fitted in the locating dowel locations and working in a criss-cross pattern, tighten the holder retaining bolts by half a turn at a time to gradually draw the holders into position. Whilst tightening the bolts make sure that each holder is being pulled squarely down onto the cylinder head and is not sticking on the locating dowels. **Caution:** *If the bolts are carelessly tightened and the holders are not drawn squarely onto the head, they are likely to break.*

61   Once all holders are in contact with the head, go around and tighten the bolts to the specified torque setting.

62   Check the 'T' mark is still correctly aligned with the index mark on the cover then check that both the camshaft index marks are still correctly aligned the holder marks **(see illustrations 8.4a, 8.4b and 8.4c)**. If the marks aren't lined up, unbolt the holder from the cylinder head and repeat the operations in Steps 57 through 61.

63   With all the index marks correctly positioned, remove the spacers from between the exhaust followers and head then adjust the valve clearances as described in Chapter 1.

64   Lubricate all bearing surfaces with clean engine oil and fit the valve covers as described in Section 7.

65   Install the spark plugs as described in Chapter 1.

Rear camshafts only - G through K models

66   Install the followers as described in Step 51 or 52 (as applicable).

67   Referring to Step 13, rotate the crankshaft clockwise until the 'T' mark of No. 1 cylinder is aligned with the index mark, in the form of a line, on the casing. Now, check the position of the index marks on the right end of the front cylinder camshafts; they should be positioned as shown in illustrations 8.13a, 8.13b and 8.13c. If the marks are not correctly positioned, turn the crankshaft through 360° (one complete turn). **Note:** *Turn the engine in the normal direction of rotation (clockwise), viewed from the right end of the engine.*

68   Install the camshafts as described in Steps 54 through 62, noting that the camshafts are marked 'RR' (instead of 'FR') to indicate that they belong to the rear cylinders. Note that it is not necessary to install spacers between the exhaust followers and cylinder head.

69   With all the index marks correctly positioned, adjust the valve clearances as described in Chapter 1.

70   Lubricate all bearing surfaces with clean engine oil and fit the valve covers as described in Section 7.

71   Install the spark plugs as described in Chapter 1.

8.77 Ensure each shim is correctly seated in the valve spring retainer . . .

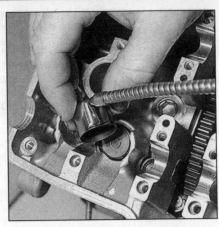

8.78 . . . then lubricate the follower and slide it into position

8.79 Ensure the 'T' mark of No. 2 cylinder is correctly aligned with the casing cutout (arrow)

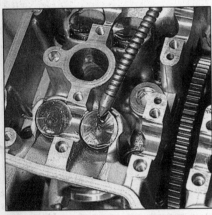

8.80 Lubricate the camshaft bearings and followers with clean engine oil

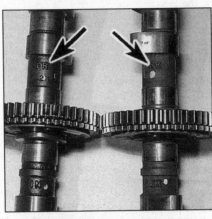

8.81a Camshafts are marked for identification purposes (rear cylinder camshafts shown)

8.81b Install the inlet camshaft . . .

8.81c . . . and engage it with the drive gear so that its arrow marking is level with the cylinder head upper surface . . .

8.81d . . . then engage the exhaust camshaft with the drive gear . . .

8.81e . . . so that its arrow is also level with the cylinder head upper surface

Front and rear camshafts - G through K models

72   Install the followers as described in Step 51 or 52 (as applicable).
73   Rotate the crankshaft clockwise until the 'T' mark of No. 1 cylinder is aligned with the index mark, in the form of a line, on the casing.
74   Install the rear camshafts as described in Steps 54 to 62, noting that the camshafts are marked 'RR' (instead of 'FR') to indicate that they belong to the rear cylinders. Note also that it is not necessary to

install spacers between the exhaust followers and cylinder head.
75   Rotate the crankshaft through 450° (1 and 1/4 turns) until the 'T' mark of No. 2 cylinder is aligned with the index mark, in the form of a line, on the casing.
76   Install the front camshafts as described in Steps 53 through 65.

Front camshafts only - L onwards models

Refer to illustrations 8.77, 8.78, 8.79, 8.80, 8.81a, 8.81b, 8.81c, 8.81d, 8.81e and 8.83

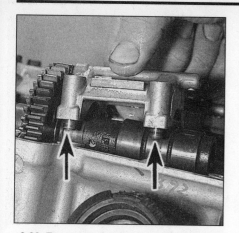

8.83 Ensure the locating dowels (arrow) are in position in the bearing holders

8.96 Crankshaft No. 1 cylinder 'T' mark aligned with the casing cutout (arrow)

8.99a Install the inlet camshaft . . .

77   Fit each shim to the top of its correct valve making sure it is correctly seated in the valve spring retainer **(see illustration)**. Note: *It is most important that the shims are returned to their original valves otherwise the valve clearances will be inaccurate.*

78   Install the followers in their respective positions in the cylinder head, making sure each one squarely enters its bore **(see illustration)**.

79   Referring to Step 21, rotate the crankshaft clockwise until the 'T' mark of No. 2 cylinder is aligned with the index mark, in the form of a cutout, on the casing **(see illustration)**. Now, check the position of the arrows on the rear cylinder camshafts; they should be aligned with the upper surface of the cylinder head as shown in illustration 8.21. If the marks are not correctly positioned, turn the crankshaft through 360° (one complete turn). **Note:** *Turn the engine in the normal direction of rotation (clockwise), viewed from the right end of the engine.*

80   Apply a smear of clean engine oil to the cylinder head camshaft bearings and followers **(see illustration)**.

81   Referring to Step 23, identify the inlet and exhaust camshafts and fit them to the cylinder head. Engage each camshaft with the drive gear so the arrow on each camshaft gear is level with the cylinder head surface and pointing away from each other **(see illustrations)**. The cam lobes of No. 2 cylinder will be pointing away from the followers.

82   With both camshafts correctly positioned, apply a smear of clean engine oil to the camshaft bearing journals.

83   Make sure the locating dowels are in position in the bearing holders or cylinder head **(see illustration)**.

84   Referring to Step 23, install the bearing holders in their original locations on the cylinder head.

85   Install the bearing holder bolts noting that the longer bolts fit into the locating dowel holes.

86   Tighten all the bearing holder bolts by hand only until all bolts are contacting the caps.

87   Starting with the intake bearing holders, working in the sequence shown in illustration 8.23a, tighten the bearing holder bolts by half a turn at a time to gradually draw the holders into position. Whilst tightening the bolts make sure that the bearing holders are being pulled squarely down onto the cylinder head and are not sticking on the locating dowels. **Caution:** *If the bolts are carelessly tightened and the bearing holders are not drawn squarely onto the head, they are likely to break. If this happens the complete cylinder head assembly must be replaced; the bearing holders are matched to the cylinder head and cannot be replaced separately.*

88   Once the caps are in contact with the head, go around again in the specified sequence and tighten the bolts to the specified torque setting.

89   Repeat the procedure in Steps 87 and 88 and tighten the exhaust camshaft bearing holder bolts.

90   Check the 'T' mark of No. 2 cylinder is still correctly aligned with the cutout in the cover, then check that the camshaft gear arrows are correctly aligned with the cylinder head upper surface **(see illustration**

8.21). If the arrows aren't lined up, unbolt the bearing holder from the cylinder head and repeat the operations in Steps 81 through 88.

91   With all the arrows correctly positioned, rotate the crankshaft through a few rotations to settle all disturbed components in position.

92   Check and, if necessary, adjust the valve clearances as described in Chapter 1.

93   Lubricate all bearing surfaces with clean engine oil and fit the valve covers as described in Section 7.

94   Install the spark plugs as described in Chapter 1.

Rear camshafts only - L models onward

Refer to illustrations 8.96, 8.99a, 8.99b, 8.99c and 8.99d

95   Install the shims and followers as described in Steps 77 and 78.

96   Referring to Step 28, rotate the crankshaft clockwise until the 'T' mark of No. 1 cylinder is aligned with the index mark, in the form of a cutout, on the casing **(see illustration)**. Now, check the position of the lines on the front cylinder camshafts; they should be aligned with the upper surface of the cylinder head as shown in illustration 8.28. If the marks are not correctly positioned, turn the crankshaft through 360° (one complete turn). **Note:** *Turn the engine in the normal direction of rotation (clockwise), viewed from the right end of the engine.*

97   Apply a smear of clean engine oil to the cylinder head camshaft bearings and followers.

98   Referring to Step 23, identify the inlet and exhaust camshafts noting that the camshafts are marked 'RR' (instead of 'FR') to indicate that they belong to the rear cylinders.

99   Fit the camshafts to the cylinder head. Engage each camshaft with the drive gear so the line on each camshaft gear is level with the cylinder head surface and is positioned on the outside of the gear **(see illustrations)**. The cam lobes of No. 1 cylinder will be pointing away

8.99b . . . and engage it with the drive gear so that its straight line marking is level with the cylinder head upper surface . . .

8.99c ... then engage the exhaust camshaft with the drive gear ...

8.99d ... so that its straight line is also level with the cylinder head upper surface

9.5 Camshaft drive gear assemblies are marked (arrows) for identification purposes

9.7a On L models onward, unscrew the upper camshaft drive gear retaining bolts ...

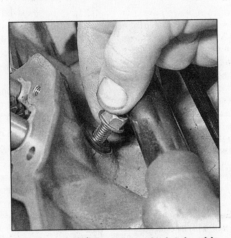

9.7b ... and the bolt from the intake side of the cylinder block ...

9.7c ... then lift the drive gear assembly out of position ...

from the followers.

100 Install the camshaft bearing caps as described in Steps 82 through 89.

101 Check that the 'T' mark of No. 1 cylinder is still correctly aligned with the cutout in the cover then check that the camshaft gear lines are correctly aligned with the cylinder head upper surface **(see illustration 8.28)**. If the lines aren't correctly positioned, unbolt the bearing cap from the cylinder head and repeat the operations in Steps 81 to 88.

102 With all the lines correctly positioned, rotate the crankshaft through a few rotations to settle all disturbed components in position.

103 Check and, if necessary, adjust the valve clearances as described in Chapter 1.

104 Lubricate all bearing surfaces with clean engine oil and fit the valve covers as described in Section 7.

105 Install the spark plugs as described in Chapter 1.

Front and rear camshafts - L models onward

106 Install the shims and followers as described in Steps 77 and 78.

107 Rotate the crankshaft clockwise until the 'T' mark of No. 1 cylinder is aligned with the cutout in the cover.

108 Install the rear camshafts as described in Steps 97 through 101.

109 Rotate the crankshaft through 450° (1 and 1/4 turns) until the 'T' mark of No. 2 cylinder is aligned with the cutout in the casing.

110 Install the front camshafts as described in Steps 80 through 94.

9 Camshaft drive gears - removal, inspection and installation

Removal

G through K models

Refer to illustration 9.5

Note: *If you intend removing the camshaft drive gear assembly and leaving the cylinder head in position, there is a slight risk of the cylinder head gasket joint being disturbed. It is highly recommended that the camshaft drive gear assembly is removed as part of the cylinder head removal procedure, and not individually.*

Caution: *The engine must be completely cool before beginning this procedure or the cylinder head may become warped.*

1   Remove the camshafts as described in Section 8.

2   Unscrew the bolt securing the camshaft drive gear to the intake side of the cylinder block/crankcase. **Note:** *In order to remove the bolt, it may be necessary to drain the cooling system and unbolt the coolant pipe from the top of the crankcase. If this is the case it is permissible to unscrew the bolt, yet leave it in position in the crankcase.*

3   Slacken and remove the four cylinder head bolts securing the camshaft drive gear in position.

4   Carefully lift the camshaft drive gear assembly out of position and remove it from the cylinder head. Recover the locating dowels and

9.7d . . . and recover the locating dowels

9.14 On installation, fit a new sealing washer to the lower retaining bolt (L models onward shown)

store them with the drive gear for safe-keeping. **Note:** *Take care not to drop the dowels down into the engine unit; if a dowel is dropped, it must be recovered before the engine can be started - drain the engine oil and remove the oil pan to recover the dowel.*

5   If both camshaft drive gear assemblies are to be removed at the same time, great care must be taken to ensure the front and rear gear assemblies are not inadvertently swapped over. The front gear assembly has an 'F' stamped on the side of its casing, and the rear gear assembly has an 'R' stamped on its casing. If the marks are no longer visible, make suitable markings as the gears are removed **(see illustration)**.

L models onward
Refer to illustrations 9.7a through 9.7d
6   Remove the cylinder head as described in Section 10.
7   Remove the camshaft drive gear assembly as described above in Steps 2 through 5. Note that the drive gear bolts are of two different lengths **(see illustrations)**.

Inspection
8   Wash the assembly in clean solvent and dry it off.
9   Check the gear teeth for cracking and other obvious damage and make sure each gear turns smoothly.
10   If wear or damage of the gears is noted the complete assembly must be replaced. *Do not* attempt to dismantle the gear assembly.

Installation

G through K models
Refer to illustration 9.14
11   Install the locating dowels in the cylinder head making sure each one is pushed fully into position.
12   Install the camshaft drive gear assembly, making sure it is correctly engaged with the crankshaft gear. Locate the gear assembly on the locating dowels. If both gear assemblies have been removed, make sure the assembly is being installed in its original location (see Step 5).
13   Install the retaining bolts and tighten them lightly.
14   Fit a new sealing washer (where possible) and screw in the bolt securing the gear assembly to the cylinder block/crankcase **(see illustration)**. Tighten the bolt lightly only at this stage.
15   With all bolts in position, working in a diagonal sequence, tighten the four upper bolts to the specified torque setting.
16   Tighten the camshaft gear to cylinder block/crankcase bolt to the specified torque.
17   Install the camshafts as described in Section 8.

L models onward
18   Install the camshaft drive gear as described in Steps 11 through 16, noting that the longer gear retaining bolts are fitted to the locating dowel holes.
19   Install the cylinder head as described in Section 10.

10 Cylinder head - removal and installation

Caution: *The engine must be completely cool before beginning this procedure or the cylinder head may become warped.*

Removal

Front cylinder head only - G through K models
Note: *This procedure can be performed with the engine in the frame. If the engine has already been removed, ignore the preliminary steps which don't apply.*
1   Remove the radiator as described in Chapter 3.
2   Remove the carburetors and the exhaust system front pipes as described in Chapter 4.
3   Slacken and remove the left and right upper front engine mounting bolts and washers which screw into the cylinder head. Note that it may be necessary to remove the ignition HT coils to allow the bolts to be withdrawn (see Chapter 5).
4   On California models, unbolt the secondary air injection system pipes from the front of the cylinder head (see Chapter 4).
5   Slacken the clips and disconnect the cooling system hoses from the thermostat housing. Disconnect the wiring connector from the coolant temperature sender, then undo the mounting bolts and remove the complete thermostat housing from the engine unit. Recover the O-ring from behind the housing.
6   Remove the camshafts as described in Section 8.
7   Unscrew the four bolts securing the two coolant outlet unions to the top of the crankcase. Free the left union from the metal coolant pipe and remove both unions and the joining metal pipe as an assembly. Recover the sealing rings.
8   Undo the two bolts and remove the oil pipe joining the cylinder head to the crankcase, taking great care not to bend the pipe. Recover the locating dowels from each end of the pipe and the O-rings.
9   Slacken and remove the bolt and sealing washer securing the camshaft drive gear to the intake side of the cylinder block/crankcase.
10   On G models, trace the wiring back from the camshaft pulse generator to its wiring connector. Disconnect the connector and free the wiring from any relevant clips so that it is free to be removed with the head.

10.33 Do not forget to remove the two 6 mm cylinder head bolts (arrow)

11   Unscrew the three 6 mm cylinder head bolts from each side of the camshaft drive gear.

12   Working from the outside to the inside in a criss-cross pattern, slacken the 9 mm cylinder head bolts by half a turn at a time. Once all pressure is released from the bolts, fully unscrew them and remove along with their washers.

13   Carefully lift the camshaft drive gear assembly out of position and remove it from the cylinder head. Recover the locating dowels and keep them with the drive gear for safe-keeping. **Note:** *Take care not to drop the dowels down into the engine unit; if a dowel is dropped, it must be recovered before the engine can be started - drain the engine oil and remove the oil pan to recover the dowel.*

14   Tap around the joint faces of the cylinder head with a soft-faced mallet to free the head. Don't attempt to free the head by inserting a screwdriver between the head and cylinder block - you'll damage the sealing surfaces.

15   Lift the head off the block, and remove it from the engine.

16   Remove the old head gasket and discard it. If loose, remove the cylinder head locating dowels from the cylinder block and store them with the head for safe-keeping.

17   Check the cylinder head gasket and the mating surfaces on the cylinder head and block for signs of leakage, which could indicate warpage. Check the flatness of the head as described in Section 12.

Rear cylinder head only - G through K models

18   The rear cylinder head cannot be removed with the engine in the frame. In order to remove the cylinder head, the engine must first be removed as described in Section 5.

19   Remove the exhaust rear pipes as described in Chapter 4.

20   The cylinder head can then be removed as described above in Steps 6 through 17, ignoring Step 10.

Front and rear cylinder heads - G through K models

21   Since the rear cylinder head cannot be removed with the engine in the frame, it will be necessary to remove the engine as described in Section 5.

22   Remove the rear exhaust pipes as described in Chapter 4.

23   Remove the camshafts (see Section 8).

24   Remove the front cylinder head as described above in Steps 7 through 17, ignoring Step 10.

25   Repeat the procedure and remove the rear cylinder head taking great care to ensure all components are kept separate and are not interchanged. Note that the front and rear camshaft drive gear assemblies are different; the front gear assembly has an 'F' stamped on the side of its casing, and the rear gear assembly has an 'R' stamped on its casing. If the marks are no longer visible, make suitable markings as the gears are removed.

Front cylinder head only - L models onward

Refer to illustration 10.33

Note: *This procedure can be performed with the engine in the frame. If the engine has already been removed, ignore the preliminary steps which don't apply.*

26   Remove the radiator and coolant reservoir as described in Chapter 3.

27   Remove the exhaust system front pipes as described in Chapter 4.

28   Remove the carburetors as described in Chapter 4.

29   On US models, unbolt the secondary air injection system pipes from the front of the head (see Chapter 4).

30   Slacken and remove the left and right front engine mounting bolts which screw into the cylinder head.

31   Undo the two bolts and free the coolant outlet union from the rear of the cylinder head.

32   Remove the camshafts and followers as described in Section 8.

33   Unscrew the two 6 mm cylinder head bolts from each side of the camshaft drive gear **(see illustration)**. **Note:** *Take care not to drop the bolts down into the engine unit; if a bolt is dropped, it must be recovered before the engine can be started - drain the engine oil and remove the oil pan to recover the bolt.*

34   Working from the outside to the inside in a criss-cross pattern, slacken the cylinder head bolts by half a turn at a time. Once all pressure is released from the bolts, fully unscrew them and remove along with their washers.

35   Tap around the joint faces of the cylinder head with a soft-faced mallet to free the head. Don't attempt to free the head by inserting a screwdriver between the head and cylinder block - you'll damage the sealing surfaces.

36   Lift the head off the block, and remove it from the engine.

37   Remove the old head gasket and discard it. If loose, remove the cylinder head locating dowels from the cylinder block and store them with the head for safe-keeping.

38   Check the cylinder head gasket and the mating surfaces on the cylinder head and block for signs of leakage, which could indicate warpage. Check the flatness of the head as described in Section 12.

Rear cylinder head only - L models onward

Note 1: *This procedure can be performed with the engine in the frame. If the engine has already been removed, ignore the preliminary steps which don't apply.*

Note 2: *A suitable peg wrench will be required to slacken and tighten the engine mounting adjuster locknut. In the absence of the special Honda service tool (Part No. 07HMA-MR70200), it will be necessary to fabricate a suitable alternative before starting work.*

39   Drain the cooling system as described in Chapter 1

40   Remove the exhaust rear pipes as described in Chapter 4.

41   Remove the carburetors as described in Chapter 4.

42   On US models, unbolt the secondary air injection system pipes from the head (see Chapter 4).

43   Slacken and remove the upper, rear right mounting bolt. Slacken the adjuster locknut, then unscrew the adjuster.

44   Unscrew the upper, rear left mounting bolt.

45   Remove the cylinder head as described above in Steps 31 through 38.

Front and rear cylinder heads - L models onward

Note 1: *This procedure can be performed with the engine in the frame. If the engine has already been removed, ignore the preliminary steps which don't apply.*

Note 2: *A suitable peg wrench will be required to slacken and tighten the engine mounting adjuster locknut. In the absence of the special Honda service tool (Part No. 07HMA-MR70200), it will be necessary to fabricate a suitable alternative before starting work.*

46   Remove the radiator and coolant reservoir as described in Chapter 3.

47   Remove the complete exhaust system as described in Chapter 4.

48   Remove the carburetors as described in Chapter 4.

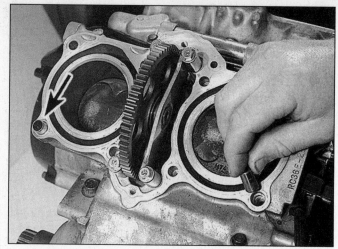

10.85 Fit the two locating dowels to the block (arrow) . . .

10.86 . . . then install the gasket, making sure its UP mark (arrow) is the correct way up

49   On US models, unbolt the secondary air injection system pipes from each cylinder head (see Chapter 4).
50   Slacken and remove the left and right engine front mounting bolts which screw into the cylinder head.
51   Slacken and remove the upper, rear right mounting bolt. Slacken the adjuster locknut using the peg wrench, then unscrew the adjuster.
52   Unscrew the upper, rear left mounting bolt.
53   Undo the bolts and free the coolant outlet union from the each cylinder head.
54   Remove the camshafts and followers as described in Section 8.
55   Remove the front cylinder head as described above in Steps 32 through 38.
56   Repeat the procedure and remove the rear cylinder head. Take great care to ensure all components are kept separate and are not interchanged.

Installation

Front cylinder head only - G through K models

57   Ensure both cylinder head and block mating surfaces are clean and fit the locating dowels to the block (if removed). Apply a smear of engine oil to the surface of each cylinder bore.
58   Fit the new head gasket over the locating dowels making sure its 'UP' mark is facing up.
59   Carefully lower the cylinder head onto the block and align it with the locating dowels.
60   Install the three 6 mm cylinder head bolts, tightening them by hand only at this stage
61   Fit the camshaft drive gear locating dowels to the head.
62   Install the camshaft drive gear assembly, making sure it is correctly engaged with the crankshaft gear. Locate the gear assembly on the locating dowels.
63   Apply a smear of clean engine oil to the threads and undersides of the cylinder head bolts. Install the bolts and washers, noting that the four longer bolts are fitted to the camshaft drive gear holes, and tighten them lightly.
64   Fit a new sealing washer and screw in the bolt securing the drive gear assembly to the cylinder block/crankcase. Tighten the bolt lightly only at this stage.
65   Working from the inside to the outside in a criss-cross pattern, tighten the eight 9 mm cylinder head bolts to approximately half the specified torque setting given in the Specifications. Then go around in the same sequence and tighten the bolts to the full specified torque setting.
66   With the 9 mm bolts tightened, tighten the three 6 mm bolts to the specified torque setting.
67   Tighten the camshaft gear to cylinder block/crankcase bolt to the

specified torque.
68   Insert the oil pipe locating dowel then fit a new O-ring to each dowel and install the oil pipe.
69   Wipe clean the oil pipe bolts then apply a smear of fresh sealant to their threads. Install the bolts and tighten them securely.
70   Fit a new sealing ring to each of the coolant outlet unions and one to the metal pipe. Install the union and metal pipe assembly and securely tighten the retaining bolts.
71   Install the camshafts as described in Section 8.
72   On G models, reconnect the camshaft pulse generator wiring, making sure the wire is correctly routed.
73   Fit a new O-ring to the thermostat housing and fit the housing assembly, tightening its retaining bolts securely. Connect the coolant hoses and tighten their clips.
74   Install the left and right upper front engine mounting bolts and tighten them to the specified torque. Where necessary, install the HT coils as described in Chapter 5.
75   Install the carburetors and exhaust front pipes as described in Chapter 4. On California models, also connect the air pipes to the head.
76   Fit the radiator and refill the cooling system as described in Chapter 3.

Rear cylinder head only - G through K models

77   Install the head as described above in Steps 57 through 71.
78   Install the rear exhaust pipes as described in Chapter 4.
79   Install the engine as described in Section 5.

Front and rear cylinder head - G through K models

80   Install the front cylinder head as described in Steps 57 through 69, ensuring that the correct camshaft drive gear assembly is being installed (see Step 25).
81   Install the rear cylinder head as described in Steps 57 through 70.
82   Install the camshafts as described in Section 8.
83   Install the rear exhaust pipes as described in Chapter 4.
84   Install the engine as described in Section 5.

Front cylinder head only - L models onward
Refer to illustrations 10.85, 10.86, 10.88 and 10.89
85   Ensure both cylinder head and block mating surfaces are clean and fit the locating dowels to the block (if removed) **(see illustration)**. Apply a smear of engine oil to the surface of each cylinder bore.
86   Fit the new head gasket over the locating dowels making sure its 'UP' mark is facing up **(see illustration)**.
87   Carefully lower the cylinder head onto the block and align it with the locating dowels.

2

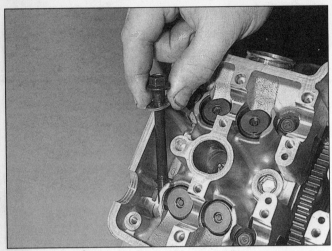

10.88 Lubricate the threads and underside of the heads of the cylinder head bolts and screw them into position

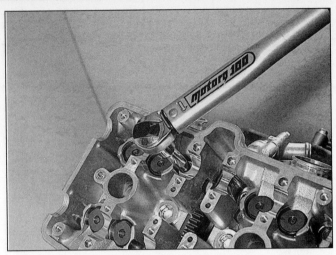

10.89 Tighten the heads bolts to the specified torque setting as described in text

88   Apply a smear of clean engine oil to the threads and undersides of the cylinder head bolt heads. Install the bolts and washers and tighten them lightly **(see illustration)**.

89   Working from the inside to the outside in a criss-cross pattern, tighten the cylinder head bolts to approximately half the specified torque setting given in the Specifications. Then go around in the same sequence and tighten the bolts to the full specified torque setting **(see illustration)**.

90   Fit the two 6 mm cylinder head bolts and tighten them to the specified torque.

91   Fit a new sealing ring to the coolant union. Fit the union to the head and securely tighten its retaining bolts.

92   Install the camshafts and followers as described in Section 8.

93   Fit the left and right front engine mounting bolts and tighten them to the specified torque.

94   Install the carburetors and exhaust front pipes as described in Chapter 4. On US models, also connect the air pipes to the head.

95   Fit the radiator and coolant reservoir as described in Chapter 3 and refill with coolant.

Rear cylinder head only - L models onward

96   Install the cylinder head as described above in Steps 85 through 92.

97   Fit the upper, rear left mounting bolt and tighten it to the specified torque.

98   Using an Allen wrench, tighten the upper, rear right mounting adjuster to the specified torque setting. Hold the adjuster stationary, then tighten the adjuster locknut to the specified torque setting with the peg wrench.

99   Install the upper, rear right mounting bolt and tighten it to the specified torque setting.

100 Install the carburetors and exhaust rear pipes as described in Chapter 4. On US models, also connect the air pipes to the head.

101 Refill the cooling system as described in Chapter 1.

Front and rear cylinder head - L models onward

102 Install the rear cylinder head as described above in Steps 85 through 91.

103 Repeat the procedure and install the front cylinder head as described in Steps 85 through 91.

104 Install the camshafts and followers as described in Section 8.

105 Fit the left and right front engine mounting bolts and tighten them to the specified torque.

106 Fit the upper, rear left mounting bolt and tighten it to the specified torque.

107 Using an Allen wrench, tighten the upper, rear right mounting adjuster to the specified torque setting. Hold the adjuster stationary,

then tighten the adjuster locknut to the specified torque setting with the peg wrench.

108 Install the upper, rear right mounting bolt and tighten it to the specified torque setting.

109 Install the carburetors and exhaust system as described in Chapter 4. On US models, also connect the air pipes to the head.

110 Fit the radiator and coolant reservoir as described in Chapter 3, and refill the cooling system.

11   Valves/valve seats/valve guides - servicing

1   Because of the complex nature of this job and the special tools and equipment required, servicing of the valves, the valve seats and the valve guides (commonly known as a valve job) is best left to a professional.

2   The home mechanic can, however, remove and disassemble the head, do the initial cleaning and inspection, then reassemble and deliver the head to a dealer service department or properly equipped motorcycle repair shop for the actual valve servicing. Refer to Section 12 for those procedures.

3   The dealer service department will remove the valves and springs, recondition or replace the valves and valve seats, replace the valve guides, check and replace the valve springs, spring retainers and keepers (collets) (as necessary), replace the valve seals with new ones and reassemble the valve components.

4   After the valve job has been performed, the head will be in like-new condition. When the head is returned, be sure to clean it again very thoroughly before installation on the engine to remove any metal particles or abrasive grit that may still be present from the valve service operations. Use compressed air, if available, to blow out all the holes and passages.

12   Cylinder head and valves - disassembly, inspection and reassembly

1   As mentioned in the previous Section, valve servicing and valve guide replacement should be left to a dealer service department or motorcycle repair shop. However, disassembly, cleaning and inspection of the valves and related components can be done (if the necessary special tools are available) by the home mechanic. This way no expense is incurred if the inspection reveals that service work is not required at this time.

2   To properly disassemble the valve components without the risk of damaging them, a valve spring compressor is absolutely necessary.

12.3 Exploded view of the cylinder head components - L models onward

1   Follower
2   Shim
3   Keepers (collets)
4   Spring retainer
5   Outer valve spring
6   Inner valve spring
7   Valves
8   Inner spring seat
9   Outer spring seat
10   Valve stem oil seal
11   Valve guide
12   Intake joint
13   Head gasket
14   Locating dowels

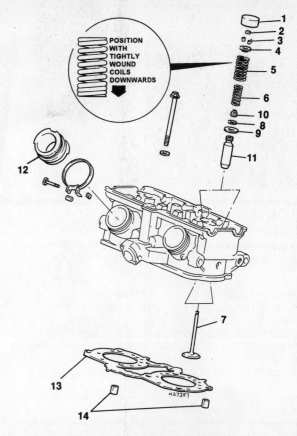

This special tool can usually be rented, but if it's not available, have a dealer service department or motorcycle repair shop handle the entire process of disassembly, inspection, service or repair (if required) and reassembly of the valves.

Disassembly

Refer to illustrations 12.3, 12.7a and 12.7b

3   Remove the followers if you haven't already done so (see Section 8). Store the components in such a way that they can be returned to their original locations without getting mixed up **(see illustration)**.
4   Before the valves are removed, scrape away any traces of gasket material from the head gasket sealing surface. Work slowly and do not nick or gouge the soft aluminum of the head. Gasket removing solvents, which work very well, are available at most motorcycle shops and auto parts stores.
5   Carefully scrape all carbon deposits out of the combustion chamber area. A hand held wire brush or a piece of fine emery cloth can be used once the majority of deposits have been scraped away. Do not use a wire brush mounted in a drill motor, or one with extremely stiff bristles, as the head material is soft and may be eroded away or scratched by the wire brush.
6   Before proceeding, arrange to label and store the valves along with their related components so they can be kept separate and reinstalled in the same valve guides they are removed from (labeled plastic bags work well for this).
7   Compress the valve spring on the first valve with a spring compressor, then remove the keepers (collets) from the valve assembly. **Note:** *On L models onward, take great care not to mark the cylinder head follower bore with the spring compressor.* Do not compress the springs any more than is absolutely necessary to remove the keepers (collets). Slowly release the valve spring compressor and remove the retainer, springs and the valve from the head. If the valve binds in the guide (won't pull through), push it back into the head and deburr the area around the keeper (collet) groove with a very fine file or whetstone **(see illustrations)**.

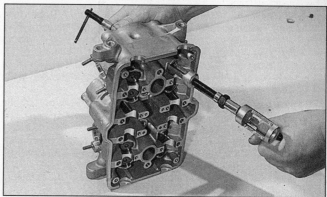

12.7a Using a spring compressor to compress a valve spring

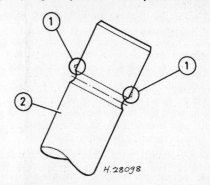

12.7b Don't force the valves out of their guides; check the area around the keeper (collet) groove for burrs and remove any that you find

1   Burrs (remove)   2   Valve stem

12.14 Checking cylinder gasket face for distortion

12.15 Measuring valve seat width

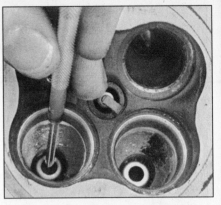

12.16a Insert small hole gauge into the valve guide and expand it so there's a slight drag when it's pulled out

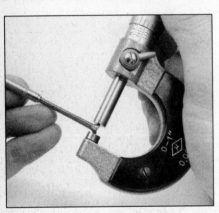

12.16b Measure the small hole gauge with a micrometer

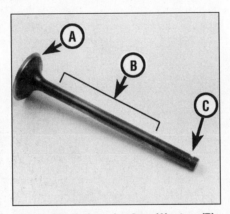

12.17 Check the valve face (A), stem (B) and keeper/collet groove (C) for signs of damage or wear

12.18 Measure the valve stem diameter with a micrometer

8   Repeat the procedure for the remaining valves. Remember to keep the parts for each valve together so they can be reinstalled in the same location.

9   Once the valves have been removed and labeled, pull off the valve stem seals with pliers and discard them (the old seals should never be re-used), then remove the spring seats.

10   Next, clean the cylinder head with solvent and dry it thoroughly. Compressed air will speed the drying process and ensure that all holes and recessed areas are clean.

11   Clean all of the valve springs, keepers (collets), retainers and spring seats with solvent and dry them thoroughly. Do the parts from one valve at a time so that no mixing of parts between valves occurs.

12   Scrape off any deposits that may have formed on the valve, then use a motorized wire brush to remove deposits from the valve heads and stems. Again, make sure the valves do not get mixed up.

Inspection

Refer to illustrations 12.14, 12.15, 12.16a, 12.16b, 12.17, 12.18, 12.19a and 12.19b

13   Inspect the head very carefully for cracks and other damage. If cracks are found, a new head will be required. Check the cam bearing surfaces for wear and evidence of seizure. Check the camshafts and followers for wear as well (see Section 8).

14   Using a precision straightedge and a feeler gauge, check the head gasket mating surface for warpage. Lay the straightedge lengthwise, across the head and diagonally (corner-to-corner), intersecting the head stud holes, and try to slip a feeler gauge under it, on either side of each combustion chamber **(see illustration)**. The gauge should be the same thickness as the cylinder head warp limit listed in this Chapter's Specifications. If the feeler gauge can be

inserted between the head and the straightedge, the head is warped and must either be machined or, if warpage is excessive, replaced with a new one.

15   Examine the valve seats in each of the combustion chambers. If they are pitted, cracked or burned, the head will require valve service that's beyond the scope of the home mechanic. Measure the valve seat width and compare it to this Chapter's Specifications **(see illustration)**. If it exceeds the service limit, or if it varies around its circumference, valve service work is required.

16   Clean the valve guides to remove any carbon build-up, then measure the inside diameters of the guides (at both ends and the center of the guide) with a small hole gauge and micrometer **(see illustrations)**. Record the measurements for future reference. These measurements, along with the valve stem diameter measurements, will enable you to compute the valve stem-to-guide clearance. This clearance, when compared to the Specifications, will be one factor that will determine the extent of the valve service work required. The guides are measured at the ends and at the center to determine if they are worn in a bell-mouth pattern (more wear at the ends). If they are, guide replacement is an absolute must.

17   Carefully inspect each valve face for cracks, pits and burned spots **(see illustration)**. Check the valve stem and the keeper (collet) groove area for cracks. Rotate the valve and check for any obvious indication that it is bent. Check the end of the stem for pitting and excessive wear. The presence of any of the above conditions indicates the need for valve servicing.

18   Measure the valve stem diameter **(see illustration)**. By subtracting the stem diameter from the valve guide diameter, the valve stem-to-guide clearance is obtained. If the stem-to-guide clearance is greater than listed in this Chapter's Specifications, the guides and valves will have to be replaced with new ones.

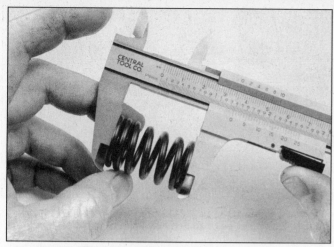

12.19a Measure the free length of the valve springs

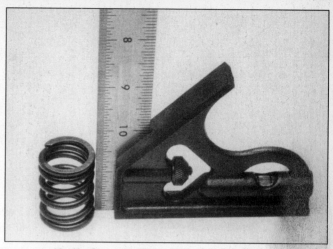

12.19b Check the valve springs for squareness

12.23 Apply lapping compound very sparingly, in small dabs, to the valve face only

12.24a After lapping, the valve face should exhibit a uniform, unbroken contact pattern (arrow) . . .

2

19   Check the end of each valve spring for wear and pitting. Measure the free length and compare it to this Chapter's Specifications. Any springs that are shorter than specified have sagged and should not be re-used. Stand the spring on a flat surface and check it for squareness **(see illustrations)**.

20   Check the spring retainers and keepers (collets) for obvious wear and cracks. Any questionable parts should not be re-used, as extensive damage will occur in the event of failure during engine operation.

21   If the inspection indicates that no service work is required, the valve components can be reinstalled in the head.

Reassembly

Refer to illustrations 12.23, 12.24a, 12.24b, 12.27a, 12.27b, 12.27c and 12.28a through 12.28e

22   Before installing the valves in the head, they should be lapped to ensure a positive seal between the valves and seats. This procedure requires coarse and fine valve lapping compound (available at auto parts stores) and a valve lapping tool. If a lapping tool is not available, a piece of rubber or plastic hose can be slipped over the valve stem (after the valve has been installed in the guide) and used to turn the valve.

23   Apply a small amount of coarse lapping compound to the valve face, then slip the valve into the guide **(see illustration)**. **Note:** *Make sure the valve is installed in the correct guide and be careful not to get any lapping compound on the valve stem.*

24   Attach the lapping tool (or hose) to the valve and rotate the tool

12.24b . . . and the seat should be the specified width (arrow) with a smooth, unbroken appearance

between the palms of your hands. Use a back-and-forth motion rather than a circular motion. Lift the valve off the seat and turn it at regular intervals to distribute the lapping compound properly. Continue the lapping procedure until the valve face and seat contact area is of uniform width and unbroken around the entire circumference of the valve face and seat **(see illustrations)**.

25   Carefully remove the valve from the guide and wipe off all traces

12.27a Fit the outer spring seat . . .

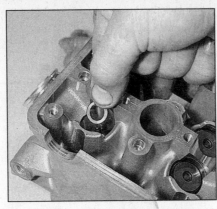

12.27b . . . followed by the inner spring seat . . .

12.27c . . . then press the valve stem seal into position using a suitable deep socket

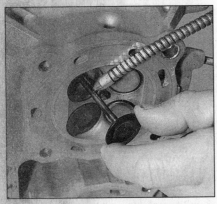

12.28a Lubricate the stem and slide the valve into its correct location

12.28b Fit the inner valve spring . . .

12.28c . . . and outer valve spring making sure their tightly wound coils are at the bottom

12.28d Fit the spring retainer . . .

12.28e . . . then compress the springs and install the keepers (collets) using grease to help keep them in position

of lapping compound. Use solvent to clean the valve and wipe the seat area thoroughly with a solvent soaked cloth.

26   Repeat the procedure with fine valve lapping compound, then repeat the entire procedure for the remaining valves.

27   Lay the spring seats in place in the cylinder head, then install new valve stem seals on each of the guides. Use an appropriate size deep socket to push the seals into place until they are properly seated **(see illustrations)**. Don't twist or cock them, or they will not seal properly against the valve stems. Also, don't remove them again or they will be damaged.

28   Coat the valve stems with clean engine oil, then install one of

them into its guide. Next, install the springs and retainer, compress the springs and install the keepers (collets). **Note:** *Install the springs with their tightly wound coils at the bottom toward the spring seats* **(see illustration 12.3)**. When compressing the springs with the valve spring compressor, depress them only as far as is absolutely necessary to slip the keepers (collets) into place. **Note:** *On L models onward, take great care not to mark the cylinder head follower bore with the spring compressor.* Apply a small amount of grease to the keepers (collets) to help hold them in place as the pressure is released from the springs. Make certain that the keepers (collets) are securely locked in their retaining grooves **(see illustrations)**.

13.8a Withdraw the shaft then remove the starter motor idler gear . . .

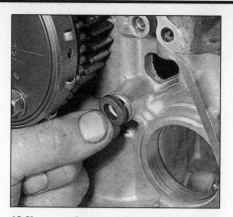

13.8b . . . and recover the washer which is fitted behind the gear

13.11 Remove the starter clutch retaining bolt and washer . . .

29 Support the cylinder head on blocks so the valves can't contact the workbench top, then very gently tap each of the valve stems with a soft-faced hammer. This will help seat the keepers (collets) in their grooves.

30 Once all of the valves have been installed in the head, check for proper valve sealing by pouring a small amount of solvent into each of the valve ports. If the solvent leaks past the valve(s) into the combustion chamber area, disassemble the valve(s) and repeat the lapping procedure, then reinstall the valve(s) and repeat the check. Repeat the procedure until a satisfactory seal is obtained.

13 Starter motor clutch - removal, inspection and installation

Note: *The starter motor clutch can be removed with the engine in the frame.*

Removal

Refer to illustrations 13.8a, 13.8b, 13.11, 13.13, 13.14 and 13.15

1 Remove the right lower fairing panel or lower fairing (as applicable) as described in Chapter 8.

2 Drain the engine oil as described in Chapter 1.

3 Working in a criss-cross pattern, evenly slacken the right crankcase cover retaining bolts, noting the correct fitted positions of all wiring retaining clamps.

4 Lift the cover away from the engine, being prepared to catch any residual oil which may be released as the cover is removed.

5 Remove the gasket and discard it. Note the two locating dowels fitted to the crankcase; remove these for safe-keeping if they are loose.

6 On G models, unscrew the four retaining bolts and release the pulse generator assembly from the engine.

7 On H models onward, unscrew the three retaining bolts and release the pulse generator assembly from the engine unit. Remove the generator assembly locating dowels from the crankcase for safe-keeping.

8 Withdraw the starter idler gear shaft and recover the washer which will fall from behind the gear. Rotate the starter clutch clockwise and remove the idler gear **(see illustrations)**.

9 In the absence of the special Honda gear locking tool (Part No. 07724-0010100) some means of preventing the starter clutch from rotating must be found. This can be achieved by jamming a piece of stout cloth, such as a piece of denim, between the top of the primary drive and clutch drum gears.

10 Slacken the starter clutch retaining bolt, then rotate the clutch clockwise and withdraw the cloth. Make sure that any fibers from the cloth are removed from between the gears.

11 Unscrew and remove the retaining bolt and washer **(see illustration)**.

12 Check for alignment marks between the starter clutch and

13.13 . . . and slide off the starter clutch assembly

13.14 Remove the flanged spacer, noting which way around it is fitted . . .

crankshaft. On G through K models, the punch mark on the crankshaft should align with the circular pin on the starter clutch; on J and K models there is also a wide master spline on the starter clutch which aligns with the mark. As an aid to ensure correct installation, using a dab of white paint, make your own alignment marks between the clutch and crankshaft. **Note:** *If the starter clutch is not correctly installed on the crankshaft the engine will not run due to the pulse generator triggers on the clutch being wrongly positioned and preventing correct ignition timing.* On L models onward, both the starter clutch and crankshaft have one wide spline making it impossible to install the clutch incorrectly.

13 Remove the starter clutch assembly from the crankshaft, then lift off the driven gear and needle roller bearing from the rear of the starter clutch **(see illustration)**.

14 Slide off the flanged spacer, noting which way around it is fitted **(see illustration)**.

2

13.15 ... followed by the primary drive gear

13.17a Inspect the starter clutch driven gear contact surface ...

13.17b ... and rollers (arrows) for signs of wear

13.19a Exploded view of starter clutch components

1   *Driven gear*
2   *Needle roller bearing*
3   *Bolt - 3 off*
4   *Cover*
5   *Rollers*
6   *Plungers*
7   *Springs*
8   *Starter clutch body*
9   *Locating pin*

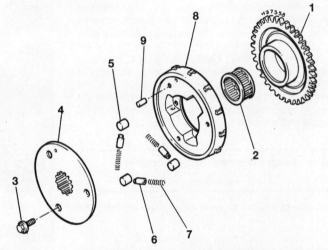

15   Remove the primary drive gear, noting which way around it is installed **(see illustration)**.

Inspection

Refer to illustrations 13.17a, 13.17b, 13.19a and 13.19b

16   Inspect the starter idler gear and driven gear teeth and replace them as a pair if any teeth are chipped or missing. Check the idler shaft and gear bearing surfaces for signs of wear or damage, and replace if necessary.

17   Inspect the starter clutch rollers and driven gear contact surfaces for signs of wear and scoring **(see illustrations)**. The starter clutch rollers should be unmarked with no signs of wear such as pitting or flat spots. The degree of wear on the driven gear can be assessed by measuring the outside diameter of its boss and comparing it to the service limit given in the Specifications.

18   Inspect the needle roller bearing and driven gear contact surfaces for wear or scoring. Replace worn components as necessary.

19   To replace the starter clutch rollers, clamp the body in a vise equipped with soft jaws. Undo the three bolts and remove the cover from the clutch **(see illustrations)**.

20   Remove the rollers, plungers and springs from the starter clutch, noting each component's correct fitted location.

21   Install the new springs, plungers and rollers.

22   Ensure all components are correctly positioned then install the cover, aligning its hole with the locating pin on the clutch body.

23   Clean the cover bolts and apply a drop of locking compound to their threads. Install the bolts and tighten them to the specified torque setting.

Installation

Refer to illustrations 13.26a, 13.26b, 13.27 and 13.29

13.19b Undo the three retaining bolts and lift off the cover; note the cover locating pin hole (arrow)

24   Position the primary drive gear with its small tensioning gear facing out and engage it with the crankshaft splines. Align the tensioning gear teeth with those of the main gear, using a large flat-bladed screwdriver, and mesh the gear with the clutch drum.

25   Slide on the flanged spacer so that its flange is facing outs.

26   Apply a smear of clean engine oil to the driven gear and needle roller bearing and fit them to the rear of the starter clutch body, turning it clockwise to help it engage with the starter clutch rollers **(see illustrations)**.

27   Referring to Step 12, align the starter clutch assembly correctly with the crankshaft and slide the assembly onto the splines **(see illustration)**.

28   On G through K models, clean the starter clutch retaining bolt and

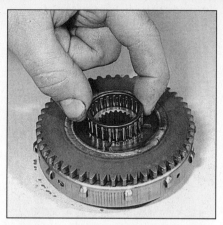

13.26a Fit the driven gear to the rear of the starter clutch body . . .

13.26b . . . then slide the needle roller bearing into position

13.27 On L models onward align the wide spline of the clutch with that of the crankshaft on installation

13.29 Tighten the starter clutch retaining bolt to the specified torque setting (note use of cloth to prevent rotation)

14.1 Special Honda service tool or suitable alternative will be required to slacken and tighten the clutch center nut

apply a drop of locking compound to its threads.

29   On all models, fit the washer and bolt and tighten it to the specified torque setting. Prevent starter clutch rotation using a piece of stout cloth, such as denim, jammed between the bottom of the primary drive gear and clutch drum gear **(see illustration)**.

30   With the bolt correctly tightened, rotate the clutch counter-clockwise (anti-clockwise) and remove the cloth. Make sure that any fibers from the cloth are removed from between the gears.

31   Apply a smear of clean engine oil to the idler gear shaft. Slide the shaft into the gear and fit the washer to the rear of the gear. Engage the idler gear with the starter clutch and starter motor gear and locate the shaft in the crankcase, making sure the washer stays correctly positioned between the gear and crankcase.

32   Apply a smear of suitable sealing compound to the pulse generator wiring grommets.

33   On G models, locate the grommets in position in the crankcase then install the generator retaining bolts, tightening them securely.

34   On H models onward, fit the locating dowels to the crankcase then install the generator assembly, locating the wiring grommets in the crankcase cutouts. Ensure the front generator wiring is correctly routed through the bracket clamp, then securely tighten the retaining bolts.

35   Remove all traces of old gasket from the crankcase and cover mating surfaces.

36   Install the locating dowels and fit a new gasket to the crankcase.

37   Fit the cover and install the bolts, making sure all the wiring clamps are correctly positioned. Tighten the cover bolts evenly and progressively to the specified torque setting.

38   Fill the engine with the correct type and amount of oil as described in Chapter 1.

39   Install the fairing panel(s) as described in Chapter 8.

14   Clutch - removal, inspection and installation

Note 1: *A suitable peg wrench will be required to slacken and tighten the clutch center nut. In the absence of the special Honda service tool (Part No. 07716-0020203), it will be necessary to fabricate a suitable alternative before starting work* **(see illustration)**. *Some means of holding the clutch center will also be required if the engine has been removed from the frame (see Step 8).*

Note 2: *This procedure can be performed with the engine in the frame. If the engine has already been removed, ignore the preliminary steps which don't apply.*

Removal

Refer to illustrations 14.1, 14.2a, 14.2b, 14.3, 14.4 and 14.8

1   Remove the starter motor clutch and primary drive gear as described in Section 13.

2   Working in a criss-cross pattern, gradually slacken the clutch spring retaining bolts until spring pressure is released. Unscrew the

14.2a Exploded view of the clutch components

1   Spring bolts
2   Springs
3   Pressure plate
4   Bearing
5   Lifter guide
6   Snap-ring
7   Pushrod
8   Friction and plain plates
9   Inner friction plate
10 Anti-judder spring
11 Spring seat
12 Center nut
13 Washer
14 Clutch center
15 Clutch drum
16 Needle roller bearing
17 Oil pump driven sprocket
18 Center bush
19 Oil pump drive sprocket and chain
20 Spacer

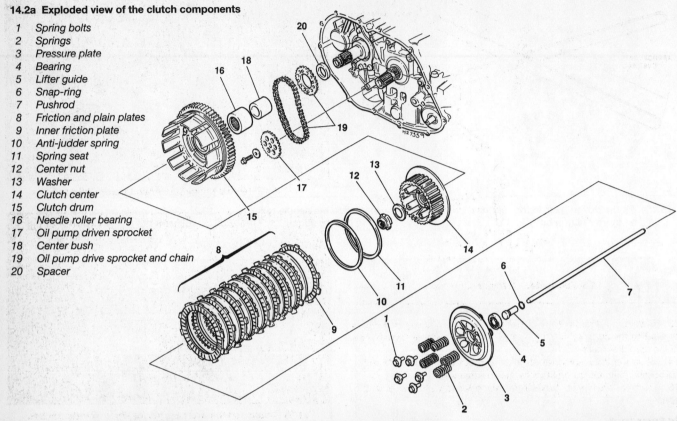

14.2b Unscrew the bolts as described in text and remove them along with the springs

14.3 Remove the pressure plate, complete with bearing and lifter guide . . .

14.4 . . . then withdraw the pushrod

bolts and remove them along with the springs **(see illustrations)**. **Note:** *Do not operate the clutch lever from this point in the removal procedure.*

3   Remove the pressure plate from the clutch and recover the lifter guide from the plate bearing **(see illustration)**.

4   Withdraw the pushrod from the center of the mainshaft **(see illustration)**.

5   Withdraw the clutch friction plates and plain plates. **Note:** *The inner friction plate is different to the others. Mark the plate in some way to ensure that it is fitted in its original position.*

6   Remove the anti-judder spring and spring seat from the clutch center, noting which way around the spring is fitted.

7   Unstake the clutch center nut using a hammer and suitable pointed-nose chisel, taking care not to damage the mainshaft end.

8   In the absence of the Honda service tool (Part Number 07724-0050001) it will be necessary to devise some method of

preventing the clutch center rotating as the center nut is slackened. If the engine is in the frame, lock the clutch through the transmission, by selecting top gear and applying the rear brake hard whilst the nut is slackened. If the engine is out of the frame, pass a close-fitting box wrench (ring spanner) over the countershaft (output shaft) splines, select top gear and hold the wrench (spanner) whilst the nut is slackened. Alternatively, a tool similar to the Honda service tool can be fabricated from some steel strap, bent at the ends and bolted together in the middle **(see illustration)**.

9   Remove the nut and discard it; a new one must be used on installation.

10   Remove the washer noting which way around it is fitted. **Note:** *The washer should be marked 'OUTSIDE'.*

11   Remove the clutch center.

12   Slide off the clutch drum and remove the needle roller bearing from its center.

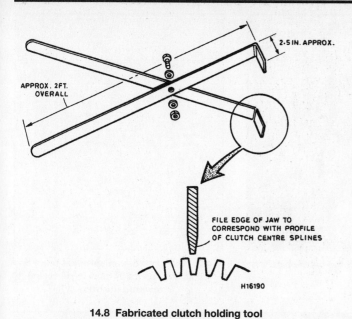

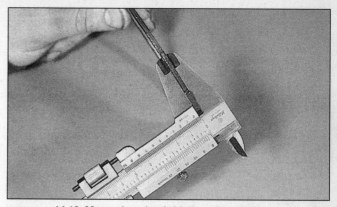

14.16 Measuring clutch friction plate thickness

14.8 Fabricated clutch holding tool

13   Slacken and remove the oil pump sprocket retaining bolt whilst preventing the sprocket turning by inserting a screwdriver through one of the sprocket holes.
14   Slide the drive sprocket off the mainshaft and remove the drive sprocket, chain and pump sprocket as an assembly.
15   Remove the center bush from the mainshaft and slide off the spacer.

Inspection

Refer to illustrations 14.16, 14.18, 14.21 and 14.22

16   After an extended period of service the clutch friction plates will wear and promote clutch slip. Measure the thickness of each friction plate using a vernier caliper **(see illustration)**. If any plate has worn to or beyond the service limit given in the Specifications, the friction plates must be replaced as a set.
17   The plain plates should not show any signs of excess heating (bluing). Check for warpage using a flat surface and feeler gauges. If any plate exceeds the maximum permissible amount of warpage, or shows signs of bluing, all plain plates must be replaced as a set.
18   Inspect the clutch assembly for burrs and indentations on the edges of the protruding tangs of the friction plates and/or slots in the edge of the clutch drum with which they engage **(see illustration)**. Similarly check for wear between the inner tongues of the plain plates and the slots in the clutch center. Wear of this nature will cause clutch drag and slow disengagement during gear shifting, since the plates will snag when the pressure plate is lifted. With care, a small amount of wear can be corrected by dressing with a fine file, but if this is excessive the worn components must be replaced.
19   Also inspect the anti-judder spring and seat for signs of wear or distortion and replace if necessary.
20   Inspect the mainshaft, center bush and clutch drum bearing surfaces, along with the needle bearing, for signs of wear and damage. If any component shows signs of wear or damage, it must be replaced.
21   Check the clutch pressure plate bearing for wear **(see illustration)**. Ensure that the inner race of the bearing spins freely without any sign of notchiness and that there is no freeplay between the inner and outer races or the outer race and plate. If necessary, replace the bearing by driving the old bearing out of the plate and tapping the new bearing into position using a hammer and suitable tubular drift which bears only on the bearing's outer race.
22   Measure the free length of each clutch spring **(see illustration)**. If any one has settled to less than the service limit, the clutch springs must be replaced as a set.
23   Remove the snap-ring from the clutch lifter guide and discard it;

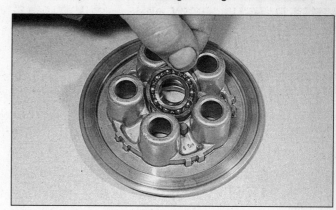

14.18 Inspect clutch drum edges for signs of indentations

14.21 Check the pressure plate bearing for wear as described in text

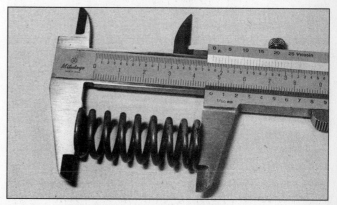

14.22 Measuring clutch spring free length

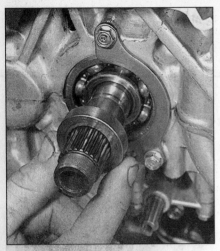

14.26a Slide the spacer onto
the mainshaft . . .

14.26b . . . then fit the center bush

14.27 Oil pump driven sprocket must be
positioned so its IN marking is facing
towards the pump

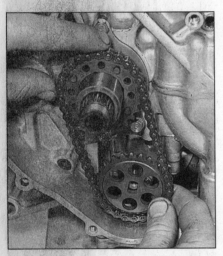

14.28 Engage the oil pump sprockets with
the chain and install them as an assembly

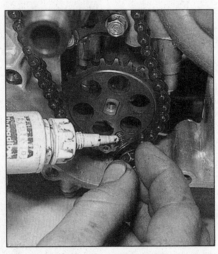

14.29 Apply thread locking compound to
the oil pump sprocket bolt . . .

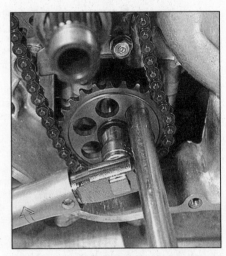

14.30 . . . and tighten it to the specified
torque setting; note method of locking the
sprocket in position

14.31 Lubricate the needle roller bearing and slide it over the
mainshaft center bush

14.32a Align the clutch drum holes with the oil pump sprocket
dogs (arrows) . . .

14.32b . . . then slide the drum into
position

14.33 Fit the clutch center . . .

14.34 . . . then fit the washer making sure
it is the correct way around

14.35a Fit the new center nut . . .

14.35b . . . then tighten it to the specified
torque setting (note the use of the clutch
holding tool)

14.35c Secure the center nut in position
by staking it . . .

the snap-ring **must** be replaced whenever it is disturbed.
24 Check the pushrod for signs of damage and straightness by
rolling it on a flat surface. Replace the pushrod if it's bent.

Installation

Refer to illustrations 14.26a, 14.26b, 14.27, 14.28, 14.29, 14.30, 14.31,
14.32a, 14.32b, 14.33, 14.34, 14.35a through 14.35d, 14.36a, 14.36b,
14.36c, 14.37, 14.38, 14.40a, 14.40b, 14.42a and 14.42b
25 Remove all traces of gasket from the crankcase and cover sealing
surfaces.
26 Apply a smear of clean engine oil to the spacer and center bush
and slide them on the mainshaft **(see illustrations)**.
27 Engage the oil pump drive and driven sprockets with the chain.
Make sure that the 'IN' mark on the driven sprocket is positioned so
that it will be facing towards the pump when the chain is installed, and
the drive sprocket is installed so that its drive dogs will be facing
towards the clutch drum **(see illustration)**.
28 Slide the drive sprocket and chain assembly onto the mainshaft.
Engage the driven sprocket with the oil pump driveshaft and check
both sprockets are fitted the correct way around **(see illustration)**.
29 Clean the sprocket bolt and apply a few drops of a suitable
locking compound to its threads **(see illustration)**.
30 Fit the oil pump sprocket bolt and tighten it to the specified
torque. Prevent the sprocket from rotating by inserting a screwdriver
through one of the sprocket holes **(see illustration)**.
31 Apply a smear of clean engine oil to the needle roller bearing and
slide it over the center bush **(see illustration)**.
32 Maneuver the clutch drum into position, aligning it with the dogs
on the oil pump drive sprocket **(see illustrations)**. **Note:** *Rotate the oil*

14.35d . . . into the mainshaft groove as shown

pump sprocket to ensure the drum is correctly engaged with its drive
sprocket before proceeding.
33 Fit the clutch center **(see illustration)**.
34 Fit the washer, ensuring that the OUTSIDE mark is facing out
(away from crankcase). If the washer is not marked, it must be installed
with its convex face outermost **(see illustration)**.
35 Fit a **new** clutch nut and tighten it to the specified torque setting
whilst holding the clutch center using the method employed on
removal. Secure it in position by staking it into the groove in the
mainshaft using a suitable hammer and punch **(see illustrations)**.

2

14.36a Fit the spring seat to the clutch center . . .

14.36b . . . then fit the anti-judder spring with its convex side facing the spring seat

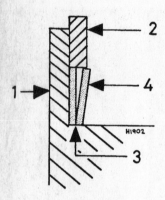

14.36c Correct fitting of anti-judder spring

1 *Clutch center*	3 *Spring seat*
2 *Inner friction plate*	4 *Anti-judder spring*

36   Fit the spring seat to the clutch center followed by the anti-judder spring. **Note:** *The anti-judder spring must be fitted with its convex side facing the spring seat* **(see illustrations)**.

37   Using the identification mark made on dismantling, fit the inner friction plate to the clutch center **(see illustration)**. **Note:** *The inner friction plate has a slightly larger internal diameter than the other plates to allow it to fit over the anti-judder spring and its seat.*

38   Install a plain plate followed by one of the ordinary friction plates, then alternately install all the remaining plain and friction plates **(see illustration)**. **Note:** *If new clutch plates are being fitted, apply a coating*

of engine oil to their surfaces to prevent seizure.

39   Insert the pushrod into the center of the mainshaft, ensuring it is installed the correct way around.

40   Fit a **new** snap-ring to the clutch lifter guide making sure it is securely located in the guide groove. Slide the rod into position in the pressure plate bearing **(see illustrations)**.

41   Install the pressure plate making sure the lifter guide engages correctly with the pushrod end.

42   Install the clutch springs and retaining bolts. Gradually tighten the bolts evenly in a criss-cross pattern until they are all securely tightened **(see illustrations)**.

43   Install the primary drive gear and starter clutch as described in Section 13.

15   Clutch master cylinder - removal, overhaul and installation

1   If the master cylinder is leaking fluid, or if the clutch does not function when the lever is applied, and bleeding the system does not help, master cylinder overhaul is recommended. Before disassembling the master cylinder, read through the entire procedure and make sure that you have the correct rebuild kit. Also, you will need some new, clean fluid of the recommended type, some clean shop towels and internal snap-ring pliers. **Note:** *To prevent damage to the paintwork from spilled fluid, always cover the fuel tank when working on the master cylinder.*

2   **Caution:** *Disassembly, overhaul and reassembly of the master cylinder must be done in a spotlessly clean work area to avoid contamination and possible failure of the hydraulic system components.*

14.37 Fit the inner friction plate to the clutch center . . .

14.38 . . . followed by a plain plate

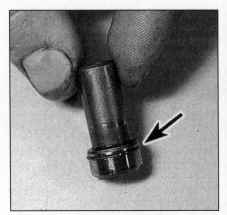

14.40a Fit a new snap-ring (arrow) to the lifter guide groove . . .

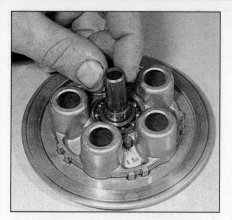

14.40b . . . then fit the guide to the pressure plate bearing

14.42a Install the springs . . .

14.42b . . . and tighten the bolts evenly and progressively in a criss-cross pattern

Removal

Refer to illustration 15.5

3   Loosen, but do not remove, the screws holding the reservoir cover in place.

4   Disconnect the electrical connectors from the clutch switch.

5   Pull back the rubber boot, loosen the banjo fitting bolt and separate the clutch hose from the master cylinder **(see illustration)**. Wrap the end of the hose in a clean rag and suspend the hose in an upright position or bend it down carefully and place the open end in a clean container. The objective is to prevent excessive loss of fluid, fluid spills and system contamination.

6   Remove the locknut from the underside of the clutch lever pivot bolt, then unscrew the bolt and remove the clutch lever.

7   Remove the master cylinder mounting bolts then remove the clamp and lift the master cylinder away from the handlebar. **Caution:** *Do not tip the master cylinder upside down or fluid will run out.*

Overhaul

Refer to illustration 15.8

8   Detach the reservoir cover and remove the plate and rubber

15.5 Peel back the rubber boot then undo the clutch hose banjo fitting bolt

2

15.8 Exploded view of the clutch master cylinder assembly

1	Banjo fitting bolt and hose
2	Sealing washers
3	Reservoir cover
4	Plate
5	Rubber diaphragm
6	Clutch switch
7	Clutch lever pivot bolt
8	Clutch lever
9	Pushrod and dust boot
10	Snap-ring
11	Piston assembly
12	Spring
13	Seals

15.19 Install the mounting clamp so that its UP mark is the correct way around

16.3a Undo the three retaining bolts . . .

16.3b . . . then withdraw the clutch release cylinder and recover its locating dowels (arrows)

diaphragm, then drain the fluid into a suitable container **(see illustration)**. Wipe any remaining fluid out of the reservoir with a clean rag.

9   Undo the screw and remove the clutch switch.

10   Carefully remove the rubber dust boot and pushrod from the end of the piston.

11   Using snap-ring pliers, remove the snap-ring and slide out the piston assembly and the spring. Lay the parts out in the proper order to prevent confusion during reassembly.

12   Clean all of the parts with brake system cleaner (available at auto parts stores), isopropyl alcohol or clean brake fluid. **Caution:** *Do not, under any circumstances, use a petroleum-based solvent to clean hydraulic parts.* If compressed air is available, use it to dry the parts thoroughly (make sure it's filtered and unlubricated).

13   Check the master cylinder bore for corrosion, scratches, nicks and score marks. If damage is evident, the master cylinder must be replaced with a new one. If the master cylinder is in poor condition, then the release cylinder should be checked as well.

14   If the necessary measuring equipment is available, compare the dimensions of the master cylinder bore and piston to those given in the Specifications Section of this Chapter, replacing any component that it is worn beyond the service limit.

15   The dust boot, piston assembly and spring are included in the rebuild kit. Use all of the new parts, regardless of the apparent condition of the old ones.

16   Before reassembling the master cylinder, soak the piston and the rubber cup seals in clean fluid for ten or fifteen minutes. Lubricate the master cylinder bore with clean fluid, then carefully insert the piston and related parts in the reverse order of disassembly. Make sure the lips on the cup seals do not turn inside out when they are slipped into the bore and ensure the spring is fitted the correct way around.

17   Depress the piston, then install the snap-ring (make sure the snap-ring is properly seated in the groove). Install the rubber dust boot (make sure the lip is seated properly in the piston groove) and pushrod.

18   Install the clutch switch and securely tighten its retaining screw.

Installation

Refer to illustration 15.19

19   Attach the master cylinder to the handlebar then fit the clamp, making sure the 'UP' mark is facing up **(see illustration)**. Securely tighten the clamp bolts.

20   Connect the clutch hose to the master cylinder, using new sealing washers. Tighten the banjo fitting bolt to the specified torque setting.

21   Install the lever and pivot bolt. Install the pivot bolt locknut and tighten it to the specified torque setting. Connect the clutch switch wiring.

22   Refer to Section 17 and bleed the air from the system.

16   Clutch release cylinder - removal, overhaul and installation

Removal

Refer to illustrations 16.3a and 16.3b

1   Remove the left lower fairing panel or left middle fairing panel (as applicable) as described in Chapter 8.

2   Remove the clutch hose banjo fitting bolt and separate the hose from the cylinder. Plug the hose end or wrap a plastic bag tightly around it to minimize fluid loss and prevent dirt entering the system. Discard the sealing washers; new ones must be used on installation.

Note: *If you're planning to overhaul the cylinder and don't have a source of compressed air to blow out the piston, just loosen the banjo bolt at this stage and retighten it lightly. The bike's hydraulic system can then be used to force the piston out of the body once the cylinder*

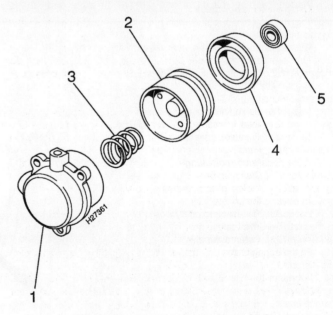

16.5 Clutch release cylinder components

1 Release cylinder	4 Piston fluid seal
2 Piston	5 Pushrod seal
3 Spring	

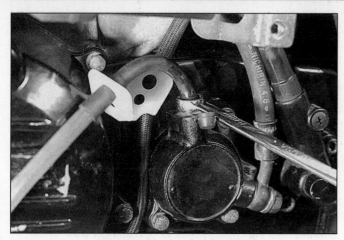

17.6 Bleeding the clutch system

has been unbolted. Disconnect the hose once the piston has been sufficiently displaced.

3   Unscrew the three mounting bolts and remove the cylinder from the sprocket cover. If the cylinder locating dowels are a loose fit, remove them and store them with the cylinder for safe-keeping **(see illustrations)**.

4   Remove the gasket and discard it.

Overhaul

Refer to illustration 16.5

5   Clean the exterior of the cylinder with denatured alcohol or brake system cleaner **(see illustration)**.

6   If the piston wasn't forced out using the bike's hydraulic system, wrap the cylinder in a wad of rag, then use compressed air directed into the fluid inlet to force the piston out of the body. **Warning:** *Use only low pressure to ease the piston out. If the air pressure is too high the piston will be forcibly expelled and serious injury could result.*

7   Recover the spring from the cylinder, noting which way around it is fitted.

8   Using a wooden or plastic tool, remove the pushrod seal and fluid seal from the piston. If a metal tool is being used, take great care not to damage the piston.

9   Clean the piston and bores with denatured alcohol, clean fluid or brake system cleaner. **Caution:** *Do not, under any circumstances, use a petroleum-based solvent to clean hydraulic parts.* If compressed air is available, use it to dry the parts thoroughly (make sure it's filtered and unlubricated).

10   Inspect the cylinder bore and piston for signs of corrosion, nicks and burrs and loss of plating. If surface defects are present, the cylinder assembly must be replaced. If the cylinder is in bad shape the master cylinder should also be checked.

11   If the necessary measuring equipment is available, compare the dimensions of the cylinder bore and piston to those given in the Specifications Section of this Chapter, replacing any component that is worn beyond the service limit.

12   Lubricate the new piston fluid seal with clean fluid. Install the seal in the piston groove making sure it is fitted the correct way around. Fit the new pushrod seal to the piston.

13   Fit the spring to the cylinder making sure its tapered end is facing the piston.

14   Lubricate the piston with clean fluid and install it in the cylinder bore. Make sure the spring remains correctly positioned and take great care to ensure the fluid seal is not damaged as it enters the bore. Using your thumbs, push the piston all the way in, making sure it enters the bore squarely.

Installation

15   Remove all traces of gasket from the cylinder and cover sealing surfaces.

16   Ensure the locating dowels are correctly fitted and fit a new gasket to the sprocket cover.

17   Fit the clutch release cylinder, aligning it with the pushrod and locating dowels. Install the retaining bolts and tighten them securely.

18   Connect the clutch hose to the cylinder, using new sealing washers on each side of the fitting. Tighten the banjo fitting bolt to the specified torque setting.

19   Fill the master cylinder with the recommended clutch fluid (see Chapter 1) and bleed the hydraulic system as described in Section 17.

20   Check for leaks and thoroughly test the operation of the clutch before installing the fairing panel.

17   Clutch system - bleeding

Refer to illustration 17.6

1   Bleeding the clutch is simply the process of removing all the air bubbles from the clutch fluid reservoir, the line and the release cylinder. Bleeding is necessary whenever a clutch system hydraulic connection is loosened, when a component or hose is replaced, or when the master cylinder or release cylinder is overhauled. Leaks in the system may also allow air to enter, but leaking clutch fluid will reveal their presence and warn you of the need for repair.

2   To bleed the clutch, you will need some new, clean fluid of the recommended type (see Chapter 1), a length of clear vinyl or plastic tubing, a small container partially filled with clean fluid, some shop towels and a wrench to fit the release cylinder bleeder valve.

3   Cover the fuel tank and other painted components to prevent damage in the event that fluid is spilled.

4   Remove the left lower fairing panel or left middle fairing panel (as applicable) as described in Chapter 8.

5   Support the motorcycle in an upright position then remove the reservoir cap, plate and rubber diaphragm and slowly pump the clutch lever a few times, until no air bubbles can be seen floating up from the holes at the bottom of the reservoir. Doing this bleeds the air from the master cylinder end of the line.

6   Attach one end of the clear vinyl or plastic tubing to the bleeder valve and submerge the other end in the fluid in the container **(see illustration)**. Check the fluid level in the reservoir. Do not allow the fluid level to drop below the lower mark during the bleeding process.

7   Carefully pump the clutch lever three or four times and hold it in against the handlebar whilst opening the cylinder bleeder valve. When the valve is opened, fluid will flow out of the cylinder into the clear tubing.

8   Retighten the bleeder valve, then release the lever gradually. Repeat the process until no air bubbles are visible in the fluid leaving the cylinder and the clutch action feels smooth and progressive.

9   Replace the rubber diaphragm, plate and reservoir cover and securely tighten its retaining screws. Wipe up any spilled fluid and check the entire system for leaks.

18   Oil pan - removal and installation

Note: *The oil pan can be removed with the engine in the frame. If work is being carried out with the engine removed ignore the preliminary steps.*

Removal

Refer to illustration 18.6

1   On G through K models remove the exhaust system front pipes. On L models onward remove the exhaust system collector box assembly; see Chapter 4 for further information.

2   Drain the engine oil as described in Chapter 1.

3   Working in a criss-cross pattern, gradually loosen the oil pan retaining bolts.

4   Remove all the bolts and lower the oil pan away from the crankcase. If the engine is in the frame, note that as the oil pan is

18.6 Remove the three oil pipes (arrows) from the engine unit

18.9a Fit a new O-ring to each end of the oil pipes and install the right pipe . . .

18.9b . . . center oil pipe . . .

18.9c . . . and small rear oil pipe to the engine unit

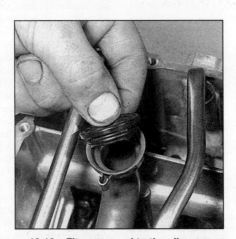

18.10a Fit a new seal to the oil pump pick-up strainer pipe . . .

18.10b . . . then fit the strainer, aligning its fork with the oil pump pipe tang (arrows)

removed, the oil pump pick-up strainer, oil pressure relief valve and oil pipes may fall out of the bottom of the crankcase.

5   Recover the gasket and discard it.

6   If they were not released when the oil pan was removed, remove the oil pump pick-up strainer, the oil pressure relief valve and the three loose oil pipes from the base of the engine. Remove the seal from the pick-up and the O-rings from the pressure relief valve and each end of the oil pipes **(see illustration)**. Discard all seals and O-rings.

7   Clean the pick-up strainer mesh in solvent. Check it for clogging or splitting and replace if necessary.

Installation

Refer to illustrations 18.9a, 18.9b, 18.9c, 18.10a, 18.10b, 18.11, 18.12a and 18.12b

8   Remove all traces of gasket from the oil pan and crankcase mating surfaces.

9   Fit a new O-ring to each end of the oil pipes and install them in their original locations in the crankcase **(see illustrations)**.

10   Fit a new seal to the oil pump pick-up strainer making sure its flange is facing the strainer. Fit the strainer to the oil pump pipe, engaging its fork with the tang on the pipe **(see illustrations)**.

11   Fit a new O-ring to the oil pressure relief valve groove. Apply a smear of oil to the O-ring and ease the relief valve into position in the base of the crankcase **(see illustration)**.

12   Position a new gasket on the oil pan and fit the pan to the engine **(see illustrations)**. If the engine is in the frame, use a smear of grease on the gasket to hold it in place as the oil pan is installed.

13   Make sure the gasket is correctly positioned then insert the retaining bolts and tighten them by hand.

14   Working in a criss-cross pattern, tighten all the oil pan retaining bolts to the specified torque setting.

15   Install the front pipes/collector box (as applicable) as described in Chapter 4.

16   Fill the engine with the correct type and quantity of oil as described in Chapter 1. Start the engine and check for leaks.

17   If all is well, fit the fairing panels as described in Chapter 8.

19 Oil pump - pressure check, removal, inspection and installation

Pressure check

1   To check the oil pressure, a suitable gauge and adapter piece (which screws into the oil pressure switch threads) will be needed.

2   Warm the engine up to normal operating temperature then stop it.

3   Remove the oil pressure switch as described in Chapter 9.

4   Screw the adapter into the oil pressure switch threads in the top of the crankcase and connect the gauge to the adapter.

5   Start the engine and increase its speed to 5000 rpm whilst watching the gauge reading. The oil pressure should be similar to that given in the Specifications at the start of this Chapter.

6   If the pressure is significantly lower than specified, either the relief valve is stuck open, the oil pump is faulty, the oil pump pick-up strainer

18.11 Fit a new O-ring (arrow) to the pressure relief valve and install it in the crankcase

18.12a Fit a new gasket . . .

18.12b . . . then install the oil pan

19.15 Undo the two bolts and remove the main oil pipe from the base of the crankcase

19.17 Undo the three bolts and remove the oil pump assembly

2

is blocked or there is other engine damage. Begin diagnosis by checking the oil pump pick-up strainer and relief valve (see Sections 18 and 20), then the oil pump. If those items check out okay, chances are the bearing oil clearances are excessive and the engine needs to be overhauled.

7   If the pressure is too high, the relief valve is stuck closed. To check it, see Section 20.

8   Stop the engine and unscrew the gauge and adapter from the crankcase.

9   Install the oil pressure switch as described in Chapter 9.

Removal

Note: *The oil pump can be removed with the engine in the frame.*
Refer to illustrations 19.15 and 19.17

10   Remove the oil pan and associated components as described in Section 18.

11   Working in a criss-cross pattern, evenly slacken the right crankcase cover retaining bolts, noting the correct fitted positions of all wiring retaining clamps.

12   Lift the cover away from the engine, being prepared to catch any residual oil which may be released as the cover is removed.

13   Remove the gasket and discard it. Note the two locating dowels fitted to the crankcase and store these with the cover for safe-keeping

if they are loose.

14   Slacken and remove the oil pump driven sprocket retaining bolt whilst preventing the sprocket turning by inserting a screwdriver through one of the sprocket holes **(see illustration 14.30)**. Access to the bolt is awkward with the clutch in position; if it proves impossible to remove the bolt, the clutch will have to be removed (see Section 14).

15   Undo the two mounting bolts and remove the remaining oil pipe from the base of the crankcase. Recover the seals from each end of the pipe and discard them **(see illustration)**.

16   Rotate the oil pump shaft and position it so its drive slot, which engages with the water pump, is positioned vertically; this will allow the two to disengage as the pump is removed.

17   Undo the three bolts and remove the oil pump from the crankcase. Recover the locating dowels and store them with the pump for safe-keeping **(see illustration)**.

Inspection

Refer to illustrations 19.18, 19.19, 19.21, 19.22, 19.23a, 19.23b, 19.24, 19.26, 19.28, 19.29, 19.30, 19.33, 19.34, 19.35, 19.38, 19.41a and 19.41b

Note: *The pump has two sets of rotors. The thinner set circulates oil around the oil cooler and the thicker set functions as the main oil pump supply to the engine.*

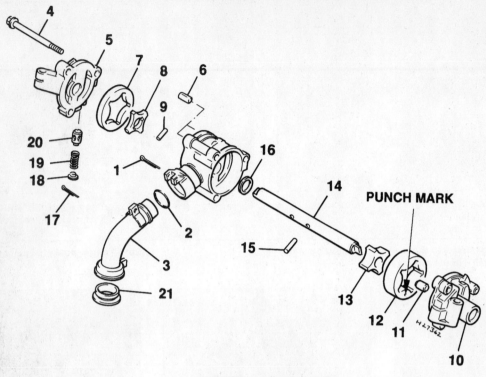

19.18 Oil pump components

1	Cotter (split) pin	8	Oil cooler pump inner rotor	15	Drive pin
2	O-ring	9	Drive pin	16	Thrust washer
3	Metal pipe	10	Main pump cover	17	Cotter (split) pin
4	Cover bolts	11	Locating dowels	18	Spring seat
5	Oil cooler pump cover	12	Main pump outer rotor	19	Spring
6	Locating dowels	13	Main pump inner rotor	20	Oil cooler relief valve piston
7	Oil cooler pump outer rotor	14	Driveshaft	21	Strainer seal

18   Wash the oil pump in solvent, then dry it off **(see illustration)**.
19   Remove the cotter (split) pin, then remove the metal pipe and O-ring from the pump **(see illustration)**.
20   Remove the cotter (split) pin and withdraw the spring seat, spring and oil cooler relief valve piston from the oil cooler pump cover, noting each component's correct fitted direction.
21   Remove the three pump cover bolts **(see illustration)**.
22   Lift off the oil cooler pump cover and recover the locating dowels **(see illustration)**.
23   Remove the oil cooler pump inner and outer rotors from the pump

body. Slide the drive pin out from the pump driveshaft **(see illustrations)**.
24   Remove the main pump cover from the opposite end of the pump and recover the locating dowels **(see illustration)**.
25   Remove the main pump inner and outer rotors.
26   Slide out the driveshaft, noting which way around it is fitted, and remove the drive pin and thrust washer **(see illustration)**.
27   Check the pump body and rotors for scoring and wear. If any damage or uneven or excessive wear is evident, replace the pump (individual parts aren't available). If you are rebuilding the engine, it's a

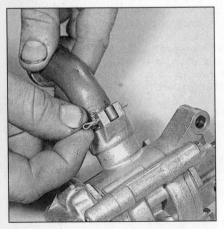

19.19 Remove the cotter (split) pin and remove the metal pipe from the oil pump

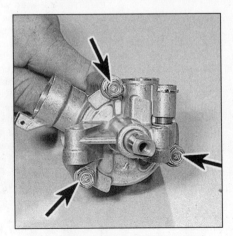

19.21 Undo the three bolts (arrows) . . .

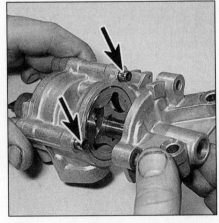

19.22 . . . then lift off the oil cooler pump cover and recover the dowels (arrows)

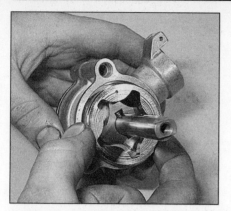

19.23a Remove the oil cooler pump outer rotor (note punch mark) and inner rotor . . .

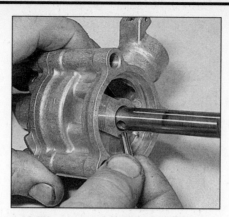

19.23b . . . then withdraw the drive pin

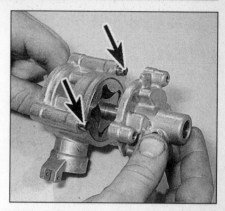

19.24 Remove the main pump cover and recover the dowels (arrows)

19.26 Slide out the driveshaft and remove the drive pin and thrust washer

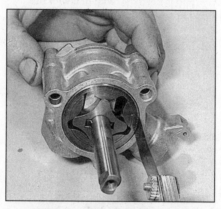

19.28 Checking outer rotor-to-body clearance

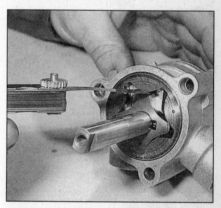

19.29 Checking inner rotor tip-to-outer rotor clearance

19.30 Checking rotor endfloat

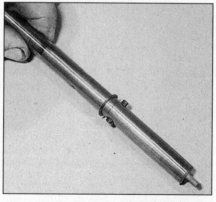

19.33 Fit the drive pin and thrust washer to the driveshaft

19.34 Fit the main pump inner rotor, making sure it is correctly engaged with the drive pin . . .

good idea to install a new oil pump.

28 Install the rotors in the pump body and measure the clearance between the outer rotor and body with a feeler gauge **(see illustration)**. Compare it to the value listed in this Chapter's Specifications. If it's excessive, replace the pump.

29 Measure the clearance between the inner rotor tip and the outer rotor **(see illustration)**. Again, replace the pump if the clearance is excessive.

30 Lay a straightedge across the rotors and pump body and measure the rotor endfloat (gap between the rotors and pump body) with a feeler gauge **(see illustration)**. If it's outside the limits listed in this Chapter's Specifications, replace the pump.

31 If the clutch has been removed, inspect the pump drive chain and

sprockets for wear and damage and replace if necessary. If replacement is necessary note that both sprockets and the chain should be replaced as a set.

32 If the pump is good make sure all components are clean and lubricate them with clean engine oil. Reassemble the pump as follows.

33 Fit the main pump drive pin to the driveshaft and slide on the thrust washer. Insert the driveshaft into the pump body, making sure it is fitted the correct way around so that the thrust washer is positioned between the main pump drive pin and the pump body **(see illustration)**.

34 Install the main pump inner rotor, making sure its punch mark is facing away from the pump body, and engage its slot with the drive pin **(see illustration)**.

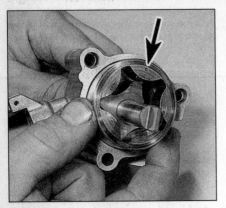

19.35 ... then install the outer rotor, making sure its punch mark (arrow) is facing out

19.38 Make sure the oil cooler inner rotor is fitted with its punch mark facing out and is correctly engaged with the drive pin

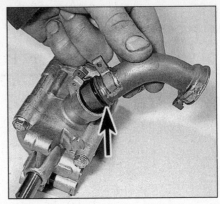

19.41a Fit a new O-ring (arrow) ...

19.41b ... then fit the metal pipe to the oil pump and secure it in position with a new cotter (split) pin

19.43 Fit the pump locating dowels (arrows) to the crankcase

19.46 Locate the oil pump on its dowels then fit the mounting bolts and tighten them to the specified torque setting

35   Install the main pump outer rotor making sure its punch mark is facing away from the pump body **(see illustration)**.

36   Install the locating dowels and fit the main pump cover.

37   Working at the opposite end of the pump, insert the oil cooler pump drive pin in the driveshaft.

38   Install the oil cooler pump components as described in Steps 34 through 36 **(see illustration)**.

39   Fit the pump cover bolts and tighten them to the specified torque.

40   Insert the relief valve piston, spring and spring seat making sure the piston and spring seat are fitted the correct way around. Secure the components in position with a new cotter (split) pin.

41   Fit a new O-ring to the metal pipe and fit the pipe to the pump, positioning its tang between the pump lugs. Secure the pipe in position with a new cotter (split pin) **(see illustrations)**.

Installation

Refer to illustrations 19.43 and 19.46

42   Lubricate the pump rotors with clean engine oil and check that the pump driveshaft rotates freely.

43   Install the pump locating dowels in the crankcase **(see illustration)**.

44   Position the water pump and oil pump driveshaft slots vertically so that they will mesh correctly as the pump is installed.

45   Maneuver the pump into position, engaging it with the water pump shaft, and locate it on the dowels.

46   Fit the pump mounting bolts and tighten them to the specified torque setting **(see illustration)**.

47   Engage the sprocket with the pump driveshaft. Clean the sprocket bolt and apply a drop of thread locking compound to it. Install

the bolt and tighten it to the specified torque. Where the clutch assembly has been removed, install it as described in Section 14.

48   Fit a new seal to each end of the main oil pipe. Fit the pipe to the engine unit and securely tighten its retaining bolts.

49   Remove all traces of old gasket from the crankcase and cover mating surfaces.

50   Install the locating dowels and fit a new gasket to the crankcase.

51   Fit the cover and install the bolts, making sure all the wiring clamps are correctly positioned. Tighten the cover bolts evenly and progressively to the specified torque setting.

52   Install the oil pan and associated components as described in Section 18.

20 Oil pressure relief valve - removal, inspection and installation

Note: *The pressure relief valve can be removed with the engine in the frame.*

Removal

1   Remove the oil pan and pressure relief valve as described in Section 18.

Inspection

2   Push the plunger into the relief valve body and check for free movement. If the valve operation is sticky it must be replaced (individual parts are not available).

21.3 Oil cooler mounting bolt (1) and hose unions (2)

21.7 Disconnect the oil cooler hose from the front of the
crankcase and recover the O-ring (arrow)

Installation

3   Install the pressure relief valve and oil pan as described in Section 18.

21 Oil cooler and hoses - removal and installation

Note: *The oil cooler can be removed with the engine in the frame.*

Removal

Oil cooler

Refer to illustration 21.3

1   Remove the lower fairing panel(s) as described in Chapter 8. On some models it will also be necessary to remove the upper fairing to gain access to the oil cooler.
2   Drain the engine oil as described in Chapter 1.
3   Undo the two bolts securing each hose union to the oil cooler. Free each hose from the cooler and recover the O-rings **(see illustration)**.
4   Slacken and remove the mounting bolt(s) and remove the oil cooler from the bike. Recover the spacers from the cooler mounting dampers.
5   Check the oil cooler rubber mounts for signs of damage or deterioration and replace if necessary.

Oil cooler hoses

Refer to illustration 21.7

6   Disconnect the upper hose union from the oil cooler as described in Steps 1 through 3.
7   Undo the bolts securing the hose to the front of the crankcase and recover the O-ring from the lower hose union **(see illustration)**.
8   Free the hose from its retaining clips, noting how it is routed, and remove it from the bike.

Installation

9   Installation is the reverse of the removal procedure using new O-rings. Fill the engine with the correct type and amount of oil (see Chapter 1).

22 Gearshift mechanism - removal, inspection and installation

Note: *The gearshift mechanism components can be removed with the engine in the frame. If work is being carried out with the engine removed ignore the preliminary steps.*

22.9 Gearshift mechanism cover bolts (arrows)

Removal

G and H models

Refer to illustrations 22.9, 22.10a, 22.10b, 22.11 and 22.12

1   Remove the left lower fairing panel as described in Chapter 8.
2   Place the bike on its centerstand (where fitted). Where no stand is fitted, support the bike safely in an upright position so there is no danger of the machine falling over.
3   Undo the lower engine mounting bolt locknut and the sidestand bracket retaining bolt and remove the sidestand assembly.
4   Drain the engine oil as described in Chapter 1.
5   Undo the three bolts securing the clutch release cylinder to the sprocket cover. Withdraw the cylinder and recover its gasket and locating dowels from the sprocket cover. Position the cylinder clear of the engine unit. **Note:** *Do not operate the clutch lever whilst the release cylinder is disconnected from the engine. Wrap a stout elastic band around the cylinder to prevent the piston being accidentally expelled.*
6   Unscrew the remaining screws securing the sprocket cover to the engine unit. Remove the sprocket cover and gasket and recover the two cover locating dowels.
7   Remove the water pump as described in Chapter 3.
8   Ensure the transmission is positioned in neutral, then undo the clamp bolt and disconnect the gearshift lever pedal from the engine.
9   Undo the retaining bolts and slide the gearshift mechanism cover off the gearshift shaft. Remove the cover locating dowels and gasket **(see illustration)**.
10   Remove the return spring from the gearshift lever shaft assembly **(see illustrations)**.

2

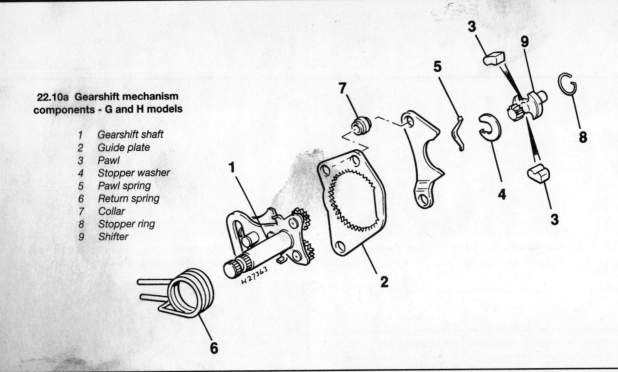

22.10a Gearshift mechanism components - G and H models

1   Gearshift shaft
2   Guide plate
3   Pawl
4   Stopper washer
5   Pawl spring
6   Return spring
7   Collar
8   Stopper ring
9   Shifter

11   Undo the guide plate nut and bolts and withdraw the guide plate and gearshift shaft assembly **(see illustration)**. Recover the plate spacers and locating dowels and separate the guide plate assembly from the shaft.

12   Remove the shifter assembly from the center of the shift drum, taking care to ensure none of the assembly components spring out as it is removed. If necessary, fit a cable tie around the circumference of the shifter assembly to hold all components in position **(see illustration)**.

13   Slacken and remove the nut and washer then slide off the stopper arm and spring, followed by the neutral arm and spring. **Note:** *The neutral arm and stopper arm are different.*

14   If necessary, the shifter assembly can be disassembled. Noting each component's correct fitted position, remove the spring clip and stopper washer, then recover the spring and ratchet pawls from the shifter.

22.10b Removing the gearshift shaft return spring

22.11 Guide plate retaining nut and bolts (arrows)

22.12 Shifter assembly can be held together by fitting a cable tie around its circumference as shown

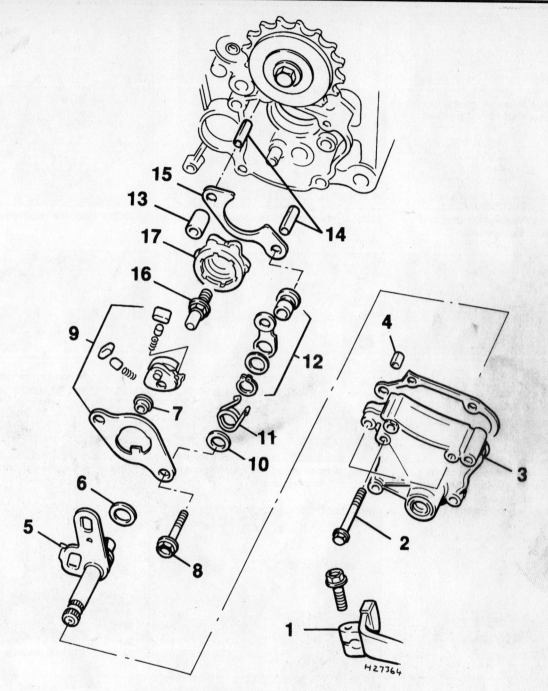

22.18 Gearshift mechanism components - L onwards models

1	Gearshift lever pedal	7	Collar	13	Spacer
2	Cover bolts	8	Shifter retaining plate bolts	14	Dowels
3	Cover	9	Shifter assembly components	15	Shift drum retaining plate
4	Dowels	10	Washer	16	Shift drum cam bolt
5	Gearshift lever	11	Stopper arm spring	17	Shift drum cam
6	Washer	12	Stopper arm components		

J models onward

Refer to illustrations 22.18, 22.19, 22.20, 22.21a, 22.21b, 22.22a, 22.22b, 22.23 and 22.25

15   Remove the lower fairing as described in Chapter 8.

16   On J and K models, undo the lower engine mounting bolt locknut and the sidestand bracket retaining bolt, then position the sidestand assembly clear of the cover.

17   On L models onward, undo the two retaining screws and release the speedometer drive from the sprocket cover. Recover the gasket.

18   On all models carry out the operations described above in Steps 4 through 9 **(see illustration)**.

19   Remove the gearshift shaft assembly and recover the washer

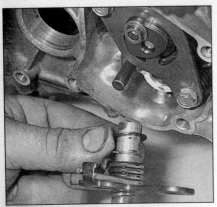

22.19 Remove the gearshift shaft and recover the washer . . .

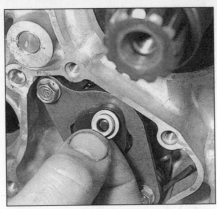

22.20 . . . then remove the collar from the shifter pin

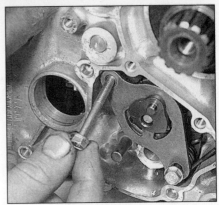

22.21a Undo the retaining bolts . . .

22.21b . . . then remove the shifter assembly from the center of the shift drum cam

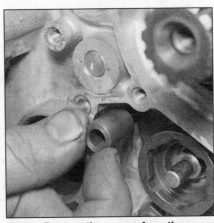

22.22a Remove the spacer from the upper locating dowel . . .

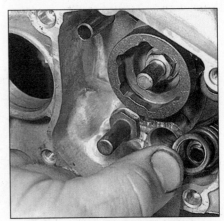

22.22b . . . and the washer from the lower dowel

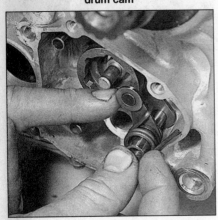

22.23 Removing the stopper arm and spring assembly

22.25 Remove the locating pin from the shift drum and store it with the cam for safe-keeping

22.29 On G and H models inspect the shift mechanism gear teeth for signs of damage; if worn all components must be replaced as a set

from the inner end of its shaft (see illustration).

20   Remove the collar from the shifter assembly pin (see illustration).

21   Undo the two bolts and remove the retaining plate and shifter assembly from the shift drum. Take care not to allow the shifter assembly to spring apart as it is removed (see illustrations).

22   Remove the spacer from the upper plate locating dowel and remove the washer from the lower locating dowel (see illustrations).

23   Unhook the stopper arm from the shift drum cam and slide off the arm and spring (see illustration).

24   Pull out the locating dowels and remove the shift drum retaining plate.

25   Unscrew the shift drum cam bolt and remove the cam. Remove the locating pin from the shift drum and store it with the cam for safe-keeping (see illustration).

26   If necessary, disassemble the shifter assembly and plate as follows, noting each component's correct fitted positions. Press the pawls into the shifter and separate the assembly from the plate. Gently release the pawls and remove the pawls, plungers and springs from the shifter.

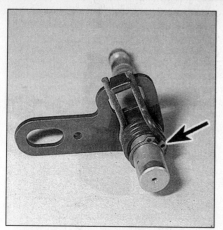

22.34 On J models onward, ensure the return spring is correctly fitted before securing it in position with the snap-ring (arrow)

22.35 Stopper arm assembly

22.38a On G and H models make sure the shifter assembly components are correctly fitted . . .

22.38b . . . so that the assembly looks like this

Inspection

G and H models

Refer to illustration 22.29

27 Inspect the gearshift shaft return spring post. If it's worn or damaged, replace it. If it's loose, unscrew it, apply a few drops of thread locking compound to the threads, reinstall the post and tighten it securely.

28 Check the gearshift shaft for straightness and damage to its splines. If the shaft is bent, you can attempt to straighten it, but if the splines are damaged it will have to be replaced.

29 Inspect the gearshift shaft, guide plate and shifter gears for signs of wear or damage to the teeth. If damaged, all components should be replaced as a matched set **(see illustration)**.

30 Check the condition of the neutral and stopper arms and springs. Replace the arm(s) if they are worn and the spring(s) if they are distorted.

31 Inspect the gearshift shaft return spring for wear or damage and replace it if necessary.

32 Check the shifter assembly components for wear or damage and replace them as necessary.

33 Check the condition of the seal in the cover and the cover needle roller bearing. If the bearing is worn or damaged the cover must be replaced; it is not possible to replace the bearing separately. If the seal has been leaking, pry it out. It's a good idea to replace it in any case,

since gaining access to it requires a fair amount of work. Install a new seal with its sealing lip facing ins. It should be possible to install the seal with thumb pressure, but if necessary, drive it in with a socket the same diameter as the seal's outer edge.

J models onward

Refer to illustrations 22.34 and 22.35

34 Inspect the gearshift shaft return spring and splines for damage. The return spring can be replaced individually, but if the splines are damaged the complete shaft must be replaced. To replace the return spring, remove the snap-ring and slide off the spring. Fit the new spring, making sure it is the correct way around and thus correctly engaged with the shaft, and secure it in position with the snap-ring **(see illustration)**. **Note:** *The snap-ring should be fitted with its chamfered edge facing the return spring and must be correctly located in the shaft groove.*

35 Check the condition of the stopper arm and spring. Replace the stopper arm if it's worn where it contacts the shift cam. Replace the spring if it's distorted. To replace the stopper arm, remove the snap-ring and slide the washer and arm off the spacer. Fit the new arm, making sure it is the correct way around, then slide on the washer and secure it with the snap-ring; note that the snap-ring should be fitted with its chamfered edge facing the washer and be correctly located in the spacer groove **(see illustration)**.

36 Inspect the shifter pawls and the shift cam for signs of wear on their contact surfaces. If they're worn or damaged, replace the cam and both pawls. Replace the pawl springs if there is any doubt to their condition.

37 Check the cover components as described in Step 33.

Installation

G and H models

Refer to illustrations 22.38a, 22.38b, 22.41, 22.42, 22.43a, 22.43b, 22.43c, 22.44a, 22.44b, 22.44c, 22.45, 22.47, 22.48, 22.50, 22.51, 22.52 and 22.54

38 Where necessary, fit the pawls and spring to the shifter, making sure they are fitted the correct way around. Install the stopper washer and position the washer tabs against the pawls. Check that each pawl moves freely and is forced out by spring pressure, then fit the spring clip **(see illustrations)**.

39 Engage the spring correctly with the neutral arm. Slide the arm and spring assembly into position and engage it with the shift drum cam. **Note:** *The neutral arm can be distinguished from the stopper arm by the size of its circular contact pad; the neutral arm pad is much larger.*

2

22.41 Ensure the neutral and stopper arms are correctly fitted before proceeding

22.42 Position the shifter assembly as described in text and lock it in position by inserting a suitable diameter rod as shown

22.43a Fit the locating dowels (arrows) . . .

22.43b . . . then fit the long spacer over the stud . . .

22.43c . . . and fit the shorter spacer on the upper dowel

22.44a Ensure the guide plate assembly is correctly assembled . . .

22.44b . . . then engage it with the gearshift shaft . . .

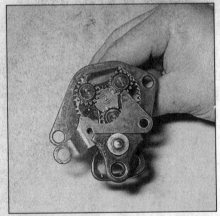

22.44c . . . so that the two are correctly joined as shown

22.45 Maneuver the shaft and guide plate assembly into position and locate it on the dowels

40   Repeat the operation and install the stopper arm and spring.

41   Ensure both the neutral and stopper arms are correctly engaged with the shift drum, then fit the washer and securely tighten the retaining nut **(see illustration)**.

42   Depress the pawls and install the shifter assembly on the shift drum, aligning the dot on the shifter with the dot on the drum. Lock the shifter assembly in position by inserting a 3 mm (0.12 in) rod into the groove between the two dots **(see illustration)**.

43   Install the guide plate locating dowels and slide on the spacers, positioning the long spacer on the plate stud and the shorter one on the upper locating dowel **(see illustrations)**.

44   Fit the guide plate assembly to the rear of the gearshift shaft assembly, engaging it with its gears **(see illustrations)**.

45   Install the shaft and guide plate assembly, aligning it with the return spring post and the locking rod. Make sure the assembly is correctly engaged with the shifter gear and locate the guide plate on its locating dowels **(see illustration)**.

46   Clean the guide plate retaining nut and apply a smear of locking

22.47 Fit the guide plate nut and bolts and tighten them securely

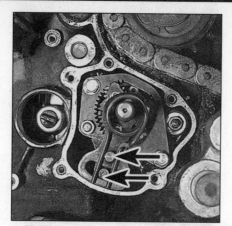

22.48 Install the return spring making sure it is correctly engaged with both the shaft and return spring post (arrows)

22.50 Ensure the dowels (arrows) are in position then fit a new gasket to the crankcase

compound to its threads.

47   Install the guide plate retaining nut and bolts and tighten them securely **(see illustration)**.

48   Withdraw the locking pin from between the shifter and shift drum and install the return spring. Make sure the return spring is correctly engaged with the shaft and return spring post **(see illustration)**.

49   Temporarily fit the gearshift lever pedal to the shaft and check the operation of the shift mechanism components.

50   If all is well, ensure the crankcase and cover surfaces are clean and dry, then fit the cover locating dowels to the crankcase. Fit a new gasket over the dowels **(see illustration)**.

51   Apply a smear of grease to the lip of the gearshift shaft oil seal and wrap the splines of the gearshift shaft with electrical tape, so the splines don't damage the seal as the cover is installed **(see illustration)**.

52   Slide the cover along the gearshift shaft and onto the crankcase. Locate the cover on the dowels and remove the tape from the shaft splines **(see illustration)**.

53   Fit the cover bolts and tighten them securely.

54   Align the punch marks on the gearshift lever pedal and shaft and locate the gearshift pedal on the shaft splines. Fit the clamp bolt and tighten it to the specified torque setting **(see illustration)**.

55   Install the water pump as described in Chapter 3.

56   Fit the sprocket cover locating dowels to the crankcase and fit a new gasket over the dowels.

22.51 Wrap tape around the shaft splines to protect the cover seal . . .

2

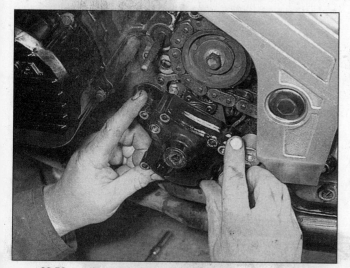

22.52 . . . then slide the mechanism cover into position

22.54 Slide the gearshift lever pedal on the shaft, aligning its marking with the shaft punch mark (arrow)

22.62a **Shifter assembly components - J models onward**

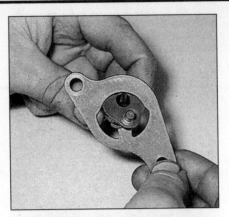

22.62b **Depress the pawls then engage the shifter assembly with the retaining plate . . .**

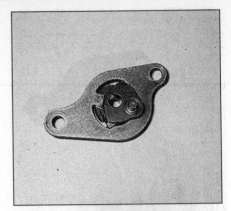

22.62c **. . . and position it as shown**

22.64a **Fit the shift drum retaining plate . .**

22.64b **. . . and slide the locating dowels into position**

22.65 **Fit the shift drum cam aligning its cutout with the locating pin (arrows)**

57 Fit the clutch release cylinder dowels to the sprocket cover and fit a new gasket.

58 Locate the clutch release cylinder on its dowels, ensuring it is correctly engaged with the pushrod. Fit the cylinder and sprocket cover bolts and tighten them securely.

59 Fit the sidestand and tighten its mounting bolt and the lower engine mounting bolt locknut to the specified torque setting.

60 Fill the engine with the correct type and quantity of oil as described in Chapter 1. Start the engine and check for leaks.

61 If all is well, fit the fairing panel as described in Chapter 8.

J models onward

Refer to illustrations 22.62a, 22.62b, 22.62c, 22.64a, 22.64b, 22.65, 22.66a, 22.66b, 22.68, 22.70 and 22.72

62 If disassembled, fit the springs to the shifter then install the plungers. Install the pawls, making sure they are the correct way around (with their rounded ends facing the shifter and the plungers correctly aligned with the pawl cutouts). Depress the pawls and engage the shifter assembly with the retaining plate **(see illustrations)**.

63 Fit the locating pin into the shift drum.

64 Fit the shift drum retaining plate and install its locating dowels **(see illustrations)**.

65 Fit the shift cam to the drum, aligning its cutout with the locating pin **(see illustration)**.

66 Clean the shift cam bolt and apply a drop of locking compound to its threads. Install the bolt and tighten it to the specified torque setting **(see illustrations)**.

67 Engage the spring with the stopper arm assembly.

68 Slide the stopper arm and spring assembly onto the lower locating dowel and engage the arm with the shift drum cam **(see illustration)**.

69 Fit the washer to the lower locating dowel and slide the spacer onto the upper dowel.

70 Install the shifter and retaining plate assembly into the center of the shift drum cam. Locate the plate on the dowels and install the retaining bolts, tightening them securely **(see illustration)**.

71 Fit the collar to the shifter assembly pin.

72 Fit the washer to the rear of the gearshift shaft and slide the shaft into the crankcase. As the shaft is installed, make sure the return spring engages correctly with the post and the shaft slot engages correctly with the shifter pin collar **(see illustration)**.

73 Install all the remaining components as described in Steps 49 through 61. On L models onward, ignore Step 59, but fit the speedometer drive to the sprocket cover, ensuring it is correctly aligned with the sprocket bolt head.

23 Alternator rotor - removal and installation

Note: *To remove the alternator rotor the special Honda rotor puller (Part No. 07733-0020001) or a pattern equivalent will be required. Do not attempt to remove the rotor using any other method. The alternator rotor can be removed with the engine in the frame. If work is being carried out with the engine removed, ignore the preliminary steps.*

Removal

G and H models

1 Remove the left lower fairing panel as described in Chapter 8.

2 Drain the engine oil as described in Chapter 1.

3 Unscrew the cover retaining bolts and withdraw the cover squarely from the engine unit. Recover the gasket.

4 Slacken and remove the rotor retaining bolt and washer whilst

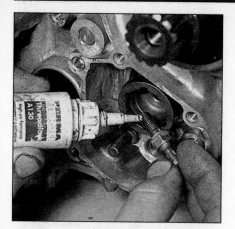

22.66a Apply locking compound to the retaining bolt . . .

22.66b . . . and tighten it to the specified torque setting

22.68 Fit the stopper arm and spring assembly positioning them as shown

22.70 Fit the shifter and retaining plate assembly and securely tighten the retaining bolts

22.72 Install the gearshift shaft making sure it is correctly engaged with the shifter pin collar and return spring post (arrows)

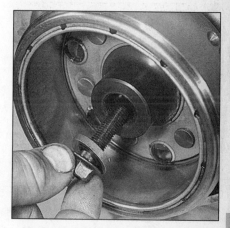

23.12a Unscrew the retaining bolt and washer . . .

holding the rotor to prevent it turning. The rotor can be retained using a large strap wrench or by fitting a suitable socket and bar to the starter clutch bolt (accessed through the center cap on the right crankcase cover). Alternatively, if the engine is still in the frame, the engine can be locked through the transmission by selecting top gear and applying the rear brake hard.

5   Screw the rotor puller tool into the center of the rotor and tighten it securely. Tap sharply on the end of puller tool to release the rotor's grip on the tapered crankshaft end. Remove the rotor.

6   Recover the Woodruff key from the crankshaft slot and store it safely inside the rotor.

J models onward

Refer to illustrations 23.12a and 23.12b

7   Remove the lower fairing as described in Chapter 8.

8   Drain the engine oil as described in Chapter 1.

9   Trace the wiring back from the left crankcase cover to its wiring connector. Disconnect the alternator wiring connector and work back along the wiring, noting its routing whilst releasing it from any relevant ties or clips.

10   Unscrew the cover retaining bolts and withdraw the cover squarely from the engine unit. **Note:** *Due to the magnetic pull of the rotor, the cover may prove difficult to remove. Do not pry the cover away with a screwdriver as the mating surfaces will be damaged.*

11   Remove the cover locating dowels from the crankcase and discard the gasket.

12   Remove the rotor as described in Steps 4 through 6 **(see illustrations)**.

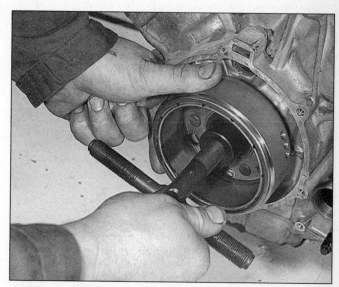

23.12b . . . then release the alternator rotor from the shaft using the special Honda tool (L model shown)

23.21 On fitting tighten the rotor retaining bolt to the specified torque

23.22 Make sure the dowels (arrows) are in position and fit a new gasket to the crankcase

Installation

G and H models

13 Degrease the rotor and crankshaft tapers and remove any metal particles or swarf from the rotor magnet. Remove all traces of gasket from the cover and crankcase mating surfaces.

14 Install the Woodruff key in the crankshaft slot.

15 Align the slot in the rotor taper with the Woodruff key and gently push the rotor on the crankshaft. Gently tap the rotor center with a soft-faced hammer to seat it on the crankshaft taper.

16 Fit the rotor bolt and washer and tighten it to the specified torque whilst holding the rotor using the method employed on removal.

17 Fit a new gasket to the crankcase and install the cover.

18 Install the cover bolts and tighten them to the specified torque.

19 Fill the engine with the correct type and amount of oil as described in Chapter 1.

20 Fit the fairing panel as described in Chapter 8.

J models onward

Refer to illustrations 23.21 and 23.22

21 Install the rotor as described in Steps 13 through 16 **(see illustration)**.

22 Install the locating dowels in the crankcase and fit a new gasket **(see illustration)**.

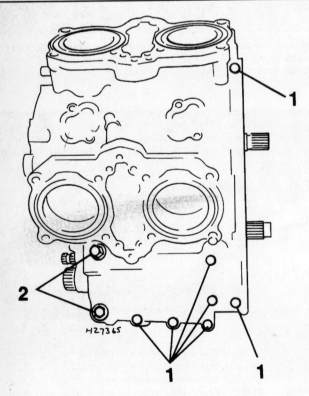

24.5 Upper crankcase bolt locations

1   6 mm bolts
2   10 mm bolts (with sealing washers)

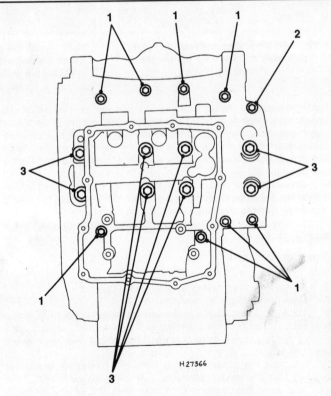

24.6 Lower crankcase bolt locations

1   6 mm bolts   *3   9 mm bolts*
2   8 mm bolt

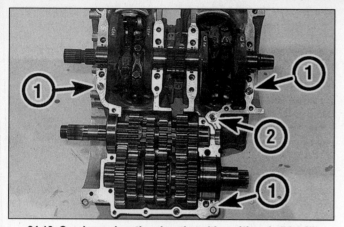

24.10 Crankcase locating dowel positions (1) and oil jet (2)

23   Fit the cover and locate it on the dowels. Fit the cover retaining bolts and tighten them to the specified torque.
24   Make sure the wiring is correctly routed and reconnect the wiring connector. Secure the wiring in position with all the necessary clips and ties.
25   Fill the engine with the correct type and amount of oil as described in Chapter 1.
26   Fit the fairing panel as described in Chapter 8.

24 Crankcase - separation and reassembly

Separation

Refer to illustrations 24.5, 24.6 and 24.10
1   To examine and repair or replace the crankshaft, pistons and connecting rods, bearings and transmission components, the crankcase must be split into two parts.
2   To enable the crankcases to be split the engine must be removed from the frame (see Section 5) and the following components first removed with reference to the relevant Sections.

   a) *Camshafts and followers*
   b) *Camshaft drive gears*
   c) *Cylinder heads*
   d) *Clutch*
   e) *Oil pan*
   f) *Oil pump*
   g) *Gearshift mechanism components*
   h) *Alternator rotor*
   i) *Alternator stator plate - G and H models (Chapter 9).*
   j) *Starter motor (Chapter 9)*

Note: *If the crankcase halves are being separated just to examine the transmission shafts, crankshaft or connecting rod/pistons then there is no need to remove the gearshift mechanism components.*
3   With all the relevant components removed proceed as follows.
4   Undo the three retaining bolts and remove the mainshaft bearing retaining plate from the right side of the crankcase.
5   With the crankcase the right way up, slacken and remove the two 10 mm bolts and the seven 6 mm bolts from the top of the upper crankcase half **(see illustration). Note:** *As each bolt is removed, store it in its relative position in a cardboard template of the crankcase halves. This will ensure that each bolt is returned to its original location on reassembly.* Discard the sealing washers fitted to the two 10 mm bolts; new ones must be used on reassembly.
6   Turn the crankcase upside down, and unscrew the eight 6 mm lower crankcase bolts **(see illustration).**
7   Unscrew the single 8 mm bolt from the front of the crankcase.
8   Working in a criss-cross pattern, starting from the outside and working in, gradually slacken the eight 9 mm lower crankcase bolts. Once all the bolts are loose, unscrew and remove them (see note in

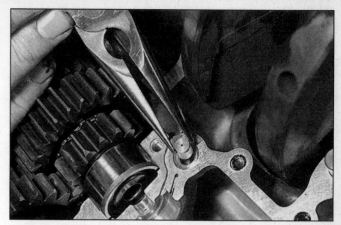

24.16a Fit the oil jet to the upper crankcase making sure its smaller diameter orifice is facing the lower crankcase . . .

24.16b . . . and fit a new O-ring

Step 5).
9   Carefully lift the lower crankcase half off, leaving the crankshaft and transmission shafts in the upper half of the crankcase. As the lower half is lifted away take care not to dislodge or lose any main bearing inserts. **Note:** *If it won't come away easily, make sure all fasteners have been removed. Don't pry against the crankcase mating surfaces or they will leak; initial separation can be achieved by tapping gently with a soft-faced mallet.*
10   Remove the three locating dowels from the upper crankcase half **(see illustration).**
11   Remove the oil jet and its O-ring from the upper crankcase half, noting which way around the jet is fitted **(see illustration 24.10).**

Reassembly

Refer to illustrations 24.16a, 24.16b, 24.17, 24.20a, 24.20b, 24.22, 24.23, 24.24, 24.25, 24.27a, 24.27b, 24.29a and 24.29b
12   Check that the transmission shafts and crankshaft are correctly installed in the upper crankcase half as described in Sections 30 and 31.
13   Remove all traces of sealant from the crankcase mating surfaces, being careful not to let any fall into the case as this is done.
14   Check that all components are installed and that they can rotate smoothly and easily.
15   Lubricate the transmission shafts and crankshaft with clean engine oil then use a rag soaked in high flash-point solvent to wipe over the gasket surfaces of both halves to remove all traces of oil.
16   Make sure the oil jet hole is clear. Fit the jet to the upper crankcase half so that its smaller diameter orifice is facing the lower

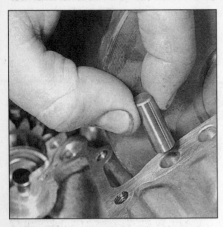

24.17 Fit the locating dowels to their original locations in the crankcase

24.20a Guide the lower crankcase half into position . . .

24.20b . . . making sure the shift forks engage correctly with the gear slots

24.22 Oil the threads and heads of the 9 mm lower crankcase bolts . . .

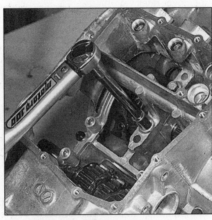

24.23 . . . and tighten them to the specified torque setting as described in text

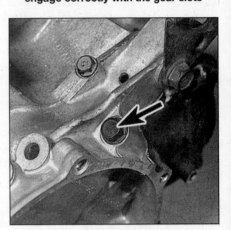

24.24 Fit the 8 mm bolt (arrow) to the crankcase and tighten it to the specified torque . . .

24.25 . . . then tighten all the 6 mm bolts to the specified torque

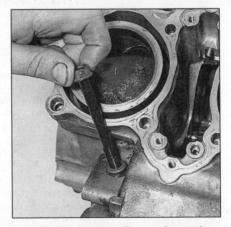

24.27a Fit a new sealing washer to the two 10 mm upper crankcase bolts . . .

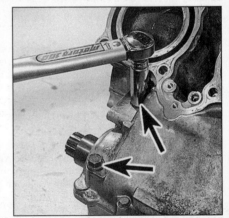

24.27b . . . and tighten them to the specified torque

crankcase half. Fit a new O-ring to the outside of the jet **(see illustrations)**.

17   Install the three locating dowels in the upper crankcase half **(see illustration)**.

18   Apply a small amount of suitable sealant to the mating surface of the upper crankcase half. **Caution:** *Don't apply sealant to the area around the main bearing inserts. Do not use an excessive amount of sealant, as it will ooze out when the case halves are assembled and may obstruct oil passages and prevent the bearings from seating.*

19   Check the position of the shift drum cam, shift forks and transmission shafts - make sure they're in the neutral position.

20   Make sure that the main bearing inserts are in position and carefully install the lower crankcase half on the upper half. The shift forks must engage with their respective slots in the transmission gears as the halves are joined **(see illustrations)**.

21   Check that the lower crankcase half is correctly seated and that all shafts are free to rotate. **Note:** *If the casings are not correctly seated, remove the lower crankcase half and investigate the problem.*

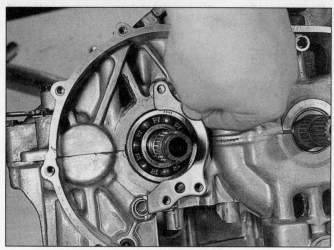

24.29a Offer up the mainshaft bearing retaining plate . . .

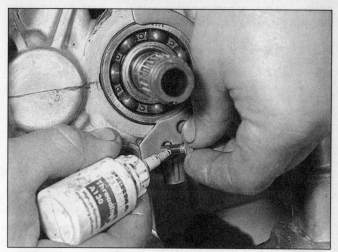

24.29b . . . and install its retaining bolts, having applied thread locking compound to them

Do not attempt to pull them together using the crankcase bolts as the casing will crack and be ruined.

22   Apply a smear of engine oil to the threads and undersides of the heads of the eight 9 mm lower crankcase bolts and install the bolts in their original locations **(see illustration)**.

23   Starting from the center and working out in a criss-cross pattern, tighten all the bolts to approximately half the specified torque. Go around a second time in the same sequence and tighten them to the full torque setting given in the Specifications at the start of this Chapter **(see illustration)**.

24   Fit the single 8 mm crankcase bolt and tighten it to the specified torque setting **(see illustration)**.

25   Fit the eight 6 mm bolts in their original locations and evenly and progressively tighten them to the specified torque setting **(see illustration)**.

26   Turn the crankcase over so that it is upright.

27   Fit a new sealing washer to the two 10 mm upper crankcase bolts, then install the bolts and tighten them to the specified torque setting **(see illustrations)**.

28   Install the seven 6 mm upper crankcase bolts and tighten them to the specified torque.

29   Clean the threads of the mainshaft bearing retaining plate bolts and apply locking compound to their threads. Install the retaining plate, making sure it is correctly engaged with the shift fork shaft cut-out, and securely tighten its retaining bolts **(see illustrations)**.

30   With all crankcase fasteners tightened, check that the crankshaft and transmission shafts rotate smoothly and easily. If there are any signs of undue stiffness or of any other problem, the fault must be rectified before proceeding further.

31   Install all other removed assemblies in the reverse of the sequence given in Step 2.

25   Crankcase components - inspection and servicing

1   After the crankcases have been separated and the crankshaft and transmission components have been removed, the crankcases should be cleaned thoroughly with new solvent and dried with compressed air.

Cylinder bores

Note: *Don't attempt to separate the liners from the cylinder block.*

2   Check the cylinder walls carefully for scratches and score marks.

3   Using the appropriate precision measuring tools, check each cylinder's diameter. Measure near the top, center and bottom of the cylinder bore, parallel to the crankshaft axis. Next, measure each cylinder's diameter at the same three locations across the crankshaft axis. Compare the results to this Chapter's Specifications. If the cylinder bores are tapered, out-of-round, worn beyond the specified limits, or badly scuffed or scored, have them rebored and honed by a dealer service department or a motorcycle repair shop. If a rebore is done, oversize pistons and rings will be required as well. Honda produce two sizes of oversize pistons (see Section 28).

4   As an alternative, if the precision measuring tools are not available, a dealer service department or motorcycle repair shop will make the measurements and offer advice concerning servicing of the cylinders.

5   If they are in reasonably good condition and not worn to the outside of the limits, and if the piston-to-cylinder clearances can be maintained properly (see Section 28), then the cylinders do not have to be rebored; honing is all that is necessary.

6   To perform the honing operation you will need the proper size flexible hone with fine stones, or a 'bottle brush' type hone, plenty of light oil or honing oil, some shop towels and an electric drill motor. Hold the upper crankcase half in a vise (cushioned with soft jaws or wood blocks) when performing the honing operation. Mount the hone in the drill motor, compress the stones and slip the hone into the top of the cylinder. Lubricate the cylinder thoroughly, turn on the drill and move the hone up and down in the cylinder at a pace which will produce a fine crosshatch pattern on the cylinder wall with the crosshatch lines intersecting at approximately a 60° angle. Be sure to use plenty of lubricant and do not take off any more material than is absolutely necessary to produce the desired effect. Do not withdraw the hone from the cylinder while it is running. Instead, shut off the drill and continue moving the hone up and down in the cylinder until it comes to a complete stop, then compress the stones and withdraw the hone. Wipe the oil out of the cylinder and repeat the procedure on the other cylinders. Remember, do not remove too much material from the cylinder wall. If you do not have the tools, or do not desire to perform the honing operation, a dealer service department or motorcycle repair shop will generally do it for a reasonable fee.

7   Next, the cylinders must be thoroughly washed with warm soapy water to remove all traces of the abrasive grit produced during the honing operation. Be sure to run a brush through the bolt holes and flush them with running water. After rinsing, dry the cylinders thoroughly and apply a coat of light, rust-preventative oil to all machined surfaces.

Crankcase castings

8   Remove any oil passage plugs that haven't already been removed. All oil passages should be blown out with compressed air.

9   All traces of old gasket sealant should be removed from the mating surfaces. Minor damage to the surfaces can be cleaned up with a fine sharpening stone or grindstone. **Caution:** *Be very careful not to*

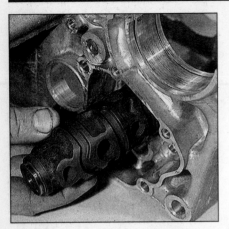

26.10a Install the shift drum . . .

26.10b . . . then fit the bearing (J models onward)

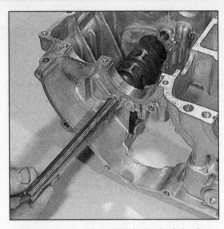

26.11 Locate the shift fork shaft in the crankcase half

nick or gouge the crankcase mating surfaces or leaks will result. Check both crankcase halves very carefully for cracks and other damage.

10   Small cracks or holes in aluminum castings may be repaired with an epoxy resin adhesive as a temporary measure. Permanent repairs can only be effected by argon-arc welding, and only a specialist in this process is in a position to advise on the economy or practical aspect of such a repair. If any damage is found that can't be repaired, replace the crankcase halves as a set.

11   Damaged threads can be economically reclaimed by using a diamond section wire insert, of the Helicoil type, which is easily fitted after drilling and re-tapping the affected thread. Most motorcycle dealers and small machine shops (engineering firms) offer a service of this kind.

12   Sheared studs or screws can usually be removed with screw extractors, which consist of a tapered, left thread screw of very hard steel. These are inserted into a pre-drilled hole in the stud, and usually succeed in dislodging the most stubborn stud or screw. If a problem arises which seems beyond your scope, it is worth consulting a professional before condemning an otherwise sound casing. Many of these firms advertise regularly in the motorcycle press.

26   Shift drum and forks - removal, inspection and installation

Removal

1   Separate the crankcase halves as described in Section 24.

2   On G and H models, unscrew the shift drum retaining plate stud and remove the retaining plate. The stud can be removed using two nuts screwed onto its thread and locked together or by using a universal stud extractor.

3   On all models, withdraw the shift fork shaft slowly and remove the shift forks from the crankcase as they are released from the end of the shaft. When all three shift forks have been removed, fully withdraw the shaft from the crankcase.

4   Remove the shift drum and bearing from the crankcase.

Inspection

5   The shift forks and shaft should be closely inspected to ensure that they are not badly damaged or worn.

6   Measure the width of both fork ends and the internal diameter of the shaft bore. If either fork end or the shaft bore has worn beyond its service limit the shift fork(s) must be replaced.

7   The shift fork shaft can be checked for trueness by rolling it along a flat surface. A bent shaft will cause difficulty in selecting gears and make the gearshift action heavy. Measure the diameter of the shaft at the points where it is in contact with the shift forks. If the shaft is bent or has worn beyond its service limit at any point it must be replaced.

8   Inspect the shift drum grooves and selector fork guide pins for signs of wear or damage. If either component shows signs of wear or damage the shift fork(s) and drum must be replaced.

9   Check that the shift drum bearing rotates freely and has no sign of freeplay between its inner and outer race. Replace the bearing if necessary. **Note:** On G and H models it is not possible to replace the bearing separately; if damaged the complete shift drum assembly must be replaced.

Installation

Refer to illustrations 26.10a, 26.10b, 26.11, 26.12, 26.13a, 26.13b and 26.13c

10   Lubricate the bearing and shift drum grooves with clean engine oil and insert the shift drum and bearing into position in the crankcase **(see illustrations)**.

11   Apply a smear of engine oil to the shift fork shaft and slide the shaft partially into the crankcase **(see illustration)**.

12   The shift forks can be identified by the letter cast on each one; L denotes the left fork, C the center, and R the right **(see illustration)**. **Note:** All shift forks must be installed in the crankcase so that the letter on each one faces towards the right side of the casing (clutch).

13   Locate the right fork with its groove in the shift drum and slide in the shift fork shaft until it engages the fork. Repeat the process for the center and left fork and push the shaft fully home, making sure each fork is positioned as described in Step 12 **(see illustrations)**.

14   On G and H models, slide the shift drum bearing retaining plate into position. Clean the thread of its retaining stud, then screw in the stud and tighten it securely (see Step 2).

15   Join the crankcase halves as described in Section 24.

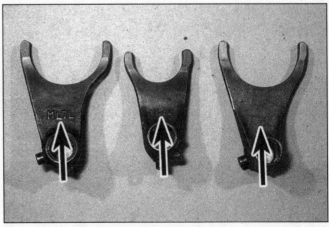

26.12 Each shift fork is marked with a letter to identify its correct fitted position (arrows)

26.13a Making sure all shift forks are fitted with their markings facing the right, install the right fork . . .

26.13b . . . followed by the center fork . . .

26.13c . . . and finally the left fork

27 Main and connecting rod bearings - general note

1   Even though main and connecting rod bearings are generally replaced with new ones during the engine overhaul, the old bearings should be retained for close examination as they may reveal valuable information about the condition of the engine.

2   Bearing failure occurs mainly because of lack of lubrication, the presence of dirt or other foreign particles, overloading the engine and/or corrosion. Regardless of the cause of bearing failure, it must be corrected before the engine is reassembled to prevent it from happening again.

3   When examining the bearings, remove the main bearings from the case halves and the rod bearings from the connecting rods and caps and lay them out on a clean surface in the same general position as their location on the crankshaft journals. This will enable you to match any noted bearing problems with the corresponding crankshaft journal.

4   Dirt and other foreign particles get into the engine in a variety of ways. It may be left in the engine during assembly or it may pass through filters or breathers. It may get into the oil and from there into the bearings. Metal chips from machining operations and normal engine wear are often present. Abrasives are sometimes left in engine components after reconditioning operations such as cylinder honing, especially when parts are not thoroughly cleaned using the proper cleaning methods. Whatever the source, these foreign objects often end up imbedded in the soft bearing material and are easily recognized. Large particles will not imbed in the bearing and will score or gouge the bearing and journal. The best prevention for this cause of bearing failure is to clean all parts thoroughly and keep everything spotlessly clean during engine reassembly. Frequent and regular oil and filter changes are also recommended.

5   Lack of lubrication or lubrication breakdown has a number of interrelated causes. Excessive heat (which thins the oil), overloading (which squeezes the oil from the bearing face) and oil leakage or throw off from excessive bearing clearances, worn oil pump or high engine speeds all contribute to lubrication breakdown. Blocked oil passages will also starve a bearing and destroy it. When lack of lubrication is the cause of bearing failure, the bearing material is wiped or extruded from the steel backing of the bearing. Temperatures may increase to the point where the steel backing and the journal turn blue from overheating.

6   Riding habits can have a definite effect on bearing life. Full throttle low speed operation, or lugging (laboring) the engine, puts very high loads on bearings, which tend to squeeze out the oil film. These loads cause the bearings to flex, which produces fine cracks in the bearing face (fatigue failure). Eventually the bearing material will loosen in pieces and tear away from the steel backing. Short trip riding leads to corrosion of bearings, as insufficient engine heat is produced to drive off the condensed water and corrosive gases produced. These

products collect in the engine oil, forming acid and sludge. As the oil is carried to the engine bearings, the acid attacks and corrodes the bearing material.

7   Incorrect bearing installation during engine assembly will lead to bearing failure as well. Tight fitting bearings which leave insufficient bearing oil clearances result in oil starvation. Dirt or foreign particles trapped behind a bearing insert result in high spots on the bearing which lead to failure.

8   To avoid bearing problems, clean all parts thoroughly before reassembly, double check all bearing clearance measurements and lubricate the new bearings with clean engine oil during installation.

28 Piston/connecting rod assemblies - removal, inspection, bearing selection, oil clearance check and installation

Removal

Refer to illustrations 28.1, 28.3, and 28.8

1   Separate the crankcase halves as described in Section 24. Before removing the piston/connecting rods from the crankshaft measure the side clearance of each pair of rods with a feeler gauge **(see illustration)**. If the clearance is greater than the service limit listed in this Chapter's Specifications, both rods will have to be replaced with a new ones.

2   Using a center punch or paint, mark the relevant cylinder number

28.1 Checking connecting rod big-end side clearance

2

28.3 On removal make sure the bearing shell stays in the cap

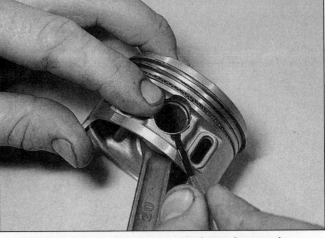

28.8 Using a scriber to pry out a piston pin snap-ring

on each connecting rod and bearing cap (see specifications for cylinder identification details).

3   Unscrew the bearing cap nuts and withdraw the cap, complete with the lower bearing insert, from each of the four connecting rods **(see illustration)**. Push the connecting rods up and off their crankpins, then remove the upper bearing insert. Keep the cap, nuts and (if they are to be re-used) the bearing inserts together in their correct sequence.

4   Remove the ridge of carbon from the top of each cylinder bore. If there is a pronounced wear ridge on the top of each bore, remove with a ridge reamer.

5   Push each piston/connecting rod assembly up and remove it from the top of the bore making sure the connecting rod does not mark the cylinder bore walls.

6   Immediately install the relevant bearing cap, inserts and nuts on each piston/connecting rod assembly so that they are all kept together as a matched set.

7   Using a sharp scriber, scratch the number of each piston into its crown (or use a suitable marker pen if the piston is clean enough).

8   Support the first piston and, using a small screwdriver or scriber, carefully pry out a snap-ring from the piston groove **(see illustration)**.

9   Push the piston pin out from the opposite end to free the piston from the rod. You may have to deburr the area around the groove to enable the pin to slide out (use a triangular file for this procedure). If the pin is tight, tap it out using a suitable hammer and punch, taking care not to damage the piston. Repeat the procedure for the other pistons.

Inspection

Pistons

Refer to illustrations 28.11, 28.18, 28.19 and 28.20

10   Before the inspection process can be carried out, the pistons must be cleaned and the old piston rings removed.

11   Using a piston ring removal and installation tool, carefully remove the rings from the pistons **(see illustration)**. Do not nick or gouge the pistons in the process.

12   Scrape all traces of carbon from the tops of the pistons. A hand-held wire brush or a piece of fine emery cloth can be used once most of the deposits have been scraped away. Do not, under any circumstances, use a wire brush mounted in a drill motor to remove deposits from the pistons; the piston material is soft and will be eroded away by the wire brush.

13   Use a piston ring groove cleaning tool to remove any carbon deposits from the ring grooves. If a tool is not available, a piece broken off an old ring will do the job. Be very careful to remove only the carbon deposits. Do not remove any metal and do not nick or gouge the sides of the ring grooves.

14   Once the deposits have been removed, clean the pistons with solvent and dry them thoroughly. Make sure the oil return holes below the oil ring grooves are clear.

15   If the pistons are not damaged or worn excessively and if the cylinders are not to be rebored, new pistons will not be necessary. Normal piston wear appears as even, vertical wear on the thrust surfaces of the piston and slight looseness of the top ring in its groove. New piston rings, on the other hand, should always be used when an engine is rebuilt.

16   Carefully inspect each piston for cracks around the skirt, at the pin bosses and at the ring lands.

17   Look for scoring and scuffing on the thrust faces of the skirt, holes in the piston crown and burned areas at the edge of the crown. If the skirt is scored or scuffed, the engine may have been suffering from overheating and/or abnormal combustion, which caused excessively high operating temperatures. The oil pump and oil cooler should be checked thoroughly. A hole in the piston crown, an extreme to be sure, is an indication that abnormal combustion (pre-ignition) was occurring. Burned areas at the edge of the piston crown are usually evidence of spark knock (detonation). If any of the above problems exist, the causes must be corrected or the damage will occur again.

18   Measure the piston ring-to-groove clearance by laying a new piston ring in the ring groove and slipping a feeler gauge in beside it **(see illustration)**. Check the clearance at three or four locations around the groove. Be sure to use the correct ring for each groove;

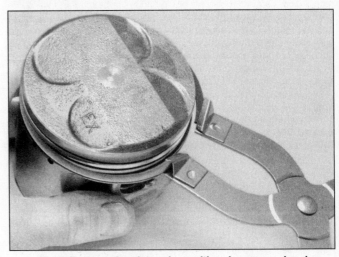

28.11 Remove the piston rings with a ring removal and installation tool

28.18 Measuring piston ring-to-groove clearance

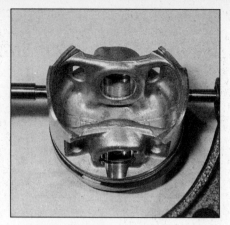

28.19 Measuring piston diameter

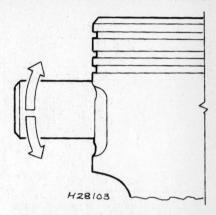

28.20 Slip the pin into the piston and try to wiggle it back-and-forth; if it's loose, replace the piston and pin

they are different. If the clearance is greater than the service limit, new pistons will have to be used when the engine is reassembled.

19   Calculate the piston-to-bore clearance by measuring the bore (see Section 25) and the piston diameter. Make sure that the pistons and cylinders are correctly matched. Measure the piston across the skirt on the thrust faces at a 90° angle to the piston pin, 10 mm (0.4 in) up from the bottom of the skirt **(see illustration)**. Subtract the piston diameter from the bore diameter to obtain the clearance. If it is greater than specified in the Specifications at the beginning of this Chapter, the cylinders will have to be rebored and new oversized pistons and rings installed.

20   Apply clean engine oil to the pin, insert it into the piston and check for freeplay by rocking the pin back-and-forth **(see illustration)**. If the pin is loose, new pistons and pins must be installed. If the necessary measuring equipment is available measure the pin diameter and piston pin bore and check the readings obtained do not exceed the limits given in this Chapter's Specifications. Replace components that are worn beyond the specified limit.

21   If the pistons are to be replaced, ensure the correct size of piston is ordered. Honda produce two oversizes of piston as well as standard pistons. The piston oversizes available are: +0.25 mm and +0.50 mm. **Note:** *Oversize pistons have their size stamped on top of the piston crown, e.g. a +0.25 mm oversize piston will be marked 0.25.*

22   Install the rings on the pistons as described in Section 29.

Connecting rods

Refer to illustration 28.23

23   Check the connecting rods for cracks and other obvious damage. Lubricate the piston pin for each rod, install it in its original rod and check for play. If it wobbles, replace the connecting rod and/or the pin **(see illustration)**. If the necessary measuring equipment is available measure the pin diameter and connecting rod bore and check the readings obtained do not exceed the limits given in this Chapter's Specifications. Replace components that are worn beyond the specified limit.

24   Refer to Section 27 and examine the connecting rod bearing inserts. If they are scored, badly scuffed or appear to have been seized, new bearings must be installed. Always replace the bearings in the connecting rods as a set. If they are badly damaged, check the corresponding crankpin. Evidence of extreme heat, such as discoloration, indicates that lubrication failure has occurred. Be sure to thoroughly check the oil pump and pressure relief valve as well as all oil holes and passages before reassembling the engine.

25   Have the rods checked for twist and bending at a dealer service department or other motorcycle repair shop.

26   If a connecting rod is to replaced, it is essential that the new rod is of the correct weight group to minimize vibration. The weight is indicated by a letter stamped on the big-end cap of each rod (see

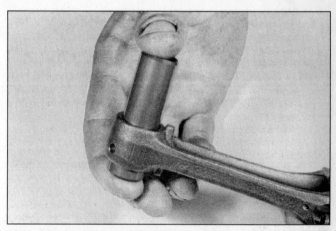

28.23 Slip the piston pin into the rod and rock it back-and-forth to check for looseness

illustration 28.29). This letter together with the connecting rod size mark (see Step 29) should be quoted when purchasing new connecting rod(s), also state whether it is a front or rear cylinder connecting rod. **Note:** *The front and rear connecting rods are not interchangeable as their oil holes are offset. The front cylinder connecting rods are marked `ML7-F' on their shafts, and the rear connecting rods are marked `ML7-R'.* Since the rods run in pairs on the crankpins, it is essential that each pair of rods is correctly matched as shown in the following table.

Code of rod	Code of other rod to be replaced on same crankpin	Permitted code of new rod
A	B	A, B or C
A	C	A or B
B	A	B or C
B	B	A, B or C
B	C	A or B
C	A	B or C
C	B	A, B or C

Bearing selection

Refer to illustrations 28.27, 28.28a, 28.28b, 28.28c and 28.29

27   The connecting rod bearing running clearance is controlled in production by selecting one of five grades of bearing insert. The grades are indicated by a color-coding marked on the edge of each insert **(see illustration)**. **Note:** *The front and rear connecting rod bearing inserts are not interchangeable because the insert oil holes are offset. The front cylinder bearing inserts have one paint marking, and*

2

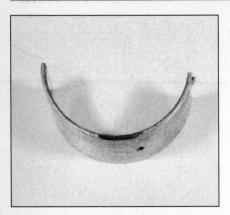

28.27 The color code is painted on the side of the bearing

28.28a Crankpin journal identification marks and main bearing journal identification marks are stamped on each crank web (arrows)

28.28b The letters indicate the crankpin sizes and the numbers the main bearing journal sizes

the rear bearing inserts have two paint marking0s. In order, from the thickest to the thinnest, the insert grades are: Blue, Black, Brown, Green and Yellow. New bearing inserts are selected as follows using the crankpin and connecting rod size markings.

28   The standard crankpin journal diameter is divided into three size groups to allow for manufacturing tolerances. The size group of each crankpin can be determined by the letters which are stamped on the crank web next to the crankpin. **Note:** *Ignore the numbers as these refer to the main bearing journals.* If the equipment is available, these marks can be checked by direct measurement **(see illustrations)**.

29   The connecting rods are also divided into three size groups to allow for manufacturing tolerances. The size group is in the form of a number stamped on the rod (either 1, 2 or 3) **(see illustration)**. **Note:** *Ignore the letter as this indicates the weight group of the connecting rod.* If the equipment is available, these marks can be checked by direct measurement.

30   Match the relevant connecting rod code with its crankshaft code and select a new set of bearing inserts using the following table.

Connecting rod mark	Crankshaft mark	Insert color
1	A	Yellow
1	B	Green
1	C	Brown
2	A	Green
2	B	Brown
2	C	Black
3	A	Brown
3	B	Black
3	C	Blue

Oil clearance check

Refer to illustration 28.37

31   Whether new bearing inserts are being fitted or the original ones are being re-used, the connecting rod bearing oil clearance should be checked prior to reassembly.

32   Clean the backs of the bearing inserts and the bearing locations in both the connecting rod and bearing cap.

33   Press the bearing inserts into their locations, ensuring that the tab on each insert engages the notch in the connecting rod/bearing cap. Make sure the bearings are fitted in the correct locations and take care not to touch any insert's bearing surface with your fingers.

34   There are two possible ways of checking the oil clearance. The first method is by direct measurement (see Steps 35 and 38) and the second by the use of a product known as Plastigage (see Steps 36 through 38).

35   If the first method is to be used, fit the bearing cap to the connecting rod, with the bearing inserts in place. Make sure the cap is fitted the correct way around so the connecting rod and bearing cap weight/size markings are correctly aligned. Tighten the cap retaining

28.28c Using a micrometer to measure a crankpin diameter

nuts to the specified torque and measure the internal diameter of each assembled pair of bearing inserts. If the diameter of each corresponding crankpin journal is measured and then subtracted from the bearing internal diameter, the result will be the connecting rod bearing oil clearance.

36   If the second method is to be used, cut lengths of the appropriate size Plastigage (they should be slightly shorter than the width of the crankpin). Place a strand of Plastigage on each (cleaned) crankpin journal and fit the (clean) piston/connecting rod assemblies, inserts and bearing caps. Make sure the cap is fitted the correct way around so the connecting rod and bearing cap weight/size markings are correctly aligned and tighten the bearing cap nuts to the specified torque whilst ensuring that the connecting rod does not rotate. Take care not to disturb the Plastigage. Slacken the bearing cap nuts and remove the connecting rod assemblies, again taking great care not to rotate the crankshaft.

37   Compare the width of the crushed Plastigage on each crankpin to the scale printed on the Plastigage envelope to obtain the connecting rod bearing oil clearance **(see illustration)**.

38   If the clearance is not within the specified limits, the bearing inserts may be the wrong grade (or excessively worn if the original inserts are being re-used). Before deciding that different grade inserts are needed, make sure that no dirt or oil was trapped between the bearing inserts and the connecting rod or bearing cap when the clearance was measured. If the clearance is excessive, even with new inserts (of the correct size), the crankpin is worn and the crankshaft should be replaced.

28.29 Connecting rod bearing diameter number and weight group letter

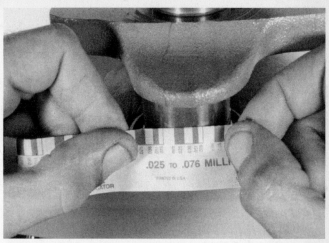

28.37 Place the Plastigage scale next to the flattened Plastigage to measure the bearing clearance

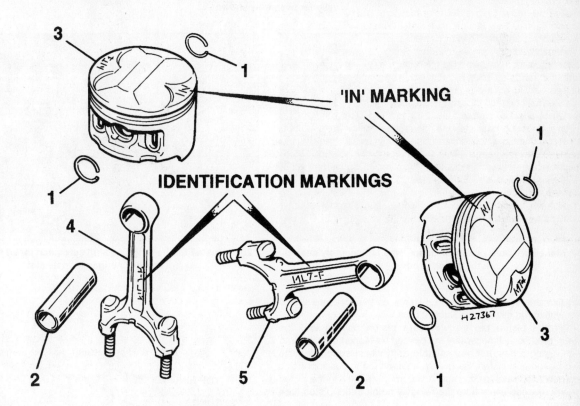

'IN' MARKING

IDENTIFICATION MARKINGS

28.41a Connecting rod and piston mating details

1 Snap-rings
2 Piston pin
3 Piston
4 Rear cylinder connecting rod
5 Front cylinder connecting rod

39   On completion, carefully scrape away all traces of the Plastigage material from the crankpin and bearing inserts using a fingernail or other object which is unlikely to score the inserts.

Installation

Refer to illustrations 28.41a through 28.41d, 28.42, 28.44, 28.46, 28.47, 28.48, 28.49, 28.51a and 28.51b

40   Check that each piston has one new snap-ring fitted to it and that it is correctly seated in the piston groove with its gap away from the removal notch in the piston. Insert the piston pin from the opposite side. If it is a tight fit, the piston should be warmed first. If the original pistons/connecting rods are being installed, use the marks made on disassembly to ensure each piston is fitted to its correct connecting rod (see Step 26).

41   Lubricate the piston pin and connecting rod bores with clean engine oil. On the front cylinders, fit the piston to its respective connecting rod making sure that the IN mark on the crown of the piston is on the **same** side as the connecting rod oilway. On the rear cylinders, fit the piston to its respective connecting rod making sure

28.41b Rear cylinder connecting rod identification marking (arrow)

28.41c On assembly, make sure the connecting rod oilway and piston IN marking are correctly positioned in relation to each other (arrows) - front cylinder assembly shown . . .

28.41d . . . then slide in the piston pin

28.42 Make sure both piston pin snap-rings are securely seated in the piston grooves

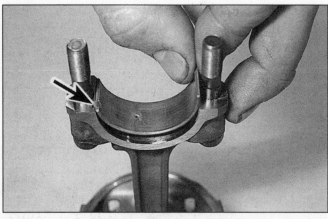

28.44 Install the bearings making sure each insert tab (arrow) is correctly engaged in its slot

that the IN mark on the crown of the piston is on the **opposite** side to the connecting rod oilway **(see illustrations)**.

42   Push the piston pin through both piston bosses and the connecting rod bore. If necessary the pin can be tapped carefully into position, using a hammer and suitable drift, whilst supporting the connecting rod and piston. Secure each piston pin in position with a second new snap-ring, making sure it is correctly seated in the piston groove with its gap away from the removal notch in the piston **(see illustration)**.

43   Clean the backs of the bearing inserts and the bearing recesses in both the connecting rod and bearing cap. If new inserts are being fitted, ensure that all traces of the protective grease are cleaned off using kerosene (paraffin). Wipe dry the inserts and connecting rods with a lint-free cloth.

44   Press the bearing inserts into their locations. Make sure the tab on each insert engages the notch in the connecting rod or bearing cap **(see illustration)**. Make sure the bearings are fitted in the correct locations (see Step 27) and take care not to touch any insert's bearing surface with your fingers.

45   Lubricate the cylinder bores, the pistons and piston rings then lay out each piston/connecting rod assembly in its respective position.

46   Starting with assembly number 1, position the piston rings so their end gaps are positioned at the specified intervals **(see illustration)**.

47   With the piston rings correctly positioned, clamp them in position

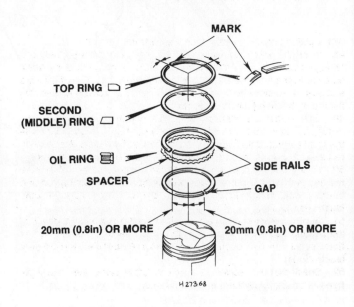

28.46 Piston ring end gap positioning diagram

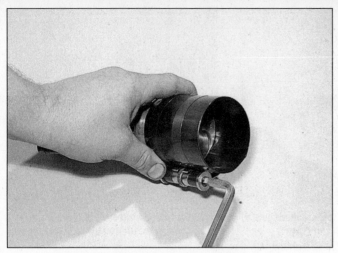

28.47 Clamp the piston rings in position with a ring compressor . . .

28.48 . . . and insert the piston/connecting rod assembly, making sure each piston IN mark is on the intake side of the bore

28.49 Lubricate the crankpins with fresh engine oil

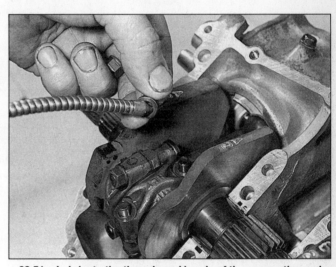

28.51a Lubricate the threads and heads of the connecting rod bearing cap nuts . . .

2

with a piston ring compressor **(see illustration)**.

48   Insert the piston/connecting rod assembly into the top of its bore, taking care not to allow the connecting rod to mark the bore. Make sure the IN mark on the piston crown is on the intake side of the bore and push the piston into the position until the piston crown is flush with the top of the bore **(see illustration)**.

49   Ensure that the connecting rod bearing insert is still correctly installed. Taking care not to mark the cylinder bores, liberally lubricate the crankpin and both bearing inserts, then pull the piston/connecting rod assembly down its bore and onto the crankpin **(see illustration)**.

50   Fit the bearing cap and insert to the connecting rod. Make sure the cap is fitted the correct way around so the connecting rod and bearing cap weight/size markings are correctly aligned **(see illustration 28.29)**.

51   Apply a smear of clean engine oil to the threads and underside of the bearing cap nuts. Fit the nuts to the connecting rod and tighten them evenly, in two or three stages, to the specified torque **(see illustrations)**.

52   Check that the crankshaft is free to rotate easily, then install the three remaining assemblies in the same way.

28.51b . . . and tighten the nuts to the specified torque as described in text

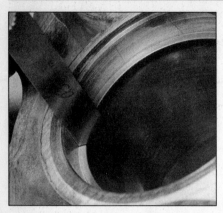

29.3 Measuring piston ring end gap

29.5 If the end gap is too small, clamp a file in a vise and file the ring ends (from outside in only) to enlarge the gap slightly

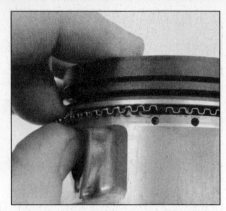

29.9a Installing the oil expander ring - make sure the ends don't overlap

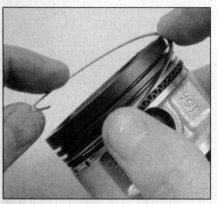

29.9b Installing an oil ring side rail - don't use a ring installation tool to do this

30.3 Lifting the crankshaft out of position

30.10 Using a micrometer to measure a main bearing journal

29 Piston rings - installation

Refer to illustrations 29.3, 29.5, 29.9a and 29.9b

1   Before installing new piston rings, their end gaps must be checked.

2   Lay out the pistons and the new ring sets so the rings will be matched with the same piston and cylinder during the end gap measurement procedure and engine assembly.

3   Insert the top ring into the top of the first cylinder and square it up with the cylinder walls by pushing it in with the top of the piston. The ring should be about 25 mm below the top edge of the cylinder. To measure the end gap, slip a feeler gauge between the ends of the ring and compare the measurement to that given in the Specifications at the beginning of this Chapter **(see illustration)**.

4   If the gap is larger or smaller than specified, double check to make sure that you have the correct rings before proceeding.

5   If the gap is too small, it must be enlarged or the ring ends may come in contact with each other during engine operation, which can cause serious damage. The end gap can be increased by filing the ring ends very carefully with a fine file. When performing this operation, file only from the outside in **(see illustration)**.

6   Excess end gap is not critical unless it is greater than 1 mm 0.04 in. Again, double check to make sure you have the correct rings for your engine.

7   Repeat the procedure for each ring that will be installed in the first cylinder and for each ring in the remaining cylinders. Remember to keep the rings, pistons and cylinders matched up.

8   Once the ring end gaps have been checked/corrected, the rings can be installed on the pistons.

9   The oil control ring (lowest on the piston) is installed first. It is composed of three separate components. Slip the expander into the groove, then install the upper side rail. Do not use a piston ring installation tool on the oil ring side rails as they may be damaged. Instead, place one end of the side rail into the groove between the expander and the ring land. Hold it firmly in place and slide a finger around the piston while pushing the rail into the groove. Next, install the lower side rail in the same manner **(see illustrations)**.

10   After the three oil ring components have been installed, check to make sure that both the upper and lower side rails can be turned smoothly in the ring groove.

11   Install the second (middle) ring next. **Note:** *The second ring and top ring are different and cannot be interchanged. The second ring is easily identified by its tapered outer edge.* To avoid breaking the ring, use a piston ring installation tool and make sure that the ring is fitted the correct way up with its widest point at the bottom **(see illustration 28.46)**. Fit the ring into the middle groove on the piston. Do not expand the ring any more than is necessary to slide it into place.

12   Finally, install the top ring in the same manner. Make sure the identifying mark (either a T or R) is facing up.

13   Repeat the procedure for the remaining pistons and rings.

30 Crankshaft and main bearings - removal, inspection, bearing selection, oil clearance check and installation

Removal

Refer to illustration 30.3

1   Separate the crankcase halves as described in Section 24.

30.11 On L models onward, the crankcase main bearing bore diameter marks (arrow) are stamped on the right side of the upper crankcase half

2   Remove the piston/connecting rod assemblies as described in Section 28. **Note:** *If no work is to be carried out on the piston/connecting rod assemblies there is no need to remove them from the bores. However, the connecting rod bearing caps should be removed and the pistons pushed up to the top of the bores so that the connecting rod ends are positioned clear of the crankshaft.*

3   Lift the crankshaft out of the upper crankcase half, taking care not to dislodge the bearing inserts **(see illustration)**.

4   The main bearing inserts can be removed from the crankcase halves by pushing their centers to the side, then lifting them out. Keep the bearing inserts in order.

Inspection

5   Clean the crankshaft with solvent, using a rifle-cleaning brush to scrub out the oil passages. If available, blow the crank dry with compressed air.

6   Refer to Section 27 and examine the main bearing inserts. If they are scored, badly scuffed or appear to have been seized, new bearings must be installed. Always replace the main bearings as a set. If they are badly damaged, check the corresponding crankshaft journal. Evidence of extreme heat, such as discoloration, indicates that lubrication failure has occurred. Be sure to thoroughly check the oil pump and pressure relief valve as well as all oil holes and passages before reassembling the engine.

7   The crankshaft journals should be given a close visual examination, paying particular attention where damaged bearing inserts have been discovered. If the journals are scored or pitted in any way a new crankshaft will be required. Note that undersizes are not available, precluding the option of re-grinding the crankshaft.

8   Set the crankshaft on V-blocks and check the runout with a dial indicator touching the center main bearing journal, comparing your findings with this Chapter's Specifications. If the runout exceeds the limit, replace the crankshaft.

Bearing selection

Refer to illustrations 30.10 and 30.11

9   The main bearing running clearance is controlled in production by selecting one of five grades of bearing insert. The grades are indicated by a color-coding marked on the edge of each insert. In order, from the thickest to the thinnest, the insert grades are: Blue, Black, Brown, Green and Yellow. New bearing inserts are selected as follows using the crankshaft journal and crankcase main bearing bore size markings.

10   The standard crankshaft journal diameter is divided into three size groups to allow for manufacturing tolerances. The size group of each journal can be determined by the numbers (either 1, 2 or 3) which are stamped on the crankshaft webs next to each journal **(see illustrations 28.28a and 28.28b)**. **Note:** *Ignore the letters as these refer to the crankpin journals.* If the equipment is available, these marks can be checked by direct measurement **(see illustration)**.

11   The crankcase main bearing bore diameters are divided into three size groups to allow for manufacturing tolerances. The size group of each main bearing bore can be determined using the four letters (made up of the letters A, B or C) stamped on the upper crankcase half; on G through K models the letters are stamped on the top of the crankcase half along its rear edge, and on L models onward the letters are stamped on the right side of the crankcase, directly above the main bearing journal **(see illustration)**. The first letter indicates the diameter of the left journal, and the last the diameter of the right journal. If the equipment is available, these marks can be checked by direct measurement.

12   Match the relevant crankcase code with its crankshaft code and select a new set of bearing inserts using the following table.

Crankshaft mark	Crankcase mark	Insert color
1	A	Yellow
1	B	Green
1	C	Brown
2	A	Green
2	B	Brown
2	C	Black
3	A	Brown
3	B	Black
3	C	Blue

Oil clearance check

13   Whether new bearing inserts are being fitted or the original ones are being re-used, the main bearing oil clearance should be checked prior to reassembly.

14   Clean the backs of the bearing inserts and the bearing locations in both crankcase halves.

15   Press the bearing inserts into their locations, ensuring that the tab on each insert engages in the notch in the crankcase. Make sure the bearings are fitted in the correct locations and take care not to touch any insert's bearing surface with your fingers.

16   There are two possible ways of checking the oil clearance. The first method is by direct measurement (see Step 17 and 23) and the second by the use of a product known as Plastigage (see Steps 18 to 23).

17   If the first method is to be used, with the main bearing inserts in position, carefully lower the lower crankcase half onto the upper half. Make sure that the shift forks (if fitted) engage with their respective slots in the transmission gears as the halves are joined. Check that the lower crankcase half is correctly seated. **Note:** *Do not tighten the crankcase bolts if the casing is not correctly seated.* Install the eight 9 mm lower crankcase bolts in their original locations and, starting from the center and working out in a criss-cross pattern, tighten them to the specified torque setting. Measure the internal diameter of each assembled pair of bearing inserts. If the diameter of each corresponding crankshaft journal is measured and then subtracted from the bearing internal diameter, the result will be the connecting rod bearing oil clearance.

18   If the second method is to be used, ensure the main bearing inserts are correctly fitted and that the inserts and crankshaft are clean and dry. Lay the crankshaft in position in the upper crankcase.

19   Cut several lengths of the appropriate size Plastigage (they should be slightly shorter than the width of the crankshaft journal). Place a strand of Plastigage on each (cleaned) crankshaft journal.

20   Carefully lower the lower crankcase half onto the upper half. Make sure that the shift forks (if fitted) engage with their respective slots in the transmission gears as the halves are joined. Check that the lower crankcase half is correctly seated. **Note:** *Do not tighten the crankcase bolts if the casing is not correctly seated.* Install the eight 9 mm lower crankcase bolts in their original locations and, starting from the center and working out in a criss-cross pattern, tighten them to the specified torque. Make sure that the crankshaft is not rotated as the bolts are tightened.

21   Slacken and remove the crankcase bolts, working in a criss-cross pattern from the outside in, then carefully lift off the lower crankcase half, making sure the Plastigage is not disturbed.

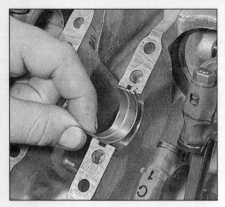

30.26 Install the main bearing inserts making sure each insert tab (arrow) is correctly engaged in the crankcase slot

31.2 Lift the mainshaft and countershaft out of the crankcase

31.6a Install the countershaft bearing half ring . . .

31.6b . . . and dowel pin in the upper crankcase half

31.7 Fit a new oil seal to the countershaft making sure its sealing lip is facing in

31.8a Lower the countershaft into position making sure the bearing race and dowel pin are correctly aligned . . .

22   Compare the width of the crushed Plastigage on each crankshaft journal to the scale printed on the Plastigage envelope to obtain the main bearing oil clearance.

23   If the clearance is not within the specified limits, the bearing inserts may be the wrong grade (or excessively worn if the original inserts are being re-used). Before deciding that different grade inserts are needed, make sure that no dirt or oil was trapped between the bearing inserts and the crankcase halves when the clearance was measured. If the clearance is excessive, even with new inserts (of the correct size), the crankshaft journal is worn and the crankshaft should be replaced.

24   On completion carefully scrape away all traces of the Plastigage material from the crankshaft journal and bearing inserts; use a fingernail or other object which is unlikely to score the inserts.

Installation

Refer to illustration 30.26

25   Clean the backs of the bearing inserts and the bearing recesses in both crankcase halves. If new inserts are being fitted, ensure that all traces of the protective grease are cleaned off using kerosene (paraffin). Wipe dry the inserts and crankcase halves with a lint-free cloth.

26   Press the bearing inserts into their locations. Make sure the tab on each insert engages in the notch in the casing **(see illustration)**. Make sure the bearings are fitted in the correct locations and take care not to touch any insert's bearing surface with your fingers.

27   Lubricate the bearing inserts in the upper crankcase with clean engine oil.

28   Lower the crankshaft into position in the upper crankcase making sure it is fitted the correct way around.

29   Fit the piston/connecting rod assemblies to the crankshaft as

31.8b . . . and the oil seal lip and bearing pin are correctly engaged with the crankcase (arrows)

described in Section 28.

30   Reassemble the crankcase halves as described in Section 24.

31   Transmission shafts - removal and installation

Removal

Refer to illustration 31.2

1   Separate the crankcase halves as described in Section 24.

2   Lift the mainshaft and countershaft out of the crankcase **(see**

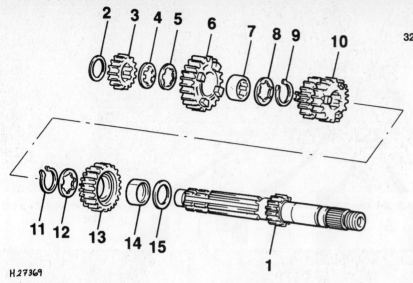

32.2a Mainshaft components - G and H models

1   Mainshaft
2   Thrust washer
3   2nd gear
4   Lock washer
5   Special splined washer
6   6th gear
7   6th gear bushing
8   Splined thrust washer
9   Snap-ring
10 3rd/4th gear
11 Snap-ring
12 Splined thrust washer
13 5th gear
14 5th gear bushing
15 Thrust washer

H.27369

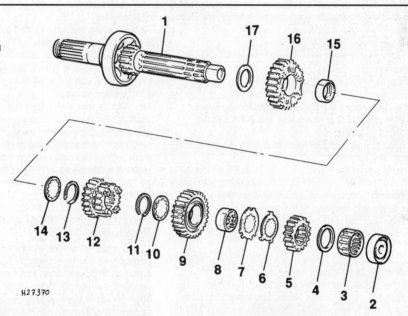

32.2b Mainshaft components - J
models onward

1   Mainshaft
2   Bearing cage
3   Needle roller bearing
4   Thrust washer
5   2nd gear
6   Lock washer
7   Special splined washer
8   6th gear bushing
9   6th gear
10 Splined thrust washer
11 Snap-ring
12 3rd/4th gear
13 Snap-ring
14 Splined thrust washer
15 5th gear bushing
16 5th gear
17 Thrust washer   H27370

illustration). On G through K models, take care not to lose the end plate from the left end of the mainshaft.

3   Recover the countershaft bearing half ring and dowel pin from the upper crankcase half and store them with the transmission shafts for safe-keeping.

4   Remove the oil seal from the end of the countershaft and discard it, as a new one must be used on installation.

5   If necessary, the transmission shafts can be disassembled and inspected for wear or damage as described in Section 32.

Installation

Refer to illustrations 31.6a, 31.6b, 31.7, 31.8a and 31.8b

6   Install the countershaft bearing half ring and dowel pin in the upper crankcase (see illustrations).

7   Slide a new oil seal on the end of the countershaft making sure it is fitted with its sealing lip facing in (see illustration).

8   Lower the countershaft into position in the crankcase half. As the shaft is fitted, align the bearing groove with the half ring, making sure the bearing pin is correctly aligned with the casing cutout. At the same time, align the oil seal lip with the casing groove and engage the needle bearing race with the dowel pin (see illustrations).

9   Lower the mainshaft into position in the upper crankcase.
10   Make sure both transmission shafts are correctly seated. **Caution:** *If the countershaft bearing pin, half ring or dowel pin are not correctly engaged, the crankcase halves will not seat correctly.*
11   Position the gears in the neutral position and check that the shafts are free to rotate freely before proceeding further.

32   Transmission shafts - disassembly, inspection and reassembly

Note: *When disassembling the transmission shafts, place the parts on a long rod or thread a wire through them to keep them in order and facing the proper direction.*

1   Remove the shafts from the casing as described in Section 31.

Mainshaft

Disassembly

Refer to illustrations 32.2a and 32.2b

2   Remove the end plate (G through K models only) and slide off the

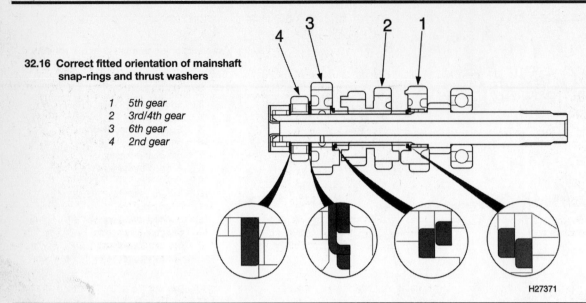

32.16 Correct fitted orientation of mainshaft snap-rings and thrust washers

1   5th gear
2   3rd/4th gear
3   6th gear
4   2nd gear

H27371

needle roller bearing and thrust washer from the left end of the shaft **(see illustrations)**.

3   Slide off the 2nd gear.

4   Disengage the lock washer from the special splined washer and slide both off the mainshaft.

5   Remove the 6th gear followed by its splined bushing and thrust washer.

6   Remove the snap-ring using a suitable pair of snap-ring pliers.

7   Remove the 3rd/4th gear, noting which way around it is fitted.

8   Remove the second snap-ring.

9   Slide off the splined thrust washer followed by the 5th gear, 5th gear bushing and thrust washer.

Inspection

10   Wash all of the components in clean solvent and dry them off.

11   Check the gear teeth for cracking and other obvious damage. Check the gear bushings and the surface in the inner diameter of each gear for scoring or heat discoloration. If the gear or bushing is damaged, replace it.

12   Inspect the dogs and the dog holes in the gears for excessive wear. Replace the paired gears as a set if necessary.

13   The shaft is unlikely to sustain damage unless the engine has seized, placing an unusually high loading on the transmission, or the machine has covered a very high mileage. Check the surface of the shaft, especially where a pinion turns on it, and replace the shaft if it has scored or picked up. Inspect the threads of the shafts and check them for trueness by setting them up in V-blocks and measuring any runout with a dial gauge. Damage of any kind can only be cured by

replacement.

14   Measure the internal diameter of all gears which run on bushings and the external diameter of the bushings which they run on. If either component has worn to or beyond its service limit it must be replaced. Using the above measurements calculate the gear-to-bushing clearance; if this exceeds the specified limit replace the relevant gear and bushing as a pair.

15   Check that the outer race of the bearing fitted to the end of the shaft rotates freely and has no sign of freeplay between its inner and outer races. If the bearing requires replacement, a bearing puller will be required to extract the bearing from its shaft. Pull the bearing off of the shaft and fit the new bearing using a hammer and tubular drift which bears only on the inner race of the bearing.

Reassembly

Refer to illustrations 32.16, 32.17, 32.18a, 32.18b, 32.18c, 32.19, 32.20, 32.21, 32.22, 32.23a, 32.23b, 32.24a, 32.24b, 32.24c, 32.25a, 32.25b and 32.26

16   During reassembly, always use new snap-rings. Lubricate the components with engine oil before assembling them. **Note:** *If the thrust washers and snap-rings are examined closely it will be seen that they are chamfered on one side. During reassembly it is essential that each thrust washer and snap-ring is fitted so its chamfer is on the correct side; also ensure the snap-ring ends are positioned in the shaft grooves* **(see illustration)**.

17   Slide on the thrust washer making sure its chamfered edge is facing away from the integral 1st gear **(see illustration)**.

18   Slide on the 5th gear bushing then fit the 5th gear with its dogs

32.17 Slide on the thrust washer . . .

32.18a . . . followed by the 5th gear bushing

32.18b Fit the 5th gear with its dogs facing as shown . . .

32.18c ... then fit the splined thrust washer

32.19 Secure 5th gear components in position with a snap-ring making sure it is correctly seated in the mainshaft groove

32.20 Align the gear oil hole with the mainshaft oilway when installing the 3rd/4th gear. Gear must be fitted with the larger 4th gear facing the 5th gear

32.21 Fit a second snap-ring to the next groove ...

32.22 ... then slide on a splined thrust washer

32.23a Fit the 6th gear splined bushing, aligning its oil holes with the shaft oilways ...

2

32.23b ... and fit the 6th gear with its dogs facing the 3rd/4th gear

32.24a Slide on the special splined washer ...

32.24b ... then fit the lock washer ...

facing away from the 1st gear. Fit the splined thrust washer with its chamfered edge facing away from the 5th gear **(see illustrations)**.
19   Secure the 5th gear components in position with a new snap-ring making sure its chamfered edge is facing away from the thrust washer. Check the snap-ring is correctly located in the mainshaft groove **(see illustration)**.
20   Install the 3rd/4th gear with its larger 4th gear facing the 5th gear. Engage the gear on the shaft splines ensuring that its oil holes are correctly aligned with the shaft oilways **(see illustration)**.

21   Fit a second new snap-ring to the shaft with its chamfered edge facing away from the 3rd/4th gear pinion. Make sure the snap-ring is correctly located in the shaft groove **(see illustration)**.
22   Slide on the splined thrust washer with its chamfered edge facing away from the snap-ring **(see illustration)**.
23   Align the 6th gear splined bushing oil holes with the shaft oilways and slide it along the shaft. Fit the 6th gear so that its dogs are facing the 3rd/4th gear **(see illustrations)**.
24   Slide the special splined washer along until it abuts the 6th gear,

32.24c ... engaging its tabs with the splined washer slots (arrows)

32.25a Fit the 2nd gear ...

32.25b ... followed by the thrust washer ...

followed by the lock washer. Rotate the splined washer until its cutouts align with the lock washer tabs, then engage the lock washer with the splined washer to lock it in position (**see illustrations**).

25　Fit the 2nd gear followed by the thrust washer, making sure the thrust washer chamfered edge faces the gear (**see illustrations**).

26　Liberally oil the needle roller bearing assembly and install it on the end of the shaft (**see illustration**). On G through K models fit the end plate to the needle roller bearing.

Countershaft

Disassembly

Refer to illustrations 32.27a and 32.27b

27　Slide the needle roller bearing off the right end of the countershaft (**see illustrations**).

32.26 ... then install the needle roller bearing assembly

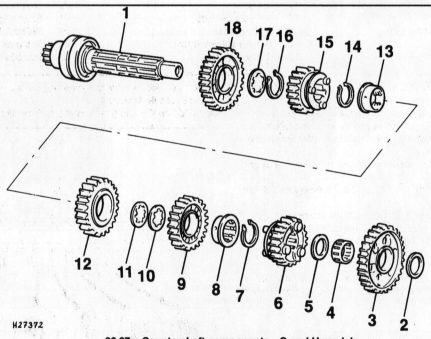

H27372

32.27a Countershaft components - G and H models

1	Countershaft	7	Snap-ring	14	Snap-ring
2	Thrust washer	8	4th gear bushing	15	6th gear
3	1st gear	9	4th gear	16	Snap-ring
4	1st gear needle roller bearing	10	Special lock washer	17	Splined thrust washer
		11	Splined thrust washer	18	2nd gear
5	Thrust washer	12	3rd gear		
6	5th gear	13	3rd gear bushing		

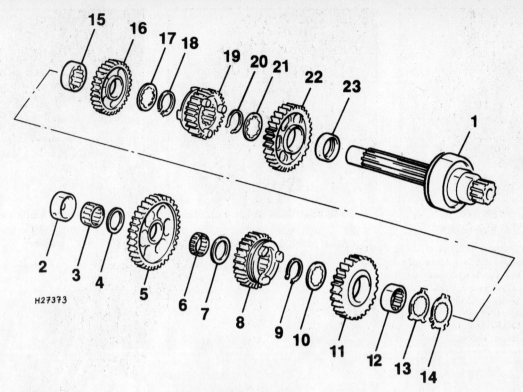

32.27b Countershaft components - J models onward

1	Countershaft	8	5th gear	16	3rd gear	
2	Bearing cage	9	Snap-ring	17	Splined thrust washer	
3	Needle roller bearing	10	Splined thrust washer	18	Snap-ring	
4	Thrust washer	11	4th gear	19	6th gear	
5	1st gear	12	4th gear bushing	20	Snap-ring	
6	1st gear needle roller bearing	13	Lock washer	21	Splined thrust washer	
7	Thrust washer	14	Special splined washer	22	2nd gear	
		15	3rd gear bushing	23	2nd gear bushing	

28   Remove the thrust washer followed by the 1st gear, needle roller bearing and second thrust washer.

29   Remove the 5th gear noting which way around it is fitted.

30   Remove the snap-ring with a suitable pair of snap-ring pliers.

31   Slide off the splined washer followed by the 4th gear and splined bushing.

32   Disengage the lock washer from the special splined washer and slide both off the countershaft.

33   Remove the 3rd gear along with its splined bushing and thrust washer.

34   Remove the second snap-ring and slide off the 6th gear.

35   Remove the third snap-ring and slide off the splined thrust washer followed by the 2nd gear and 2nd gear bushing.

Inspection

36   Refer to Steps 10 through 15 noting that it is not possible to replace the shaft bearing. If the bearing is worn, the complete shaft assembly must be replaced.

Reassembly

Refer to illustrations 32.37, 32.38a through 32.38d, 32.39, 32.40, 32.41, 32.42a, 32.42b, 32.43a, 32.43b, 32.43c, 32.45a, 32.45b, 32.45c, 32.46, 32.47, 32.48a, 32.48b, 32.49a, 32.49b and 32.50

37   During reassembly, always use new snap-rings. Lubricate the components with engine oil before assembling them. **Note:** *If the thrust washers and snap-rings are examined closely it will be seen that they are chamfered on one side. During reassembly it is essential that each thrust washer and snap-ring is fitted so its chamfer is on the*

correct side. Also ensure the snap-ring ends are positioned in the shaft grooves **(see illustration)**.

38   Slide on the 2nd gear bushing and install the 2nd gear so that its

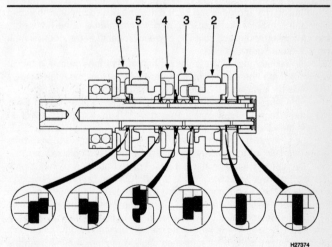

32.37 Correct fitted orientation of countershaft snap-rings and thrust washers

1	1st gear	4	3rd gear	
2	5th gear	5	6th gear	
3	4th gear	6	2nd gear	

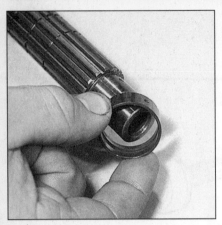
32.38a Fit the 2nd gear bushing . . .

32.38b . . . and install the 2nd gear so that its side on which the gear hub protrudes the most is facing the countershaft bearing

32.38c Slide on a splined thrust washer . . .

32.38d . . . and secure the 2nd gear components with the snap-ring

32.39 Slide on the 6th gear as shown making sure its oil holes are correctly aligned with the shaft oilways

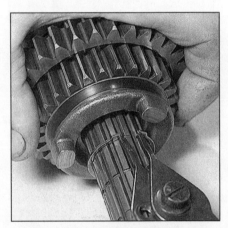
32.40 Fit a second snap-ring to the countershaft groove

side on which the gear hub protrudes the most is facing the countershaft bearing. Fit the splined thrust washer with its chamfered edge facing the 2nd gear and secure the 2nd gear components with a new snap-ring. Fit the snap-ring with its chamfered edge facing the thrust washer and make sure it is correctly located in the countershaft groove (see illustrations).

39   Fit the 6th gear to the shaft so that its shift fork groove is facing away from the 2nd gear. Align the gear oil holes with the shaft oilways and slide the gear onto the shaft (see illustration).

40   Fit a second new snap-ring with its chamfered edge facing away from the 6th gear. Ensure the snap-ring is correctly located in the shaft groove (see illustration).

41   On J models onward, slide on the splined thrust washer with its chamfered edge facing away from the snap-ring (see illustration).

42   On all models, align the 3rd gear splined bushing oil holes with the shaft oilways and slide it along the shaft. **Note:** *On G and H models make sure the bush flange is facing the 6th gear.* Fit the 3rd gear so that its dog holes are facing the 6th gear (see illustrations).

43   Slide the special splined washer along until it abuts the 3rd gear, followed by the lock washer. Rotate the splined washer until its cutouts align with the lock washer tabs then engage the lock washer with the splined washer to lock it in position (see illustrations).

44   On G and H models, fit the 4th gear so that its dog holes are facing away from the 3rd gear. Align the 4th gear splined bushing oil holes with the shaft oilways then slide it along the shaft and engage it with the gear.

45   On J models onward, align the 4th gear splined bushing oil holes

32.41 On J models onward, slide on a splined thrust washer

with the shaft oilways and slide it along the shaft. Fit the 4th gear so that its dog holes are facing away from the 3rd gear, then slide on the splined thrust washer with its chamfered edge facing the 4th gear (see illustrations).

46   On all models, secure the 3rd gear components in position with a new snap-ring. Fit the snap-ring with its chamfered edge facing the thrust washer and make sure it is correctly located in the countershaft groove (see illustration).

32.42a Fit the 3rd gear bushing, aligning its oil holes with the shaft oilways . . .

32.42b . . . and install the 3rd gear with its dog holes facing the 6th gear (J models onward shown)

32.43a Fit the special splined washer . . .

32.43b . . . and lock washer . . .

32.43c . . . engaging the lock washer tabs with the splined washer cutouts (arrows)

32.45a On J models onward, slide on the 4th gear bushing, aligning its oil holes with the shaft oilways . . .

32.45b . . . and fit the 4th gear with its dog holes facing away from the 3rd gear

32.45c Slide on a splined thrust washer . . .

32.46 . . . and secure it in position with another snap-ring

2

32.47 Fit the 5th gear as shown

32.48a Install the thrust washer . . .

32.48b . . . followed by the 1st gear needle
roller bearing . . .

32.49a . . . then fit the 1st gear so that its
side on which the gear hub protrudes the
most is facing away from the 5th gear

32.49b Slide on another thrust washer . . .

32.50 . . . and install the needle roller
bearing and end plate

47   Fit the 5th gear to the shaft so that its shift fork groove is facing
the 4th gear. Align the gear oil holes with the shaft oilways and slide
the gear on the shaft (see illustration).
48   Fit the thrust washer to the countershaft with its chamfered edge
facing away from the 5th gear, then install the 1st gear needle roller
bearing (see illustrations).
49   Liberally lubricate the bearing, then fit the 1st gear so that its side
on which the gear hub protrudes the most is facing away from the 5th
gear. Slide on the second thrust washer with its chamfered edge facing
the 1st gear (see illustrations).
50   Lubricate the needle roller bearing assembly and fit it to the end
of the countershaft (see illustration).

33 Initial start-up after overhaul

1   Make sure the engine oil and coolant levels are correct (see
Chapter 1), then remove the spark plugs from the engine. Place the
engine kill switch in the OFF position.
2   Turn on the ignition switch and crank the engine over with the
starter until the oil pressure indicator light goes off (which indicates
that oil pressure exists). Reinstall the spark plugs, connect the plug
wires (HT leads) and turn the kill switch to RUN.
3   Make sure there is fuel in the tank, then turn the fuel tap to the ON
position and operate the choke.
4   Start the engine and allow it to run at a moderately fast idle until it
reaches operating temperature. **Warning:** *If the oil pressure indicator
light doesn't go off, or it comes on while the engine is running, stop the
engine immediately.*
5   Check carefully for oil leaks and make sure the transmission and
controls, especially the brakes, function properly before road testing
the machine. Refer to Section 34 for the recommended break-in
procedure.

6   Upon completion of the road test, and after the engine has cooled
down completely, recheck the valve clearances and check the engine
oil and coolant levels (see Chapter 1).

34 Recommended break-in procedure

1   Any rebuilt engine needs time to break-in, even if parts have been
installed in their original locations. For this reason, treat the machine
gently for the first few miles to make sure oil has circulated throughout
the engine and any new parts installed have started to seat.
2   Even greater care is necessary if the engine has been rebored or a
new crankshaft has been installed. In the case of a rebore, the engine
will have to be broken in as if the machine were new. This means
greater use of the transmission and a restraining hand on the throttle
until at least 500 miles (800 km) have been covered. There's no point in
keeping to any set speed limit - the main idea is to keep from lugging
(laboring) the engine and to gradually increase performance until the
500 mile (800 km) mark is reached. These recommendations can be
lessened to an extent when only a new crankshaft is installed.
Experience is the best guide, since it's easy to tell when an engine is
running freely. The following recommendations, which Honda provide
for new motorcycles, can be used as a guide.
   a) *0 to 600 miles (0 to 1000 km): Keep engine speed below 5,000
       rpm. Vary the engine speed and don't use full throttle.*
   b) *600 to 1000 miles (1,000 to 1,600 km): Keep engine speed below
       7,000 rpm. Rev the engine freely through the gears, but don't use
       full throttle for prolonged periods.*
   c) *After 1000 miles (1,600 km): Full throttle can be used. Don't
       exceed maximum recommended engine speed (redline).*
3   If a lubrication failure is suspected, stop the engine immediately
and try to find the cause. If an engine is run without oil, even for a short
period of time, severe damage will occur.

Chapter 3   Cooling system

Note: *Refer to 'Identification numbers' at the beginning of this Manual to establish the model code of your motorcycle.*

Contents

Specifications

Coolant

Mixture type .... 50% distilled water, 50% corrosion-inhibited ethylene glycol antifreeze

Capacity
    Radiator and engine .... 2.30 liters (2.43 US qt, 4.0 Imp pt)
    Coolant reservoir .... 0.33 liters (0.35 US qt, 0.6 Imp pt)
    Total .... 2.63 liters (2.78 US qt, 4.6 Imp pt)

Radiator

Cap valve opening pressure .... 14 to 18 psi (0.95 to 1.25 Bars)

Thermostat

Opening temperature .... 80 to 84°C (176 to 183°F)
Fully open .... 95°C (203°F)
Minimum valve lift .... 8 mm (0.32 in) @ 95°C (203°F)

Torque settings

	Nm	Ft-lbs
Water pump and cover bolts	13	9
Coolant outlet union bolts	18	13
Cooling fan thermostatic switch*	18	13
Temperature gauge sender unit*	10	7

*Apply sealant to threads, leaving sensor tip clear of sealant.

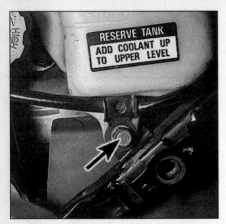

3.4a Unscrew the coolant reservoir mounting bolt (arrow) - G through K models

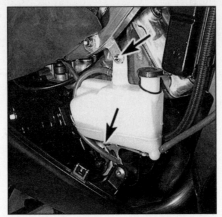

3.4b On L models onward the reservoir is secured by two bolts (arrows)

4.2 The cooling fan thermostatic switch is screwed into the left side of the radiator

1   General information

The cooling system uses a water/antifreeze coolant to carry away in the form of heat excess energy created by the engine. The cylinders are surrounded by a water jacket from which the heated coolant is circulated by thermo-siphonic action in conjunction with a water pump, driven off the oil pump. The hot coolant passes up to the thermostat and through to the radiator (mounted on the frame's front downtubes to take maximum advantage of the passing airflow); a thermostatically-controlled cooling fan is fitted to provide assistance in extreme conditions. The coolant then flows across the radiator core, where it is cooled by the passing air, down to the water pump and back up to the engine where the cycle is repeated. The thermostat is fitted in the system to prevent the coolant flowing through the radiator when the engine is cold, therefore accelerating the speed at which the engine reaches normal operating temperature.

The complete cooling system is partially sealed and pressurized, the pressure being controlled by a valve contained in the spring-loaded radiator cap. By pressurizing the coolant the boiling point is raised, preventing premature boiling in adverse conditions. The overflow pipe from the system is connected to a reservoir into which excess coolant is expelled under pressure. The discharged coolant automatically returns to the radiator when the engine cools.

Warning 1: *Do not allow antifreeze to come in contact with your skin or painted surfaces of the motorcycle. Rinse off any spills immediately with plenty of water. Antifreeze is highly toxic if ingested. Never leave antifreeze lying around in an open container or in puddles on the floor; children and pets are attracted by its sweet smell and may drink it. Check with the local authorities about disposing of used antifreeze. Many communities will have collection centers which will see that antifreeze is disposed of safely.*

Warning 2: *Do not remove the pressure cap from the radiator when the engine is hot. Scalding hot coolant and steam may be blown out under pressure, which could cause serious injury. To reach the pressure cap, remove the upper fairing right inner panel on G through K models; on L onwards models, move aside the fuse box (undoing its retaining screw and removing the fuse box access panel from the right side of the upper fairing, where necessary). See Chapter 8 if required. When the engine has cooled, place a thick rag, like a towel, over the radiator cap; slowly rotate the cap counterclockwise (anti-clockwise) to the first stop. This procedure allows any residual pressure to escape. When the steam has stopped escaping, press down on the cap while turning it counterclockwise (anti-clockwise) and remove it.*

2   Radiator pressure cap - check

If problems such as overheating or loss of coolant occur, check

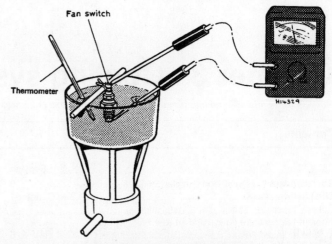

4.6 Fan switch testing set-up

the entire system as described in Chapter 1. The radiator cap opening pressure should be checked by a dealer service department or service station equipped with the special tester required to do the job. If the cap is defective, replace it with a new one.

3   Coolant reservoir - removal and installation

Removal

Refer to illustrations 3.4a and 3.4b

1   Drain the cooling system as described in Chapter 1.
2   On G through K models remove the left side cover. On L models onward remove the right middle fairing panel, then release the cable ties and withdraw the rubber sheet. See Chapter 8, if necessary.
3   Disconnect the two hoses from the top and bottom of the reservoir and allow any residual coolant to drain from the reservoir.
4   Unbolt the coolant reservoir and remove it from the machine. On G through K models, it may be necessary to unbolt and move aside components such as the fuel pump to permit the reservoir to be removed **(see illustrations)**.

Installation

5   Installation is the reverse of the removal sequence, noting that on G through K models the reservoir bolt retains a wire clamp. On completion refill the cooling system as described in Chapter 1.

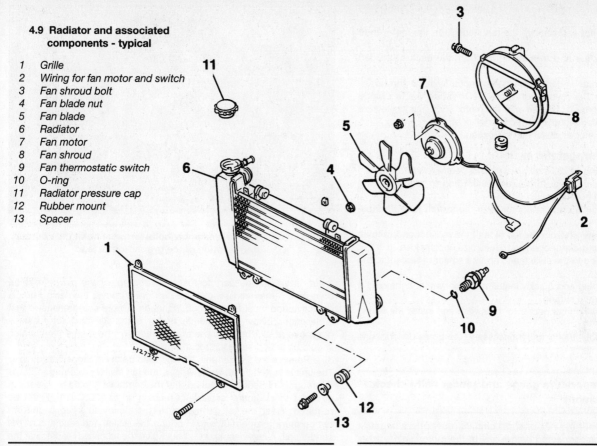

4.9 Radiator and associated components - typical

1   Grille
2   Wiring for fan motor and switch
3   Fan shroud bolt
4   Fan blade nut
5   Fan blade
6   Radiator
7   Fan motor
8   Fan shroud
9   Fan thermostatic switch
10 O-ring
11 Radiator pressure cap
12 Rubber mount
13 Spacer

4   Cooling fan and thermostatic switch - check and replacement

Warning: *To prevent the risk of short circuits, the battery negative cable should be disconnected before any of the motorcycle's other electrical components are disturbed. Don't forget to reconnect the cable securely once work is finished.*

Check

Refer to illustrations 4.2 and 4.6

1   If the engine is overheating and the cooling fan isn't coming on, first check the cooling fan switch fuse. If the fuse is blown, check the fan circuit for a short to ground/earth (see the wiring diagrams at the end of this book).

2   If the fuse is sound, remove the left lower (or middle, according to model) fairing panel as described in Chapter 8, then disconnect the wire from the fan switch which is fitted to the left side of the radiator **(see illustration)**. Turn the ignition switch ON and ground (earth) the fan switch wire - the fan should come on. If it does the fan switch is defective and must be replaced, although a more comprehensive test is described below in Steps 5 through 7.

3   If the fan does not come on the fault lies in either the cooling fan motor or relevant wiring. The wiring can be tested as described in Chapter 9.

4   To test the cooling fan motor, remove the upper fairing right inner panel and lower (or middle, according to model) fairing panel as described in Chapter 8. Depending on model, it may also be necessary to remove the fuel tank (see Chapter 4) to reach the fan motor wiring connector, mounted on the right side of the frame, just above the radiator pressure cap. Disconnect the connector and, using a 12 volt battery and two jumper wires, connect the battery across the terminals of the cooling fan block connector. Once connected the fan should operate. If this is not the case the fan motor is faulty and must be replaced.

5   To fully test the cooling fan switch, a heat-proof container (do not use a cooking pan for this test), a small gas-powered camping stove, a thermometer capable of reading up to 110°C (230°F) and an ohmmeter or multimeter will be required. Remove the switch as described in Steps 16 through 18.

6   Fill the container with coolant of the specified type and strength and suspend the switch on some wire so that just the sensing portion and threads are submerged. Connect one probe of the meter to the switch terminal and the other to the body of the switch. Suspend the thermometer so that its bulb is close to the switch **(see illustration)**. **Note:** *No components should be allowed to touch the container.*

7   Set the meter to the ohms x 1 scale and start to heat the coolant, stirring it gently, until the coolant is between 97 - 103°C (207 - 217°F). **Warning:** *This must be done very carefully to avoid the risk of personal injury. If it is found that the coolant temperature cannot be raised above 100°C (212°F), the switch must be heated in oil, which will require even greater care - for normal testing purposes a sufficiently accurate result can be deduced from noting the switch's performance when heated to 100°C (212°F) in coolant.* With the coolant at this temperature the meter should show a reading of 0 ohms indicating that the switch has closed. Carry on heating the coolant until it reaches 103°C (217°F) then turn the stove off. Note the resistance reading of the switch as the temperature falls. When the coolant cools to 92°C (198°F) there should no longer be continuity between the meter probes. If this is not the case the fan switch is defective and must be replaced.

Replacement

Fan motor

Refer to illustrations 4.9, 4.10 and 4.11

8   Remove the radiator as described in Section 7.

9   Disconnect the wiring connector from the fan switch **(see illustration)**.

10 Unscrew the bolt(s) and nuts (according to model) from the top and bottom of the radiator. Separate the fan assembly from the

3

radiator noting the correct position of the fan motor ground/earth lead **(see illustration)**.

11   Unscrew the nut and remove the fan blade from the motor **(see illustration)**.

12   Release the clips and free the wiring from the back of the fan motor shroud.

13   Unscrew the nuts and separate the fan motor from the shroud.

14   Installation is the reverse of removal. On fitting the fan blade ensure its slot is correctly aligned with the motor shaft and make sure the motor ground/earth lead is correctly positioned.

15   Install the radiator as described in Section 7.

Cooling fan thermostatic switch

Warning: *The engine must be completely cool before this procedure.*

16   Remove the left lower (or middle, according to model) fairing panel as described in Chapter 8.

17   Disconnect the wiring connector from the switch **(see illustration 4.2)**.

18   Unscrew the switch from the left side of the radiator and recover the O-ring. Plug the radiator opening to minimize coolant loss.

19   Fit a new O-ring to the switch and apply a smear of sealant to the switch threads.

20   Remove the plug and quickly install the new switch, tightening it to the specified torque setting.

21   Connect the wiring connector to the switch and install the fairing panel.

22   Check the coolant level and if necessary, top up as described in Chapter 1.

5   Coolant temperature gauge and sender unit - check and replacement

Warning: *To prevent the risk of short circuits, the battery negative cable should be disconnected before any of the motorcycle's other electrical components are disturbed. Don't forget to reconnect the cable securely once work is finished.*

Check

Refer to illustration 5.2

1   The circuit consists of the sender unit screwed into the thermostat housing and the gauge assembly mounted in the instrument panel. If the system malfunctions check first that the battery is fully charged and that all fuses are in good condition.

2   To test the circuit, first remove the right lower (or middle, according to model) fairing panel, as described in Chapter 8, to reach the sender unit wiring connector **(see illustration)**. Turn the ignition switch ON and disconnect the wire from the sender unit. Ground (earth) the sender unit wire - the needle should swing immediately over to the 'H' on the gauge. **Caution:** *Do not ground (earth) the wire for any*

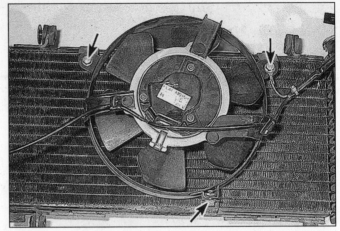

4.10 Unscrew the fan assembly bolts (arrows) noting the correct fitted position of the ground/earth lead

longer than is necessary to take the reading, or the gauge may be damaged. If the needle moves as described above, the sender unit is defective and must be replaced, although a more comprehensive test is described below. If the needle movement is still faulty, or if it does not move at all, the fault lies in the wiring or the gauge itself which should be tested as described in Step 4.

3   Remove the sender unit as described below in Steps 5 through 7. The unit is tested in the same way as the fan switch, referring to Steps 5 through 7 of Section 4, noting that the container should be filled with oil and a thermometer capable of reading up to 120°C (248°F) will be required. Heat the oil gently, stirring it slowly to keep a uniform temperature throughout, whilst noting the resistance readings of the sender unit. A serviceable unit should give the following readings at the specified temperatures:

Temperature	85°C (185°F)	120°C (248°F)
Resistance	39 to 49 ohms	14 to 18 ohms

If the sender unit does not produce the specified resistances at the stated temperatures it must be replaced.

4   If the gauge appears to be faulty, remove the instrument cluster as described in Chapter 9, and check the relevant wiring connectors. If all appears to be well, the gauge is defective and must be replaced.

Replacement

Temperature sender unit

Warning: *The engine must be completely cool before this procedure.*

5   Remove the right lower (or middle, according to model) fairing panel, as described in Chapter 8, to reach the unit. Depending on

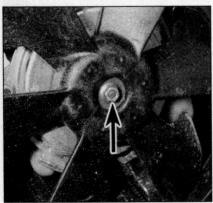

4.11 Fan blade is retained by a nut (arrow)

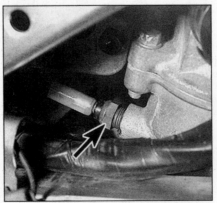

5.2 Temperature gauge sender unit (arrow) is screwed into thermostat housing - at the front, or at the rear (as shown)

6.4 Unbolt the thermostat housing cover support bracket from cylinder head - L models onward

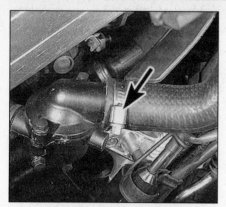

6.5 Slacken the clip (arrow) and disconnect the coolant hose from the thermostat housing

6.6a Unscrew the two bolts . . .

6.6b . . . then withdraw the cover and lift out the thermostat

model, it may also be necessary to improve access by removing the fuel tank (see Chapter 4).

6   Disconnect the wiring connector from the unit **(see illustration 5.2)**.

7   Unscrew the unit and plug the opening to minimize coolant loss.

8   Apply a smear of sealant to the switch threads.

9   Remove the plug and quickly install the new unit, tightening it to the specified torque setting.

10   Connect the wiring to the unit. Install the fuel tank as described in Chapter 4 and the fairing panel as described in Chapter 8.

11   Check the coolant level and, if necessary, top up as described in Chapter 1.

Temperature gauge

12   See Chapter 9.

6   Thermostat - removal, check and installation

Removal

Refer to illustrations 6.4, 6.5, 6.6a and 6.6b

1   The thermostat is automatic in operation and should give many years service without requiring attention. In the event of a failure, the valve will probably jam open, in which case the engine will take much longer than normal to warm up. Conversely, if the valve jams shut, the coolant will be unable to circulate and the engine will overheat. Neither condition is acceptable, and the fault must be investigated promptly.

2   Drain the cooling system as described in Chapter 1.

3   On G through K models (if not already done), remove the right lower (or middle, according to model) fairing panel, as described in Chapter 8, to reach the thermostat. Depending on the model, it may also be necessary to improve access to the cover bolts by removing the fuel tank (see Chapter 4).

4   On L models onward, remove the fuel tank and the carburetors as described in Chapter 4. Depending on the model, it may also be necessary to improve access to the thermostat by removing the right middle fairing panel (see Chapter 8 if necessary). Unbolt the thermostat housing cover support bracket from the cylinder head **(see illustration)**.

5   On all models, slacken the clip and disconnect the coolant hose from the thermostat housing cover **(see illustration)**.

6   Unscrew the two bolts and remove the thermostat housing cover. Recover the sealing O-ring **(see illustrations)**.

7   Remove the thermostat from the housing, noting the alignment of its small bypass hole.

Check

Refer to illustration 6.9

8   Examine the thermostat visually before carrying out the test. If it remains in the open position at room temperature, it should be replaced.

9   Suspend the thermostat by a piece of wire in a container of cold water. Place a thermometer in the water so that its bulb is close to the thermostat. Heat the water, noting when the thermostat opens and how much valve lift it has when it is fully open, and compare the results with those given in the Specifications **(see illustration)**. If the readings obtained differ from those given, the thermostat is faulty and must be replaced.

10   In the event of thermostat failure, as an emergency measure only, it can be removed and the machine used without it. **Note:** *Take care when starting the engine from cold as it will take much longer than usual to warm up. Ensure that a new unit is installed as soon as possible.*

Installation

Refer to illustrations 6.11 and 6.12

11   Fit a new O-ring to the housing groove **(see illustration)**.

12   Fit the thermostat so that its small bypass hole is positioned as

3

THERMOMETER

THERMOSTAT

6.9 Testing the thermostat

6.11 Always install a new sealing O-ring whenever the thermostat housing cover is disturbed

6.12 When installing the thermostat make sure that its bypass hole (arrow) is aligned as detailed in the text - L models onward shown

7.4a Slacken the clips and disconnect the top hose and reservoir hose (arrow) from the filler neck . . .

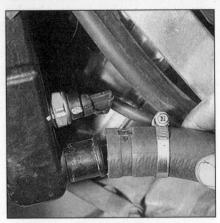

7.4b . . . and the bottom hose from the radiator

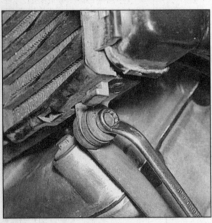

7.8a Unscrew the radiator mounting bolts . . .

7.8b . . . and recover the spacer from each mounting

7.8c On L models onward, move the radiator to the right to disengage it from its right upper locating peg . . .

noted on removal. On G through K models, this is next to the rear cover bolt location, while on L models onward, the bypass hole should be at the front **(see illustration)**.

13 Install the housing cover and securely tighten the cover bolts. Install the support bracket (L models onward) to the thermostat cover and cylinder head, tightening the bolts securely.

14 Reconnect the coolant hose and tighten its clip securely.

15 Refill the cooling system as described in Chapter 1.

16 If removed, install the carburetors and fuel tank as described in Chapter 4, and all disturbed fairing sections as described in Chapter 8.

7 Radiator - removal and installation

Warning: *To prevent the risk of short circuits, the battery negative cable should be disconnected before any of the motorcycle's other electrical components are disturbed. Don't forget to reconnect the cable securely once work is finished.*

Removal

Refer to illustrations 7.4a, 7.4b and 7.8a through 7.8d

1 Remove both lower (or middle, according to model) fairing panels as described in Chapter 8. On G through K models, remove also the seat and the left side cover (see Chapter 8) and the fuel tank (see Chapter 4).

2 To reach the pressure cap, remove the upper fairing right inner panel on G through K models; on L models onward, move aside the

fuse box (undoing its retaining screw and removing the fuse box access panel from the right side of the upper fairing, where necessary).

3 Drain the cooling system as described in Chapter 1.

4 Slacken the clips and disconnect the top and bottom hoses from the radiator **(see illustrations)**.

5 Release the clip and disconnect the coolant reservoir hose from the radiator filler neck **(see illustration 7.4a)**.

6 Free the fan motor wiring connector from the top of the frame and disconnect the connector.

7 On G through K models, unscrew the four radiator mounting bolts and recover the spacer from each mounting. Carefully remove the radiator, taking great care not to damage the radiator fins.

8 On L models onward, unscrew the two radiator mounting bolts and recover the spacer from each mounting **(see illustrations)**. Move the radiator to the right to disengage it from its right upper locating peg, then carefully remove the radiator, taking great care not to damage the radiator fins **(see illustrations)**.

9 On all models, check the radiator mounting dampers for signs of damage or deterioration and replace if necessary.

Installation

10 Installation is the reverse of the removal sequence noting the following.

a) Locate the radiator on its mounting peg (L models onward), fit the spacer to each mounting rubber and securely tighten the mounting bolts.

b) Make sure that the fan wiring is correctly routed, is in no danger of being caught by the fan and is retained by any relevant clips.

7.8d . . . then remove the radiator assembly

8.6a Note routing of wiring lead and location of clip when unscrewing water pump and pump cover bolts (arrows)

8.6b Note cover locating dowels (arrows) - discard cover O-ring

8.7 Slacken both clips to disconnect coolant hose from water pump body

8.10 Install and lubricate new O-ring (A), then align water pump shaft slot (B) with oil pump shaft projection (C) when installing water pump

3

c) Ensure the coolant hoses are securely retained by their clips and that the reservoir hose in particular is routed correctly, is not trapped and that it is clear of kinks.
d) On completion refill the cooling system as described in Chapter 1.

8 Water pump - check, removal and installation

Check

1   Remove the (left side) lower fairing panel as described in Chapter 8. Wash thoroughly the whole area around the water pump, the gearbox sprocket and the engine unit's underside to be sure of determining exactly the source of any oil or coolant leakage. Visually check the area around the water pump for signs of leakage.
2   To prevent leakage of water or oil from the cooling system to the lubrication system and vice versa, two seals are fitted on the pump shaft. On the underside of the pump body there is also a drainage hole. If either seal fails this hole should allow the coolant or oil to escape and prevent the oil and coolant mixing.
3   The seal on the water pump side is of the mechanical type which bears on the rear face of the impeller. The second seal, which is mounted behind the mechanical seal is of the normal feathered lip type; neither seal is available as a separate item as the pump is a sealed unit. Therefore, if on inspection the drainage hole shows signs of leakage, the pump must be removed and replaced.

Removal

Refer to illustrations 8.6a, 8.6b and 8.7

4   If not already done, remove the (left side) lower fairing panel as described in Chapter 8.
5   Drain the cooling system as described in Chapter 1.
6   Unscrew the four pump and pump cover mounting bolts (noting the routing of the wiring lead and the location of its clip) and withdraw the pump cover; the radiator bottom hose need not be disconnected unless required **(see illustration)**. Recover the O-ring from the water pump cover. Note the cover's two locating dowels in the pump body mating surface; if these are loose, they should be removed and kept with the cover to prevent their loss **(see illustration)**.
7   Slacken both clips and disconnect the coolant hose from the water pump body **(see illustration)**.
8   Withdraw the water pump from the engine unit. Recover the O-ring from the pump body.
9   Wiggle the water pump impeller back-and-forth and in-and-out. If there is excessive movement the pump must be replaced.

Installation

Refer to illustrations 8.10, 8.11 and 8.13

10   Fit a new O-ring to the rear of the pump body, smear it with clean engine oil and install the pump, aligning the slot in the pump shaft with the projection on the oil pump shaft **(see illustration)**.
11   Ensure the two locating dowels are inserted in their locations. Fit

a new sealing O-ring (using grease to stick it in place) and install the cover to the pump body **(see illustration)**.

12   Install the cover/pump bolts, ensuring that the wiring lead is correctly routed and its clip is correctly installed. Tighten the bolts securely and evenly to the specified torque wrench setting.

13   Reconnect the coolant hoses to the pump and cover, making sure each one is securely retained by its clip(s) **(see illustration)**.

14   Refill the cooling system as described in Chapter 1.

---

9   Coolant hoses - removal and installation

Note: *This Section describes removal and installation of the cooling system flexible hoses; for details of the metal coolant pipe and coolant outlet unions on the crankcase top surface, refer to Chapter 2, Sections 5 and 10 respectively.*

Removal

1   Before removing a hose, drain the coolant as described in Chapter 1.

2   Use a screwdriver to slacken the hose clamps, then slide them back along the hose and clear of the union spigot.

3   **Caution:** *The radiator unions are fragile. Do not use excessive force when attempting to remove the hoses.* If a hose proves stubborn, release it by rotating it on its union before working it off. If all else fails, cut the hose with a sharp knife then slit it at each union so that it can be peeled off in two pieces. Whilst this is expensive it is preferable to buying a new radiator.

Installation

4   Slide the clips onto the hose and then work it on to its respective union. **Note:** *Do not use a lubricant of any kind. If necessary the hose can be softened by soaking it in very hot water before installing, although care is obviously necessary to prevent the risk of personal injury whilst doing this.*

5   Rotate the hose on its unions to settle it in position before sliding the clips into place and tightening them securely.

8.11 Fit a new sealing ring to the pump cover

8.13 Ensure coolant hose clips are securely fastened on installation

Chapter 4 Fuel and exhaust systems

Note: *Refer to 'Identification numbers' at the beginning of this Manual to establish the model code of your motorcycle.*

Contents

Specifications

Fuel grade ... Unleaded or leaded (according to local regulations), minimum 91 octane (Research method)

Fuel tank capacity

G to K models ... 20 lit (5.3 US gal, 4.4 Imp gal)
L to P models ... 19 lit (5.0 US gal, 4.2 Imp gal)
R models ... 21 lit (5.5 US gal, 4.6 Imp gal)

Carburetor

Identification code
  G and H models
    California models ... VDBCA (700 F, FII) or VDBBA (750)
    US models (except California) ... VDBAB (700 F, FII) or VDBAA (750)
    UK models ... VDBOB
  J and K models ... VDJOA
  L and M models
    California models ... VDJCA
    US models (except California) ... VDJBA
    UK models ... VDJ4A
  N and P models
    California models ... VDJKA
    US models (except California) ... VDJJA
    UK models ... VDJ6A
  R models
    California models ... VP33A
    US models (except California) ... VP34A
    UK models ... VP35A

Jet sizes

G and H models
  Main jet 118
  Slow jet .... N/A
J and K models
  Main jet .... 125 (front) 122 (rear)
L to P models
  Main jet 130
  Slow jet
    California models 38
    All other models 40
R models
  Main jet
    California models .... 128 (front) 125 (rear)
    US models (except California) 125
    UK models 130
  Slow jet 40

Note: *Where jet sizes are not quoted, refer to your Honda dealer*

Carburetor adjustments

Float height
  G models
    US models .... 9.0 mm (0.36 in)
    UK models .... 7.0 mm (0.28 in)
  H models .... 7.0 mm (0.28 in)
  K models onward .... 9.0 mm (0.36 in)
Pilot screw - initial setting (turns out)
  G and H models 2 1/2
  J and K models 2 3/8
  L and M models
    California models 2 1/2
    US models (except California) 1 1/2
    UK models 2 1/4
  N and P models
    California models 2
    US models (except California) 1 7/8
    UK models 1 7/8
  R models
    California models 2 3/8
    US models (except California) 1 5/8
    UK models 1 3/8
Idle speed .... See Chapter 1

---

1 General information and precautions

General information

The fuel system consists of the fuel tank, the fuel tap and filter, the fuel pump, the carburetors and the connecting lines, hoses and control cables.

Various types of carburetors have been used on this motorcycle since its introduction, all of which are of the CV type. For cold starting, an enrichment circuit is actuated by a cable and the choke lever on the left handlebar.

Air is drawn to the carburetors from a molded plastic air filter housing containing a pleated paper type element.

The exhaust system design varies depending on the model. On G through K models a 4-into-2 system is fitted, and on all L models onward the exhaust system is of the 4-into-1 type.

Many of the fuel system service procedures are considered routine maintenance items and for that reason are included in Chapter 1.

Precautions

Warning: *Gasoline (petrol) is extremely flammable, so take extra precautions when you work on any part of the fuel system. Don't smoke or allow open flames or bare light bulbs near the work area, and don't work in a garage where a natural gas-type appliance (such as a water heater or clothes dryer) is present. If you spill any fuel on your skin, rinse it off immediately with soap and water. When you perform any kind of work on the fuel system, wear safety glasses and have a fire extinguisher suitable for a class B type fire (flammable liquids) on hand.*

Always perform service procedures in a well-ventilated area to prevent a build-up of fumes.

Never work in a building containing a gas appliance with a pilot light, or any other form of naked flame. Ensure that there are no naked light bulbs or any sources of flame or sparks nearby.

Do not smoke (or allow anyone else to smoke) while in the vicinity of gasoline (petrol) or of components containing it. Remember the possible presence of vapor from these sources and move well clear before smoking.

Check all electrical equipment belonging to the house, garage or

2.11 On UK L through P models ensure the triangular mark (arrowed) on the fuel tap valve is pointing towards the front of the bike

2.12a Slacken and remove the nut . . .

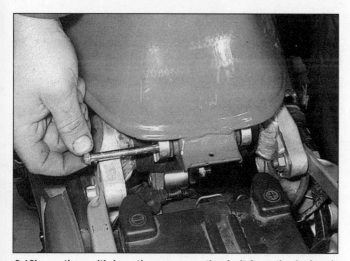

2.12b . . . then withdraw the rear mounting bolt from the fuel tank

workshop where work is being undertaken (see the Safety first! section of this manual). Remember that certain electrical appliances such as drills, cutters etc. create sparks in the normal course of operation and must not be used near gasoline (petrol) or any component containing it. Again, remember the possible presence of fumes before using electrical equipment.

Always mop up any spilt fuel and safely dispose of the shop towel or rag used.

Any stored fuel that is drained off during servicing work, must be kept in sealed containers that are suitable for holding gasoline (petrol), and clearly marked as such; the containers themselves should be kept in a safe place. Note that this last point applies equally to the fuel tank, if it is removed from the machine; also remember to keep its cap closed at all times.

Note that the fuel system consists of the fuel tank, with its cap and related vent hoses, the fuel pump and filters. On US California models, this includes the Evaporative Emission Control (EVAP) System components.

Read the Safety first! section of this manual carefully before starting work.

Owners of machines used in the US, particularly California, should note that their machines must comply at all times with Federal or state legislation governing the permissible levels of noise and of pollutants such as unburned hydrocarbons, carbon monoxide etc. that can be emitted by those machines. All vehicles offered for sale must comply with legislation in force at the date of manufacture and must not subsequently be altered in any way which will affect their emission of noise or of pollutants.

In practice, this means that adjustments may not be made to any part of the fuel, ignition or exhaust systems by anyone who is not authorized or mechanically qualified to do so, or who does not have the tools, equipment and data necessary to properly carry out the task. Also if any part of these systems is to be replaced it must be replaced with only genuine Honda components or by components which are approved under the relevant legislation. The machine must never be used with any part of these systems removed, modified or damaged.

2 Fuel tank - removal and installation

Warning: *Refer to the precautions given in Section 1 before starting work*

Removal

1   Set the bike on its centerstand (where fitted) or sidestand.
2   Remove the seat as described in Chapter 8.

G through K models

3   Remove the left and right side covers (see Chapter 8, if necessary).
4   Unscrew the fuel tank rear mounting bolt and washer and remove the spacer from the center of the tank rubber mount.
5   Unscrew the fuel tank front mounting nut and remove its washer.
6   Disconnect the fuel gauge sender unit wiring connector at the connector situated at the rear of the fuel tank.
7   Ensure the fuel tap is turned OFF.
8   Lift up the rear of the fuel tank and disconnect the fuel hose and the various breather and drain hoses from the underside of the tank. Note the correct fitted position of each hose as it is disconnected.
9   Lift the fuel tank away from the machine taking care not to lose the rubber mount from each side of the tank. Recover the spacer from the front mount.
10   Inspect the tank mounts for signs of damage or deterioration and replace if necessary.

L through P models

Refer to illustrations 2.11, 2.12a, 2.12b, 2.13a, 2.13b, 2.13c, 2.14, 2.15 and 2.16

11   Ensure the fuel valve is turned to OFF. On UK models, with the valve set to the off position, the triangular mark on the fuel tap valve operating cam should be pointing forwards **(see illustration)**.
12   Slacken and remove the mounting nut and bolt from the rear of the fuel tank. If the spacer and rubber mounts are loose, remove them for safe-keeping **(see illustrations)**.

4

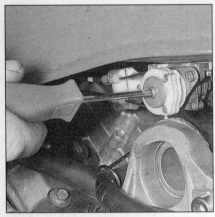

2.13a On UK L through P models, undo the screw and remove the collar . . .

2.13b . . . then unscrew the two screws (arrowed) . . .

2.13c . . . and free the bracket and operating cam assembly from the fuel tap

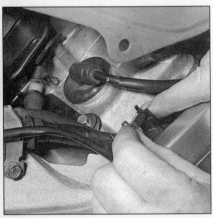

2.14 Trace the wiring back from the tank and disconnect the fuel gauge sender unit wiring connector

2.15 Release the retaining clip and disconnect the fuel hose from the tank

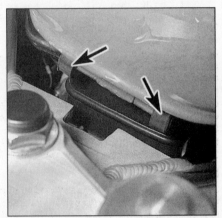

2.16 Release the front of the tank from the frame and recover the rubber mounts (arrowed)

13   On UK models, lift up the fuel tank then slacken and remove the screw and collar securing the operating cam to the fuel tap. Undo the screws securing the cable mounting bracket to the fuel tap and free the bracket and operating cam from the tap (see illustrations). It is not necessary to disconnect the cables.

14   On all models, disconnect the fuel gauge sender unit wiring connector situated at the rear of the fuel tank (see illustration).

15   Lift up the rear of the fuel tank and disconnect the fuel hose and the various breather and drain hoses from its underside. Note the correct fitted position of each hose as it is disconnected (see illustration).

16   Unhook the tank from its front retaining hook and lift the fuel tank away from the machine. Take care not to lose the rubber mounts from each side of the tank (see illustration).

17   Inspect the rubber tank mounts for signs of damage or deterioration and replace if necessary.

R models

Refer to illustration 2.22

18   Remove the side cover/tail cowl assembly as described in Chapter 8.

19   Disconnect the fuel gauge sender unit wiring connector at the connector situated at the rear of the fuel tank, on the right side.

20   Slacken and remove the mounting nut and bolt from the rear of the fuel tank. If the spacer and rubber mounts are loose, remove them for safe-keeping.

21   Ensure the fuel tap is turned OFF.

22   Lift up the rear of the fuel tank and disconnect the fuel hose and the various breather and drain hoses from the underside of the tank. Note the correct fitted position of each hose as it is disconnected (see illustration).

23   Unhook the tank from its front retaining hook and lift the fuel tank away from the machine. Take care not to lose the rubber mount from each side of the tank.

24   Inspect the tank mounts for signs of damage or deterioration and replace if necessary.

Installation

G through K models

25   Fit the spacer to the front rubber mount and lower the fuel tank into position, making sure the rubber mounts remain in position.

26   Reconnect the breather and drain hoses to the rear of the tank.

27   Connect the fuel hoses to the fuel tap, ensuring it is securely retained by their clips.

28   Ensure the wiring is correctly routed and reconnect the fuel gauge sender unit wiring.

29   Install the front mounting nut and washer and tighten securely.

30   Fit the spacer to the rear rubber mount then fit the washer and mounting bolt and tighten it securely.

31   Start the engine and check for leaks then install the side covers and seat.

L through P models

Refer to illustration 2.36

32   Lower the fuel tank into position, making sure the rubber mounts remain in position. Engage the front of the tank with the frame.

33   Reconnect the breather and drain hoses to the rear of the tank.

34   Connect the fuel hose to the fuel tap, ensuring it is securely retained by the clip.

2.22 Fuel tap and fuel tank breather and drain hoses - R models

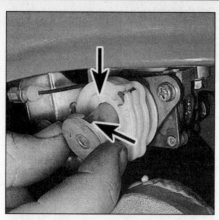

2.36 On UK L through P models, ensure the tap collar cutout is correctly aligned with the cam lug (arrows)

6.2 Release the retaining clip and disconnect the fuel hose from the carburetors

35   Ensure the wiring is correctly routed and reconnect the fuel gauge sender unit wiring.
36   On UK models, fit the cable mounting bracket to the tap and securely tighten its screws. Align the operating cam lug with the cutout and engage it with the fuel tap. Apply a smear of multi-purpose grease to the operating cam collar and install the collar, aligning its cutout with the cam lug, and securely tightening the retaining screw (see illustration). Check the operation of the fuel tap and if necessary adjust.
37   On all models, ensure the rubbers and spacer are correctly fitted, then install the rear mounting bolt and tighten it securely.
38   Start the engine and check for leaks then install the seat.

R models
39   Carry out the operations described in Steps 32 to 35.
40   Ensure the rubbers and spacer are correctly fitted, then install the rear mounting bolt and tighten it securely.
41   Start the engine and check for leaks then install the side cover/tail cowl assembly as described in Chapter 8.

3   Fuel tank - cleaning and repair

1   All repairs to the fuel tank should be carried out by a professional who has experience in this critical and potentially dangerous work. Even after cleaning and flushing of the fuel system, explosive fumes can remain and ignite during repair of the tank.
2   If the fuel tank is removed from the vehicle, it should not be placed in an area where sparks or open flames could ignite the fumes coming out of the tank. Be especially careful inside garages where a natural gas-type appliance is located, because the pilot light could cause an explosion.

4   Idle fuel/air mixture adjustment - general information

1   Due to the increased emphasis on controlling motorcycle exhaust emissions, certain governmental regulations have been formulated which directly affect the carburation of this machine. In order to comply with the regulations, the carburetors on some models have a plastic limiter cap stuck onto the end of the pilot screw (which controls the idle fuel/air mixture) on each carburetor, so they can't be tampered with. These should only be removed in the event of a complete carburetor overhaul, and even then the screws should be returned to their original settings. The pilot screws on other models are accessible, but the use of an exhaust gas analyzer is the only accurate way to adjust the idle fuel/air mixture and be sure the machine doesn't exceed the emissions regulations. Note: On US R models a special wrench is needed to turn the pilot screw. See your Honda dealer for details.
2   If the engine runs extremely rough at idle or continually stalls, and if a carburetor overhaul does not cure the problem, take the

motorcycle to a Honda dealer service department or other repair shop equipped with an exhaust gas analyzer. They will be able to properly adjust the idle fuel/air mixture to achieve a smooth idle and restore low speed performance.

5   Carburetor overhaul - general information

1   Poor engine performance, hesitation, hard starting, stalling, flooding and backfiring are all signs that major carburetor maintenance may be required.
2   Keep in mind that many so-called carburetor problems are really not carburetor problems at all, but mechanical problems within the engine or ignition system malfunctions. Try to establish for certain that the carburetors are in need of maintenance before beginning a major overhaul.
3   Check the fuel filter, the fuel pump, the fuel lines, the tank cap vent (except California models), the intake manifold hose clamps, the vacuum hoses, the air filter element, the cylinder compression, the spark plugs and carburetor synchronization before assuming that a carburetor overhaul is required.
4   Most carburetor problems are caused by dirt particles, varnish and other deposits which build up in and block the fuel and air passages. Also, in time, gaskets and O-rings shrink or deteriorate and cause fuel and air leaks which lead to poor performance.
5   When the carburetor is overhauled, it is generally disassembled completely and the parts are cleaned thoroughly with a carburetor cleaning solvent and dried with filtered, unlubricated compressed air. The fuel and air passages are also blown through with compressed air to force out any dirt that may have been loosened but not removed by the solvent. Once the cleaning process is complete, the carburetor is reassembled using new gaskets and O-rings.
6   Before disassembling the carburetors, make sure you have a carburetor rebuild kit (which will include all necessary O-rings and other parts), some carburetor cleaner, a supply of rags, some means of blowing out the carburetor passages and a clean place to work. It is recommended that only one carburetor be overhauled at a time to avoid mixing up parts.

6   Carburetors - removal and installation

Warning: Refer to the precautions given in Section 1 before starting work

Removal
Refer to illustrations 6.2, 6.3, 6.4, 6.6, 6.7a, 6.7b and 6.7c
1   Remove the air filter housing as described in Section 12.
2   Release the retaining clip and disconnect the fuel hose from the carburetors (see illustration). On California models, disconnect the

6.3 Slacken the clip securing the intake joint to each carburetor

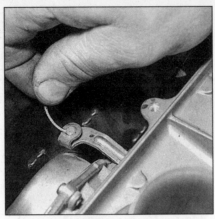

6.4 Loosen the retaining clamp and detach the choke cable from the carburetor linkage

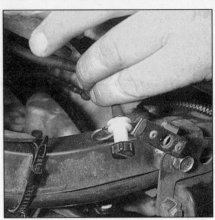

6.6 Where necessary, release the idle speed adjusting screw from the frame

6.7a Removing the carburetors from the motorcycle

6.7b If necessary, release the retaining clips . . .

6.7c . . . and remove the carburetor heatshield from the top of the engine

relevant emission (EVAP) system hoses from the carburetors noting the correct fitted position of each hose.

3   Slacken the four retaining clips securing the carburetor intake joints to the carburetors **(see illustration)**. To improve access to the clip screws remove the middle or lower fairing panels (as applicable) as described in Chapter 8.

4   Slacken the choke outer cable clamp screw and detach the inner cable from the carburetor lever **(see illustration)**.

5   Slacken the throttle cable locknuts then free each outer cable from its mounting bracket.

6   Where necessary, free the idle speed adjusting screw from its mounting bracket on the frame **(see illustration)**.

7   Ease the carburetors away from the cylinder head, then detach the inner cables from the throttle cam and remove the carburetors from the motorcycle. **Note:** *Keep the carburetors upright to prevent fuel spillage from the float chambers and the possibility of the piston diaphragms being damaged.* If necessary, release the retaining clips and remove the carburetor heatshield from the top of the engine **(see illustrations)**.

8   With the carburetors removed, place a suitable container below the carburetor float chambers then slacken the drain screws and drain all the fuel from the carburetors. Once all the fuel has been drained, tighten all the drain screws securely.

Installation

9   Installation is the reverse of removal making sure the carburetors are fully engaged with the intake joints and their retaining clips are securely tightened. Prior to installing the air filter housing, adjust the throttle and choke cables as described in Chapter 1.

10   Due to the nature of the fuel system (fuel only flows when the starter button is pressed), it will take some time for the carburetors to refill with fuel and for the engine to start. During this period do not operate the starter motor continuously. Operate the motor in short bursts (approximately 5 seconds), allowing time for it to cool down in between bursts. With the engine running, check thoroughly for fuel leaks before riding the machine on the road.

7   Carburetors - disassembly, cleaning and inspection

Warning: *Refer to the precautions given in Section 1 before proceeding*

Disassembly

1   Remove the carburetors from the machine as described in the previous Section. **Note:** *Do not separate the carburetors unless absolutely necessary; each carburetor can be dismantled sufficiently for all normal cleaning and adjustments while in place on the mounting brackets. Dismantle the carburetors separately to avoid interchanging parts.* Note that it is necessary to separate the carburetors to remove the choke plungers from Nos. 2 and 3 carburetors.

G through K models

Refer to illustrations 7.2a, 7.2b, 7.3, 7.5a, 7.5b, 7.6a, 7.6b, 7.7, 7.8, 7.9, 7.10 and 7.12

2   Slacken and remove the top cover retaining screws. Lift off the cover and remove the spring from inside the piston **(see illustrations)**.

7.2a Undo the retaining screws . . .

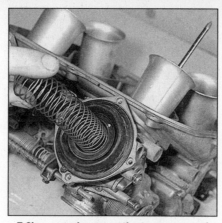

7.2b . . . and remove the top cover and spring from the carburetor

7.3 Carefully withdraw the diaphragm and piston assembly

7.5a Undo the retaining screws . . .

7.5b . . . then lift off the float chamber and recover its rubber seal

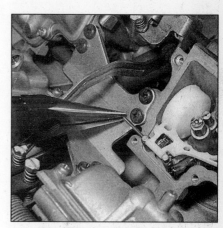

7.6a Withdraw the pivot pin . . .

7.6b . . . and remove the float and needle valve assembly

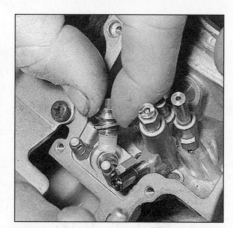

7.7 Unscrew the needle valve seat and remove it along with its sealing washer and filter

7.8 Unscrew the main jet from the base of the needle jet . . .

4

3   Carefully peel the diaphragm away from its sealing groove in the carburetor and withdraw the diaphragm and piston assembly **(see illustration)**. **Caution:** *Do not use a sharp instrument to displace the diaphragm as it is easily damaged.*

4   To remove the needle from the piston, using an 8 mm socket, push down on the needle holder and turn it 90° counterclockwise (anti-clockwise). Pull the needle holder out of the piston and recover the spring. Tip the needle and sealing washer out of the piston.

5   Remove the retaining screws and remove the float chamber from the base of the carburetor. Recover the rubber seal **(see illustrations)**.

6   Withdraw the float pivot pin, using a pair of pointed-nose pliers, and remove the float and needle valve assembly **(see illustrations)**.

7   Unscrew the needle valve seat from the carburetor and remove it along with its sealing washer and filter **(see illustration)**.

8   Unscrew the main jet from the base of the needle jet **(see illustration)**.

7.9 . . . then unscrew the needle jet from the carburetor

7.10 Unscrew the slow jet; do not attempt to remove the starter jet (arrow)

7.12 Remove the pilot screw along with its O-ring, washer and spring

7.14 Exploded view of a carburetor - L through P models; inset shows spring holder tangs which must be aligned with the piston slots

1   Top cover screws
2   Top cover
3   Spring
4   Diaphragm and piston assembly
5   Needle holder
6   Spring
7   Spring holder
8   Needle
9   Sealing washer
10   Float chamber screw
11   Float pivot pin
12   Float
13   Needle valve
14   Needle valve seat
15   Sealing washer
16   Filter
17   Main jet
18   Needle jet
19   Slow jet
20   Choke plunger nut
21   Spring
22   Choke plunger
23   Pilot screw
24   Spring
25   Washer
26   O-ring
27   Air cut-off valve cover
28   Spring
29   O-ring
30   Air cut-off valve

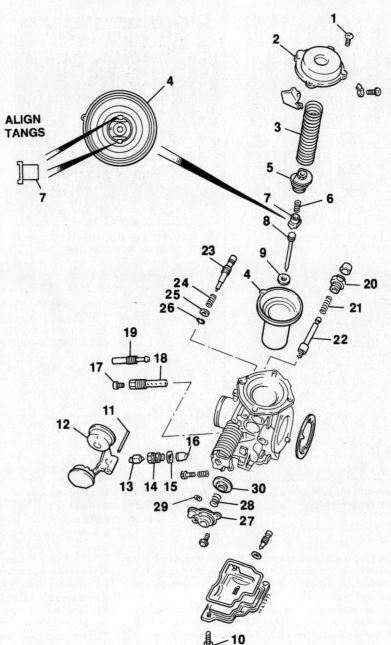

7.16a Undo the two retaining screws . . .

7.16b . . . then carefully remove the cover . . .

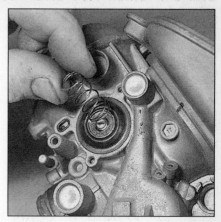

7.16c . . . and recover the spring, valve and O-ring(s) from the carburetor

7.17a On R models undo the choke linkage shaft screws . . .

7.17b . . . then recover the washers . . .

7.17c . . . lift off the shaft and recover the spacers . . .

7.17d . . . and return spring positioned beneath it

9   Unscrew the needle jet from the carburetor **(see illustration)**.
10   Unscrew the slow jet, situated next to the starter jet, from the carburetor **(see illustration)**. **Note:** *Do not attempt to remove the starter jet from the carburetor body.*
11   Remove the plastic limiter cap (where fitted) from the pilot screw which is screwed into the side of the carburetor. The cap will be cemented in place and can be removed using a pair of pliers.

12   Screw the pilot screw in until it seats lightly, counting the number of turns necessary to achieve this, then remove the screw along with its spring, flat washer and O-ring **(see illustration)**. If the screw is bent or damaged in any way, all the pilot screws must be replaced as a set.
13   If necessary, unscrew the valve nut and remove the choke plunger and spring from the carburetor.

L through P models

Refer to illustrations 7.14, 7.16a, 7.16b and 7.16c
14   Refer to the information given above in Steps 2 through 13, noting that the needle is removed from the piston as follows **(see illustration)**.
15   Using an 8 mm socket, push down on the needle holder and turn it 90° counterclockwise (anti-clockwise). Lift the needle holder out of the piston and recover the spring. Pull the spring holder out of the piston then tip out the needle and sealing washer.
16   Undo the retaining screws and carefully ease the air cut-off valve cover away from the side of the carburetor, taking great care not to lose the spring. Remove the valve, noting which way around it is fitted, and recover its O-ring(s) **(see illustrations)**.

R models

Refer to illustrations 7.17a, 7.17b, 7.17c, 7.17d, 7.18a, 7.18b, 7.19, 7.20a, 7.20b, 7.21a, 7.21b, 7.22a, 7.22b, 7.23, 7.25, 7.26 and 7.27
17   Undo the two screws and washers securing the choke linkage shaft to the top of the relevant pair of carburetors then lift off the linkage shaft and recover the spacers and return spring from underneath the shaft **(see illustrations)**.

4

**7.18a Exploded view of a carburetor
- R models**

1   Top cover screw
2   Top cover
3   Spring
4   Diaphragm and piston assembly
5   Needle holder
6   Spring
7   Needle and sealing washer
8   Float chamber screw
9   Float chamber
10 Seal
11 Float pivot pin
12 Float
13 Needle valve
14 Main jet
15 Needle jet
16 Slow jet
17 Pilot screw
18 Spring
19 Washer
20 O-ring
21 Choke plunger nut
22 Spring
23 Choke plunger
24 Air cut-off valve cover screw
25 Air cut-off valve cover
26 O-rings
27 Air cut-off valve

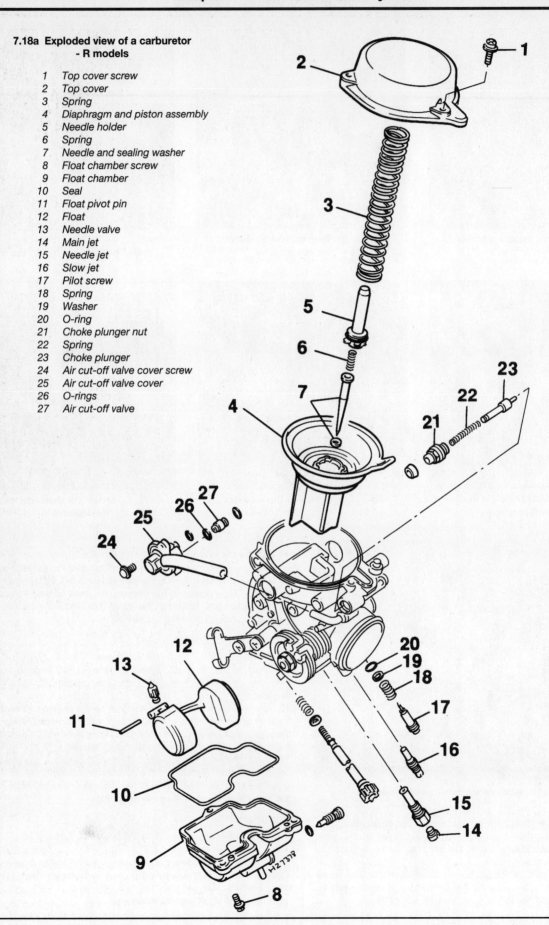

7.18b Undo the retaining screws and remove the top cover

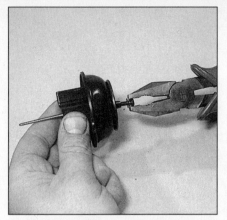

7.19 Using a top cover screw and pair of pliers to remove the needle holder from the piston

7.20a Undo the retaining screws . . .

7.20b . . . then lift off the float chamber and recover the rubber seal (arrowed)

7.21a Withdraw the pivot pin . . .

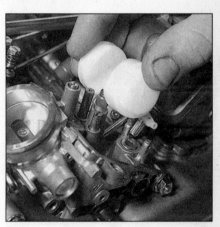

7.21b . . . and remove the float and needle valve assembly

7.22a Unscrew the main jet from the base of the needle jet . . .

7.22b . . . then unscrew the needle jet from the carburetor

18   Slacken and remove the top cover retaining screws (see illustrations). Lift off the cover and remove the spring from inside the piston. Carefully peel the diaphragm away from its sealing groove in the carburetor and withdraw the diaphragm and piston assembly. Caution: *Do not use a sharp instrument to displace the diaphragm as it is easily damaged.*

19   To remove the needle from the piston, screw a 4 mm bolt into the thread in the center of the needle holder (one of the top cover retaining screws will do), then use a pair of pliers to pull the needle holder out of the piston. Recover the O-ring and spring then tip the needle and sealing washer out of the piston (see illustration).

20   Remove the retaining screws and remove the float chamber from the base of the carburetor. Recover the rubber seal (see illustrations).

21   Withdraw the float pivot pin, using a pair of pointed-nose pliers, and remove the float and needle valve assembly (see illustrations). Note: *Do not attempt to remove the needle valve seat from the carburetor.*

22   Unscrew the main jet from the base of the needle jet, then unscrew the needle jet from the carburetor (see illustrations).

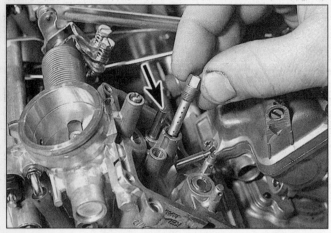

7.23 Unscrew the slow jet; do not attempt to remove the starter jet (arrow)

7.25 Remove the pilot screw as described in text

7.26 Air cut-off valve cover is retained by a single screw

7.27 Unscrew the nut (arrow) and remove the choke plunger components

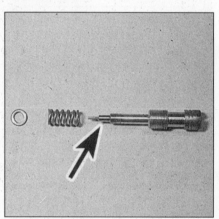

7.31 Inspect the pilot screw tapered portion for wear (arrow)

23   Unscrew the slow jet, situated next to the starter jet, from the carburetor **(see illustration)**. **Note:** *Do not attempt to remove the starter jet from the carburetor body.*

24   Remove the plastic limiter cap (where fitted) from the pilot screw which is screwed into the base of the carburetor. The cap will be cemented in place and can be removed using a pair of pliers.

25   Screw the pilot screw in until it seats lightly, counting the number of turns necessary to achieve this, then remove the screw along with its spring, flat washer and O-ring. If the screw is bent or damaged in any way, all the pilot screws must be replaced as a set **(see illustration)**.

26   Undo the retaining screw and carefully ease the air cut-off valve cover away from the side of the carburetor, taking great care not to lose the spring **(see illustration)**. Remove the valve, noting which way around it is fitted, and recover its O-rings.

27   If necessary, unscrew the valve nut and remove the choke plunger and spring from the carburetor **(see illustration)**.

Cleaning

Caution: *Use only a petroleum based solvent for carburetor cleaning. Don't use caustic cleaners.*

28   Submerge the metal components in the solvent for approximately thirty minutes (or longer, if the directions recommend it).

29   After the carburetor has soaked long enough for the cleaner to loosen and dissolve most of the varnish and other deposits, use a brush to remove the stubborn deposits. Rinse it again, then dry it with compressed air. Blow out all of the fuel and air passages in the main and upper body. **Caution:** *Never clean the jets or passages with a piece of wire or a drill bit, as they will be enlarged, causing the fuel and air metering rates to be upset.*

Inspection

Refer to illustrations 7.31, 7.33, 7.36a and 7.36b

30   Check the operation of the choke plunger. If it doesn't move smoothly, replace it along with the return spring. Inspect the needle on the end of the choke plunger and replace the plunger if it's worn or bent.

31   Check the tapered portion of the pilot screw for wear or damage **(see illustration)**. Replace the pilot screw if necessary.

32   Check the carburetor body, float chamber and top cover for cracks, distorted sealing surfaces and other damage. If any defects are found, replace the faulty component, although replacement of the entire carburetor will probably be necessary (check with your parts supplier for the availability of separate components).

33   Check the diaphragm for splits, holes and general deterioration **(see illustration)**. Holding it up to a light will help to reveal problems of this nature.

34   Insert the diaphragm piston in the carburetor body and check that it moves up-and-down smoothly. Check the surface of the piston for wear. If it's worn excessively or doesn't move smoothly in the bore, replace the carburetor.

35   Check the jet needle for straightness by rolling it on a flat surface (such as a piece of glass). Replace it if it's bent or if the tip is worn.

36   Check the tip of the float needle valve. If it has grooves or scratches in it, it must be replaced. Push in on the rod in the other end of the needle valve, then release it - if it doesn't spring back, replace the needle valve. Also examine the needle valve seat and on G through P models, examine the filter for signs of damage and replace if necessary; clean the filter with high flash-point solvent and blow it dry

7.33 Check the piston diaphragm for signs of damage and splits

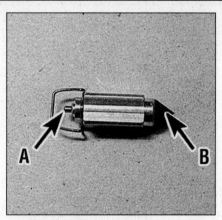

7.36a Check the needle valve's spring-loaded rod (A) and tip (B) for wear or damage

7.36b If the needle tip is worn check the seat carefully for wear; ensure the filter is clean on G through P models

8.11 On L through P models, undo the retaining screws and remove the joining bracket from the base of the carburetors

8.12 Bend up the lockplate tabs and remove the air filter housing plate screws

with compressed air (see illustrations). Note: On R models, if the needle valve seat is damaged the carburetor assembly must be replaced; it is not possible to replace the seat individually.

37   Check the float chamber seal and replace it if it's damaged.

38   Operate the throttle shaft to make sure the throttle butterfly valve opens and closes smoothly. If it doesn't, replace the carburetor.

39   Check the floats for damage. This will usually be apparent by the presence of fuel inside one of the floats. If the floats are damaged, they must be replaced.

8   Carburetors - separation and reassembly

Warning: Refer to the precautions given in Section 1 before proceeding

Separation

1   The carburetors do not need to be separated for normal overhaul. If you need to separate them (to replace a carburetor body, for example), refer to the following procedure.

2   Remove the carburetors from the machine as described in Section 6. Mark the body of each carburetor with its cylinder number to ensure that it is positioned correctly on reassembly. Proceed as described under the relevant sub-heading.

G through K models

3   Slacken and remove the screw from either end of the carburetor assembly.

4   Bend up the lockplate tabs then undo the eight screws securing the air filter housing mounting plate to the carburetors. Remove the screws

and lockplates then lift the mounting plate away from the carburetors. Recover the sealing ring from each carburetor and, on J and K models, recover the rubber air funnels from the plate.

5   Noting their correct routing, disconnect the fuel and breather hoses from the carburetor.

6   Make a note of how the throttle linkage springs are arranged to ensure that they are fitted correctly on reassembly.

7   Loosen the choke linkage clamp screws then separate No. 1 and 4 carburetors from No. 2 and 3 carburetors. Ensure the carburetors are separated squarely to prevent damage to the air and fuel joints. Keep a careful watch on all springs as the carburetors are separated, they should stay with the adjusting screws, but if they don't, find them and install them as shown in the illustration so they aren't lost.

8   Noting the correct fitted positions of the linkage components, remove the cotter (split) pins and washers and remove the throttle and choke linkage components from No. 2 and 3 carburetors.

9   Undo the joining bracket retaining screws and separate No. 2 and 3 carburetors.

10   If necessary, undo the retaining nut and washers and remove the choke lever assembly from No. 2 carburetor.

L through P models

Refer to illustrations 8.11, 8.12, 8.14, 8.15 and 8.17

11   Undo the retaining screws and remove the joining bracket from the base of the carburetors (see illustration).

12   Bend up the lockplate tabs then slacken and remove the eight screws securing the air filter housing mounting plate to the carburetors (see illustration).

4

8.14 Note the correct fitted location of all throttle linkage springs prior to separation (L model shown)

8.15 Slackening a choke linkage clamp screw

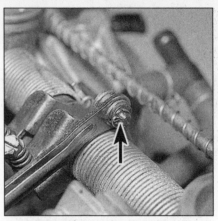

8.17 Remove the cotter (split) pin (arrow) and separate the throttle linkage rod

8.23 Note the correct fitted location of all throttle linkage springs prior to separation (R model shown)

8.24 Unscrew the retaining nuts from all the carburetor connecting studs

9.8 Checking the float height (L model shown)

13   Lift the mounting plate away from the carburetors and recover its locating dowels. Remove the air funnels and recover the sealing ring from each carburetor.

14   Make a note of how the throttle linkage springs are arranged to ensure that they are fitted correctly on reassembly **(see illustration)**.

15   Loosen the choke linkage clamp screws then free the linkage from each carburetor **(see illustration)**.

16   Noting the correct fitted location of each washer, remove the cotter (split) pins and remove the choke linkage rod, linking No. 1 and 2 carburetors.

17   Noting the correct fitted location of each washer, remove the cotter (split) pins and remove the throttle linkage rod, linking No. 1 and 2 carburetors **(see illustration)**.

18   Separate Nos. 2 and 4 carburetors from Nos. 1 and 3 carburetors.

19   Carefully separate each pair of carburetors whilst taking care not to damage the fuel and air vent joints between each carburetor nor lose the screws from the throttle linkages. Keep a careful watch on all springs as the carburetors are separated; they should stay with the adjusting screws, but if they don't, find them and install them as shown in the illustration so they aren't lost.

R models

Refer to illustrations 8.23 and 8.24

20   Bend up the lockplate tabs, then slacken and remove the sixteen screws securing the air filter housing mounting plate to the carburetors.

21   Lift the mounting plate away from the carburetors and recover the air funnels and sealing rings from each carburetor.

22   Undo the two screws and washers securing the choke linkage

shaft to the top of one pair of carburetors, then lift off the linkage shaft and recover the spacers and return spring from underneath the shaft **(see illustrations 7.17a through 7.17d)**. Repeat the operation on the other pair of carburetors.

23   Make a note of how the throttle linkage springs are arranged to ensure that they are fitted correctly on reassembly **(see illustration)**.

24   Evenly and progressively slacken and remove the six nuts securing the carburetors together but do not withdraw the connecting studs yet **(see illustration)**.

25   Carefully ease No. 4 carburetor away from the others and recover the thrust spring.

26   Carefully remove No. 3 carburetor and recover the thrust spring.

27   Remove the various fuel and air joints from the carburetors and recover the spacers.

28   Remove the choke linkage assembly from the side of the carburetors.

29   Noting the correct fitted location of each washer, remove the cotter (split) pins and remove the throttle linkage rod, linking Nos. 1 and 2 carburetors.

30   Withdraw the three connecting studs and separate Nos. 1 and 2 carburetors.

Joining

31   Joining is the reverse of the separation procedure. Use new O-rings on the fuel and air joint fittings. Check the operation of both the choke and throttle linkages ensuring that both operate smoothly and return quickly under spring pressure before installing the carburetors on the machine. Check carburetor synchronization (see Chapter 1).

9.11 Ensure the diaphragm tongue is correctly aligned with the carburetor valve cutout (arrowed)

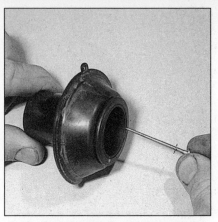

9.14a On L through P models, insert the needle and sealing washer into the piston . . .

9.14b . . . and fit the spring holder . . .

9.14c . . . making sure its tabs are correctly seated in the piston slots

9.14d Fit the spring and needle holder . . .

9.14e . . . and secure it in position by depressing and twisting it 90° clockwise

9   Carburetors - reassembly and float height check

Note: *When reassembling the carburetors, be sure to use the new O-rings, gaskets and other parts supplied in the rebuild kit. Do not overtighten the carburetor jets and screws as they are easily damaged.*

G through K models

Refer to illustrations 9.8 and 9.11

1   Install the choke plunger in its bore, followed by its spring and nut. Tighten the nut securely and install the cap.
2   Install the pilot screw (if removed) along with its spring, washer and O-ring, turning it in until it seats lightly. Now, turn the screw out the number of turns previously recorded. Where fitted, install a new limiter cap on the screw, applying a little bonding agent to hold it in position.
3   Screw the needle jet into position in the carburetor.
4   Screw the main jet into the end of the needle jet.
5   Screw the slow jet into position.
6   Fit a new sealing washer to the needle valve seat and install the filter on the end of the seat. Screw the seat assembly into the carburetor,
7   Hook the needle valve over the float, then install the float and secure it with the pivot pin.
8   To check the float height, hold the carburetor so the float hangs down, then tilt it back until the needle valve is just seated, but not so far that its spring-loaded rod is compressed. Measure the distance between the gasket face and the bottom of the float with an accurate ruler **(see illustration)**. The correct setting should be as given in the Specifications Section. Where the float tang is made of metal, the float

height can be adjusted by carefully bending the tang as required. Where the float tang is made of plastic, no adjustment is possible; if the height is incorrect the float must be replaced. Repeat the procedure for all carburetors.
9   With the float height correct, fit the rubber seal to the float chamber and install the chamber on the carburetor.
10   Fit the washer to the needle and insert the needle into the piston. Locate the spring in the holder and insert the holder into the piston. Secure the holder in position by depressing it and turning it 90° clockwise.
11   Insert the piston assembly into the carburetor body and lightly push it down, ensuring the needle is correctly aligned with the needle jet. Press the diaphragm outer edge into its groove, ensuring the diaphragm tongue is correctly seated in the cutout on the carburetor. Check the diaphragm is not creased, and that the piston moves smoothly up and down the bore **(see illustration)**.
12   Insert the spring and fit the top cover to the carburetor.

L through P models

Refer to illustrations 9.14a through 9.14e

13   Refer to the information given above in Steps 1 through 12, noting the needle and associated components are fitted to the piston as follows.
14   Fit the sealing washer to the needle and insert the needle into the piston. Slide the spring holder into the piston aligning its tangs with the piston slots. Insert the spring into the spring holder then install the needle holder, securing it in position by depressing it and turning it 90° clockwise **(see illustrations)**.

4

9.24a On R models, fit the needle and sealing washer . . .

9.24b . . . and install the needle holder, making sure its O-ring (arrow) is correctly fitted

9.25 Ensure the diaphragm is correctly seated in the carburetor groove . . .

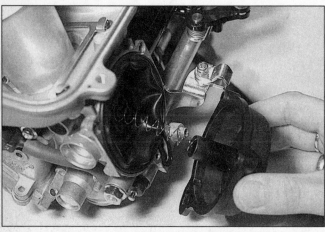

9.26 . . . and refit the spring and top cover

15   If the air cut-off valve was removed, install the valve on the carburetor ensuring that it is positioned the correct way around. Install a new O-ring, then fit the spring and cover; tighten the cover retaining screws securely.

R models

Refer to illustrations 9.24a, 9.24b, 9.25 and 9.26
16   Install the choke plunger in its bore, followed by its spring and nut. Tighten the nut securely and install the cap.
17   Fit new O-rings to the air cut-off valve positioning each one so that its flat surface faces the carburetor body. Fit the valve to the carburetor, making sure it is fitted the correct way around, and install the valve cover and spring. Securely tighten the cover screw and reconnect the valve hose to the carburetor.
18   Install the pilot screw (if removed) along with its spring, washer and O-ring, turning it in until it seats lightly. Now, turn the screw out the number of turns previously recorded. Where fitted, install a new limiter cap on the screw, applying a little bonding agent to hold it in position.
19   Screw the needle jet into position in the carburetor, then screw the main jet into the end of the needle jet.
20   Screw the slow jet into position.
21   Hook the needle valve over the float, then install the float and secure it with the pivot pin.
22   Check the float height as described in Step 8.
23   With the float height correct, fit the rubber seal to the float chamber and install the chamber on the carburetor.
24   Fit the washer to the needle and insert the needle into the piston. Position a new O-ring in the groove on the inside of the piston and fit the spring. Insert the needle holder into the center of the piston and press it into position until the O-ring is fully seated against the base of

the piston and clicks into position **(see illustrations)**.
25   Insert the piston assembly into the carburetor body and lightly push it down, ensuring the needle is correctly aligned with the needle jet. Press the diaphragm outer edge into its groove, ensuring the diaphragm tongue is correctly seated in the cutout on the carburetor **(see illustration)**. Check the diaphragm is not creased, and that the piston moves smoothly up and down the bore.
26   Insert the spring and fit the top cover to the carburetor **(see illustration)**.
27   Fit the choke linkage shaft return spring and install the spacers on the carburetors. Install the linkage shaft, making sure it is correctly engaged with the plungers and return spring, then fit the washers and screws. Securely tighten the screws then check the shaft moves smoothly and returns quickly under spring pressure.

10 Throttle cables - removal and installation

Warning: *Refer to the precautions given in Section 1 before proceeding.*

Removal

Refer to illustrations 10.2a and 10.2b
1   Remove the fuel tank as described in Section 2.
2   Slacken the throttle cable locknuts then free each outer cable from its mounting bracket. Detach the inner cables from the throttle cam. If necessary, to improve access to the throttle cables, remove the left lower or middle fairing panel (as applicable) as described in Chapter 8 **(see illustrations)**.
3   Unscrew the two right handlebar switch screws and free the switch from the handlebar.
4   Disconnect the throttle cables from the throttle grip and unscrew each cable from the lower half of the handlebar switch. Mark each cable to ensure it is connected correctly on installation.
5   Remove the cables from the machine noting the correct routing of each cable.

Installation

6   Install the cables making sure they are correctly routed. The cables must not interfere with any other component and should not be kinked or bent sharply.
7   Screw the cables into the lower half of the handlebar switch, making sure they are correctly connected. Lubricate the end of each cable with multi-purpose grease and attach the cables to the throttle grip.
8   Fit the switch lower half to the handlebar, locating its peg in the handlebar hole. Fit the top half of the switch and securely tighten the screws.
9   Lubricate the end of each cable with multi-purpose grease and attach them to the carburetor throttle cam.

10.2a Slacken the locknuts . . .

10.2b . . . then free the cables from the left side of the carburetors

11.2 Slacken the retaining screw and detach the choke cable from the carburetor linkage

12.2 Release the retaining clip and detach the breather hose from the rear of the air filter housing

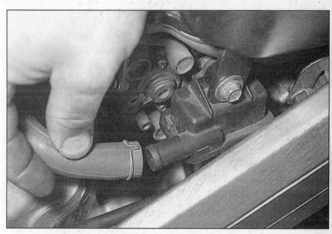

12.3 On L models onward, disconnect the hose from the air vent filter

10 Make sure the cables are correctly connected and locate the outer cable adjusters in the mounting bracket.

11 Adjust the cables as described in Chapter 1. Turn the handlebars back and forth to make sure the cables don't cause the steering to bind.

12 Install the fuel tank as described in Section 2. Prior to fitting the fuel tank, start the engine and turn the handlebars back and forth to make sure the idle speed doesn't rise as the bars are turned. If it does, the cables are incorrectly routed. Sort out the problem before riding the motorcycle.

11 Choke cable - removal and installation

Removal

Refer to illustration 11.2

1 Remove the air filter housing as described in Section 12. Note that on some models it will only be necessary to remove the lid, and not the complete housing, to gain access to the cable.

2 Slacken the screw then free the choke outer cable from its retaining clamp and detach the inner cable from the carburetor choke linkage **(see illustration)**.

3 Unscrew the two left handlebar switch screws and free the switch from the handlebar.

4 Disconnect the choke cable from the choke lever and unscrew the cable from the lower half of the handlebar switch.

5 Remove the cable from the machine noting its correct routing.

Installation

6 Install the cable making sure it is correctly routed. The cable must not interfere with any other component and should not be kinked or bent sharply.

7 Screw the cable into the lower half of the handlebar switch. Lubricate cable end with multi-purpose grease and attach it to the choke lever.

8 Fit the switch lower half to the handlebar, locating its peg in the handlebar hole. Fit the top half of the switch and securely tighten the screws.

9 Lubricate the cable end with multi-purpose grease and attach it to the choke linkage.

10 Locate the outer cable in the retaining clamp and adjust the cable as described in Chapter 1.

11 Install the air filter housing components as described in Section 12.

12 Air filter housing - removal and installation

Removal

Refer to illustrations 12.2, 12.3, 12.4a and 12.4b

1 Remove the air filter element as described in Chapter 1.

2 Release the retaining clip and disconnect the breather hose from the rear of the air filter housing **(see illustration)**.

3 On L models onward, release the retaining clip and disconnect the hose from the air vent filter which is mounted on the rear of the air filter housing **(see illustration)**.

4

12.4a Remove the retaining screws . . .

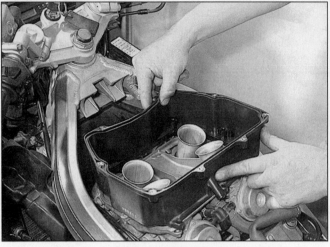

12.4b . . . and lift the air filter housing from the top of the carburetors

13.1 Exhaust system components - G and H models

1 Muffler (silencer) mounting bolt
2 Muffler (silencer)
3 Clamps
4 Front pipe nuts
5 Front pipes
6 Gaskets
7 Rear pipes
8 Rear pipe nuts

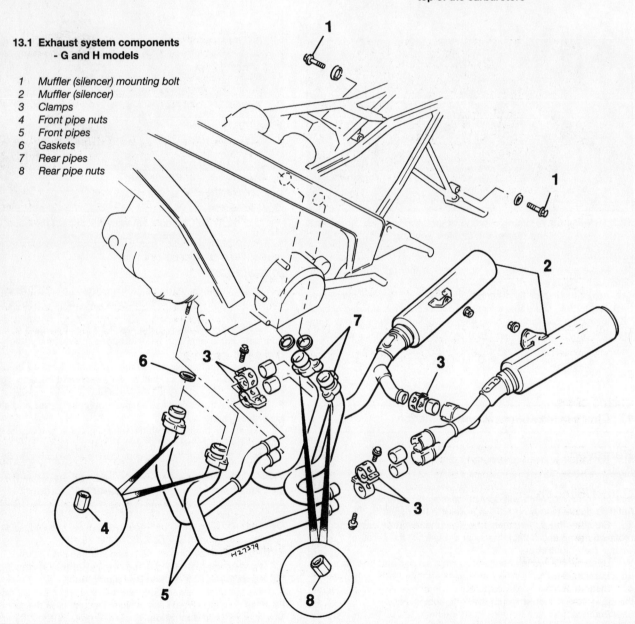

13.8 Unscrew the nuts securing the front pipe to the cylinder head

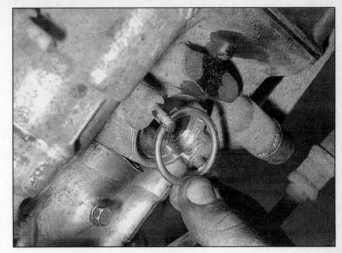

13.11a On installation, fit a new gasket to the cylinder head port . . .

13.11b . . . and a new sealing ring to the front pipe

4   On all models, undo the screws which secure the filter housing base in position and remove it from the bike **(see illustrations)**. On all California models and all US L models onward, it will also be necessary to disconnect the pulse secondary air injection suction hoses from the housing.

Installation

5   Installation is the reverse of removal.

13 Exhaust system - removal and installation

G and H models

Refer to illustrations 13.1, 13.8, 13.11a and 13.11b

1   Set the bike on its centerstand (where fitted) or sidestand **(see illustration)**.

Mufflers (silencers)

2   Loosen the four clamps securing both left and right mufflers (silencers) to the front and rear pipes.

3   Slacken and remove the left and right mounting bolts and washers.

4   Free the mufflers (silencers) from the front and rear pipes and remove them from the bike. Recover the sealing rings from each of the front and rear pipes.

5   If necessary, loosen the clamp and separate the left and right mufflers (silencers). Recover the sealing ring.

6   Installation is the reverse of removal using new sealing rings.

Front pipes

7   Remove the lower fairing panel(s) as described in Chapter 8.

8   Unscrew the two nuts securing the relevant front pipe to the cylinder head and release the collar from the head studs **(see illustration)**.

9   Loosen the clamp and remove the front pipe from the bike. Recover the sealing ring and the gasket from the cylinder head port.

10   If necessary, repeat the operation and remove the remaining front pipe.

11   Installation is the reverse of removal using a new gasket and sealing ring **(see illustrations)**.

Rear pipes

12   Remove the engine unit from the frame as described in Chapter 2 then unscrew the retaining nuts and remove the rear pipes from the engine unit. Recover the gaskets from the cylinder head ports.

13   Installation is the reverse of removal using new gaskets.

J and K models

Refer to illustration 13.14

14   Set the bike on its centerstand (where fitted) or sidestand **(see illustration)**.

Muffler (silencer)

15   Loosen the clamp securing the relevant muffler (silencer) to the collector box.

16   Unscrew the mounting bolt and washer then free the muffler (silencer) from the collector box and remove it from the bike. Recover the sealing ring.

17   If necessary, repeat the operation and remove the remaining muffler (silencer).

18   Installation is a reverse of removal using a new sealing ring.

Collector box

19   Remove both mufflers (silencers) as described above.

20   Loosen the clamps securing the collector box to the rear exhaust pipes.

21   Remove the collector box and recover the sealing rings.

22   Installation is the reverse of removal using new sealing rings.

4

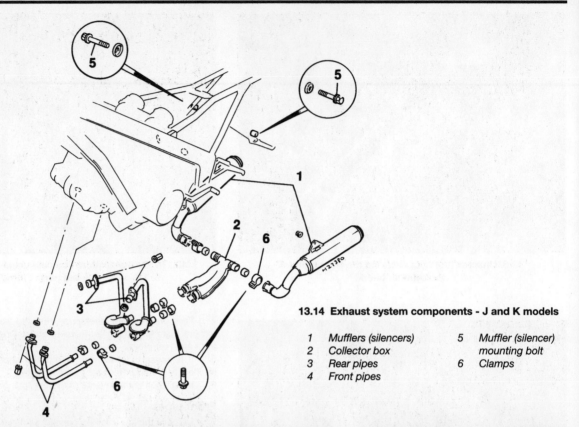

13.14 Exhaust system components - J and K models

1	Mufflers (silencers)	5	Muffler (silencer)
2	Collector box		mounting bolt
3	Rear pipes	6	Clamps
4	Front pipes		

13.28a Unscrew the silencer to collector box bolts . . .

13.28b . . . and recover their spacers and springs

13.29a Slacken and remove the nut and mounting bolt . . .

Front pipes

23   Refer to the information given in Steps 7 to 11.

Rear pipes

24   Remove the engine unit from the frame as described in Chapter 2.
25   Remove the front pipes (see above) then unscrew the retaining nuts and remove the rear pipes from the engine unit. Recover the gaskets from the cylinder head ports.
26   Installation is the reverse of removal using new gaskets.

L through P models

Refer to illustrations 13.28a, 13.28b, 13.29a, 13.29b, 13.32, 13.35, 13.36 and 13.43

Muffler (silencer)

27   Set the bike on its centerstand (where fitted) or sidestand.

28   Slacken and remove the two bolts securing the muffler (silencer) to the collector box. Recover the spacers and springs from the bolts **(see illustrations)**.
29   Undo the retaining bolt and remove the muffler (silencer). Recover the spacer from the mounting and the sealing ring **(see illustrations)**.
30   Installation is the reverse of removal using a new sealing ring.

Front pipes

31   Refer to the information given in Steps 7 to 11.

Collector box assembly

32   Support the motorcycle in an upright position, ideally using a hoist and suitable lifting gear. Make sure the motorcycle is securely supported before proceeding **(see illustration)**.
33   Remove the rear wheel as described in Chapter 7.
34   Remove the muffler (silencer) and front pipes as described above then undo the three bolts and remove the exhaust cover from the left

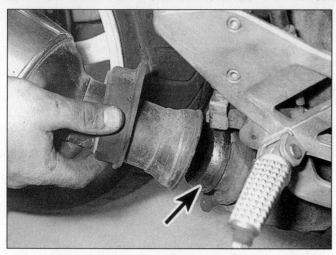

13.29b . . . then remove the silencer and recover its sealing ring (arrow)

13.32 The motorcycle can be supported by positioning axle stands under the passenger footpeg brackets

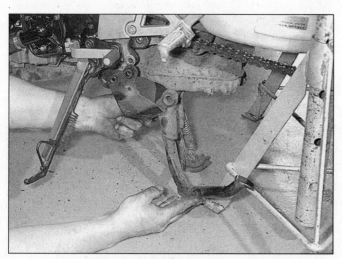

13.35 Undo the retaining bolts and remove the centerstand assembly

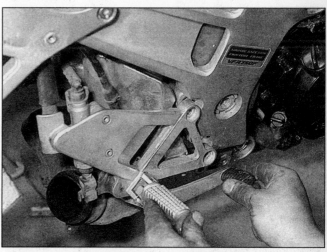

13.36 Undo the two bolts and free the right side footpeg bracket from the frame to improve access

4

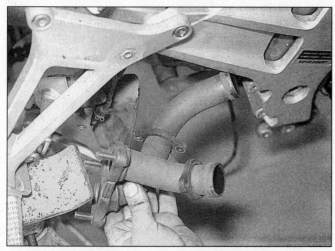

13.43 Removing the rear exhaust pipes (L model shown)

side of the machine.

35 Undo the four bolts securing the centerstand mounting bracket (where fitted) to the frame and remove the stand assembly **(see illustration)**.

36 Slacken and remove the rider's right footpeg bracket retaining bolts and free the bracket from the frame **(see illustration)**.

37 Undo the two bolts and remove the heatshield from the top of the left rear collector box pipe.

38 Undo the three nuts securing the collector box pipes to the rear exhaust pipes.

39 Free the collector box from the rear exhaust pipes and maneuver the assembly out from underneath the bike.

40 Recover the gaskets from the collector box to rear pipe joint.

41 Installation is the reverse of removal using new gaskets and sealing rings.

Rear pipes

42 Remove the collector box assembly as described in Steps 32 to 40.

43 Unscrew the four nuts securing the rear pipes to the cylinder head. Remove the rear pipes and recover the gaskets from the cylinder head ports **(see illustration)**.

44 Installation is the reverse of removal using new gaskets.

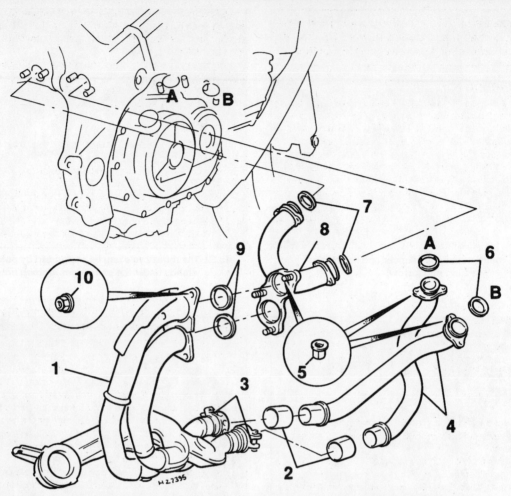

13.45 Exhaust system components - R models (muffler/silencer not shown)

1	Collector box assembly	6	Front pipe to cylinder head gaskets
2	Sealing rings	7	Rear pipe to cylinder head gaskets
3	Clamps	8	Rear pipes
4	Front pipes	9	Rear pipe to collector box gaskets
5	Pipe to cylinder head nuts	10	Collector box to rear pipe nuts

R models

Refer to illustration 13.45

Muffler (silencer)

45   Set the bike on its centerstand **(see illustration)**.
46   Unscrew the two bolts and washers and remove both halves of the clamp securing the muffler (silencer) to the collector box.
47   Undo the mounting bolt and remove the muffler (silencer). Recover the spacers from the mounting and the sealing ring from the collector box.
48   Installation is the reverse of removal using a new sealing ring. Note that the silencer must be positioned so that the clearance between its inside edge and the edge of the rear tire is 25 to 35 mm (1 to 1 1/2 inch).

Front pipes

49   Refer to the information given in Steps 7 to 11.

Collector box assembly

50   Support the motorcycle in an upright position, ideally using a hoist and suitable lifting gear. Make sure the motorcycle is securely supported before proceeding.

51   With the motorcycle securely supported, unhook the centerstand return spring and remove the spring bracket from underneath the bike.
52   Undo the centerstand pivot shaft retaining bolt then withdraw the shaft and remove the centerstand.
53   Remove the muffler (silencer) and front pipes as described above.
54   Slacken and remove the right rider's footpeg bracket retaining bolts and free the bracket from the frame.
55   Undo the three nuts securing the collector box pipes to the rear exhaust pipes.
56   Free the collector box from the rear exhaust pipes and maneuver the assembly out from underneath the bike.
57   Recover the gaskets from the collector box to rear pipe joint.
58   Installation is the reverse of removal using new gaskets and sealing rings.

Rear pipes

59   Remove the collector box assembly as described in Steps 50 to 57.
60   Unscrew the four nuts securing the rear pipes to the cylinder head.
61   Remove the rear pipes and recover the gaskets from the cylinder head ports.
62   Installation is the reverse of removal using new gaskets.

14 Pulse secondary air (PAIR) injection system (G and H California models and all L models onward US models only) - general information, removal and installation

General information

1   On all California models and all US L models onward, to reduce the amount of unburned hydrocarbons released in the exhaust gases, a pulse secondary air injection system is fitted. The system consists of the air control valve assemblies, which are mounted on each side of the engine unit (one for the rear cylinders and one for the front cylinders), and the air feed pipes linking the control valves to the cylinder heads. Each control valve is linked to one of the intake ducts by a vacuum hose and to the air filter housing by a suction hose.

2   When the engine is running, the depression present in the intake duct acts on the vacuum diaphragm in the control valve and opens up the valve.

3   With the valve open, whenever there is a negative pulse in the exhaust system, filtered air is drawn from the air filter housing through the control valve and into the exhaust ports in the cylinder head. This fresh air promotes the burning of any excess fuel present in the exhaust gases, so reducing the amount of harmful hydrocarbons emitted into the atmosphere via the exhaust gases.

4   The control valve assembly is fitted with a pair of one-way check valves to prevent the exhaust gases passing through the control valve and into the air filter housing.

5   The system is not adjustable and can be tested only by a Honda dealer. Checks which can be performed by the owner are given in Chapter 1.

Removal

6   Remove the lower fairing panel(s) as described in Chapter 8. If the rear cylinder control valve is to be removed, also remove the fuel tank as described in Section 2.

7   Release the retaining clips and disconnect the vacuum hose and air hose from the relevant control valve.

8   Undo the mounting bolts and release the control valve from the bike.

9   Unscrew the retaining bolts and release the air feed pipes from the relevant cylinder head.

10   Remove the control valve assembly, complete with pipes and hoses, from the bike.

11   Recover the gaskets from the air feed pipe joints and discard them.

12   Inspect the pipes and hoses for signs of cracks and splits and replace damaged components.

Installation

13   Ensure the air feed pipe and cylinder head mating surfaces are clean and dry.

14   Fit a new gasket to each of the cylinder head unions, making sure each gasket is fitted the correct way around.

15   Install the control valve assembly, aligning the feed pipes with their cylinder head unions. Fit the feed pipe and control valve bolts and tighten them securely.

16   Connect the vacuum hose and air suction hose to the control valve and secure in position with the retaining clips.

17   Fit the fairing panels as described in Chapter 8 and, where necessary, the fuel tank as described in Section 2.

15 Evaporative emission control system (EVAP) (California models only) - general information

1   On all California models, an evaporative emission control (EVAP) system is fitted. This system prevents the escape of fuel vapors into the atmosphere. The system functions as follows.

2   When the engine is stopped, fuel vapor from the tank is directed into a charcoal canister where it is absorbed and stored whilst the motorcycle is standing. When the engine is started, inlet manifold depression opens the purge control valve diaphragm. The vapors which are stored in the canister are then drawn into the engine to be burned during the normal combustion process.

3   The system is not adjustable and can be tested only by a Honda dealer. Checks which can be performed by the owner are given in Chapter 1.

4

Notes

Chapter 5   Ignition system

Note: *Refer to 'Identification numbers' at the beginning of this Manual to establish the model code of your motorcycle.*

Contents

Specifications

Firing order
1-3-2-4

Cylinder identification
No. 1 .... Left rear cylinder
No. 2 .... Left front cylinder
No. 3 .... Right rear cylinder
No. 4 .... Right front cylinder

Ignition timing
Initial
  K models .... 12° BTDC @ specified idle speed
  All other models .... 15° BTDC @ specified idle speed
Full advance
  G, H and J models .... 37° BTDC @ 3300 rpm
  K models .... 35° BTDC @ 4000 rpm
  L, M, N and P models........................ Not available
  R models .... 36° BTDC @ 6000 rpm

Pulse generator
Resistance
  L models.. 200 to 400 ohms @ 20°C (68°F)
  All other models .... 450 to 550 ohms @ 20°C (68°F)

5

Camshaft pulse generator - G models
Resistance .... 405 to 495 ohms @ 20°C (68°F)

Ignition HT coils
Primary winding resistance.................................... 2 to 4 ohms @ 20°C (68°F)
Secondary winding resistance
   With plug wires (HT leads) and plug caps......................... 17 to 24 K ohms @ 20°C (68°F)
   Without plug wires (HT leads) .... 13 to 17 K ohms @ 20°C (68°F)

Spark plugs .... See Chapter 1

Torque settings
	Nm	Ft-lbs
Crankcase right cover		
Retaining bolts	12	9
Center cap...	18	13

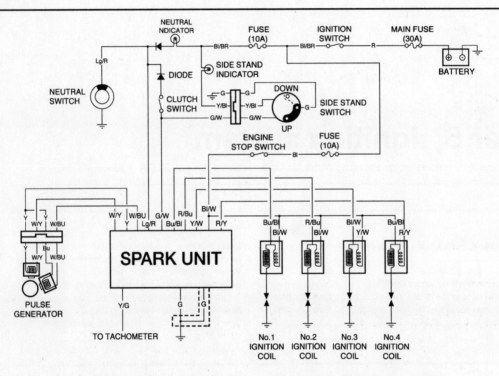

1.1a Ignition system wiring diagram - G models (H through K models similar)

See wiring diagram at the end of this manual for wire color codes

---

1   General information

Refer to illustrations 1.1a and 1.1b

These models are fitted with a magnetically-triggered electronic ignition system, which due to its lack of mechanical parts is totally maintenance-free except for spark plug replacement. The system comprises a rotor, pulse generator, spark unit and four ignition HT coils. On G models there is also a camshaft pulse generator in the ignition system **(see illustrations)**.

The raised triggers on the rotor, fitted to the right end of the crankshaft, magnetically operate the pulse generators as the crankshaft rotates. The pulse generators send signals to the spark unit which then supplies the ignition coils with the power necessary to produce the spark at the plugs. There are four coils, one for each cylinder.

On G models a camshaft pulse generator is also included in the ignition system; the generator is magnetically operated by the camshaft drive gear.

Because of their nature, the individual ignition system components can be checked but not repaired. If ignition system troubles occur, and

the faulty component can be isolated, the only cure for the problem is to replace the part with a new one. Keep in mind that most electrical parts, once purchased, can't be returned. To avoid unnecessary expense, make very sure the faulty component has been positively identified (have this confirmed by a Honda dealer) before buying a replacement part.

---

2   Ignition system - check

Warning: *The energy levels in electronic systems can be very high. On no account should the ignition be switched on whilst the plugs or plug caps are being held. Shocks from the secondary (HT) circuit can be most unpleasant. Secondly, it is vital that the plugs are soundly grounded (earthed) when the system is checked for sparking. The ignition system components can be seriously damaged if the secondary (HT) circuit becomes isolated.*

1   As no means of adjustment is available, any failure of the system can be traced to failure of a system component or a simple wiring fault. Of the two possibilities, the latter is by far the most likely. In the event of failure, check the system in a logical fashion, as described below.

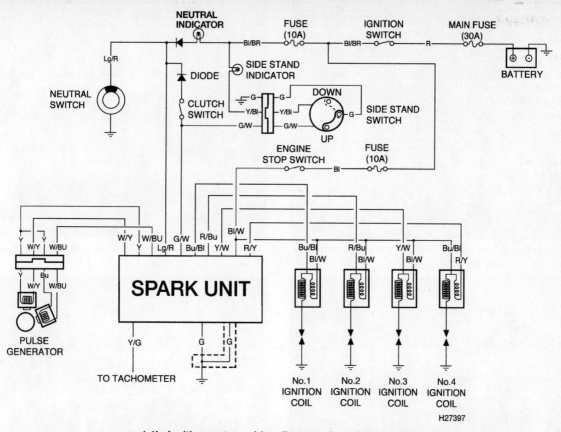

1.1b Ignition system wiring diagram - L models onward

See wiring diagram at the end of this manual for wire color codes

2   Disconnect the plug wires (HT leads) from the spark plugs and connect each lead to a spare spark plug. Lay each plug on the engine with the threads contacting the engine. If necessary, hold each spark plug with an insulated tool. **Warning:** *Don't remove one of the spark plugs from the engine to perform this check - atomized fuel being pumped out of the open spark plug hole could ignite, causing severe injury!*

3   Having observed the above precautions, check that the kill switch is in the RUN position, turn the ignition switch to ON and turn the engine over on the starter motor. If the system is in good condition a regular, fat blue spark should be evident at each plug electrode. If the spark appears thin or yellowish, or is non-existent, further investigation will be necessary. Before proceeding further, turn the ignition OFF and remove the key as a safety measure.

4   Ignition faults can be divided into two categories, namely those where the ignition system has failed completely, and those which are due to a partial failure. The likely faults are listed below, starting with the most probable source of failure. Work through the list systematically, referring to the subsequent sections for full details of the necessary checks and tests. **Note:** *Before checking the following items ensure that the battery is fully charged and that all fuses are in good condition.*

a) *Loose, corroded or damaged wiring connections, broken or shorted wiring between any of the component parts of the ignition system (see Chapter 9).*
b) *Faulty ignition or engine kill switch (see Chapter 9).*
c) *Faulty sidestand switch - J models onward (see Chapter 9).*
d) *Faulty neutral switch - L models onward (See Chapter 9).*
e) *Faulty pulse generator or damaged rotor.*
f) *Faulty camshaft pulse generator - G models.*
g) *Faulty ignition HT coil(s).*
f) *Faulty spark unit.*

3   Ignition HT coils - check, removal and installation

Check

Refer to illustrations 3.3a, 3.3b, 3.3c and 3.3d

1   In order to determine conclusively that the ignition coils are defective, they should be tested by a Honda dealer service department which is equipped with the special electrical tester required for this check.

2   However, the coils can be checked visually (for cracks and other damage) and the primary and secondary coil resistances can be measured with an ohmmeter. If the coils are undamaged, and if the resistances are as specified, they are probably capable of proper operation.

3   The ignition HT coil locations are as follows.

G through K models

Cylinder No. 1 coil - situated underneath the seat (remove the seat to gain access to the coil, and the left side cover to gain access to the spark plug cap).
Cylinder No. 2 coil - mounted on the frame left front downtube (remove the left side lower or middle fairing (as applicable) to gain access to the coil. If necessary, to improve access to the spark plug cap, undo the lower radiator mounting bolts and swing the radiator forwards).
Cylinder No. 3 coil - situated underneath the seat (remove the seat to gain access to the coil, and the right side cover to gain access to the spark plug cap).
Cylinder No. 4 coil - mounted on the frame right front downtube (remove the right side lower or middle fairing (as applicable) to gain access. If necessary, to improve access to the spark plug cap, undo the lower radiator mounting bolts and swing the radiator forwards).

5

3.3a No. 1 cylinder ignition HT coil location - L through P models (viewed from above)

3.3b No. 2 cylinder ignition HT coil location - L through P models

3.3c No. 3 cylinder ignition HT coil location - L through P models

3.3d No. 4 cylinder ignition HT coil location - L through P models

L through P models

Cylinder No. 1 coil - mounted on the left side of the frame (remove the left middle fairing panel to gain access to the coil. To access the spark plug cap, remove the fuel tank rear mounting nut and bolt then raise the tank and hold it in position with the U-shaped tool supplied in the bike's tool kit) **(see illustration)**.

Cylinder No. 2 coil - mounted on the left side of the frame (remove the left middle fairing panel to gain access to the coil **(see illustration)**. If necessary, to improve access to the spark plug cap, undo the lower radiator mounting bolts and swing the radiator forwards).

Cylinder No. 3 coil - mounted on the right side of the frame (remove the right middle fairing panel to gain access to the coil **(see illustration)**. To access the spark plug cap, remove the fuel tank rear mounting nut and bolt then raise the tank and hold it in position with the U-shaped tool supplied in the bike's tool kit).

Cylinder No. 4 coil - mounted on the right side of the frame (remove the right middle fairing panel to gain access to the coil **(see illustration)**. If necessary, to improve access to the spark plug cap, undo the lower radiator mounting bolts and swing the radiator forwards).

R models

Cylinder No. 1 coil - situated underneath the seat (remove the side cover/tail cowl assembly to gain access to the coil. To access the spark plug cap, remove the fuel tank rear mounting nut and bolt, then raise the tank and hold it in position with the U-shaped tool supplied in the bike's tool kit).

Cylinder No. 2 coil - mounted on the left side of the frame (remove the upper fairing to gain access to the coil. If necessary, to improve access to the spark plug cap, undo the lower radiator mounting bolts and swing the radiator forwards).

Cylinder No. 3 coil - situated underneath the seat (see coil No. 1 for access details).

Cylinder No. 4 coil - mounted on the right side of the frame (see coil No. 2 for access details).

4   Remove the component(s) listed to gain access to the relevant coil and spark plug cap.

5   Disconnect the primary circuit electrical connectors from the coil, noting the correct fitted position of each wire, and disconnect the spark plug cap from the engine.

6   Set the meter to the ohms x 1 scale and measure the resistance between the primary (low tension) terminals. This will give a resistance reading for the primary windings and should be within the limits given in the Specifications.

7   To check the condition of the secondary windings, set the meter to the K ohm scale and connect the meter to the spark plug cap and coil primary (low tension) positive terminal. Note the reading obtained. If this reading is not within the range shown in the Specifications, unscrew the plug wire (HT lead) from the coil then measure the resistance between the secondary (HT) coil terminal and positive primary (low tension) terminal. If both values obtained differ greatly from those specified it is likely that the coil is defective. **Note:** *If only the first reading obtained is suspect, then the fault lies in the plug wire (HT lead)/spark plug cap rather than the coil itself.*

8   Should any of the above checks not produce the expected result,

4.4 Pulse generator wiring connector (arrowed) (L model shown)

4.14a Remove the screw (arrowed) and disconnect the wiring connectors from the oil pressure switch . . .

4.14b . . . and the neutral switch

the coil should be taken to a Honda dealer or auto-electrician for a more thorough check. If the coil is confirmed to be faulty, it must be replaced; the coil is a sealed unit and cannot therefore be repaired.

Removal

9   Referring to Step 3, remove the necessary components to gain access to the relevant coil and its spark plug cap.
10   Disconnect the primary (low tension) wire connectors from the coil, noting the correct fitted position of each wire, and disconnect the spark plug cap from the engine.
11   Unscrew the retaining bolts and remove the coil. Note that on G through K models, and R models, coils 1 and 3 are mounted onto a bracket and should both be removed as an assembly.

Installation

12   Installation is the reverse of removal making sure the primary (low tension) wiring connectors are connected to the correct coil terminals and the plug wires (HT leads) are securely connected.

---

4   Pulse generator - check, removal and installation

Check

G through K models

1   Remove the right side cover as described in Chapter 8.
2   Disconnect the six-pin block connector, situated just in front of

the battery. Using a multimeter set to the ohms x 100 scale make the following tests on the generator side of the connector. Measure the resistance between the white/yellow and yellow wires, then between the white/blue and blue wires. Record both the readings obtained.

L models onward

Refer to illustration 4.4
3   Remove the right middle fairing section as described in Chapter 8.
4   Disconnect the black four-pin block connector which is clipped to the frame (see illustration). Using a multimeter set to the ohms x 100 scale make the following tests on the generator side of the connector. Measure the resistance between the white/yellow and yellow wires, then between the white/blue and blue wires. Record both readings obtained.

All models

5   Compare the readings obtained with those given in the Specifications at the start of this Chapter. If either reading differs greatly from that given, particularly if the meter indicates a short circuit (no measurable resistance) or an open circuit (infinite, or very high resistance), both pulse generators must be replaced. It is not possible to replace the generators individually.
6   If either generator is thought to be faulty, first check that this is not due to a damaged or broken wire from the generator to the connector; pinched or broken wires can usually be repaired.

Removal

Refer to illustrations 4.14a, 4.14b, 4.16a, 4.16b and 4.16c
7   On G and H models, remove the right lower fairing panel and the right side cover as described in Chapter 8.
8   On J models onward, remove the lower fairing as described in Chapter 8.
9   On all models, drain the engine oil as described in Chapter 1.
10   Trace the wiring back from the right crankcase cover to its wiring connector(s). Disconnect the pulse generator wiring connector(s) and work back along the wiring, noting its routing whilst releasing it from any relevant ties or clips.
11   Unscrew the right crankcase cover retaining bolts, noting the correct fitted positions of all wiring retaining clamps.
12   Withdraw the cover squarely from the engine unit.
13   Remove the cover locating dowels from the crankcase and discard the gasket. Free the pulse generator wiring grommet from the crankcase.
14   Disconnect the wiring from the oil pressure switch and the neutral switch (see Chapter 9, if necessary); the wires from both switches run in the same harness as those of the pulse generators (see illustrations).
15   On G models, unscrew the four retaining bolts then remove the

4.16a On H models onward, undo the three
retaining bolts (arrowed) . . .

4.16b . . . then remove the pulse generator assembly . . .

4.16c . . . and recover the locating dowels (arrowed)

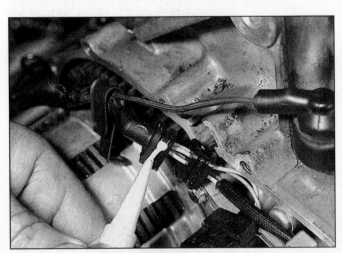

4.18 On installation, apply a smear of sealant to the pulse
generator wiring grommets

pulse generator assembly from the engine.
16   On H models onward, unscrew the three retaining bolts then
remove the pulse generator assembly from the engine unit. Remove
the generator assembly locating dowels from the crankcase for safe-
keeping **(see illustrations)**.
17   Examine the generator triggers on the starter clutch for signs of
damage such as chipped or missing teeth. If necessary, replace the
starter clutch as described in Chapter 2.

Installation

Refer to illustration 4.18
18   Apply a smear of suitable sealing compound to the pulse
generator wiring grommets **(see illustration)**.
19   On G models, locate the grommets in position in the crankcase
then install the generator retaining bolts, tightening them securely.
20   On H models onward, fit the locating dowels to the crankcase then
install the generator assembly, locating the wiring grommets in the
crankcase cutouts. Ensure the front generator wiring is correctly routed
through the bracket clamp then securely tighten the retaining bolts.
21   Remove all traces of old gasket from the crankcase and cover
mating surfaces.
22   Install the locating dowels and fit a new gasket to the crankcase.
23   Fit the cover and tighten the cover bolts evenly and progressively
to the specified torque setting.
24   Make sure the wiring is correctly routed and reconnect the wiring
connector. Secure the wiring in position with all the necessary clips

and ties.
25   Reconnect the wiring to the oil pressure and neutral switches (see
Chapter 9).
26   Fill the engine with the correct type and amount of oil as
described in Chapter 1.
27   Install the fairing panel(s) as described in Chapter 8.

5   Camshaft pulse generator (G models) - check, removal and installation

Check

1   Remove the right side cover (see Chapter 8).
2   Disconnect the two-pin block connector, situated just in front of
the battery. Using a multimeter set to the ohms x 100 scale, measure
the resistance between the connector terminals on the generator side
of the connector, and note the reading obtained.
3   Compare the reading obtained with that given in the Specifications at the start of this Chapter. If the reading differs greatly from
that given, particularly if the meter indicates a short circuit (no
measurable resistance) or an open circuit (infinite, or very high
resistance), the camshaft pulse generator must be replaced.
4   If the generator is thought to be faulty, first check that this is not
due to a damaged or broken wire from the generator to the connector;
pinched or broken wires can usually be repaired.

6.6 On L models onward the spark unit is mounted on the left side of the rear subframe

7.9 Ignition timing rotor marking and cover index mark (arrows) (No. 1 cylinder shown)

Removal

5   Remove the fuel tank as described in Chapter 4 and the right side cover.
6   Trace the wiring back from the generator, fitted to the rear of the front cylinder head (cylinder Nos. 2 and 4), to the connector. Disconnect the wiring connector and work back along the wiring, noting its routing whilst releasing it from any relevant ties or clips.
7   Unscrew the two retaining bolts and withdraw the generator from the cylinder head. Recover the O-ring and discard it; a new one must be used on installation.

Installation

8   Fit a new O-ring to the camshaft pulse generator and install it in the cylinder head. Fit the retaining bolts and tighten them securely.
9   Ensure the wiring is correctly routed, and retained by all the relevant clips and ties, and reconnect it to the main harness.
10   Install the fuel tank as described in Chapter 4 and the right side cover.

6   Spark unit - removal, check and installation

Removal

G through K models

1   Remove the left and right side covers and the tail cowl as described in Chapter 8.
2   Disconnect the rear turn signal wiring connectors then undo the four bolts and remove the turn signal mounting bracket assembly from the bike.
3   Undo the two screws then remove the cover from the fender/mudguard.
4   Lift the spark unit out of position and disconnect its wiring connector.

L models onward

Refer to illustration 6.6
5   Remove the side cover/tail cowl assembly as described in Chapter 8.
6   Disconnect the wiring connector from the spark unit **(see illustration)**.
7   Slide the spark unit out of its rubber retainer and remove it from the motorcycle.

Check

8   If the tests shown in the preceding Sections have failed to isolate the cause of an ignition fault, it is likely that the spark unit itself is faulty.

However, to assess the condition of the spark unit a special electronic test unit and adapter, only available to a Honda dealer will be required.

Installation

9   Installation is the reverse of removal ensuring the wiring connector is securely connected.

7   Ignition timing - general information and check

General information

1   Since no provision exists for adjusting the ignition timing and since no component is subject to mechanical wear, there is no need for regular checks; only if investigating a fault such as a loss of power or a misfire, should the ignition timing be checked.
2   The ignition timing can only be checked whilst the engine is running using a stroboscopic (timing) lamp. The inexpensive neon lamps should be adequate in theory, but in practice may produce a pulse of such low intensity that the timing mark remains indistinct. If possible, one of the more precise xenon tube lamps should be used, powered by an external source of the appropriate voltage. **Note:** *Do not use the machine's own battery as an incorrect reading may result from stray impulses within the electrical system.*

Check

Refer to illustrations 7.9 and 7.10
Note: *Check the ignition timing using the cylinder number specified, and then, if necessary, carry out the check on the remaining three cylinders.*
3   Warm the engine up to normal operating temperature then stop it.
4   On G and H models, remove the seat and right lower fairing section
as described in Chapter 8. Connect the timing light to the No. 1 cylinder plug wire (HT lead) as described in the manufacturer's instructions.
5   On J models onward remove the lower fairing as described in Chapter 8. Connect the timing light to the No. 4 cylinder plug wire (HT lead) as described in the manufacturer's instructions.
6   On all models, unscrew the center cap from the right crankcase cover. Recover the cap sealing ring.
7   The timing marks are stamped on the starter clutch. There are four sets of marks, one for each cylinder. The timing mark is the line next to the 'F' mark of the relevant cylinder.
8   Start the engine and aim the light at the inspection hole.
9   With the machine idling at the specified speed, the rotor timing mark for the relevant cylinder should align with the index mark, in the form of a cutout or line in the edge of the crankcase cover **(see illustration)**.

5

10   Slowly increase the engine speed whilst observing the timing mark. Starting at approximately 1800 rpm on G through K models, and 2000 rpm on L models onward, the 'F' mark should move counter-clockwise (anti-clockwise), increasing in relation to the engine speed. On some models there is a full advance marking (in the form of two straight lines) on the rotor **(see illustration)**.

11   As already stated, there is no means of adjustment of the ignition timing on these machines. If the ignition timing is incorrect one of the ignition system components is at fault, and system must be tested as described in the preceding Sections of this Chapter.

12   When the check is complete, fit a new sealing ring to the center cap and lubricate it with a smear of clean engine oil. Install the cap and tighten it to the specified torque setting.

13   Install the fairing panel(s) as described in Chapter 8.

7.10 Ignition timing full advance marking correctly aligned with cover index mark (arrows)

Chapter 6
Frame, suspension and final drive

Contents

Specifications

Front forks

Spring free length
- G and H models
  - New .... 372.4 mm (14.661 in)
  - Service limit .... 365.0 mm (14.370 in)
- J and K models
  - New .... 409.7 mm (16.130 in)
  - Service limit .... 401.5 mm (15.807 in)
- L and M models
  - New .... 413.6 mm (16.283 in)
  - Service limit .... 405.3 mm (15.957 in)
- N and P models
  - New .... 427.1 mm (16.815 in)
  - Service limit .... 418.5 mm (16.476 in)
- R models
  - New .... 340.2 mm (13.394 in)
  - Service limit .... 330.0 mm (12.992 in)

Oil capacity - per fork
- G and H models
  - Left fork .... 370 cc (12.5 US fl oz, 13.0 Imp fl oz)
  - Right fork .... 358 cc (12.1 US fl oz, 12.6 Imp fl oz)
- J and K models
  - Left fork .... 523 cc (18.4 Imp fl oz)
  - Right fork .... 513 cc (18.1 Imp fl oz)
- L and M models - both forks
  - UK models .... 394 cc (13.9 Imp fl oz)
  - US models .... 383 cc (12.9 US fl oz)
- N and P models - both forks .... 386 cc (13.1 US fl oz, 13.6 Imp fl oz)
- R models - both forks .... 412 cc (13.9 US fl oz, 14.5 Imp fl oz)

Oil level*
- G and H models .... 153 mm (6.024 in)
- J and K models .... 120 mm (4.724 in)
- L and M models .... 175 mm (6.890 in)
- N and P models .... 178 mm (7.008 in)
- R models .... 177 mm (6.969 in)

*Oil level is measured from the top of the tube with the fork spring removed and the tube fully compressed. On L onwards models the damper piston rod should also be fully inserted.

Fork oil type
- UK models, US G and H models .... ATF (Automatic Transmission Fluid)
- US L through R models .... Pro Honda Suspension Fluid SS-7

Fork tube maximum runout .... 0.2 mm (0.008 inch)

6

Rear shock absorber

Spring free length

G models

New .... 150.0 mm (5.906 in)

Service limit.. 147.0 mm (5.787 in)

H through K models

New .... 163.1 mm (6.421 in)

Service limit.. 160.0 mm (6.299 in)

L and M models

New .... 195.3 mm (7.689 in)

Service limit.. 191.4 mm (7.535 in)

N and P models

New .... 184.8 mm (7.276 in)

Service limit.. 181.1 mm (7.130 in)

R models .... Not specified

Suspension settings

Front fork air pressure - G through K models*

Standard - each fork .... 0 to 6 psi (0 to 0.04 Bars)

Maximum difference between forks .... 1.5 psi (0.01 Bars)

Pressure must be set with fork cold and motorcycle supported with front wheel clear of the ground.

Front fork spring preload standard setting

G through M models .... Not adjustable

N models onward .... 3rd position/groove from top

Front fork damping .... Not adjustable

Front fork anti-dive settings - G through K models............... According to rider's preference

Rear shock absorber spring preload standard setting

G through K models .... 2nd position from Low (L)

L through R models... STD

R model alternative .... 12 clicks back from 'Low' position, to red dot

Rear shock absorber spring standard installed length

G through K models .... Not specified

L and M models .... 181.9 mm (7.161 in)

N and P models.. 171.4 mm (6.748 in)

R models .... Not specified

Rear shock absorber compression damping .... Not adjustable

Rear shock absorber rebound (tension) damping

G through M models .... Not adjustable

N models onward .... One turn (approx.) back from fully-hard position until punch marks align

Torque settings

	Nm	Ft-lbs
Handlebar clamp bolts		
UK G through K models	27	20
US G and H models	40	29
L models onward	23	17
Triple clamp pinch bolts		
Top clamp - G through K models	11	8
Top clamp - L models onward	23	17
Bottom clamp - G through K models	33	24
Bottom clamp - L models onward	50	36
Front forks		
Top cap	23	17
Damper piston rod locknut (to top cap)	20	14
Damper rod Allen bolt	20	14
Steering stem adjuster nut (see text)	25	18
Steering stem top nut	105	76
Subframe/seat rail mounting bolts	40	29
Grab rail mounting bolts - L models onward	35	25
Shock absorber mounting bolt nuts	45	33
Rear suspension linkage pivot bolt nuts	45	33
Shock arm pinch bolt - G through K models	25	18
Swingarm pivot - G through K models		
Left pivot bolt	95	69
Right pivot bolt	60	43
Swingarm pivot - L models onward		
Left pivot bolt locknut	95	69
Right adjuster bolt (threaded sleeve)	15	11
Right adjuster bolt locknut	80	58

Front sprocket bolt	52	38
Rear sprocket nuts		
G through K models	90	65
L models onward	33	24
Drive chain adjuster locknuts - G through K models	22	16
Bearing holder clamp bolt - L models onward	55	40

3.1 Rider's right footpeg cotter pin (split pin) and washer (A), rear brake master cylinder-to-brake pedal clevis pin (B)

3.6a Unbolt (arrows) the rear brake master cylinder from the rider's right footpeg bracket . . .

3.6b . . . then unscrew the footpeg mounting bolts (other bolt arrowed) to withdraw footpeg bracket

1 General information

All models covered in this manual employ an open-diamond type frame which uses the engine unit as a stressed member. The main frame's two principal spars and their smaller-section downtubes/engine support rails are constructed of box section extruded aluminum alloy, joining forged aluminum alloy steering head and swingarm pivot sections. The separate bolt-on seat rail/subframe is of box section steel.

Front suspension is by a pair of oil-damped, coil spring, telescopic forks.

Rear suspension is by Honda's 'Pro-Link' system in which the swingarm acts on a gas-charged, hydraulically-damped suspension unit via a linkage. On G through K models the swingarm is a conventional pivoted-fork design constructed of box section extruded aluminum alloy. On later models (L onwards), Honda's 'Pro-Arm' swingarm is used, in which a single-sided member (a true 'swinging arm') is constructed of aluminum alloy and carries the rear wheel's stub axle, with the rear sprocket and brake disc attached, rotating on needle roller bearings in a housing which is set eccentrically to permit drive chain adjustment when rotated.

The final drive uses an endless chain (which means it doesn't have a master (split) link). A rubber damper (often called a cush drive) is installed between the rear sprocket coupling and the wheel.

2 Frame - inspection and repair

1   The frame should not require attention unless accident damage has occurred. In most cases, frame replacement is the only satisfactory remedy for such damage. A few frame specialists have the jigs and other equipment necessary for straightening the frame to the required standard of accuracy, but even then there is no simple way of assessing to what extent the frame may have been over stressed. Note that even fewer specialists have the ability successfully to repair/straighten aluminum alloy frames.
2   After the machine has accumulated a lot of miles, the frame should be examined closely for signs of cracking or splitting at the welded joints. Corrosion can also cause weakness at these joints. Loose engine mount bolts can cause ovaling or fracturing of the mounting tabs. Minor damage can often be repaired by welding, depending on the extent and nature of the damage and the skill of the specialist repairer entrusted with the task.
3   Remember that a frame which is out of alignment will cause handling problems. If misalignment is suspected as the result of an accident, it will be necessary to strip the machine completely so the frame can be thoroughly checked.

3 Footpegs and brackets - removal and installation

Removal

Rider's footpegs
Refer to illustration 3.1
1   Remove the cotter pin (split pin) and washer, then slide out the pivot pin and remove the footpeg from the bracket with its return spring **(see illustration)**.

Rider's left footpeg bracket
2   Place the motorcycle on its centerstand - where no centerstand is fitted, support the machine securely in an upright position.
3   Unbolt and remove the bracket assembly from the frame.

Rider's right footpeg bracket
Refer to illustrations 3.6a and 3.6b
4   Remove the seat and either the right side cover or the rear fairing panel, according to model (see Chapter 8, if necessary).
5   Trace the wiring back from the brake light switch and disconnect it at its wiring connector.
6   Unscrew the rear brake master cylinder mounting bolts and the right footpeg bracket bolts **(see illustrations)**.
7   Remove the cotter pin (split pin) and slide out the clevis pin securing the master cylinder to the brake pedal **(see illustration 3.1)**. Unhook, if required, the return springs of the brake light switch and the brake pedal to release the footpeg bracket from the master cylinder

6

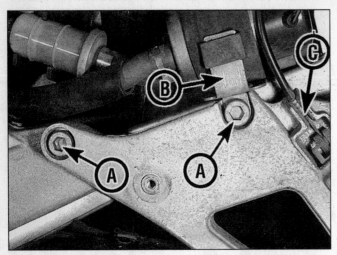

3.12 When unscrewing left passenger footpeg bracket mounting bolts (A), note fuel pump mounting (B) and disconnect seat lock cable at (C) to release bracket

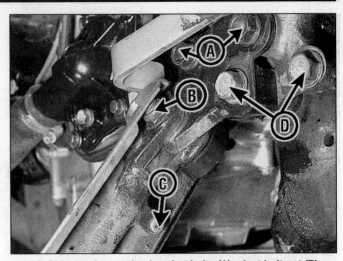

4.3 Sidestand mounting bracket bolts (A), pivot bolt nut (B), fairing panel retaining screw (C) and center stand bracket (L through P models only) bolts (D)

and frame.

8   Remove completely the master cylinder mounting bolts and separate it from the footpeg bracket.

9   Withdraw the bracket from the frame.

Passenger footpegs

10   Remove the cotter pin (split pin) and washer then slide out the pivot pin and remove the footpeg from the bracket. As the footpeg is removed, recover the footpeg detent plate, spring and ball bearing, noting the correct fitted positions of each component.

Passenger left footpeg bracket

Refer to illustration 3.12

11   Where they cover the footpeg bracket mountings, remove the seat and either the left side cover or the rear fairing panel, according to model (see Chapter 8).

12   Unbolt the footpeg bracket from the motorcycle. Note the location of components such as the fuel pump mounting and disconnect the seat lock cable to release the footpeg bracket **(see illustration)**.

Passenger right footpeg bracket

13   Where they cover the footpeg bracket mountings, remove the seat and either the right side cover or the rear fairing panel, according to model (see Chapter 8).

14   Unscrew the bolt securing the exhaust system muffler (silencer) to the footpeg bracket. Tie the muffler (silencer) to the frame to prevent strain on the exhaust system.

15   Unbolt the footpeg bracket from the motorcycle.

Installation

Rider's footpegs

16   Installation is the reverse of removal using a new cotter pin (split pin). Grease all pivot points as the various components are reassembled.

Rider's left footpeg bracket

17   Installation is the reverse of removal; tighten securely the bracket bolts.

Rider's right footpeg bracket

18   Hook up, if disconnected, the return springs of the brake light switch and the brake pedal. Install a new cotter pin (split pin) when reassembling the clevis pin securing the master cylinder to the brake pedal. Grease all pivot points as the various components are reassembled.

19   Apply a few drops of locking compound to the threads of the

master cylinder and footpeg bracket mounting bolts, then fit the bolts and tighten them securely.

20   Reconnect the brake light switch wiring, ensuring it is correctly routed.

21   Install the seat and the right side cover or rear fairing panel, according to model (see Chapter 8).

Passenger footpegs

22   Installation is the reverse of removal using a new cotter pin (split pin).

Passenger footpeg brackets

23   Installation is the reverse of removal.

---

4   Centerstand and sidestand - maintenance

Centerstand

Note: *To remove the centerstand for inspection the motorcycle must be supported securely in an upright position so that the rear wheel and stand are clear of the ground. Block the motorcycle in this position, being careful not to damage the fairing lower panels - remove them if necessary, as described in Chapter 8.*

1   The centerstand is attached to the frame as follows:

a) *On J and K models, the stand pivots on two bushings, one at each mounting point; each is secured by a bolt which passes from the outside through to the inside of each pivot, threading into a special nut located inside each bushing. To remove the stand, unscrew both bolts.* **Caution:** *The right pivot bolt uses a* **left-hand thread** *and must be unscrewed* **clockwise***. Extract the nuts and unhook the stand return springs; the stand can then be withdrawn and the bushings removed for inspection. Clean all components, check each for signs of damage or of excessive wear and replace any that warrant it. Check particularly the fit of the bushings in the stand and in the frame mounting 'ears', also the condition of the return springs. On installation, grease all components as they are reassembled, ensure that both nuts are correctly located in the frame and tighten the bolts securely.* **Caution:** *The right pivot bolt uses a* **left-hand thread** *and must be tightened* **counterclockwise (anti-clockwise)***.*

b) *On R models, the stand is retained by a pivot shaft. Periodically, undo the retaining bolt at its left end and slide out the pivot shaft, noting the washer at its right end. Inspect the shaft for signs of wear and replace if necessary. Apply a smear of grease to the shaft and fit it to the motorcycle, not forgetting the washer. Securely tighten the retaining bolt.*

5.3 Unscrew the two mounting bolts to remove the brake (or clutch) master cylinder from the handlebar . . .

5.6 . . . and remove the snap-ring from the top of the fork tube

5.9a Disconnect the clutch switch wiring (arrow)

5.9b Free the switch from the left handlebar . . .

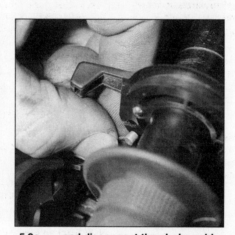

5.9c . . . and disconnect the choke cable from the lever

5.9d Handlebar end weight retaining screw

c) On all other models, refer to step [b] above, noting that the pivot shaft is secured by a cotter pin (split pin) and washer (at its left end on G and H models, at its right end on L through P models). On installation, always fit a new cotter pin (split pin), spreading its ends securely.

2   Make sure the return springs are in good condition. A broken or weak spring is an obvious safety hazard.

Sidestand

Refer to illustration 4.3

3   The sidestand is attached to a bracket on the frame. A pair of extension springs anchored to the bracket ensures that the stand is held in the retracted position **(see illustration)**.

4   Make sure the pivot bolt is tight and the extension springs are in good condition and not over-stretched. An accident is almost certain to occur if the stand extends while the machine is in motion.

5   Handlebars - removal and installation

Removal

Right handlebar

Refer to illustrations 5.3 and 5.6

1   Place the motorcycle on its centerstand - where no centerstand is fitted, support the machine securely in an upright position.

2   Disconnect the wiring connector from the front brake light switch.

3   Unbolt the master cylinder mounting clamp. Position the master

cylinder clear of the handlebar, ensuring no strain is placed on the hydraulic hose. Keep the master cylinder upright to prevent possible fluid leakage and as high as possible to prevent the entry of air into the system **(see illustration)**.

4   Unscrew the two handlebar switch screws and free the switch from the handlebar.

5   Disconnect the throttle cables from the carburetors then free the cables from the throttle grip (see Chapter 4).

6   Pry off the snap-ring from the top of the fork tube **(see illustration)**.

7   Slacken the clamp bolt and slide the handlebar off the fork.

8   If necessary, undo the retaining screw then remove the weight from the end of the handlebar and slide off the throttle twistgrip.

Left handlebar

Refer to illustrations 5.9a through 5.9d

9   Proceed as described in Steps 1 to 8 above, noting the following:

a) *Steps 1 and 2 - disconnect the clutch switch and unbolt the clutch master cylinder* **(see illustration)**.

b) *Step 5 - disconnect the choke cable from its lever* **(see illustrations)**.

c) *Step 8 - if necessary, undo the retaining screw then remove the weight from the end of the handlebar and peel or cut off the handlebar grip and remove the choke lever* **(see illustration)**.

Installation

Refer to illustrations 5.10a and 5.10b

10   Installation is the reverse of the removal procedure, noting the following points:

6

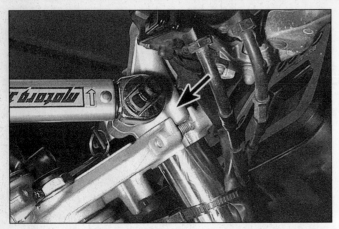

5.10a Locate the handlebar lug (arrow) in the triple clamp slot, then tighten the handlebar clamp bolt to the specified torque setting whilst pushing the handlebar forwards

a) When installing the grips to the left handlebar and to the throttle twistgrip, clean and degrease thoroughly the handlebar/twistgrip, apply a suitable adhesive to the inside of the grip and slide it into place. Rotate the grip on the handlebar/twistgrip to spread the adhesive evenly, check that the grip is straight and leave it for the specified period (see the adhesive manufacturer's instructions) to be sure that it is completely dry before using the motorcycle.

b) Align the handlebar locating lug with the slot in the triple clamp. Tighten the handlebar clamp bolt to the specified torque setting whilst pushing the handlebar fully forwards **(see illustration)**.

c) Fit the snap-ring ensuring it is correctly located in its groove.

d) Where removed, apply a smear of grease to the throttle twistgrip and choke lever before installing them.

e) Apply locking compound to the handlebar end weight retaining screws, install the weight (aligning each correctly on the inner weight) and securely tighten the screw.

f) Reconnect the throttle cables to the twistgrip or the choke cable to the lever, as appropriate.

g) Fit the switch lower half to the handlebar, locating its peg in the handlebar hole. Fit the upper half of the switch and securely tighten the screws - always tighten the front screw first, until the switch halves mate properly, then the rear screw. Don't overtighten the rear screw in an attempt to close the gap between the switch halves at the rear; you will only break the switch.

h) Adjust the throttle cables as described in Chapter 1.

i) Check the choke cable operation and, if necessary, adjust as described in Chapter 1.

j) Install the master cylinder so that its body's clamp mating surface aligns with the punch mark in the handlebar and ensure that the UP mark on the clamp is up, then tighten the mounting bolts **(see illustration)**. Always tighten the upper bolt first, to the specified torque setting (see Chapter 7) until the clamp halves mate properly, then the lower bolt. Don't overtighten the lower bolt in an attempt to close the gap between the clamp halves at the bottom; you will only break the clamp or the master cylinder.

k) Reconnect the front brake light/clutch switch wiring.

6   Forks - removal and installation

Removal

Refer to illustration 6.6

Note: *If the forks are to be dismantled it is preferable to slacken the top caps and the damper rod Allen bolts while the tubes are still held in the triple clamps. Before doing this, be sure to slacken fully the preload adjustment or release the air pressure, if appropriate - see Section 7, Step 1.*

1   Remove the front wheel as described in Chapter 7.

5.10b Install the master cylinder mounting clamps ensuring the UP mark is the correct way up

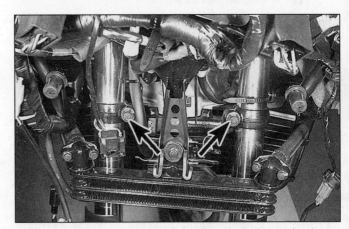

6.6 Slacken the bottom triple clamp pinch bolts (arrows) - shown with upper fairing removed

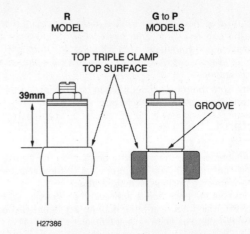

H27386

6.8 Front fork tube positions, relative to top triple clamp

2   Remove the front fender/mudguard as described in Chapter 8.

3   Carefully pry off the snap-ring from the top of each fork tube **(see illustration 5.6)**.

4   Slacken the handlebar clamp bolts. Slide the handlebars off the fork tubes and support them to prevent straining the hydraulic hoses or leakage of hydraulic fluid from the master cylinders - see Section 5, Step 3.

5   If not already done, unbolt the left brake caliper from the fork slider. Tie both calipers to the frame's front downtubes to prevent any strain

6.9a With the fork tubes correctly positioned, tighten the bottom . . .

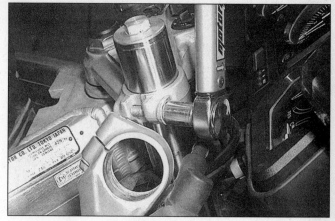

6.9b . . . and top triple clamp pinch bolts to the specified torque setting

6.12 With the tube held in the triple clamps, tighten the top cap to the specified torque setting

being placed on the hydraulic hoses or pipes. Slip clean pieces of wood between the brake pads to prevent the pistons from being ejected should the brake lever be applied inadvertently. **Caution:** *Do not operate the front brake lever with the calipers or the wheel removed.*

6   Slacken the top and bottom triple clamp bolts and remove the forks by twisting them and pulling them down **(see illustration)**. If the fork tubes are seized in the triple clamps, spray the area with penetrating oil and allow time for it to soak in before trying again.

Installation

Refer to illustrations 6.8, 6.9a, 6.9b and 6.12

7   Remove all traces of corrosion from the tubes and triple clamps and slide the fork tubes back into place. A smear of grease or similar lubricant will help installation and prevent corrosion from occurring.

8   Position each tube as shown, relative to the top triple clamp **(see illustration)**. On G through P models, align the lower groove on the fork tube with the top surface of the top triple clamp. On R models, position the tube so that its upper end (not the top cap) is 39 mm (1.53 inches) above the top surface of the top triple clamp. **Caution:** *Both tubes must be in* **exactly** *the same position relative to the top triple clamp. If the position of the top triple clamp is altered subsequently (for example, in steering stem bearing adjustment), the positions of both fork tubes must be altered accordingly.*

9   With the forks correctly positioned, tighten first the bottom triple clamp pinch bolts to the specified torque setting, then the top triple clamp pinch bolts **(see illustrations)**.

10   Install the handlebars, ensuring that the lug on the underside of each is correctly located in the slot in the top triple clamp **(see illustration 5.10a)**. Tighten the handlebar clamp bolts to the specified

torque setting whilst pushing each handlebar fully forwards.

11   Fit the snap-ring to each fork tube making sure they are correctly located in their grooves.

12   If the forks have been dismantled, the fork top caps should now be tightened to the specified torque setting **(see illustration)**.

13   Install the front fender/mudguard as described in Chapter 8.

14   Except for R models, fit the left brake caliper to the fork slider and tighten its bolts to the specified torque (see Chapter 7).

15   Install the front wheel as described in Chapter 7.

16   Adjust the fork settings as described in Section 12. Check the operation of the front forks and brake before taking the machine out on the road.

---

7   Forks - disassembly, inspection and reassembly

Disassembly

Note: *Always dismantle the forks separately to avoid interchanging parts and thus causing an accelerated rate of wear. Store all components in separate, clearly marked containers.*

1   To minimize spring pressure on the top cap, fully unscrew the preload adjuster, where fitted; refer to Section 12, if necessary. On models so equipped, remove the air valve cap and depress the valve core to equalize air pressure. **Warning:** *Keep your face, especially your eyes, away from the valve when releasing air pressure - oil droplets may be sprayed out with some force!*

2   Clamp the fork slider securely in a vise equipped with soft jaws, being careful not to overtighten it. If not already done, slacken the damper rod Allen bolt which passes up through the bottom of the slider. **Note:** *The bolt should be slackened at this point as the pressure applied by the fork spring will keep the damper rod from spinning in the fork tube as the bolt is turned. There is no need to remove the bolt completely, but make sure it's loose enough to turn easily.*

3   Release the slider from the vise and then carefully clamp the fork tube in the vise, taking care not to overtighten or score its surface, in an upright position. If not already done, slacken the top cap. Now follow the procedures given below under the relevant sub-heading.

G through K models

Refer to illustrations 7.4, 7.7 and 7.14

4   Unscrew the top cap from the tube, making sure it is not expelled forcibly by spring pressure as the last threads of the cap are unscrewed **(see illustration)**.

5   Withdraw the spacer seat (G and H models only), the spacer, the spacer/spring seat and fork spring, noting which way up the spring is fitted.

6   Invert the fork over a suitable container and pump the tube vigorously to expel as much fork oil as possible.

7   Pry out the dust seal from the slider's upper end to reach the oil

6

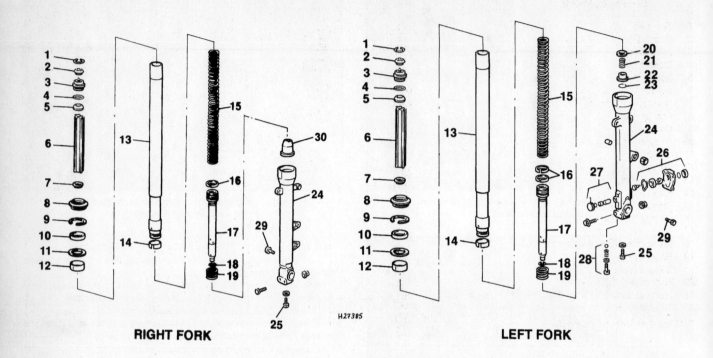

RIGHT FORK   **LEFT FORK**

7.4 Exploded view of the front forks - G through K models

1	Snap-ring	10	Oil seal
2	Pre-load adjuster	11	Washer
3	Top cap	12	Top bushing
4	O-ring	13	Fork tube
5	Spacer seat (G and H only)	14	Bottom bushing
6	Spacer*	15	Fork spring
7	Spacer/spring seat	16	Piston rings
8	Dust seal	17	Damper rod
9	Oil seal retaining snap-ring		

18	Snap-ring	26	Anti-dive assembly
19	Rebound spring	27	Anti-dive adjuster
20	Lock valve spring seat	28	Anti-dive check valve
21	Lock valve spring	29	Oil drain screw
22	Lock valve	30	Damper rod valve
23	Snap-ring		*Cruciform spacer fitted to G
24	Fork slider		models only, all others have a
25	Damper rod Allen bolt		tubular spacer.

7.7 Use a flat-bladed screwdriver to free the dust seal

7.14 Inspect the damper rod piston ring(s) for signs of damage and replace if worn - don't disturb unless they are to be replaced

seal retaining snap-ring **(see illustration)**.

8   Carefully pry out the snap-ring whilst taking care not to scratch the surface of the tube.

9   Remove the damper rod Allen bolt and washer from the bottom of the slider. **Note:** *If necessary, temporarily fit the fork spring, spring seat(s), spacer and top cap to prevent the damper rod from rotating. Failing this, insert a long wooden dowel (such as a thin broom handle)*

with a coarse taper ground on its tip into the fork tube and press it hard against the head of the damper rod to prevent it from rotating while the Allen bolt is finally unscrewed.

10   To separate the tube from the slider it will be necessary to displace the top bushing and oil seal. The bottom bushing should not pass through the top bushing, a fact which can be used to good effect. Push the tube gently ins until it stops against the damper rod valve;

**7.15a Exploded view of a front fork -
L models onward**

1   Top cap
2   O-ring
3   Locknut
4   Slotted collar
5   Spring seat*
6   Spacer*
7   Spring seat
8   Fork spring
9   Dust seal
10 Oil seal retaining snap-ring
11 Oil seal
12 Washer
13 Top bushing
14 Fork tube
15 Bottom bushing
16 Damper rod/piston assembly
17 Rebound spring
18 Damper rod/piston assembly seat
19 Fork tube protector -
    R models only
20 Fork slider
21 Damper rod Allen bolt
22 Oil drain screw

*Not fitted to N and P models.

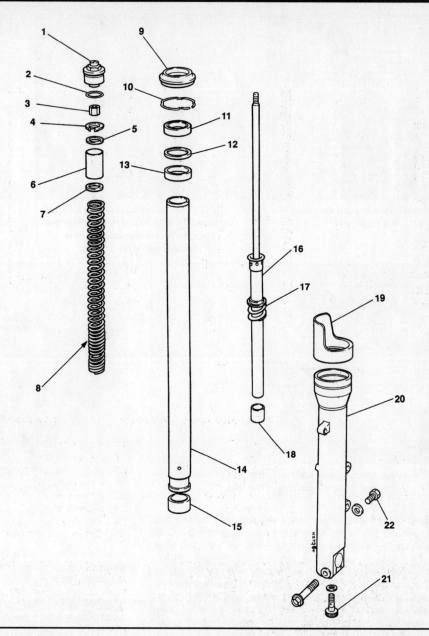

take care not to do this forcibly (especially on the left fork) or the valve may be damaged. Pull the tube sharply outs until the bottom bushing strikes the top bushing. Repeat this operation until the top bushing and seal are tapped out of the slider. Pouring hot water over the slider's upper end will cause the metal to expand, thus slackening the fit of the seal and bushing and minimizing the amount of force needed to complete this task.
11   With the tube removed, slide off the oil seal and washer, noting which way up the washer is fitted, followed by the top bushing. **Caution:** *Do not remove the bottom bushing from the tube unless it is to be replaced.*
12   On the left fork, pry out the retaining snap-ring and withdraw the damper rod valve, valve spring and spring seat from the tip of the damper rod. Pry out the remaining snap-ring, tip up the fork tube and remove the damper rod and rebound spring. **Caution:** *Do not remove the piston rings from the damper rod unless they are to be replaced.*
13   On the left fork slider, disassemble the anti-dive mechanism as follows:
a) Pry off the retaining snap-ring and withdraw the shouldered collar and the rubber bushing from the anti-dive piston.
b) Remove the rubber dust boot from the piston and cover.

c) Unscrew the four Allen screws and withdraw the anti-dive assembly cover; remove and discard its sealing O-ring.
d) Remove the piston and stopper rubber from the cover; remove and discard the piston's sealing O-ring. Withdraw the spring from the slider.
e) On G and H models only, unscrew the small grub screw securing the adjuster knob, withdraw the knob from the front of the slider and extract the adjuster spindle from the rear of the slider (noting the spindle O-ring).
f) On G and H models only, unscrew the small screw from the bottom of the protrusion on the front of the left fork slider (note the sealing washer) and extract the check valve spring and ball.
14   On the right fork, withdraw the damper rod valve from the tip of the damper rod. Pry out the retaining snap-ring, tip up the fork tube and remove the damper rod and rebound spring. **Caution:** *Do not remove the piston ring from the damper rod unless it is to be replaced* **(see illustration)**.

L models onward
Refer to illustrations 7.15a, 7.15b, 7.16, 7.20, 7.21 and 7.22
15   Unscrew the top cap from the fork tube **(see illustrations)**.

7.15b Unscrew the top cap from the tube . . .

7.16 . . . then counter-hold the locknut underneath with one wrench while the top cap is unscrewed from the damper rod with another

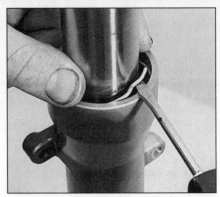

7.20 Take care not to scratch the tube when prying the snap-ring out of the slider

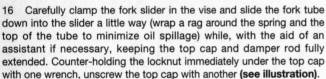

7.21 Lock the damper rod as described in the text to unscrew the Allen bolt from the bottom of the slider

7.22 These parts will come out with the fork tube

1	Oil seal	3	Top bushing
2	Washer	4	Bottom bushing

16   Carefully clamp the fork slider in the vise and slide the fork tube down into the slider a little way (wrap a rag around the spring and the top of the tube to minimize oil spillage) while, with the aid of an assistant if necessary, keeping the top cap and damper rod fully extended. Counter-holding the locknut immediately under the top cap with one wrench, unscrew the top cap with another **(see illustration)**.

17   Remove the slotted spring collar by holding down the fork spring (keep the damper rod fully extended) while the collar is slipped out to the side. **Caution:** *The fork spring may be exerting considerable pressure, making this a potentially dangerous operation. Wipe off as much oil as possible to minimize the risk of your hands slipping on oily components and enlist the aid of an assistant.* Keep the restraint on the fork spring and remove the spring seat, with the spacer and second spring seat, according to model. Slowly release the fork spring until all pressure has been relieved, then withdraw the spring from the tube.

18   Invert the fork over a suitable container and pump the damper rod piston vigorously to expel as much fork oil as possible.

19   On R models, remove the fork tube protector from the slider's upper end. On all models, pry out the dust seal from the slider's upper end to reach the oil seal retaining snap-ring.

20   Carefully pry out the snap-ring whilst taking care not to scratch the surface of the tube **(see illustration)**.

21   Remove the damper rod/piston assembly Allen bolt and washer from the bottom of the slider and withdraw the damper rod/piston assembly from the fork tube **(see illustration). Note:** *If necessary, temporarily fit the fork spring, spring seat, spacer and top cap to prevent the damper rod/piston assembly from rotating.*

22   Separate the fork tube and slider as described above in Step 10 **(see illustration)**.

23   With the tube removed, slide off the oil seal and washer, noting which way up the washer is fitted, followed by the top bushing, then

invert the slider and tip out the damper rod/piston assembly seat. **Caution:** *Do not remove the bottom bushing from the tube unless it is to be replaced.*

Inspection

Refer to illustration 7.28

24   Clean all parts in solvent and blow them dry with compressed air, if available.

25   Check the fork tube and slider, the bushings and the damper rod/piston assembly (as applicable) for score marks, scratches, flaking of the chrome and excessive or abnormal wear. Look for dents in the tubes and replace them if any are found. If either bushing is worn so badly that the copper base metal appears through the Teflon coating over more than 3/4 of the bushing's surface area, that bushing must be replaced. Check the fork seal seat for nicks, gouges and scratches. If damage is evident, leaks will occur. Replace worn or defective parts with new ones.

26   Have the fork tube checked for runout at a dealer service department or other repair shop. **Warning:** *If it is bent, it should not be straightened; replace it with a new one.*

27   Measure the overall length of the spring and check it for cracks and other damage. Compare the length to the service length listed in this Chapter's Specifications. If it's defective or sagged, replace both fork springs with new ones. Never replace only one spring.

28   If it's necessary to replace the bottom bushing, pry it apart at the slit and slide it off. Make sure the new one seats properly **(see illustration)**.

29   On G through K models, check the fit of the front left brake caliper

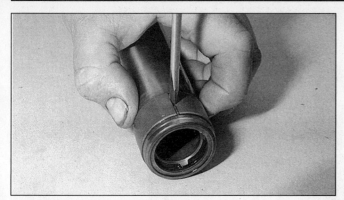

7.28 Pry the ends of the bottom bushing apart with a screwdriver and remove it from the fork tube

mounting bracket bolt and pivot collar in the needle bearing set in the rear of the left fork slider. No freeplay or other sign of wear or damage should be found; replace any of these components that warrants it. If the needle bearing is to be replaced proceed as described in Section 11 of this Chapter.

30   Also on G through K models, clean and inspect all elements of the anti-dive assembly; check particularly the adjuster spindle (where fitted), replacing it if it is worn or damaged. Replace the sealing O-rings and the rubber stopper, bushing and dust boot whenever they are disturbed. Blow clear the damping oil passages in the slider and anti-dive cover (do not probe them with bits of wire); if a passage is severely blocked, use a blast of WD-40 or similar water dispersant/penetrating lubricant applied through the thin plastic pipe usually supplied with such aerosols to dislodge the obstruction. Reassemble temporarily the components and check the piston stroke (see Step 31g below); if the stroke is incorrect, check carefully the condition of the piston and its rubber stopper, sealing O-ring and spring, or of its rubber bush, shouldered collar and the piston bolt. If there is any doubt about the condition of any of these, they must be replaced.

Reassembly

G through K models

31   On the left fork slider, assemble the anti-dive mechanism as follows:

a) On G and H models only, insert the check valve ball and spring into the passage in the bottom of the protrusion on the front of the left fork slider, fit a new sealing washer to the retaining screw and install the screw, applying thread-locking compound to its threads and tightening it securely.

b) On G and H models only, fit a new sealing O-ring to the adjuster spindle, lubricate the spindle and O-ring with clean fork oil and insert them from the rear of the slider. Fit the adjuster knob to the spindle at the front of the slider and fasten the knob by installing and tightening its grub screw. Check that the knob rotates smoothly through its full range, then set the adjustment to the setting required (see Section 12, if necessary).

c) Install the spring to the slider. Fit a new sealing O-ring to the piston, lubricate it with clean fork oil and insert the assembly into the cover. Install a new rubber stopper.

d) Locate a new sealing O-ring in the cover groove, then install the anti-dive assembly cover, ensuring that the spring engages correctly with the piston and that the rubber stopper is not displaced. Apply thread-locking compound to their threads and tighten securely the four Allen screws.

e) Install a new rubber dust boot to the piston and cover.

f) Apply a **thin** coat of PBC (Poly Butyl Cuprysil) grease, or silicone grease designed for high-temperature brake applications to the piston recess, the rubber bushing and to the shouldered collar. Install these to the piston (install the collar so that its shoulder is on the inside of the piston, nearest the wheel) and secure them by fitting the snap-ring.

g) Check the operation of the assembly by inserting the anti-dive piston bolt and pushing the piston in, then releasing it; the piston should move in smoothly and return fully under spring pressure. Measure its stroke; there should be 1.6 mm (0.063 inch) between the fully-out and the fully-in positions.

32   Install the piston ring(s) and rebound spring on the damper rod and slide it into place in the tube so that it projects fully from the bottom of the tube. Pass a long wooden dowel (such as a thin broom handle) with a coarse taper ground on its tip, or the fork spring and spacer, down the tube to hold the damper rod in place.

33   On the left fork, install the upper snap-ring to the damper rod's lower end, followed by the spring seat and valve spring, the lock valve (projecting flange at the bottom) and the remaining snap-ring.

34   On the right fork, install the snap-ring to the damper rod's lower end, followed by the damper rod valve (projecting flange at the bottom).

35   Oil the tube and bottom bushing and support the assembly horizontally with the damper rod components securely held; use grease to stick them in place if they are loose. Pass the slider over the tube and fit the damper rod Allen bolt using a new sealing washer. Apply thread locking compound to the threads of the bolt and tighten it to the specified torque setting.

36   Wrap a thin layer of adhesive tape around the top of the fork tube to cover its edges and grooves, push the tube fully into the slider, then oil the top bushing and slide it down over the tube.

37   Press the top bushing squarely into its recess in the slider as far as possible by hand, then install the washer making sure that its chamfered surface is facing the top bushing. It will be necessary to use the Honda service tool or to devise an alternative tubular drift to tap the top bushing fully into place. The best method is to use a length of tubing slightly larger in diameter than the tube, that will bear squarely on the bushing's washer (wrap adhesive tape over the tubing ends to protect the bushing). Tap the bushing home using the tube as a form of slide hammer. Take care not to scratch the tube during this operation; it is best to make sure that the fork tube is pushed fully into the slider so that any accidental scoring is confined to the area above the seal.

38   When the bushing is seated fully and squarely in its recess in the slider, so that the washer sits flat on the floor of the oil seal's recess (remove the washer to check, wipe the recess clean, then reinstall the washer), install the oil seal. Smear the seal's lips with grease and slide it over the tube so that the seal's marked surface is facing up (away from the slider).

39   Place a large plain washer against the oil seal and drive it into place as described in Step 37 above until the snap-ring groove is just visible above the seal's upper edge. Once the oil seal is correctly seated fit the snap-ring (having removed the large plain washer), ensuring that it is correctly located in its groove.

40   Lubricate the lips of the dust seal then slide it down the fork tube and press it into position.

41   Fill the fork with the specified amount and type of fork oil and pump the fork slowly to distribute the oil. Compress the assembly fully and check the oil level. Add or subtract oil, as necessary, until it is at the level given in the Specifications at the start of this Chapter.

42   Clamp the tube securely in a vise equipped with soft jaws, taking care not to overtighten it or score its surface. Remove the tape from its upper end.

43   Insert the fork spring, ensuring that its tapered end is at the bottom.

44   Insert the spacer/spring seat and spacer, followed by the spacer upper seat (G and H models only); note that the spacer seats (where appropriate) are fitted with their cupped faces against the spacer. Fit a new O-ring to the top cap, then install the top cap. **Note:** The top cap can be tightened to its specified torque setting at this stage if the tube can be held firmly enough, but do not risk distorting the tube by overtightening it. A better method is to tighten the top cap when the fork has been reinstalled and is securely held in the triple clamps.

45   Install the forks as described in Section 6.

L models onward

Refer to illustrations 7.46, 7.47, 7.48a, 7.48b, 7.48c, 7.49a through 7.49d, 7.50, 7.52a through 7.52d, 7.53a and 7.53b

46   Install the rebound spring to the damper rod/piston assembly,

6

7.46 Install the rebound spring to the damper rod/piston assembly so that its tighter-pitched coils are against the flange

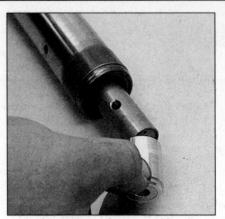

7.47 Insert the damper rod/piston assembly down through the fork tube and fit the damper rod seat

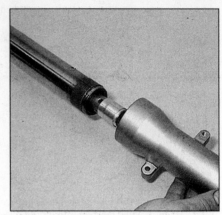

7.48a Carefully ease the slider over the end of the fork tube assembly

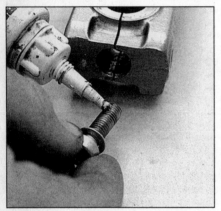

7.48b Apply thread locking compound to damper rod Allen bolt threads before installation . . .

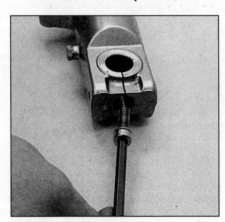

7.48c . . . tighten the bolt to the specified torque setting

7.49a Lubricate the top bushing and washer and slide them onto the tube; make sure washer is fitted the correct way around

tighter-pitched coils against the assembly's flange **(see illustration)**. If the locknut was removed from the top of the damper rod/piston assembly, it must be screwed back on, its chamfered edge down, to the bottom of the thread (i.e., tightened fully onto the rod) **(see illustration 7.53b)**.

47   Insert the damper rod/piston assembly into the fork tube and slide it into place so that it projects fully from the bottom of the tube, then install the damper rod/piston assembly seat **(see illustration)**. Pass the fork spring down the tube to hold the damper rod/piston assembly in place.

48   Oil the fork tube and bottom bushing and insert the assembly into position in the fork slider, securing it by fastening the damper rod/piston assembly Allen bolt as described in Step 35 above **(see illustrations)**.

49   Install the top bushing, washer, oil seal, snap-ring and dust seal as described above in Steps 36 through 40 **(see illustrations)**. On R models, install the fork tube protector, aligning its locating lug in the slot in the slider's upper edge; soaking the protector in hot water will soften it and ease installation, if required.

50   Slowly pour in the specified amount and type of fork oil whilst pushing the damper rod piston up and down. Once the oil has been added, slowly pump the fork tube in and out at least five times, and pump the damper rod piston at least another 10 times. This will ensure that the fork oil is evenly distributed. Fully insert both the tube and damper rod then check the fork oil level **(see illustration)**. Add or subtract fork oil until the oil is at the specified level listed in the Specifications Section of this Chapter.

51   Clamp the slider securely in a vise and fully extend the damper rod. Tie a piece of wire around the rod; the wire can then be used to hold the

7.49b Slide the seal onto the tube making sure its marked surface is facing up - note tape protecting seal lips from tube's sharp edges

rod in the extended position whilst the slotted collar is installed.

52   Insert the fork spring, ensuring that its tapered end/tighter-pitched coils (according to model) is/are at the bottom, followed by the spring seat and, according to model, the spacer and spacer upper seat **(see illustrations)**. Fit a new O-ring to the top cap and lubricate it with a smear of fork oil.

53   With the aid of an assistant push down on the spring seat/spacer upper seat, compressing the fork spring, and slide the slotted collar into position under the locknut **(see illustrations)**. Screw the top cap

7.49c Using a piece of metal tubing as a form of slide hammer to tap the fork seal into place

7.49d Secure the seal in place with the snap-ring then slide the dust seal into position

7.50 Fill the fork with the specified type and amount of fork oil then check the oil level as described in text

7.52a Install the fork spring making sure its tapered end and/or tighter-pitched coils are at the bottom

7.52b Fit the spring seat . . .

7.52c . . . followed by the spacer (where fitted) . . .

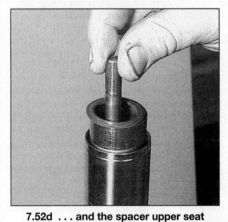

7.52d . . . and the spacer upper seat (where fitted)

7.53a Slotted collar can be slid into position under top cap locknut . . .

7.53b . . . which must be installed with its chamfered edge down and must be tightened to the bottom of the thread, fully on to the rod

6

fully on to the rod then counter-hold the locknut while the top cap is tightened to its specified torque setting against the locknut. Check that all components are correctly seated.

54   Carefully screw the top cap into the fork tube making sure it is not cross-threaded. **Note:** *The top cap can be tightened to its specified torque setting at this stage if the tube can be held firmly enough, but do not risk distorting the tube by overtightening it. A better method is to tighten the top cap when the fork has been reinstalled and is securely held in the triple clamps.*

55   Install the forks as described in Section 6.

8   Steering stem - removal and installation

Caution: *Although not strictly necessary, before removing the steering stem it is recommended that the fuel tank and fairing panels be removed. This will prevent accidental damage to the paintwork.*

Removal

Refer to illustration 8.3

1   Remove the forks as described in Section 6 of this Chapter.

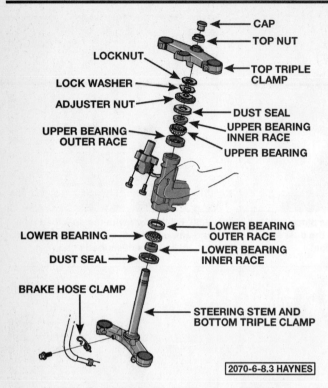

8.3 Exploded view of steering stem and bearings

2070-6-8.3 HAYNES

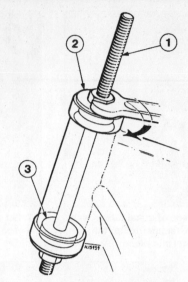

9.6 Drawbolt arrangement for fitting steering stem bearing outer races

1   *Long bolt or threaded bar*   3   *Guide for lower outer race*
2   *Thick washer*

2   Remove the ignition switch, if required; at least disconnect its wiring as described in Chapter 9.
3   On J and K models, undo the two screws and withdraw the top triple clamp cover. On all other models, pry off the cap from the steering stem top nut. Unscrew the nut and lift off the top triple clamp **(see illustration)**.
4   Unbolt the brake hose clamp and the horn, where fitted, from the bottom triple clamp.
5   Straighten the tabs of the steering stem adjuster nut lock washer.
6   Using a suitable C-wrench, unscrew the adjuster nut locknut.
7   Remove the lock washer and discard it; a new one must be fitted on reassembly.
8   Support the bottom triple clamp and slacken the adjuster nut.
9   Lift off the nut, dust seal, inner race and upper bearing from the steering head.
10   Gently lower the bottom triple clamp and steering stem out of the frame. Remove the lower bearing from the steering stem.
11   Remove all traces of old grease from the bearings and races and check them for wear or damage as described in Section 9. **Note:** *Do not attempt to remove the outer races from the frame or the lower inner race and dust seal from the steering stem unless they are to be replaced.*

Installation

12   Smear a liberal quantity of grease on both inner and outer races and the steering stem. Work the grease well into both the upper and lower bearing races.
13   Fit the lower bearing onto the steering stem.
14   Carefully lift the steering stem into position and fit the upper bearing and inner race.
15   Apply grease to the underside of the dust seal and fit it to the steering stem.
16   Apply clean engine oil to the threads of the adjuster nut and tighten it using hand pressure only.
17   To preload the bearings to the torque specified by the manufacturer (see Specifications) it will be necessary to use the service tool, Pt. No. 07916-3710100, which is a socket that fits the adjuster nut. Using the service tool, tighten the adjuster nut to the specified torque setting then turn the steering stem from lock to lock

approximately 5 times to settle the bearings and races in position. After pre-loading the bearings, slacken the adjuster nut one full turn then tighten it again to the specified torque setting. **Note:** *It is important to check the feel of the steering afterwards as described below; if it is too tight readjust the bearings as described below.*
18   If the service tool is not available, tighten the adjuster nut hard using a conventional C-wrench to preload the bearings then adjust as follows.
19   Slacken the adjuster nut slightly until pressure is just released, then turn it slowly clockwise until resistance is just evident. The object is to set the adjuster nut so that the bearings are under a very light loading, just enough to remove any freeplay. **Caution:** *Take great care not to apply excessive pressure because this will cause premature failure of the bearings.*
20   With the bearings correctly adjusted, fit a new lock washer to the adjuster nut. Bend down two opposite lock washer tabs into the grooves of the adjuster nut.
21   Install the locknut and tighten it finger-tight only.
22   Hold the adjuster nut, to prevent it from moving, and tighten the locknut approximately 90° more until its slots align with the remaining lock washer tabs. Secure the locknut in position by bending up the tabs into its slots.
23   Fit the top triple clamp to the steering stem and install the stem top nut.
24   Temporarily fit the forks, to align the triple clamps, and tighten the steering stem top nut to the specified torque setting. Fit the cap or cover.
25   Install the ignition switch as described in Chapter 9.
26   Fit the brake hose clamp and horn, tightening securely the bolts.
27   Install the forks as described in Section 6 of this Chapter.
28   Check that the steering stem bearings are correctly adjusted as soon as the forks and front wheel are installed (see Chapter 1).

9   Steering stem bearings - inspection and replacement

Inspection

1   Remove the steering stem as described in Section 8.
2   Remove all traces of old grease from the bearings and races and check them for wear or damage.
3   The ball bearing tracks of the races should be polished and free from indentations. Inspect the ball bearings for signs of wear, damage or discoloration, and examine the bearing retainer cage for signs of

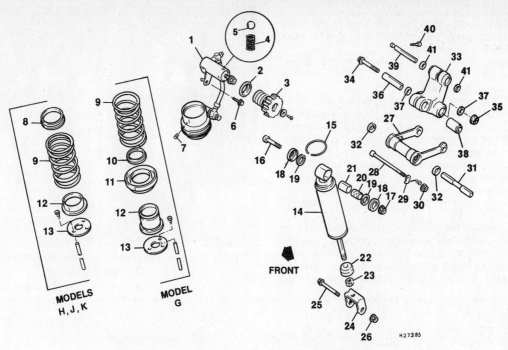

10.5a Rear shock absorber and suspension linkage - G through K models

1	Preload adjuster assembly	15	Snap-ring
2	Dust seal	16	Shock absorber upper
3	Knob		mounting bolt
4	Detent spring	17	Nut
5	Detent ball	18	Dust seal
6	Bolt	19	Grease seal
7	Grub screw	20	Inner sleeve - shock
8	Spring upper seat		absorber upper mounting
9	Spring	21	Bushing - shock absorber
10	Dust seal		upper mounting
11	Spring seat	22	Rebound rubber
12	Spring guide	23	Nut
13	Spring seat stopper	24	Lower mounting clevis
14	Damper		

25	Shock absorber lower	34	Suspension linkage front
	mounting bolt		link-to-rear link pivot bolt
26	Nut	35	Nut
27	Suspension linkage front	36	Inner sleeve - front link-to-
	(shock) link assembly		rear link pivot
28	Suspension linkage front	37	Dust seal
	pivot bolt	38	Bushing - shock absorber
29	Drain tube guide		lower mounting
30	Nut	39	Inner sleeve - rear link pivot
31	Inner sleeve - front link	40	Suspension linkage rear link
	pivot		(shock arm) pinch bolt
32	Grease seal	41	Dust seal
33	Suspension linkage rear link		
	(shock arm) assembly		

cracks or splits. If there are signs of wear on any of the above components both upper and lower bearing assemblies must be replaced as a set.

Replacement

Refer to illustration 9.6

4   The outer races are an interference fit in the steering head and can be tapped from position with a suitable drift. Tap firmly and evenly around each race to ensure that it is driven out squarely. It may prove advantageous to curve the end of the drift slightly to improve its purchase on the race.

5   Alternatively, the races can be removed using a slide-hammer type bearing extractor; these can often be hired from tool shops.

6   The new races can be pressed into the head using the drawbolt arrangement **(see illustration)**, or by using a large diameter tubular drift which bears only on the outer edge of the race. Ensure that the drawbolt washer or drift (as applicable) bears only on the outer edge of the race and does not contact the race bearing surface.

7   To remove the inner race from the steering stem, use two screwdrivers placed on opposite sides of the race to work it free.

8   With the inner race removed, lift off the dust seal. Inspect the seal for wear or damage and replace it if necessary.

9   Install the dust seal and slide on the new inner race. A length of tubing with an internal diameter slightly larger than the steering stem will be needed to tap the new race into position. Ensure that the drift bears only on the inner edge of the race and does not contact the

bearing surface.

10   Install the steering stem as described in Section 8.

10   Rear shock absorber - removal and installation

Removal

All models

1   Place the motorcycle on its centerstand - where no centerstand is fitted, support the machine securely in an upright position. Block the motorcycle (being careful not to damage the fairing lower panels - remove them if necessary, as described in Chapter 8) so that the rear wheel is just resting on the ground (i.e., so that the motorcycle's weight is off the rear suspension but also so that the rear suspension will not drop, with the possible risk of personal injury, when the shock absorber mounting bolts are removed).

2   Remove the seat (see Chapter 8, if necessary).

3   Proceed as described under the relevant sub-heading:

G through K models

Refer to illustrations 10.5a and 10.5b

Caution: *Do not attempt to separate the preload adjuster and shock absorber.*

4   Remove both side covers (see Chapter 8, if necessary).

5   Unscrew the preload adjuster mounting bolt **(see illustrations)**.

6

Release the adjuster and its hose from any securing clamps or ties.

6   Depending on access and the tools available, it may be necessary to remove the mufflers (silencers) to reach the shock absorber lower mounting bolt (see Chapter 4, if necessary).

7   Unscrew the suspension front (shock) link-to-rear link (shock arm) pivot bolt and nut and drop the front link so that the shock absorber lower mounting bolt and nut can be reached.

8   Unscrew the shock absorber lower mounting nut and bolt.

9   Unscrew the shock absorber upper mounting nut and bolt. Depending on access and the tools available, it may be necessary to unscrew the subframe/seat rail upper mounting bolts and to slacken its lower mounting bolts so that the subframe/seat rail can be pivoted gently and carefully backwards (check that components such as brake hoses and wiring are not strained or trapped) to reach the shock absorber upper mounting bolt.

10   Maneuver the shock absorber and preload adjuster assembly down out of the frame.

11   To check the operation of the preload adjuster, turn its knob from the 'Low' to the 'High' positions and measure the distance moved by the spring's top collar; this should be 7.5 mm (0.29 inch). If the distance is not as specified, or if there is any sign of fluid leakage on any part of the adjuster, its hose, or the top collar, the assembly must

10.5b Unscrew the preload adjuster mounting bolt (arrow) - G through K models

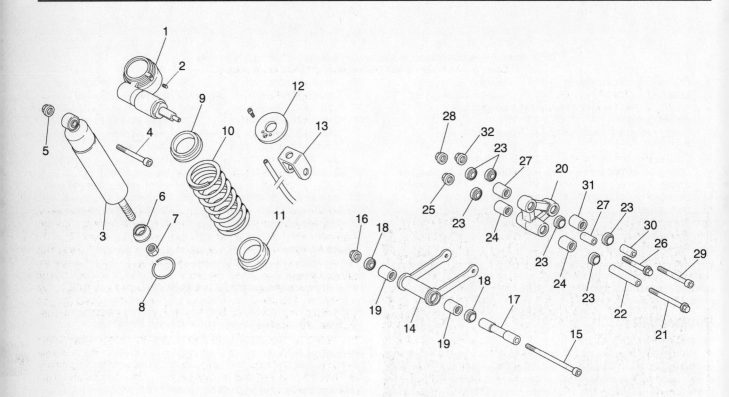

10.15a Rear shock absorber and suspension linkage - L through P models

1 Preload adjuster assembly	13 Lower mounting clevis*	24 Needle roller bearing - front/rear link pivot
2 Grub screw	14 Suspension linkage front (shock) link	25 Nut
3 Damper	15 Suspension linkage front pivot bolt	26 Shock absorber lower mounting bolt
4 Shock absorber upper mounting bolt	16 Nut	27 Inner sleeve - shock absorber lower mounting
5 Nut	17 Inner sleeve - front link pivot	
6 Rebound rubber	18 Grease seal	28 Nut
7 Nut*	19 Needle roller bearing - front link pivot	29 Suspension linkage rear pivot bolt
8 Snap-ring	20 Suspension linkage rear link (shock arm)	30 Inner sleeve - rear link pivot
9 Spring upper seat	21 Suspension linkage front link-to-rear link pivot bolt	31 Needle roller bearing - rear link pivot
10 Spring		32 Nut
11 Spring guide	22 Inner sleeve - front link-to-rear link pivot	*Not separate on N and P models - damper and bottom mounting are one-piece unit.
12 Spring seat stopper*	23 Dust seal	

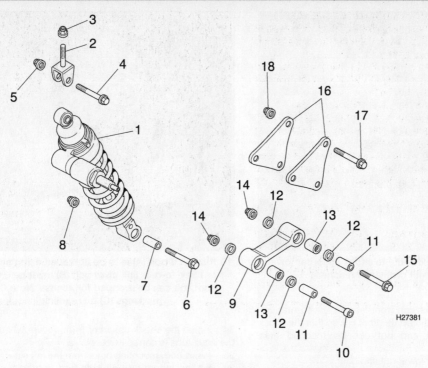

10.15b Rear shock absorber and suspension linkage - R models

1	Rear shock absorber	10	Suspension linkage front pivot bolt
2	Shock absorber upper mounting	11	Inner sleeve
3	Nut	12	Dust seal
4	Shock absorber upper mounting bolt	13	Needle roller bearing
5	Nut	14	Nut
6	Shock absorber lower mounting bolt	15	Suspension linkage rear pivot bolt
7	Inner sleeve - front link pivot	16	Suspension rear link plates
8	Nut	17	Bolts
9	Suspension linkage front (shock) link		

10.17 Undo retaining screws (other arrowed) and lift out battery box - L through R models

be replaced.

12   Check the shock for wear, damage or for signs of fluid or gas leaks and replace it if you find any. All shock absorber components are available separately, but disassembly requires the use of a suitable spring compressor. It is therefore recommended that the unit be taken to a Honda dealer who will have the necessary tools to disassemble and service the unit. If the damper is to be replaced, the gas pressure

must be released before the unit is thrown away. **Warning:** *Wear eye protection while drilling to prevent injury from flying metal chips. To release the gas pressure, drill a hole through the damper cylinder wall 13 mm (1/2 inch) below the top of the damper body - center-punch the damper cylinder to avoid the drill slipping as you start and use a sharp (to avoid heat build-up from using a blunt drill) 2 to 3 mm (5/64 to 1/8 inch) drill bit. Drill only in the specified area - any further down and you will drill into the fluid chamber, thus risking the release under high pressure of the damping fluid.*

13   Withdraw the inner sleeve from the shock absorber upper mounting. Inspect the sleeve, bushing and dust seals for signs of wear and replace worn components as necessary. The bushing is a press-fit and can be removed and installed using a drawbolt arrangement similar to that used in Section 9.

14   The bushing in the shock absorber lower mounting can be replaced (it is a press-fit and can be removed and installed using a drawbolt arrangement similar to that used in Section 9) once the suspension rear link (shock arm) has been removed. Refer to Section 11.

L models onward

Refer to illustrations 10.15a, 10.15b, 10.17, 10.18a, 10.18b and 10.20

15   Remove the fuel tank as described in Chapter 4 **(see illustrations)**.

16   On R models, remove the ignition HT coils for cylinder Nos. 1 and 3 (see Chapter 5).

17   On all models, remove the battery and unclip, then move aside the starter relay (see Chapter 9, if necessary). Undo the mounting screw(s) and withdraw the battery box **(see illustration)**.

18   On L through P models, depending on access and the tools available, it may be necessary to remove the rear wheel (see Chapter 7,

6

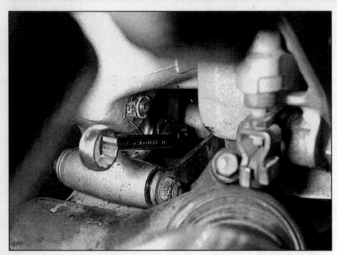

**10.18a While access may be possible to shock absorber lower
mounting bolt and nut with ordinary wrenches . . .**

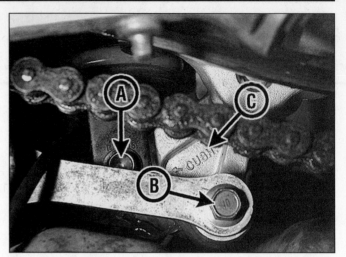

**10.18b . . . if bolt (A) is to be tightened using sockets, suspension
front link-to-rear link pivot bolt (B) must be unscrewed so that
front link can be dropped for access. Note CUSH and arrow
markings (C) on rear link (shock arm)**

if necessary). Unscrew the suspension front (shock) link-to-rear link
(shock arm) pivot bolt and nut and drop the front link so that the shock
absorber lower mounting bolt and nut can be reached **(see
illustrations)**.

19   Unscrew the shock absorber lower nut and bolt.

20   Unscrew the shock absorber upper nut and bolt and maneuver
the shock absorber up out of the frame **(see illustration)**.

21   On L through P models, inspect the shock absorber as described
above in Step 12; service its lower mounting, if required, as noted in
Step 14 - note however that a needle roller bearing with inner sleeve is
fitted on these models. With reference to Step 13, the upper mounting
components are not available separately.

22   On R models, apart from the lower mounting inner sleeve, no
shock absorber components are available separately. Damage to any
other component will require the replacement of the complete shock
absorber assembly; refer to Step 12 above. **Note:** *Do not attempt to
disassemble the shock absorber.*

Installation

G through K models

23   Check that the mounting bolts are unworn, replacing them if
necessary, and apply molybdenum disulfide grease to their shanks.

24   Lift the rear wheel and install the shock absorber from underneath
so that the preload adjuster is on the left side of the motorcycle.

25   Insert the upper and lower mounting bolts, from the right.

26   Fit the upper and lower mounting bolt nuts and tighten them to
the specified torque setting.

27   If it was moved, reposition the subframe/seat rail (check carefully
that you don't trap any wires or hoses) and insert its upper mounting
bolts. Tighten the subframe/seat rail's upper and lower mounting bolts
to the specified torque setting.

28   Install the suspension front (shock) link to the rear link (shock
arm), grease and fit the pivot bolt, from the right, then tighten to the
specified torque setting the pivot bolt and nut.

29   Install the mufflers (silencers), if removed, as described in Chapter 4.

30   Position the preload adjuster, engaging the bracket's locating pin
in the hole in the frame, then tighten securely its bolt. Set the preload
as described in Section 12.

31   Install the side covers and seat as described in Chapter 8.

32   Check the operation of the rear suspension before using the
motorcycle.

L models onward

33   Check that the mounting bolts are unworn, replacing them if
necessary, and apply molybdenum disulfide grease to their shanks.

34   Install the shock absorber from above; where fitted, ensure that
the drain tube is correctly routed.

35   Insert both mounting bolts from the left side.

36   Fit the mounting bolt nuts and tighten them to the specified torque
setting.

37   On L through P models, install the suspension front (shock) link to
the rear link (shock arm), grease and fit the pivot bolt, from the left,
then tighten to the specified torque setting the pivot bolt and nut.

38   On all models, install the battery box, battery and starter relay as
described in Chapter 9.

39   On R models, install the ignition HT coils for cylinder Nos. 1 and 3
(see Chapter 5).

40   Install the fuel tank as described in Chapter 4 and the seat as
described in Chapter 8.

41   Check the operation of the rear suspension and adjust the
suspension settings as described in Section 12.

11   Rear suspension linkage - removal, inspection and installation

Removal

Refer to illustrations 11.6a through 11.6d

1   Place the motorcycle on its centerstand - where no centerstand is
fitted (and on all R models, where the centerstand has to be removed),
support the machine securely in an upright position.

2   Block the motorcycle (being careful not to damage the fairing
lower panels - remove them if necessary, as described in Chapter 8) so
that the rear wheel is just resting on the ground (i.e., so that the
motorcycle's weight is off the rear suspension but also so that the rear
suspension will not drop, with the possible risk of personal injury, when
the suspension linkage pivot bolts are removed).

3   On G through K models, depending on access and the tools
available, it may be necessary to remove the mufflers (silencers) as
described in Chapter 4.

4   On L through P models, unbolt the rider's left footpeg bracket
(see Section 3, if necessary) and exhaust collector box cover, as
described in Chapter 4.

5   On R models, remove the centerstand as described in Section 4.

6   On all models, unscrew the pivot bolt nuts and withdraw the pivot
bolts, undo the shock absorber lower mounting nut and bolt and
disassemble the rear suspension linkage; on G through K models,
unscrew the rear link (shock arm) pinch bolt and use a hammer and
punch to drive out the rear link pivot inner sleeve **(see illustrations)**.

10.20 Withdrawing the rear shock absorber - L through P models shown

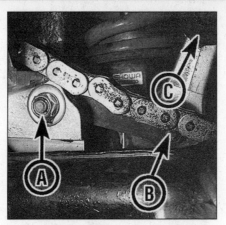

11.6a Disassembling rear suspension linkage, G through K models - unscrew nuts (A) and (B); inner sleeve (C) cannot be driven out . . .

11.6b . . . until pinch bolt (C) has been removed completely. Remove bolts (A) and (B) . . .

11.6c . . . and withdraw suspension linkage components (L model shown here, with swingarm removed for clarity)

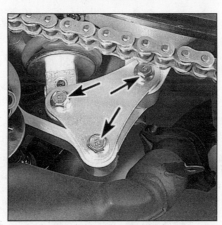

11.6d Unscrew bolts (arrows) to disassemble rear suspension linkage on R models; final bolt is obscured by centerstand pivot shaft retainer

11.7 Inspect the suspension linkage inner sleeves and bearings for wear and replace if necessary

Note any identifying marks or features which might help to ensure correct reassembly - refer to illustrations 10.5a, 10.15a and 10.15b, whichever is relevant, for details.

Inspection

Refer to illustrations 11.7, 11.16a and 11.16b

7 Withdraw the inner sleeves **(see illustration)**. Thoroughly clean all components, removing all traces of dirt, corrosion and grease.

8 Inspect all components closely, looking for obvious signs of wear such as heavy scoring, or for damage such as cracks or distortion.

9 Carefully lever out the dust seals, using a flat-bladed screwdriver, and check them for signs of wear or damage; replace them if necessary.

10 Worn bearings can be drifted out of their bores, but note that removal will destroy them; new bearings should be obtained before work commences. **Note:** *Before attempting to remove these bearings, measure their precise depth in their housings, i.e., the amount by which each bearing's outer face is recessed below the outside edge of its link/housing (usually to provide room for the grease seal).*

11 The new bearings should be pressed or drawn into their bores rather than driven into position. In the absence of a press, a suitable drawbolt arrangement can be made up as described below.

12 Obtain a long bolt or a length of threaded stud from a local engineering works or other supplier. The bolt or stud should be about one inch longer than the combined length of either link and one bearing. Also required are suitable nuts and two large and robust

washers having a larger outside diameter than the bearing housing. In the case of the threaded rod, fit one nut to one end of the rod and stake it in place for convenience.

13 Fit one of the washers over the bolt or rod so that it rests against the head, then pass the assembly through the relevant bore. Over the projecting end place the bearing, which should be greased to ease installation and have its marked end surface facing outs, followed by the remaining washer and nut.

14 Holding the bearing to ensure that it is kept square, slowly tighten the nut so that the bushing or bearing is drawn into its bore. If the bearing was recessed into its housing, insert a spacer of the same outside diameter as the bearing between the washer and bearing so that as the nut is finally tightened, the bearing is drawn inside the housing. Check carefully that the new bearing is installed to the same depth as was noted on removing the old bearing; on R models, for example, all four front (shock) link bearings and the rear link plate bearing must be seated to a depth of 5.5 mm (0.217 inch) from the outside edge of the link (or swingarm housing, as appropriate) to the outer end face of the bearing.

15 Once it is fully home, remove the drawbolt arrangement and, if necessary, repeat the procedure to fit the opposite bearing. The dust seals can then be pressed into place.

16 Lubricate all the seals, needle roller bearings, inner sleeves and the pivot bolts with molybdenum disulfide grease. Insert the sleeves into the links **(see illustrations)**.

6

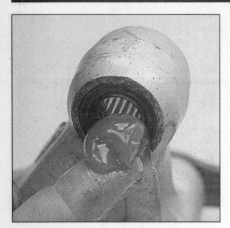
11.16a Thoroughly grease all components of rear suspension linkage on installation

11.16b Insert inner sleeves into bearings

11.19a Tighten all suspension linkage pivot bolts . . .

Installation

Refer to illustrations 11.19a and 11.19b

17   If not already done, lubricate the seals, needle roller bearings, inner sleeves and the pivot bolts with molybdenum disulfide grease.

18   Maneuver the linkage components into position making sure that marks such as the CUSH mark and arrow on the left side of the rear link (shock arm) of L through P models (see illustration 10.18b) are correctly aligned, as noted on removal.

19   Insert the pivot bolts and the shock absorber bolt from the right side of the motorcycle on G through K models and from the left side on all later models, then install their nuts. On G through K models, tap the rear link pivot inner sleeve into place from the right until its pinch bolt can be inserted (note the groove for the pinch bolt in the inner sleeve), then tighten the pinch bolt to its specified torque setting. Tighten all pivot and mounting bolt nuts to the specified torque settings **(see illustrations)**.

20   On G through K models install the mufflers (silencers) as described in Chapter 4.

21   On L through P models install the exhaust collector box cover, as described in Chapter 4, and the rider's left footpeg bracket (see Section 3, if necessary).

22   On R models, install the centerstand as described in Section 4.

23   On all models, check the operation of the rear suspension before taking the machine on the road.

12 Suspension - adjustments

Front forks

Warning: *Always ensure that both front fork settings are the same. Uneven settings will upset the handling of the machine and could cause it to become unstable.*

Air pressure - G through K models only

Refer to illustration 12.1

1   An air valve is fitted in each fork cap to enable the fork's effective spring rate to be altered, within the specified range, to suit the rider's needs **(see illustration)**. The pressure must be checked frequently (at least weekly or before any long ride) and must be exactly the same (within a narrow tolerance) in each fork. In practice the latter is very difficult to achieve and you are strongly advised to consider purchasing of one of the several aftermarket kits which are available to link the valves; these not only eliminate possible differences in pressure between the two forks, but they double the effective air volume, making checking and adjustment significantly easier.

2   A low-pressure gauge will be required to check the fork air pressure; the best type being those sold specifically for suspension applications. Tire pressure gauges are not adequate; they are unlikely to be calibrated finely enough to be of any use and also usually require so much air to operate that they will cause a large pressure drop when connected to such a small volume of air.

3   A low-pressure pump will be required to increase air pressure; hand pumps such as bicycle tire pumps or aftermarket suspension pumps being ideal. **Do not** use a high-pressure source of air such as a filling station airline; it is all too easy to exceed the maximum recommended pressure and risk popping the fork seals!

4   The air pressure must be checked when the fork is cold and with the motorcycle supported securely so that the front wheel is clear of the ground; this ensures that the pressure is not artificially increased.

5   Place the motorcycle on its centerstand - where no centerstand is fitted, support the machine securely in an upright position. Block the motorcycle (being careful not to damage the fairing lower panels - remove them if necessary, as described in Chapter 8) so that the front wheel is clear of the ground. Do not check the pressures with the motorcycle on its side stand; you will get false readings.

6   Remove the first valve cap and read the pressure recorded on the gauge, then repeat on the second valve. Both pressures should be the same (or differ by no more than the specified value) and should be within the specified range. Remember, however, that the act of connecting the gauge will itself cause a pressure drop; only practice with a particular gauge and motorcycle will enable you to know how much pressure is lost whenever a check is made and by how much, accordingly, you must compensate for this when altering the pressure.

7   To stiffen the ride increase the air pressure, up to the maximum recommended value if required. To soften the ride reduce the air pressure, to zero (i.e., atmospheric) if required.

8   If the air pressure is to be increased, it is easiest to raise it to the specified maximum (one or two strokes of most hand pumps will achieve this easily) and then very carefully to bleed the pressure back down to the required level by depressing very gently the valve core; remember to stop above your desired value to compensate for the pressure loss caused by the gauge. You will soon get the idea after the first couple of attempts!

9   Bearing in mind the warning at the beginning of this Section, it is essential to match as closely as possible (certainly within the specified tolerance) the pressures in the two forks. This will require patience to achieve, but the pressures **must** be as closely equal as possible.

10   When the air pressures are correct, refit the valve caps, tightening them securely. Do not forget these caps; they not only prevent the entry of dirt into the valves, but help to prevent pressure loss.

Spring preload - N models onward

Refer to illustrations 12.11 and 12.14

11   The preload adjuster is located in the center of each fork top cap **(see illustration)**.

12   To reduce the preload (i.e., soften the ride), rotate the adjuster

11.19b . . . and nuts to the specified torque setting

12.1 Front fork air pressure is adjustable on early models via the valve in each fork top cap

12.11 Adjusting the front fork spring preload - N models onward

12.14 Front fork spring preload adjuster in standard position - 3rd groove/position from top

12.18 Front fork anti-dive adjustment, G and H models - align number required with reference mark (arrow) cast on left fork slider; position 4 (maximum anti-dive) shown

12.23 Adjusting the rear shock absorber spring preload is done by hand on G through K models . . .

counterclockwise (anti-clockwise) using a suitably large screwdriver.

13   To increase the preload (i.e., stiffen the ride), rotate the adjuster clockwise.

14   Adjuster position is indicated by the number of grooves which are visible above the top of the fork top cap. Always ensure both adjusters are set to the same position; i.e., ensure that the same number of grooves are visible on both the left and right adjusters. The standard position is the 3rd position/groove from the top **(see illustration)**.

Compression and rebound damping - all models

15   Front fork damping is not adjustable, except by varying the viscosity of fork oil used. Always seek the advice of a Honda dealer or suspension specialist before using different fork oils.

Anti-dive settings - G and H models only

Refer to illustration 12.18

16   While Honda's TRAC (Torque Reactive Anti-dive Control) system is fitted to G through K models, it is adjustable for effect only on G and H models.

17   The system allows the front left brake caliper to pivot on its upper mounting point so that when the brakes are applied the caliper acts on the piston connected to its lower mounting point. The piston movement alters the left fork's compression damping to reduce the amount of fork dive produced by braking. The system does **not** affect fork damping under any other circumstances.

18   The adjuster knob is fitted on the front of the left fork slider **(see illustration)**. It is adjustable through four positions as follows:

Position	Anti-dive effect
1	Light
2	Medium
3	Hard
4	Maximum

19   Set the adjuster so that the number of the desired value is aligned with the reference mark cast on the slider. A distinct detent position (click) should be felt; do not leave the adjuster between detents or the compression damping will not function correctly at all.

Rear shock absorber

Spring preload - all models

20   The rear shock absorber spring preload adjuster is fitted to the top of the shock absorber, but adjustment is possible from the left side of the motorcycle.

Spring preload - G through K models

Refer to illustration 12.23

21   To reach the adjuster remove the left side cover (see Chapter 8, if necessary).

22   The preload adjuster has six positions, from 'Low' (the minimum, i.e., the softest) to 'High' (being the maximum, hardest). Honda recommend the second position from 'Low' as the standard setting.

23   The adjuster is rotated by hand **(see illustration)**. To reduce the preload (i.e., soften the ride), rotate the adjuster counterclockwise (anti-clockwise); to increase the preload (i.e., stiffen the ride), rotate the

6

12.25a . . . using an open-end wrench on L through P models . . .

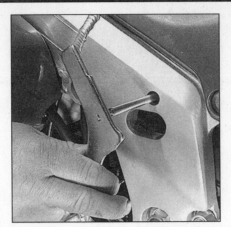
12.25b . . . and a box wrench and pin wrench/C-wrench on R models

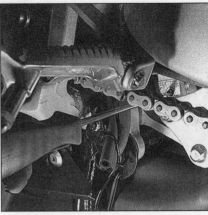
12.31 Adjusting the rear shock absorber rebound damping - N models onward

adjuster clockwise. A distinct detent (click) should be felt at each position; do not leave the adjuster between detents.
24   When the preload is correctly set, install the side cover.

Spring preload - L models onward
Refer to illustrations 12.25a and 12.25b
25   The preload is altered by applying a wrench (8 mm open-ended on L through P models, 8 mm box wrench and pin wrench/C-wrench on R models; these are included in the motorcycle's tool kit) to the adjuster's squared head, accessible through the hole in the left side of the frame **(see illustrations)**.
26   The preload adjuster has four positions, from 'Low' (the minimum, i.e., the softest) to 'High' (being the maximum, hardest). Honda recommend the second position from 'Low' as the standard (STD) setting.
27   To reduce the preload (i.e., soften the ride), rotate the adjuster counterclockwise (anti-clockwise); to increase the preload (i.e., stiffen the ride), rotate the adjuster clockwise. A distinct detent (click) should be felt at each position; do not leave the adjuster between detents.
28   On some R models the standard position may be indicated by a red dot and 12 'clicks' may be felt between each major position; a total of 36 'positions' being theoretically available and the standard setting being 12 'clicks' back from fully counterclockwise (anti-clockwise). Otherwise, adjustment is as given in Steps 25 through 27 above.

Rebound (tension) damping - N models onward
Refer to illustration 12.31
29   The rear suspension rebound damping adjuster is situated at the left bottom end of the shock absorber.
30   To establish the standard setting, turn the adjuster fully clockwise (in the direction of the H arrow) until it stops; do not force it. From this, the hardest damping setting, turn the adjuster counterclockwise (anti-clockwise) through approximately one full turn until the punch mark on the adjuster aligns with the reference mark on the shock absorber. This is the standard setting recommended by Honda.
31   To soften the damping for a smooth ride with a light load on good roads, turn the adjuster further counterclockwise (anti-clockwise), in the direction of the S arrow, using a suitably long screwdriver **(see illustration)**.
32   To stiffen the damping for a firmer ride, turn the adjuster clockwise, in the direction of the H arrow.

Compression damping - all models
33   Rear suspension compression damping is not adjustable.

13 Swingarm bearings - check

1   Refer to Chapter 7 and remove the rear wheel, then refer to Section 10 of this Chapter and remove the rear shock absorber.

2   Grasp the rear of the swingarm with one hand and place your other hand at the junction of the swingarm and the frame. Try to move the rear of the swingarm from side-to-side. Any wear (play) in the bearings should be felt as movement between the swingarm and the frame at the front. The swingarm will actually be felt to move forward and backward at the front (not from side-to-side). If any play is noted, the bearings should be replaced (see Section 15).
3   Next, move the swingarm up and down through its full travel. It should move freely, without any binding or rough spots. If it does not move freely, refer to Section 14 for servicing procedures.

14 Swingarm - removal and installation

Removal
All models
1   Place the motorcycle on its centerstand - where no centerstand is fitted, support the machine securely in an upright position.
2   Block the motorcycle (being careful not to damage the fairing lower panels - remove them if necessary, as described in Chapter 8) so that the rear wheel is just resting on the ground (i.e., so that the motorcycle's weight is off the rear suspension but also so that the rear suspension will not drop, with the possible risk of personal injury, when the suspension linkage pivot bolts are removed).

G through K models
Refer to illustration 14.8
3   Depending on access and the tools available, it may be necessary to remove the mufflers (silencers) as described in Chapter 4.
4   Remove the rear wheel as described in Chapter 7. Unbolt the drive chain guard and slip the chain off the swingarm, then withdraw the chain adjusters from the rear ends of the swingarm.
5   Unbolt the rear brake torque rod from the swingarm and move the rear brake assembly clear of the working area without straining the hydraulic hose. **Caution:** *Do not operate the rear brake pedal with the caliper removed.*
6   Unscrew the suspension front (shock) link-to-rear link (shock arm) pivot bolt and nut and drop the front link so that the shock absorber lower mounting bolt and nut can be reached.
7   Unscrew the nut and withdraw the shock absorber lower mounting bolt.
8   Carefully pry out the rubber plug from each swingarm pivot bolt, then unscrew the two bolts while an assistant supports the swingarm **(see illustration)**. Remove the swingarm, collecting the nut from the right pivot and removing the chain slider from the left pivot.
9   Remove the collars from each side of the swingarm's right pivot. Withdraw the suspension rear link as described in Section 11, Step 6. Inspect all components for wear or damage as described in the following Section.

14.8 Unscrewing the swingarm left pivot
bolt - G through K models

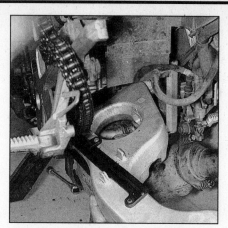

14.17 Removing the swingarm -
L model shown . . .

14.18 . . . then withdraw the collar and
unbolt the chain slider

14.21 Tightening the swingarm pivot bolt to the specified torque
setting - G through K models

L models onward

Refer to illustrations 14.17 and 14.18

10   Remove the rear shock absorber as described in Section 10.
Note: *This operation is not strictly necessary (the swingarm can be removed with the shock still in place), but installing the swingarm while trying to pass the shock through its aperture is very difficult indeed, even for two people.*

11   Remove the rear wheel as described in Chapter 7. Unbolt the drive chain guard, releasing the brake hydraulic hose from its clips, and slip the chain off the swingarm.

12   Unbolt the rear brake caliper from its stay. Unbolt the rear brake torque rod from the swingarm and remove the caliper completely, unclipping the brake hose from the brake torque rod to prevent it from being strained. Secure the caliper clear of the working area. **Caution:** *Do not operate the rear brake pedal with the caliper removed.*

13   If the rear shock absorber was not removed, unscrew the suspension linkage rear link (shock arm) or link plates-to-swingarm pivot bolt, and the shock absorber lower mounting bolt.

14   Working on the left of the motorcycle, unscrew the swingarm pivot bolt locknut.

15   Working on the right of the motorcycle, unscrew and remove the swingarm adjuster bolt locknut. This requires the use of service tool, Pt. No. 07908-4690002, which is a special wrench that fits the locknut. There is no alternative to the use of this tool; if you do not have access to it, the swingarm adjuster locknut must be unscrewed (and later tightened) by a dealer service department.

16   Using an Allen key to fit the head of the swingarm pivot bolt, unscrew the swingarm adjuster bolt by rotating counterclockwise (anticlockwise) the swingarm pivot bolt.

17   When the adjuster bolt (actually a threaded sleeve) is fully unscrewed, have an assistant support the swingarm while the pivot and adjuster bolts are removed. Remove the swingarm **(see illustration)**. If necessary, slacken the engine mounting bolt nearest the swingarm pivot to ease swingarm removal/installation.

18   Remove the collar from the left side of the swingarm and unscrew the retaining screws to withdraw the chain slider **(see illustration)**. Inspect all components for wear or damage as described in the following Section.

Installation

G through K models

Refer to illustration 14.21

19   Lubricate the dust seals, bearings, collars and both pivot bolts with grease.

20   Insert the collars (projecting flanges on the outside) into each side of the right pivot and ensure that the right pivot bolt's nut is correctly located. Install the suspension rear link as described in Section 11, then fit the chain guide over the swingarm's left pivot.

21   Offer up the swingarm, passing it through the drive chain, and insert the pivot bolts. Tighten the bolts firmly by hand, check the swingarm's movement (Section 13, Steps 2 and 3), then tighten each swingarm pivot bolt to its respective specified torque setting and recheck the swingarm's movement **(see illustration)**. Press the rubber plug into each bolt.

22   Install the shock absorber lower mounting bolt and its nut and tighten them to the specified torque setting.

23   Install the suspension front (shock) link-to-rear link (shock arm) pivot bolt and nut and tighten them to the specified torque setting.

24   Install the rear brake assembly. Secure the brake hose in its clips, tighten all nuts and bolts to their specified torque settings and fit new cotter pins (split pins) to the torque rod bolts, spreading their ends securely.

25   Install the drive chain guard, then install the rear wheel as described in Chapter 7.

26   Install, if removed, the mufflers (silencers) as described in Chapter 4.

L models onward

Refer to illustrations 14.30a, 14.30b, 14.32 and 14.33

27   Lubricate the dust seals, bearings, collar and pivot bolt with grease.

28   Insert the collar (projecting flange on the outside) into the left pivot, then fit the chain slider over the swingarm's left pivot and tighten securely its screws.

29   Offer up the swingarm, passing it through the drive chain, and have an assistant hold it in place while the adjuster bolt is inserted and tightened by hand. If you have a set of automotive drain plug keys, one of these may be the correct size to fit the adjuster bolt's internal

6

14.30a **Installing the swingarm, L models onward - screw in adjuster bolt (threaded sleeve), then install swingarm pivot bolt as shown so that its flats match those inside adjuster bolt . . .**

14.30b **. . . tighten swingarm adjuster bolt to its specified torque setting by using a torque wrench and Allen key bit applied to head of swingarm pivot bolt . . .**

14.32 **. . . next install adjuster bolt locknut and tighten using special service tool (see text) . . .**

hexagon, otherwise, simply fit the swingarm pivot bolt, engage its flats with those of the adjuster bolt and tighten the adjuster bolt by rotating the pivot bolt with an Allen key applied to its head.

30   If not already done, install the greased pivot bolt right through the swingarm pivot until its flats can be engaged with those of the adjuster bolt. Using a torque wrench and Allen key bit of suitable size applied to the head of the swingarm pivot bolt, tighten the swingarm adjuster bolt to its specified torque setting **(see illustrations)**.

31   Check the swingarm's movement (Section 13, Steps 2 and 3).

32   Next screw on the adjuster bolt's locknut and tighten it as firmly as possible by hand **(see illustration)**. Preventing the swingarm pivot bolt from rotating by applying an Allen key to its head, tighten the swingarm adjuster bolt locknut to its specified torque setting. This requires the use of service tool, Pt. No. 07908-4690002, for which there is no alternative. **Note:** *The specified torque setting takes into account the extra leverage provided by the service tool and cannot be duplicated without it.*

33   With an assistant preventing the swingarm pivot bolt from rotating by applying an Allen key to its head on the right side of the motorcycle, tighten the pivot bolt locknut on the left of the motorcycle **(see illustration)**.

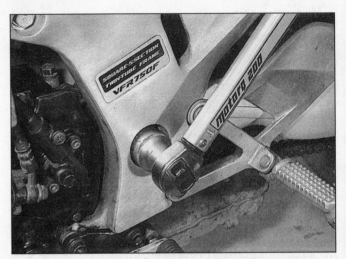

14.33 **. . . finally tighten swingarm pivot bolt locknut to specified torque setting**

15.1a Exploded view of swingarm components - G through K models

1	Swingarm
2	Rubber plug
3	Pivot bolt
4	Collar
5	Dust seal
6	Snap-ring
7	Ball bearings
8	Needle roller bearing
9	Nut
10	Thrust washers
11	Drive chain slider
12	Drive chain guard
13	Drive chain
14	Chain adjustment scale
15	Chain adjuster
16	End plate

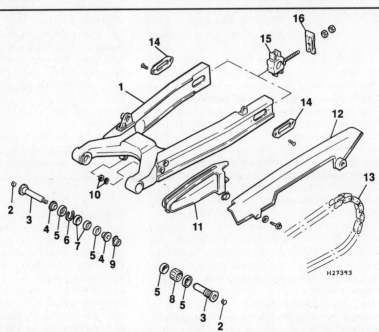

H27393

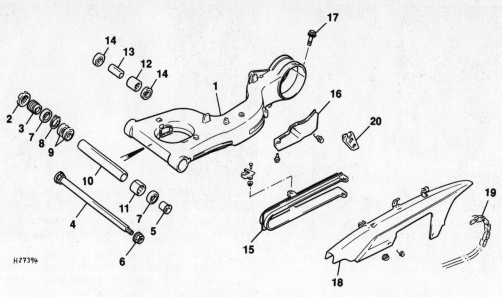

15.1b Exploded view of swingarm components - L models onward

1	Swingarm - R model shown	8	Snap-ring	14	Dust seal
2	Swingarm adjuster bolt locknut	9	Ball bearings	15	Drive chain slider
3	Swingarm adjuster bolt	10	Center spacer	16	Sprocket shield
4	Swingarm pivot bolt	11	Needle roller bearing	17	Bearing holder clamp bolt
5	Collar	12	Needle roller bearing - rear link plates	18	Drive chain guard
6	Swingarm pivot bolt locknut		pivot	19	Drive chain
7	Dust seal	13	Inner sleeve - rear link plates pivot	20	Sprocket guard

34   Recheck the swingarm's movement, then install the drive chain guard, locating its projections on the swingarm tabs. If it was slackened, tighten the engine mounting nearest the swingarm pivot as described in Chapter 2.

35   Install the rear shock absorber or the suspension linkage rear link (shock arm) or link plates-to-swingarm pivot bolt, and the shock absorber lower mounting bolt, as appropriate.

36   Install the rear brake assembly. Secure the brake hose in its clips, tighten all nuts and bolts to their specified torque settings and fit new cotter pins (split pins) to the torque rod bolts, spreading their ends securely.

37   Install the rear wheel as described in Chapter 7.

All models

38   Check the operation of the rear suspension before taking the machine on the road.

15 Swingarm - inspection and bearing replacement

Inspection

Refer to illustrations 15.1a and 15.1b

1   Thoroughly clean all components, removing all traces of dirt, corrosion and grease **(see illustrations)**.

2   Inspect all components closely, looking for obvious signs of wear such as heavy scoring, and cracks or distortion due to accident damage. Any damaged or worn component must be replaced.

Bearing replacement

Refer to illustrations 15.4 and 15.12

3   Lever out the dust seals, using a flat-bladed screwdriver, and inspect them for signs of wear or damage; replace them if necessary.

4   Using snap-ring pliers, remove the snap-ring from the right side of the swingarm's right pivot **(see illustration)**.

5   On G through K models, the two right side bearings can be driven out of position simultaneously, using a hammer and suitable drift

15.4 Swingarm right side bearings are retained by a snap-ring (arrow)

inserted through the left pivot of the swingarm. Move the drift around the face of the bearing whilst driving it out of position, so that the bearings leave the swingarm squarely. The same method can be tried on L models onward, but there is little room and the most certain means of extraction is to hire an internally-expanding bearing puller. These are available commercially or can be hired; failing this, you must have the bearings replaced by a dealer service department or motorcycle repair specialist. Once the right pivot bearings have been removed on L models onward, tip out the center spacer.

6   Wash the bearings thoroughly in a high flash-point solvent to remove all traces of the old grease.

7   Check the bearing tracks and balls for wear, pitting or damage to hardened surfaces. A small amount of side movement in the bearing is normal but no radial movement should be detectable.

8   Check the bearings for play and roughness when they are spun

6

**15.12 Press the dust seals into position with a
suitable tubular spacer**

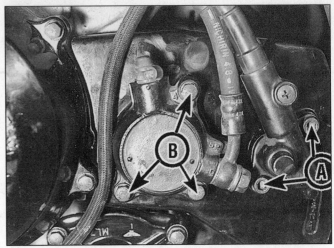

**17.2a Unscrew the bolts (A) to release the speedometer
drive/speed sensor (L models onward) - unscrew the
bolts (B) to remove the clutch release cylinder . . .**

by hand. All bearings will emit a small amount of noise when spun but they should not chatter or sound rough. If there is any doubt about the condition of the bearings they should be replaced.

9   Pack the bearings with grease and drift them separately into position using a suitable tubular drift which bears only on the outer race of the bearing. Do not forget to install the center spacer first (L models onward).

10   Secure the bearings in position with the snap-ring, ensuring that it is fitted with its chamfered side against the bearing and that it is correctly seated in its groove.

11   The needle roller bearing fitted to the swingarm's left pivot can, if necessary, be replaced as described in Section 11 of this Chapter. On L models onward the bearings must be seated to a depth of 4.0 mm (0.157 inch) from the outside edge of the swingarm housing to the outer end face of the bearing.

12   Press the dust seals into position using a suitable tubular spacer which bears only on the hard outer edge of the seal **(see illustration)**.

13   Inspect the chain slider fitted to the swingarm's left pivot. If this shows any sign of wear it should be replaced.

---

16   Drive chain - removal, cleaning and installation

Removal

Note: *All drive chains fitted as OE (original equipment) are of the endless type (which means they don't have a master (split) link) and so require the removal and installation of the swingarm, as outlined below, to allow the removal and installation of the chain itself.*

The OE drive chain fitted to R models is however connected using a staked-type of master (split) link which can be disassembled using one of several commercially-available drive chain cutting/staking tools - this means that the chain can be replaced without disturbing the swingarm. Such chains can be identified by the master link side plate's identification marks (and usually, its different color) as well as by the staked ends of the link's two pins (they look as if they have been deeply center-punched, instead of peened over as with all the other pins).

The replacement drive chain must be installed and its NEW master link assembled (with the four O-rings correctly located between the link plates) from the inside; the new side plate is installed with its identification marks facing out and must be staked to the drive chain manufacturer's specifications using the drive chain cutting/staking tool. DO NOT re-use old master link components.

If you are supplied with a replacement drive chain which uses a staked-type of master (split) link, either have the dealer's service department install it for you, or have them stake the chain then install it yourself, removing the swingarm as outlined below.

**17.2b . . . then unbolt and remove the front sprocket
cover from the engine**

Warning: *NEVER install a drive chain which uses a clip-type master (split) link. Use ONLY the correct service tools to secure the staked-type of master link - if you do not have such tools, have the chain replaced by a dealer service department or a motorcycle repair shop to be sure of having it securely installed.*

1   Remove the front sprocket cover as described in Step 2 of the following Section.

2   Remove the rear wheel as described in Chapter 7.

3   Remove the swingarm as described in Section 14.

4   Slip the chain off the front sprocket and remove it from the motorcycle.

Cleaning

5   Soak the chain in kerosene (paraffin) for approximately five or six minutes. **Caution:** *Don't use gasoline (petrol), solvent or other cleaning fluids. Don't use high-pressure water. Remove the chain, wipe it off, then blow dry it with compressed air immediately. The entire process shouldn't take longer than ten minutes - if it does, the O-rings in the chain rollers could be damaged.*

Installation

6   Installation is the reverse of the removal procedure. On completion adjust and lubricate the chain following the procedures described in Chapter 1. **Caution:** *Use only the recommended oil.*

17.6 Tighten the rear sprocket nuts to the specified torque setting

17.9 Unscrew the front sprocket bolt and washer then slide the sprocket off the shaft and disengage it from the drive chain

17.10 Tighten the front sprocket bolt to the specified torque setting . . .

17.11a . . . then fit a new gasket over the cover locating dowels (arrows) . . .

17 Sprockets - check and replacement

Check

Refer to illustrations 17.2a and 17.2b

1 Place the motorcycle on its centerstand - where no centerstand is fitted, support the machine securely in an upright position. Block the motorcycle (being careful not to damage the fairing lower panels - remove them if necessary, as described in Chapter 8) so that the rear wheel is clear of the ground.

2 To reach the front sprocket, proceed as follows:

  a) *Remove the fairing lower panels (see Chapter 8 if necessary).*
  b) *On L models onward, unscrew the two bolts and withdraw the speedometer drive/speed sensor from the front sprocket cover (see illustration).*
  c) *Unbolt the clutch slave cylinder, collecting the two locating dowels and the gasket (see Chapter 2). **Caution:** Do not operate the clutch lever while the slave cylinder is removed.*
  d) *Unbolt and remove the front sprocket cover, collecting the two locating dowels and the gasket (see Chapter 2) (see illustration).*

3 Check the wear pattern on both sprockets (see Chapter 1). If the sprocket teeth are worn excessively, replace the chain and both sprockets as a set. Whenever the drive chain is inspected, the sprockets should be inspected also. If you are replacing the chain, replace the sprockets as well.

Replacement

Refer to illustrations 17.6, 17.9, 17.10, 17.11a and 17.11b

4 To remove the rear sprocket on G through K models, remove the rear wheel as described in Chapter 7. Unscrew the nuts holding the sprocket to the coupling and lift it off. Check the condition of the rubber damper under the coupling (see Section 18).

5 To remove the rear sprocket on L models onward, slacken off the chain tension (see Chapter 1), unscrew the nuts holding the sprocket to the coupling (counterholding the bolts with an Allen key from behind/inboard of the sprocket coupling) and lift it off, disengaging it from the chain. Unbolt the chain guide if required.

6 Fit the new sprocket. Apply a smear of clean oil to the threads of the nuts prior to fitting and tighten them to the specified torque setting **(see illustration)**.

7 To replace the front sprocket, begin by installing the chain, and the rear wheel, according to model.

8 With the chain now in place, have an assistant apply the rear brake, then unscrew the sprocket bolt and washer.

9 Pull the engine sprocket and chain off the shaft, then separate the sprocket from the chain **(see illustration)**.

10 Engage the new sprocket with the chain and slide it onto the shaft. Install the washer and bolt, tightening the bolt to its specified torque setting **(see illustration)**.

11 The remainder of reassembly is the reverse of disassembly, noting the following points:

  a) *Install a new gasket on the locating dowels and fit the sprocket cover. Fit the screws and tighten them securely **(see illustrations)**.*

6

17.11b . . . and install the front sprocket cover

18.4 Remove the rubber dampers and inspect them for wear and damage

b) *Install a new gasket on the locating dowels and install the clutch slave cylinder as described in Chapter 2.*

c) *Engage the speed sensor/speedometer drive hexagon on the front sprocket bolt's head (L models onward) and tighten securely the bolts.*

12   Adjust and lubricate the chain following the procedures described in Chapter 1. **Caution:** *Use only the recommended engine oil.*

18   Rear sprocket coupling/rubber damper - check and replacement

Refer to illustration 18.4

1   Remove the rear wheel as described in Chapter 7. On L models onward, remove the rear sprocket coupling as described in Section 16 of Chapter 7.

2   On G through K models, remove the spacer from the center of the sprocket coupling. Lift the sprocket coupling away from the wheel leaving the rubber dampers in position in the wheel. Take care not to lose the spacer from the inside of the coupling bearing.

3   On L models onward pry the driven flange off the coupling, leaving the rubber dampers in position inside. Take care not to lose the spacer from the inside of the coupling bearing.

4   Lift out the rubber damper segments and check them for cracks, hardening and general deterioration **(see illustration)**. Replace the rubber dampers as a set if necessary.

5   Checking and replacement procedures for the sprocket coupling bearing are described in Section 16 of Chapter 7.

6   Installation is the reverse of the removal procedure ensuring the sprocket coupling spacers are correctly positioned.

7   Install the (rear sprocket coupling and) rear wheel as described in Chapter 7.

Chapter 7 Brakes, wheels and tires

Note: *Refer to 'Identification numbers' at the beginning of this Manual to establish the model code of your motorcycle.*

Contents

Specifications

Brakes

Brake fluid type	See Chapter 1
Front brake disc thickness*	
G and H models	
New	4.0 mm (0.158 in)
Service limit	3.5 mm (0.138 in)
J, K and R models	
New	4.5 mm (0.177 in)
Service limit	3.5 mm (0.138 in)
L through P models	
New	5.0 mm (0.197 in)
Service limit	4.0 mm (0.158 in)
Rear brake disc thickness*	
G through K models	
New	5.0 mm (0.197 in)
Service limit	4.0 mm (0.158 in)
L models onward	
New	6.0 mm (0.236 in)
Service limit	5.0 mm (0.197 in)

Refer to marks stamped in disc - if different, they supersede information given here.

Disc maximum runout (front and rear)	0.3 mm (0.012 in)
Disc maximum warpage (front and rear)	0.3 mm (0.012 in)

7

Caliper bore ID
  G and H models - front
    New .... 30.230 to 30.280 mm (1.1902 to 1.1921 in)
    Service limit... 30.290 mm (1.1925 in)
  J and K models - front, all models - rear
    New .... 27.000 to 27.050 mm (1.0629 to 1.0649 in)
    Service limit... 27.060 mm (1.0653 in)
  L models onward - front
    New .... 25.400 to 25.450 mm (0.9999 to 1.0020 in)
    Service limit... 25.460 mm (1.0024 in)
Caliper piston OD
  G and H models - front
    New .... 30.165 to 30.198 mm (1.1876 to 1.1889 in)
    Service limit... 30.160 mm (1.1874 in)
  J and K models - front, all models - rear
    New .... 26.918 to 26.968 mm (1.0598 to 1.0617 in)
    Service limit... 26.910 mm (1.0594 in)
  L models onward - front
    New .... 25.335 to 25.368 mm (0.9974 to 0.9987 in)
    Service limit... 25.330 mm (0.9972 in)
Master cylinder bore ID
  G and H models - front cylinder
    New .... 15.870 to 15.913 mm (0.6248 to 0.6265 in)
    Service limit... 15.930 mm (0.6272 in)
  All other cylinders - front and rear
    New .... 12.700 to 12.743 mm (0.4999 to 0.5017 in)
    Service limit... 12.760 mm (0.5024 in)
Master cylinder piston OD
  G and H models - front cylinder
    New .... 15.827 to 15.854 mm (0.6231 to 0.6242 in)
    Service limit... 15.820 mm (0.6228 in)
  All other cylinders - front and rear
    New .... 12.657 to 12.684 mm (0.4983 to 0.4994 in)
    Service limit... 12.650 mm (0.4980 in)

Wheels

Maximum wheel runout (front and rear)
  Axial (side-to-side)... 2.0 mm (0.079 in)
  Radial (out-of-round) .... 2.0 mm (0.079 in)
Maximum axle runout (front and rear) .... 0.2 mm (0.008 in)

Tires*

Refer to tire information/fitment label on motorcycle - if different, it supersedes information given here.

Tire pressures .... See Chapter 1
Tire sizes
  G and H models
    Front.. 110/90 V16-V250 or 110/90 V16
    Rear... 130/80 V18-V250 or 130/80 VB18
  J and K models
    Front.. 110/80 V17-V250
    Rear... 140/80 V17-V250
  L through P models
    Front.. 120/70 VR 17-V250 or 120/70 ZR 17
    Rear... 170/60 VR 17-V250 or 170/60 ZR 17
  R model
    Front.. 120/70 ZR 17
    Rear... 170/60 ZR 17
Minimum tire tread depth .... See Chapter 1

Torque settings

	Nm	Ft-lbs
Front brake caliper		
Mounting bracket bolts	27	20
Pad pins	18	13
Upper slider pin	23	17
Lower slider pin		
G through K models	12	9
L models onward	18	13
Caliper-to-anti-dive piston bolt	12	9
Brake disc mounting nuts or bolts		
Front disc bolts - R model	20	14

Rear disc nuts - L models onward	35	25
All other bolts/nuts - front or rear	43	31
Brake hose banjo fitting bolt	35	25
Brake pipe flare nuts*	17	12
Brake caliper bleeder valves	6	4
Master cylinder (front and rear) mounting bolts	12	9
Front brake lever pivot bolt locknut	6	4
Rear master cylinder fluid reservoir mounting bolt	12	9
Rear brake torque rod bolts	35	25
Rear brake caliper		
Mounting bracket/stay bolt(s)		
G through K models	23	17
L models onward	27	20
Slider pin		
G through K models	27	20
Upper/front - L models onward	23	17
Lower/rear - L models onward	18	13
Pad pins - L models onward	18	13
Pad pin retainer bolt - G through K models	11	8
Front axle bolt		
R model	40	29
All other models	60	43
Front axle clamp bolt	22	16
Rear axle nut - G through K models	100	72
Rear wheel nuts - L models onward	110	80
Rear stub axle nut - L models onward	195	141

*Oil (lightly) thread and seating before tightening.

2.2a Front brake pad replacement, G and H models - unscrew the plugs from the caliper body . . .

2.2b . . . and loosen both pad pins

1 General information

The models covered in this manual are fitted with cast aluminum wheels designed to accept tubeless tires. Both front and rear brakes are hydraulically operated disc brakes, the front using a twin disc set up and the rear a single disc. The brake calipers are of the dual piston type.

Caution: *Disc brake components rarely require disassembly. Do not disassemble components unless absolutely necessary. If any hydraulic brake line is loosened, the entire system must be disassembled, drained, cleaned and then properly filled and bled upon reassembly. Do not use solvents on internal brake components; solvents will cause the seals to swell and distort. Use only clean brake fluid or alcohol for cleaning. Use care when working with brake fluid as it can injure your eyes and it will damage painted surfaces and plastic parts.*

2 Front brake pads - replacement

Warning: *When replacing the front brake pads always replace the pads in BOTH calipers - never just on one side. The dust created by the brake system may contain asbestos, which is harmful to your health. Never blow it out with compressed air and don't inhale any of it. An approved filtering mask should be worn when working on the brakes.*

G and H models

Refer to illustrations 2.2a, 2.2b, 2.3a, 2.3b, 2.5a, 2.5b, 2.7, 2.12a, 2.12b and 2.13

1   Place the motorcycle on its centerstand - where no centerstand is fitted, support the machine securely in an upright position.
2   Unscrew both plugs from the caliper body to reveal the pad pin heads, then loosen both pad pins **(see illustrations)**.

7

2.3a On the left side, unscrew the caliper mounting bracket bolt (arrow) . . .

2.3b . . . and the caliper-to-anti-dive piston bolt (arrow)

2.5a Unscrew the pad pins . . .

2.5b . . . and withdraw the pads from the caliper

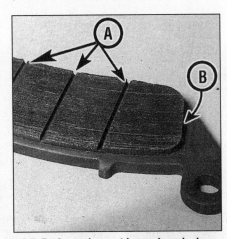

2.7 Brake pads must be replaced when the wear grooves (A) are no longer visible, or when the cutout (B) in the pad's rear edge is exposed

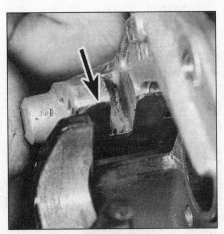

2.12a Ensure both the small pad spring (arrow) . . .

3   On the left caliper, unscrew the caliper mounting bracket bolt and the anti-dive piston bolt; on the right caliper unscrew the two caliper mounting bracket bolts **(see illustrations)**. Slide the caliper assembly off the disc, taking care not to place any undue strain on the hydraulic hose.

4   Slide the bracket off the caliper.

5   Unscrew both pad pins from the caliper and withdraw the brake pads **(see illustrations)**. On G models, note the location of the anti-squeal shim on the metal backing of the inside pad (furthest from the pistons).

6   Remove the anti-rattle springs from the caliper body and the mounting bracket, noting their correct fitted positions.

7   Inspect the surface of each pad for contamination and check that the friction material has not worn beyond its service limit groove, or down to expose the cutout in the pad's rear edge. If either pad is worn to or beyond the service limit groove (i.e. the grooves are no longer visible), fouled with oil or grease, or heavily scored or damaged by dirt and debris, both pads must be replaced as a set **(see illustration)**. Note that it is not possible to degrease the friction material; if the pads are contaminated in any way they must be replaced. **Warning:** *The wear limit described above is the absolute minimum; if the pads are near to, or approaching this limit, it is recommended that they be replaced.*

8   If the pads are in good condition clean them carefully, using a fine wire brush which is completely free of oil and grease, to remove all traces of road dirt and corrosion. Using a pointed instrument, clean out the grooves in the friction material and dig out any embedded particles of foreign matter. Any areas of glazing may be removed using emery cloth.

9   Check the condition of the brake disc (see Section 4).

10   Remove all traces of corrosion from the pad pins. Inspect the pins, slider pins, anti-rattle springs and all rubber boots for signs of damage and replace if necessary. Apply a **thin** coat of PBC (Poly Butyl Cuprysil) grease, or silicone grease designed for high-temperature brake applications, to each of the slider pins, the pad pins and all caliper/mounting bracket contact surfaces, then pack grease inside each of the rubber boots. On the left caliper, remove the collar from the caliper mounting bracket bolt location, then grease lightly both the collar and the needle bearing before reassembly. Disassemble, clean and grease the shouldered collar and anti-dive piston as described in Chapter 6, Section 7.

11   Push the pistons as far back into the caliper as possible using hand pressure only. Due to the increased friction material thickness of new pads, it may be necessary to remove the master cylinder reservoir cover, plate and diaphragm and siphon out some fluid.

12   Install the anti-rattle springs in the caliper body ensuring each one is correctly positioned **(see illustrations)**. Apply a thin smear of grease (see Step 10) to each and to the metal backing of each pad. **Caution:** *Do not leave excess lubricant on any caliper component, or allow lubricant to foul the friction material of either pad.*

13   Insert the pads into the caliper, ensuring both anti-rattle springs remain correctly positioned, so that the friction material of each pad is

2.12b . . . and large pad spring are correctly installed
in the caliper body

2.13 Position the pads in the caliper so that their friction material
is facing the brake disc

2.19a Front brake pad replacement, J models onward - unscrew
the plug from the caliper body . . .

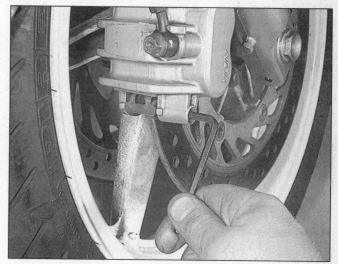

2.19b . . . and loosen the pad pin

facing the disc (see illustration). On G models, the inside pad (furthest from the pistons) must have an anti-squeal shim installed on its metal backing. Insert the pad retaining pins making sure that they pass correctly through the holes in both pads.

14   Slide the caliper assembly onto the disc so that the pad friction material is on each side of the disc. Install the bolts, tightening them to the specified torque settings.

15   Tighten the pad pins to the specified torque setting then fit the pad pin plugs, tightening them securely.

16   Top up the master cylinder reservoir (see Chapter 1) and fit the diaphragm, plate and cover.

17   Operate the brake lever several times to bring the pads into contact with the disc. Check the master cylinder fluid level (see Chapter 1) and the operation of the brake before riding the motorcycle.

J models onward

Refer to illustrations 2.19a, 2.19b, 2.25a, 2.25b and 2.25c

Note: While the brake pads can be replaced without removing the caliper, as described here, it is usually best to remove the caliper so that it can be cleaned properly and checked over whenever the pads are disturbed. Refer to the relevant Steps of Section 3 for details - there is no need to disconnect the hydraulic line or to remove the pistons,

just check, clean and lubricate the caliper slider pins, rubber boots etc.

18   Place the motorcycle on its centerstand - where no centerstand is fitted, support the machine securely in an upright position.

19   Unscrew the plug from the caliper body to reveal the pad pin head then loosen the pad pin (see illustrations).

20   Unscrew the pad pin from the caliper and withdraw the brake pads. If fitted, note the location of the anti-squeal shim on the metal backing of the inside pad (furthest from the pistons).

21   Check the thickness of each pad's friction material and inspect the surface of each pad, cleaning them as described in Steps 7 and 8 above.

22   Check the condition of the brake disc (see Section 4).

23   Prepare for reassembly as described in Steps 10 and 11 above.

24   Where fitted, install the anti-squeal shim on the metal backing of the inside pad (furthest from the pistons). Apply a thin smear of grease (see Step 10 above) to the metal backing of each pad. Caution: Do not leave excess lubricant on any caliper component, or allow lubricant to foul the friction material of either pad.

25   Insert the pads into the caliper, ensuring both anti-rattle springs remain correctly positioned, so that the squared end of each pad engages in the recess in the mounting bracket and that the friction material of each pad is facing the disc. Insert the pad retaining pin

7

2.25a Lubricate the pad metal backing as described and install pads so that their friction material is against the disc and so that the squared end (arrow) . . .

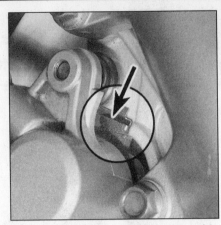

2.25b . . . engages in the recess (arrow) in the mounting bracket

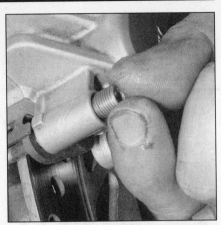

2.25c Insert the pad pin through the caliper and through the holes in both pads

making sure that it passes correctly through the holes in both pads **(see illustrations)**.

26   Tighten the pad pin to the specified torque setting then fit the pad pin plug, tightening it securely.

27   Complete reassembly as described in Steps 16 and 17 above.

3   Front brake caliper - removal, overhaul and installation

Warning: *If a caliper indicates the need for an overhaul (usually due to leaking fluid or sticky operation), all old brake fluid should be flushed from the system. Also, the dust created by the brake system may contain asbestos, which is harmful to your health. Never blow it out with compressed air and don't inhale any of it. An approved filtering mask should be worn when working on the brakes. Do not, under any circumstances, use petroleum-based solvents to clean brake parts. Use clean brake fluid, brake cleaner or denatured alcohol only.*

Removal

1   Place the motorcycle on its centerstand - where no centerstand is fitted, support the machine securely in an upright position.

2   Remove the brake hose banjo fitting bolt and separate the hose from the caliper. Plug the hose end or wrap a plastic bag tightly around it to minimize fluid loss and prevent dirt entering the system. Discard the sealing washers; new ones must be used on installation. **Note:** *If you're planning to overhaul the caliper and don't have a source of compressed air to blow out the pistons, just loosen the banjo bolt at this stage and retighten it lightly. The motorcycle's hydraulic system can then be used to force the pistons out of the body once the pads have been removed. Disconnect the hose once the pistons have been sufficiently displaced.*

3   Remove the brake pads and anti-rattle springs as described in Section 2 and remove the caliper.

Overhaul

Refer to illustrations 3.4, 3.5 and 3.12

4   Clean the exterior of the caliper with denatured alcohol or brake system cleaner **(see illustration)**.

5   Slide the caliper off the mounting bracket and recover the rubber boots from the slider pins **(see illustration)**.

6   If the pistons weren't forced out using the motorcycle's hydraulic system, place a wad of rag between the piston and caliper frame to act as a cushion, then use compressed air directed into the fluid inlet to force the pistons out of the body. Use only low pressure to ease the pistons out and make sure both pistons are displaced at the same time. If the air pressure is too high and the pistons are forced out, the caliper and/or pistons may be damaged. **Warning:** *Never place your*

fingers in front of the pistons in an attempt to catch or protect them when applying compressed air, as serious injury could result.

7   Using a wooden or plastic tool, remove the dust seals from the caliper bores. If a metal tool is being used, take great care not to damage the caliper bores.

8   Remove both the piston seals in the same way.

9   Clean the pistons and bores with denatured alcohol, clean brake fluid or brake system cleaner. **Caution:** *Do not, under any circumstances, use a petroleum-based solvent to clean brake parts.* If compressed air is available, use it to dry the parts thoroughly (make sure it's filtered and unlubricated).

10   Inspect the caliper bores and pistons for signs of corrosion, nicks and burrs and loss of plating. If surface defects are present, the caliper assembly must be replaced. If the caliper is in bad shape the master cylinder should also be checked.

11   If the necessary measuring equipment is available, compare the dimensions of the caliper bores and pistons to those given in the Specifications Section of this Chapter, replacing any component that is worn beyond the service limit.

12   Temporarily install the caliper bracket. Make sure that it slides smoothly in-and-out of the caliper and check that the pins are a snug fit in their bores. If not check the slider pins and their bores for burrs or excessive wear, replacing worn components as necessary **(see illustration)**. The slider pin boots should be replaced as a matter of course.

13   Lubricate the new piston seals with clean brake fluid and install them in their grooves in the caliper bores.

14   Lubricate the new dust seals with clean brake fluid and install them in their grooves in the caliper bores.

15   Lubricate the pistons with clean brake fluid and install them in the caliper bores. Using your thumbs, push the pistons all the way in, making sure they enter the bore squarely.

16   If the slider pins have been removed, apply a few drops of thread locking compound to the pin threads then fit the pin to the caliper body or mounting bracket (as applicable) and tighten it to the specified torque setting.

17   Install the new slider pin boots.

18   Apply a thin coat of PBC (Poly Butyl Cuprysil) grease, or silicone grease designed for high-temperature brake applications, to each of the slider pins. Install the mounting bracket on the caliper and seat the boots over the lips on the bracket.

Installation

19   Install the anti-rattle springs and brake pads as described in Section 2.

20   Connect the brake hose to the caliper, using new sealing washers on each side of the fitting. Tighten the banjo fitting bolt to the specified torque setting.

MOUNTING BRACKET

SMALL ANTI-RATTLE SPRING

UPPER SLIDER PIN BOOT

SLIDER PIN

PISTON

DUST SEAL

PISTON SEAL

BLEEDER VALVE

SLIDER PIN

LOWER SLIDER
PIN BOOT

PISTON
DUST SEAL

PISTON SEAL

LARGE ANTI-RATTLE SPRING

CALIPER BODY

2070-7-3.4 HAYNES

3.4 Exploded view of a typical front brake caliper

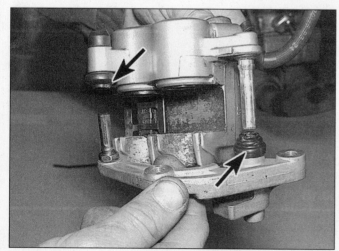

3.5 Slide the caliper off the mounting bracket and remove the
rubber boots (arrows)

3.12 Examine the slider pins for wear and replace if necessary

7

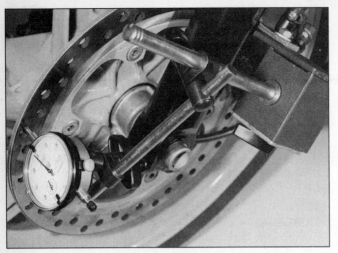

4.3 Using a dial indicator to measure disc runout

4.4 Using a micrometer to measuredisc thickness

21   Fill the master cylinder with the recommended brake fluid (see Chapter 1) and bleed the hydraulic system as described in Section 11.
22   Check for leaks and thoroughly test the operation of the brake before riding the motorcycle.

4   Front brake discs - inspection, removal and installation

Inspection

Refer to illustrations 4.3 and 4.4

1   Place the motorcycle on its centerstand - where no centerstand is fitted, support the machine securely in an upright position. Block the motorcycle (being careful not to damage the fairing lower panels - remove them if necessary, as described in Chapter 8) so that the front wheel is clear of the ground.
2   Visually inspect the surface of the discs for score marks and other damage. Light scratches are normal after use and won't   affect brake operation, but deep grooves and heavy score marks will reduce braking efficiency and accelerate pad wear. If the discs are badly grooved they must be machined or replaced.
3   To check disc runout, mount a dial indicator to a fork leg, with the plunger on the indicator touching the surface of the disc about 10 mm (1/2 inch) from the outer edge **(see illustration)**. Rotate the wheel and watch the indicator needle, comparing your reading with the limit listed in this Chapter's Specifications. If the runout is greater than allowed, check the hub bearings for play. If the bearings are worn, replace them and repeat this check. If the disc runout is still excessive, it will have to be replaced, although machining by a competent engineering shop may be a solution.
4   The disc must not be machined or allowed to wear down to a thickness less than the service limit, listed in this Chapter's Specifications (check also for wear limits stamped on the disc itself). The thickness of the disc can be checked with a micrometer **(see illustration)**. If the thickness of the disc is less than the minimum allowable, it must be replaced.

Removal

5   Remove the wheel as described in Section 14. **Caution:** *Don't lay the wheel down and allow it to rest on one of the discs - the disc could become warped. Set the wheel on wood blocks so the disc doesn't support the weight of the wheel.*
6   Mark the relationship of the disc to the wheel so it can be installed in the same position. Remove the bolts that retain the disc to the wheel. Loosen the bolts a little at a time, in a criss-cross pattern, to avoid distorting the disc.

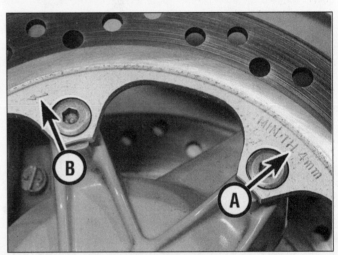

4.9 Disc minimum thickness (A) is stamped on disc; on installation ensure the arrow (B) is pointing in the normal direction of wheel rotation

7   Remove the disc and recover any shims which are positioned between the disc and wheel - usually there is one shim at each mounting point. If both discs are to be removed and are not already stamped with identifying marks, mark them 'Left' and 'Right' to ensure they are correctly positioned on installation.

Installation

Refer to illustration 4.9

8   Position the shim(s) as found on removal - usually there is one on each of the disc's threaded holes in the wheel.
9   Install the disc on the wheel, aligning the previously applied matchmarks (if you're reinstalling the original disc). Make sure the arrow (and any other marks stamped on the disc) marking the normal direction of rotation is pointing in the direction of wheel rotation and is on the outer face of the disc **(see illustration)**.
10   Install the bolts, ensuring the shims remain in position, and tighten them evenly and progressively to the specified torque setting. Clean off all grease from the brake disc(s) using acetone or brake system cleaner. If new brake discs have been installed, remove any protective coating from their working surfaces.
11   Install the wheel as described in Section 14.
12   Operate the brake lever several times to bring the pads into contact with the disc. Check the operation of the brakes carefully before riding the motorcycle.

5   Front brake master cylinder - removal, overhaul and installation

1   If the master cylinder is leaking fluid, or if the lever does not produce a firm feel when the brake is applied, and bleeding the brakes does not help, master cylinder overhaul is recommended. Before disassembling the master cylinder, read through the entire procedure and make sure that you have the correct rebuild kit. Also, you will need some new, clean brake fluid of the recommended type, some clean shop towels and internal snap-ring pliers. **Note:** *To prevent damage to the paint from spilled brake fluid, always cover the fuel tank when working on the master cylinder.*
2   **Caution:** *Disassembly, overhaul and reassembly of the brake master cylinder must be done in a spotlessly clean work area to avoid contamination and possible failure of the brake hydraulic system components.*

Removal

3   Loosen, but do not remove, the screws holding the reservoir cover in place.
4   Disconnect the electrical connectors from the brake light switch.
5   Pull back the rubber boot, loosen the banjo fitting bolt and separate the brake hose from the master cylinder. Wrap the end of the hose in a clean rag and suspend the hose in an upright position or bend it down carefully and place the open end in a clean container. The objective is to prevent excessive loss of brake fluid, fluid spills and system contamination.
6   Remove the locknut from the underside of the brake lever pivot bolt, then unscrew the bolt and remove the brake lever.
7   Remove the master cylinder mounting bolts, then remove the clamp and lift the master cylinder away from the handlebar. **Caution:** *Do not tip the master cylinder upside down or brake fluid will run out.*

Overhaul

Refer to illustration 5.8

8   Detach the reservoir cover and remove the plate, rubber diaphragm and float, then drain the brake fluid into a suitable container **(see illustration)**. Wipe any remaining fluid out of the reservoir with a clean rag.
9   Undo the screw and remove the brake light switch.
10   Carefully remove the rubber dust boot from the end of the piston.
11   Using snap-ring pliers, remove the snap-ring and slide out the piston assembly and the spring. Lay the parts out in the proper order to prevent confusion during reassembly.
12   Clean all of the parts with brake system cleaner (available at auto parts stores), isopropyl alcohol or clean brake fluid. **Caution:** *Do not, under any circumstances, use a petroleum-based solvent to clean brake parts.* If compressed air is available, use it to dry the parts thoroughly (make sure it's filtered and unlubricated).
13   Check the master cylinder bore for corrosion, scratches, nicks and score marks. If damage is evident, the master cylinder must be replaced with a new one. If the master cylinder is in poor condition, then the calipers should be checked as well.
14   If the necessary measuring equipment is available, compare the dimensions of the master cylinder bore and piston to those given in the Specifications Section of this Chapter, replacing any component that it is worn beyond the service limit.
15   The dust boot, piston assembly and spring are included in the rebuild kit. Use all of the new parts, regardless of the apparent condition of the old ones.
16   Before reassembling the master cylinder, soak the piston and the rubber cup seals in clean brake fluid for ten or fifteen minutes. Lubricate the master cylinder bore with clean brake fluid, then carefully insert the piston and related parts in the reverse order of disassembly. Make sure the lips on the cup seals do not turn inside out when they are slipped into the bore and ensure the spring is fitted the correct way around.
17   Depress the piston, then install the snap-ring (make sure the

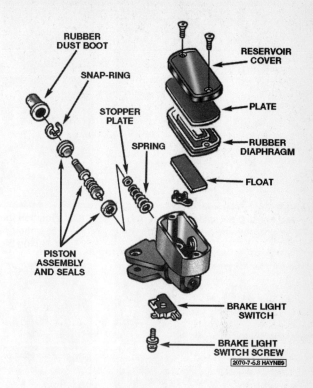

5.8 Exploded view of the front brake master cylinder

snap-ring is properly seated in the groove). Install the rubber dust boot (make sure the lip is seated properly in the piston groove).
18   Install the brake light switch and securely tighten its retaining screw.

Installation

19   Install the master cylinder so that its body's clamp mating surface aligns with the punch mark in the handlebar and ensuring that the "UP" mark on the clamp is up, then tighten the mounting bolts. Always tighten the upper bolt first, to the specified torque setting until the clamp halves mate properly, then the lower bolt. Don't overtighten the lower bolt in an attempt to close the gap between the clamp halves at the bottom; you will only break the clamp or the master cylinder.
20   Connect the brake hose to the master cylinder, using new sealing washers. Tighten the banjo fitting bolt to the specified torque setting.
21   Install the lever and pivot bolt. Install the pivot bolt locknut and tighten it to the specified torque setting. Connect the brake light switch wiring.
22   Refer to Section 11 and bleed the air from the system.

6   Rear brake pads - replacement

Warning: *The dust created by the brake system may contain asbestos, which is harmful to your health. Never blow it out with compressed air and don't inhale any of it. An approved filtering mask should be worn when working on the brakes.*

G and H models

Refer to illustrations 6.2, 6.9a, 6.9b, 6.9c and 6.10

1   Place the motorcycle on its centerstand - where no centerstand is fitted, support the machine securely in an upright position.
2   Slacken the pad pin retainer bolt **(see illustration)**.
3   Unscrew the caliper mounting bracket bolt **(see illustration 6.10)**. Pivot the caliper up - do not place any excess strain on the hydraulic hose; release the hose from its retaining clips if necessary.

7

6.2 Rear brake pad replacement, G and H models - unscrew the pad pin retainer bolt

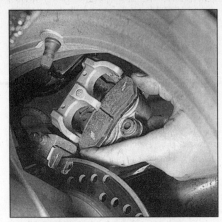

6.9a Position the pads in the caliper so that their friction material is facing the brake disc . . .

6.9b . . . insert the pad retaining pins making sure that they pass correctly through the holes in both pads . . .

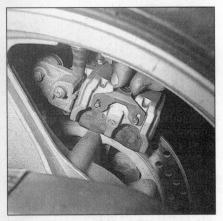

6.9c . . . and install the retainer, pressing it down to secure the ends of both pad pins

6.10 Lubricate, install and tighten the rear caliper mounting bracket bolt to its specified torque setting

6.15a Rear brake pad replacement, J models onward - pass a screwdriver through the chainguard access hole to unscrew the plug from the caliper body . . .

4   Slide the caliper off the bracket.

5   Unscrew the pad pin retainer bolt and withdraw the retainer, then pull the pad pins out of the caliper; if either is stuck, it can be tapped out with a hammer and pin punch, but both pins and the caliper must be cleaned thoroughly and lubricated on reassembly. Withdraw the brake pads, noting the location of the anti-squeal shim on the metal backing of the inside pad (furthest from the pistons), if fitted.

6   Remove the anti-rattle springs from the caliper body and the mounting bracket, noting their correct fitted positions.

7   Inspect the brake pads and associated components as described in Steps 7 through 11 of Section 2 (inspect the brake disc as described in Section 8). Clean all components, then lubricate them as outlined in Section 2 and prepare for reassembly.

8   Install the anti-rattle springs in the caliper body ensuring each one is correctly positioned **(see illustration 6.9a)**. Apply a thin smear of PBC (Poly Butyl Cuprysil) grease, or silicone grease designed for high-temperature brake applications, to each and to the metal backing of each pad. **Caution:** *Do not leave excess lubricant on any caliper component, or allow lubricant to foul the friction material of either pad.*

9   Insert the pads into the caliper, ensuring both anti-rattle springs remain correctly positioned, so that the friction material of each pad is facing the disc. Do not forget, where fitted, the inside pad (furthest from the pistons) may have an anti-squeal shim installed on its metal backing. Insert the pad retaining pins making sure that they pass correctly through the holes in both pads, then install the retainer, pushing it down to secure the pins **(see illustrations)**.

10   Slide the caliper assembly onto the mounting bracket, then pivot

the assembly down onto the disc so that the pad friction material is on each side of the disc. Install the bolt, tightening it to the specified torque setting **(see illustration)**.

11   Tighten the pad pin retainer bolt to the specified torque setting. Locate the brake hose in the retaining clips on the rear brake torque rod; ensure the hose is securely retained by each clip.

12   Top up the master cylinder reservoir (see Chapter 1) and fit the diaphragm and cap.

13   Operate the brake pedal several times to bring the pads into contact with the disc. Check the master cylinder fluid level (see Chapter 1) and the operation of the brake before riding the motorcycle.

J models onward

Refer to illustrations 6.15a, 6.15b, 6.16, 6.19a, 6.19b, 6.19c and 6.20

Note: *While the brake pads can be replaced without removing the caliper, as described here, it is usually best to remove the caliper so that it can be cleaned properly and checked over whenever the pads are disturbed - this is very important, given the amount of road dirt which is normally present around the rear wheel, and also improves access considerably. Refer to the relevant Steps of Section 7 for details - there is no need to disconnect the hydraulic line or to remove the pistons, just check, clean and lubricate the caliper slider pins, rubber boots etc.*

14   Place the motorcycle on its centerstand - where no centerstand is fitted, support the machine securely in an upright position.

15   Unscrew the plug from the caliper body to reveal the pad pin head, then loosen the pad pin **(see illustrations)**.

6.15b . . . followed by the pad pin

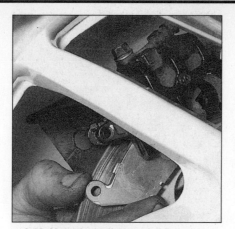

6.16 Note the anti-squeal shim on the metal backing of the inside pad furthest from the pistons) as the brake pads are removed

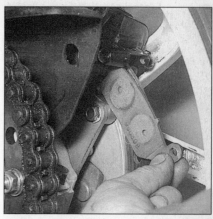

6.19a Lubricate the pad metal backing as described and install pads so that their friction material is against the disc . . .

6.19b . . . and so that the squared end engages in the recess in the mounting bracket

6.19c Insert the pad pin through the caliper and through the holes in both pads . . .

6.20 . . . then tighten the pad pin to its specified torque setting

16   Unscrew the pad pin from the caliper and withdraw the brake pads **(see illustration)**. If any is fitted, note the location of the anti-squeal shim on the metal backing of the inside pad (furthest from the pistons).

17   Inspect the brake pads and associated components as described in Steps 7 through 11 of Section 2 (inspect the brake disc as described in Section 8). Clean all components, lubricate them as outlined in Section 2 and prepare for reassembly.

18   Where fitted, install the anti-squeal shim on the metal backing of the inside pad (furthest from the pistons). Apply a thin smear of grease (see Step 8 above) to the metal backing of each pad. **Caution:** *Do not leave excess lubricant on any caliper component, or allow lubricant to foul the friction material of either pad.*

19   Insert the pads into the caliper, ensuring both anti-rattle springs remain correctly positioned, so that the squared end of each pad engages in the recess in the mounting bracket and that the friction material of each pad is facing the disc. Insert the pad retaining pin making sure that it passes correctly through the holes in both pads **(see illustrations)**.

20   Tighten the pad pin to the specified torque setting then fit the pad pin plug, tightening it securely **(see illustration)**.

21   Complete reassembly as described in Steps 12 and 13 above.

---

7   Rear brake caliper - removal, overhaul and installation

Warning: *If the caliper indicates the need for an overhaul (usually due to leaking fluid or sticky operation), all old brake fluid should be flushed*

from the system. Also, the dust created by the brake system may contain asbestos, which is harmful to your health. Never blow it out with compressed air and don't inhale any of it. An approved filtering mask should be worn when working on the brakes. Do not, under any circumstances, use petroleum-based solvents to clean brake parts. Use clean brake fluid, brake cleaner or denatured alcohol only.

Removal

Refer to illustrations 7.4a, 7.4b and 7.4c

1   Place the motorcycle on its centerstand - where no centerstand is fitted, support the machine securely in an upright position.

2   Remove the brake hose banjo fitting bolt and separate the hose from the caliper. Plug the hose end or wrap a plastic bag tightly around it to minimize fluid loss and prevent dirt entering the system. Discard the sealing washers; new ones must be used on installation. **Note:** *If you're planning to overhaul the caliper and don't have a source of compressed air to blow out the pistons, just loosen the banjo bolt at this stage and retighten it lightly. The motorcycle's hydraulic system can then be used to force the pistons out of the body once the pads have been removed. Disconnect the hose once the pistons have been sufficiently displaced.*

3   Remove the brake pads and anti-rattle springs as described in Section 6.

4   If not already done, unbolt the caliper from its mounting bracket/stay and pivot it ups off the brake disc - do not place any excess strain on the hydraulic hose; release the hose from its retaining clips if necessary. Slide the caliper away from its mounting bracket and

7

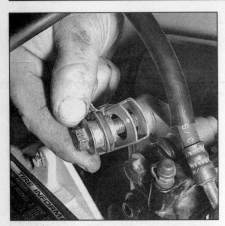
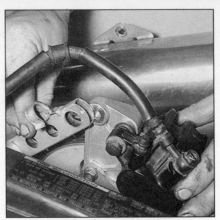

7.4a Unbolting rear brake caliper, L models onward - note arrangement of rubber washers when unbolting torque rod . . .

7.4b . . . release hydraulic hose from retaining clips to avoid straining it . . .

7.4c . . . and withdraw caliper with its mounting bracket

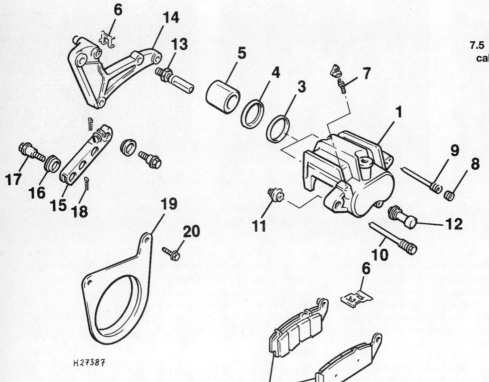

7.5 Exploded view of the rear brake caliper - L models onward shown

1 Caliper body
2 Brake pads
3 Dust seals
4 Piston seals
5 Pistons
6 Anti-rattle springs
7 Bleeder valve
8 Plug
9 Pad pin
10 Upper/front slider pin
11 Rubber boot
12 Slider bush boot
13 Lower/rear slider pin
14 Caliper mounting bracket
15 Torque rod
16 Dust seals
17 Torque rod bolts
18 Cotter pins (split pins)
19 Caliper stay
20 Stay bolts

H27387

recover the slider pin rubber boot. If required, unbolt the caliper mounting bracket from the torque rod, noting that this bolt is usually secured by a cotter pin (split pin) **(see illustrations)**.

Overhaul

Refer to illustration 7.5

5   Clean the exterior of the caliper with denatured alcohol or brake system cleaner **(see illustration)**.

6   If the pistons weren't forced out using the motorcycle's hydraulic system, place a wad of rag between the pistons and the caliper frame to act as a cushion, then use compressed air directed into the fluid inlet to force the pistons out of the body. Use only low pressure to ease

the pistons out and ensure that both pistons are displaced at the same time. If the air pressure is too high and the pistons are forced out, the caliper and/or pistons may be damaged. **Warning:** *Never place your fingers in front of the pistons in an attempt to catch or protect them when applying compressed air, as serious injury could result.*

7   Using a wooden or plastic tool, remove the dust seals from the caliper bores. If a metal tool is being used, take great care not to damage the caliper bores.

8   Remove the piston seals in the same way.

9   Clean the pistons and bores with denatured alcohol, clean brake fluid or brake system cleaner. **Caution:** *Do not, under any circumstances, use a petroleum-based solvent to clean brake parts.* If compressed air is available, use it to dry the parts thoroughly (make

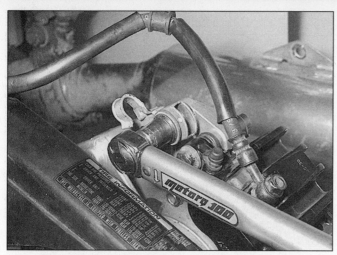

7.21a Tighten the rear brake torque rod bolts to the specified torque setting . . .

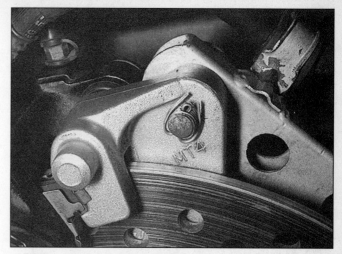

7.21b . . . and secure by installing a new cotter pin (split pin), spreading its ends as shown

sure it's filtered and unlubricated).

10   Inspect the caliper bores and pistons for signs of corrosion, nicks and burrs and loss of plating. If surface defects are present, the caliper assembly must be replaced. If the caliper is in bad shape the master cylinder should also be checked.

11   If the necessary measuring equipment is available, compare the dimensions of the caliper bores and pistons to those given in the Specifications Section of this Chapter, replacing any component that is worn beyond the service limit.

12   Temporarily install the caliper to its mounting bracket. Make sure that it slides smoothly in-and-out and check that the slider pin and the slider bushing are a snug fit in their bores. If not, check the slider pin/bushing and their bores for burrs or excessive wear, replacing worn components as necessary. The slider pin/bushing boots should be replaced as a matter of course.

13   Lubricate the new piston seals with clean brake fluid and install them in the groove in each caliper bore.

14   Lubricate the new dust seals with clean brake fluid and install them in the groove in each caliper bore.

15   Lubricate the pistons with clean brake fluid and install them in the caliper bores. Using your thumbs, push the pistons all the way in, making sure they enter their bores squarely.

16   If either slider pin has been removed, apply a few drops of thread locking compound to its threads then fit the pin to the caliper body and tighten it to the specified torque setting.

17   Install the new slider pin/bush boots.

18   Apply a thin coat of PBC (Poly Butyl Cuprysil) grease, or silicone grease designed for high-temperature brake applications, to the slider pin and bush. Slide the slider bushing into position in the caliper body ensuring the boot is correctly seated in the groove on each end of the bush.

Installation

Refer to illustrations 7.21a, 7.21b and 7.21c

19   Slide the caliper into position on the mounting bracket. Make sure the slider pin boot is correctly located in its grooves on the body and bracket.

20   Install the anti-rattle springs and brake pads as described in Section 6.

21   Refit the assembly to the torque rod (if removed), tightening the torque rod bolts to the specified torque setting and installing new cotter pins (split pins) to replace any disturbed on removal. Lower the caliper over the disc, ensuring that the disc passes correctly between the friction material of the pads, then tighten the caliper mounting bracket/stay bolt(s) to the specified torque setting **(see illustrations)**.

22   Connect the brake hose to the caliper, using new sealing washers on each side of the fitting. Tighten the banjo fitting bolt to the specified

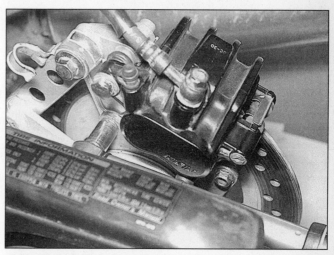

7.21c Tighten the caliper mounting bolts to the specified torque setting - caliper stay bolts, L models onward shown

torque setting.

23   Fill the master cylinder with the recommended brake fluid (see Chapter 1) and bleed the hydraulic system as described in Section 11. Operate the brake pedal several times to bring the pads into contact with the disc.

24   Check for leaks and thoroughly test the operation of the brake before riding the motorcycle.

---

8   Rear brake disc - inspection, removal and installation   **7**

Inspection

1   Refer to Section 4 of this Chapter, noting that the dial indicator should be attached to the swingarm.

Removal

Refer to illustration 8.3a and 8.3b

2   Remove the wheel as described in Section 15. **Caution:** *Don't (on G through K models) lay the wheel down and allow it to rest on the disc - the disc could become warped. Set the wheel on wood blocks so the disc doesn't support the weight of the wheel.* On L models onward, remove the rear stub axle as described in Section 16.

3   Mark the relationship of the disc to the wheel (or stub axle, according to model), so it can be installed in the same position.

**8.3a Rear brake disc is retained by four bolts (arrow) on
G through K models . . .**

8.3b . . . and by four nuts on L models onward

Remove the bolts or nuts retaining the disc. Loosen the fasteners a little at a time, in a criss-cross pattern to avoid distorting the disc, then remove the disc **(see illustrations)**.

Installation

4   Position the disc on the wheel (or stub axle, according to model), aligning the previously applied matchmarks (if you're reinstalling the original disc). Make sure the arrow (or any other marks stamped on the disc) marking the direction of rotation is pointing in the proper direction and is on the outer face of the disc **(see illustration 4.9)**.
5   Clean the threads of the disc bolts and apply a suitable thread locking compound to the threads of each bolt.
6   Install the bolts and tighten them (or the nuts, according to model) evenly and progressively to the specified torque setting. Clean off all grease from the brake disc using acetone or brake system cleaner. If a new brake disc has been installed, remove any protective coating from its working surfaces.
7   On L models onward, install the rear wheel stub axle as described in Section 16. On all models, install the wheel as described in Section 15.
8   Operate the brake pedal several times to bring the pads into contact with the disc. Check the operation of the brake carefully before riding the motorcycle.

9   Rear brake master cylinder - removal, overhaul and installation

1   If the master cylinder is leaking fluid, or if the pedal does not produce a firm feel when the brake is applied, and bleeding the brakes does not help, master cylinder overhaul is recommended. Before disassembling the master cylinder, read through the entire procedure and make sure that you have the correct rebuild kit. Also, you will need some new, clean brake fluid of the recommended type, some clean shop towels and internal snap-ring pliers.
2   **Caution:** *Disassembly, overhaul and reassembly of the brake master cylinder must be done in a spotlessly clean work area to avoid contamination and possible failure of the brake hydraulic system components.*

Removal

3   Place the motorcycle on its centerstand - where no centerstand is fitted, support the machine securely in an upright position. Remove the right side cover or the rear fairing panel, according to model (see Chapter 8 if necessary). On early models, disconnect the brake light switch wiring connector.

4   Unscrew the banjo union bolt from the top of the master cylinder. Discard the sealing washers on each side of the fitting. Wrap the end of the hose in a clean shop towel and suspend the hose in an upright position or bend it down carefully and place the open end in a clean container. The objective is to prevent excessive loss of brake fluid, fluid spills and system contamination.
5   Loosen the master cylinder mounting bolts then remove the right footpeg bracket retaining bolts (see Chapter 6).
6   Remove the bolt securing the master cylinder reservoir to the frame. Unscrew the reservoir cap and pour the contents into a container. Remove the retaining screw and disconnect the fluid reservoir hose from the master cylinder - collect and discard the sealing O-ring.
7   Remove the cotter pin (split pin) and slide out the clevis pin securing the master cylinder to the brake pedal.
8   Remove the master cylinder mounting bolts and separate it from the footpeg bracket.

Overhaul

Refer to illustration 9.9

9   Hold the clevis with a pair of pliers and loosen the locknut. Unscrew the clevis and locknut from the pushrod and carefully remove the rubber dust boot from the pushrod **(see illustration)**.
10   Depress the pushrod and, using snap-ring pliers, remove the snap-ring. Slide out the piston assembly and spring. Lay the parts out in the proper order to prevent confusion during reassembly.
11   Clean all of the parts with brake system cleaner (available at auto parts stores), isopropyl alcohol or clean brake fluid. **Caution:** *Do not, under any circumstances, use a petroleum-based solvent to clean brake parts.* If compressed air is available, use it to dry the parts thoroughly (make sure it's filtered and unlubricated).
12   Check the master cylinder bore for corrosion, scratches, nicks and score marks. If damage is evident, the master cylinder must be replaced with a new one. If the master cylinder is in poor condition, then the caliper should be checked as well.
13   If the necessary measuring equipment is available, compare the dimensions of the master cylinder bore and piston to those given in the Specifications Section of this Chapter, replacing any component that is worn beyond the service limit.
14   A new piston and spring are included in the rebuild kit. Use them regardless of the condition of the old ones.
15   Before reassembling the master cylinder, soak the piston and the rubber cup seals in clean brake fluid for ten or fifteen minutes. Lubricate the master cylinder bore with clean brake fluid, then carefully insert the parts in the reverse order of disassembly, ensuring the

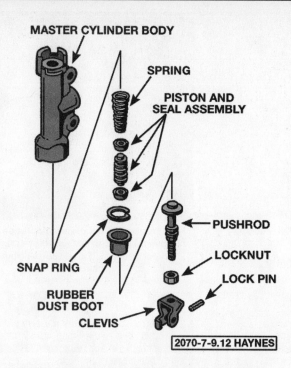

MASTER CYLINDER BODY

SPRING

PISTON AND SEAL ASSEMBLY

PUSHROD

LOCKNUT

LOCK PIN

SNAP RING

RUBBER DUST BOOT

CLEVIS

2070-7-9.12 HAYNES

9.9 Exploded view of the rear brake master cylinder

tapered end of the spring is facing the piston. Make sure the lips on the cup seals do not turn inside out when they are slipped into the bore.
16   Depress the pushrod, then install the snap-ring (make sure the snap-ring is properly seated in the groove). Note that the snap-ring must be fitted with its chamfered edge towards the master cylinder piston.
17   Install the rubber dust boot (make sure the lip is seated properly in the groove).
18   Install the locknut and clevis to the end of the pushrod. On G through K models adjust the pushrod length so that the distance from the center of the master cylinder bottom mounting bolt location to the center of the clevis holes is 80 mm (3.1 inches). On L models onward, it is sufficient to ensure that there are two or three pushrod threads exposed beyond the locknut when it is tightened. Tighten the locknut and install the lock pin (where fitted).

Installation

19   Fit the master cylinder to the footpeg bracket and lightly tighten its retaining bolts.
20   Align the pedal with the master cylinder clevis and slide in the clevis pin. Secure the clevis pin in position with a new cotter pin (split pin).
21   Fit a new O-ring to the reservoir hose union and fit the union, tightening securely the screw.
22   Apply a few drops of locking compound to the threads of the master cylinder reservoir bolt then fit the bolt and tighten it to the specified torque setting.
23   Install the footpeg bracket assembly on the frame and securely tighten its retaining bolts.
24   Tighten the master cylinder mounting bolts to the specified torque.
25   Reconnect the brake light switch wiring (where disconnected).
26   Connect the banjo fitting to the top of the master cylinder, using a new sealing washer on each side of the fitting. Tighten the banjo fitting bolt to the specified torque setting.
27   Fill the fluid reservoir with the specified fluid (see Chapter 1) and bleed the system following the procedure in Section 11.
28   Install the right side cover or the rear fairing panel, according to

model (see Chapter 8, if necessary).
29   Check the position of the brake pedal and adjust the brake light switch (see Chapter 1). Check the operation of the brake carefully before riding the motorcycle.

10   Brake pipe and hoses - inspection and replacement

Inspection

1   Once a week, or if the motorcycle is used less frequently, before every ride, check the condition of the brake hoses.
2   Twist and flex the rubber hoses while looking for cracks, bulges and seeping fluid. Check extra carefully around the areas where the hoses connect with the banjo fittings, as these are common areas for hose failure.
3   Inspect the metal banjo union fittings connected to brake hoses. If the fittings are rusted, scratched or cracked, replace them.
4   Inspect the metal pipe linking the two front brake caliper hoses. If the plating on the metal pipe is chipped or scratched, the lines may rust. If the fittings are rusted, scratched or cracked, replace the pipe assembly.

Replacement

5   The brake hoses have banjo union fittings on each end of the hose. Cover the surrounding area with plenty of shop towels and unscrew the banjo bolt on each end of the hose. Detach the hose from any clips that may be present and remove the hose. Discard the sealing washers.
6   Position the new hose, making sure it isn't twisted or otherwise strained, between the two components. Make sure the metal tube portion of the banjo fitting is located between the protrusions on the component it's connected to, if equipped. Install the banjo bolts, using new sealing washers on both sides of the fittings, and tighten them to the specified torque setting.
7   The metal pipe has a flare nut at each end, and can be removed once both nuts have been slackened. Apply a few drops of locking compound to each of the flare nut threads then install the new pipe and tighten the flare nuts to the specified torque.
8   Flush the old brake fluid from the system, refill the system with the recommended fluid (see Chapter 1) and bleed the air from the system (see Section 11). Check the operation of the brakes carefully before riding the motorcycle.

11   Brake system bleeding

Refer to illustration 11.5
1   Bleeding the brakes is simply the process of removing all the air bubbles from the brake fluid reservoirs, the lines and the brake calipers. Bleeding is necessary whenever a brake system hydraulic connection is loosened, when a component or hose is replaced, or when the master cylinder or caliper is overhauled. Leaks in the system may also allow air to enter, but leaking brake fluid will reveal their presence and warn you of the need for repair.
2   To bleed the brakes, you will need some new, clean brake fluid of the recommended type (see Chapter 1), a length of clear vinyl or plastic tubing, a small container partially filled with clean brake fluid, some shop towels and a wrench to fit the brake caliper bleeder valves.
3   Cover the fuel tank and other painted components to prevent damage in the event that brake fluid is spilled.
4   Remove the reservoir cap or cover and slowly pump the brake lever or pedal a few times, until no air bubbles can be seen floating up from the holes at the bottom of the reservoir. Doing this bleeds the air from the master cylinder end of the line. Reinstall the reservoir cap or cover.
5   Attach one end of the clear vinyl or plastic tubing to the bleeder valve and submerge the other end in the brake fluid in the container

7

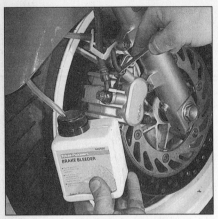

11.5 Bleeding the brakes

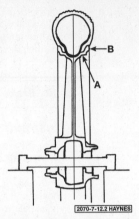

2070-7-12.2 HAYNES

12.2 Use a dial indicator to measure wheel runout

A   Radial runout
B   Axial runout

14.2 To gain the necessary clearance to remove the front wheel, unbolt the right caliper (or both, if an R model) from the fork

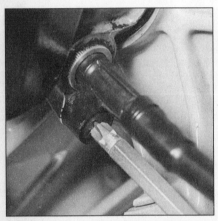

14.3a Unscrew the retaining screw . . .

14.3b . . . and detach the speedometer cable from its drive unit

14.4 Unscrew the axle bolt from the right side, loosen the clamp bolts . . .

(see illustration).

6   Remove the reservoir cap or cover and check the fluid level. Do not allow the fluid level to drop below the lower mark during the bleeding process.

7   Carefully pump the brake lever or pedal three or four times and hold it in (front) or down (rear) while opening the caliper bleeder valve. When the valve is opened, brake fluid will flow out of the caliper into the clear tubing and the lever will move toward the handlebar or the pedal will move down.

8   Retighten the bleeder valve, then release the brake lever or pedal gradually. Repeat the process until no air bubbles are visible in the brake fluid leaving the caliper and the lever or pedal is firm when applied.

9   Replace the reservoir cap or cover, wipe up any spilled brake fluid and check the entire system for leaks. **Note:** *If bleeding is difficult, it may be necessary to let the brake fluid in the system stabilize for a few hours (it may be aerated). Repeat the bleeding procedure when the tiny bubbles in the system have settled out.*

12 Wheels - inspection and repair

Refer to illustration 12.2

1   Place the motorcycle on its centerstand - where no centerstand is fitted, support the machine securely in an upright position. Block the motorcycle (being careful not to damage the fairing lower panels -

remove them if necessary, as described in Chapter 8) so that the front/rear wheel is clear of the ground. Clean the wheels thoroughly to remove mud and dirt that may interfere with the inspection procedure or mask defects. Make a general check of the wheels and tires as described in Chapter 1.

2   With the motorcycle supported and the wheel in the air, attach a dial indicator to the fork slider or the swingarm and position its stem against the side of the rim **(see illustration)**. Spin the wheel slowly and check the side-to-side (axial) runout of the rim, then compare your readings with the value listed in this Chapter's Specifications. To accurately check radial runout with the dial indicator, the wheel would have to be removed from the machine. With the axle clamped in a vise, the wheel can be rotated to check the runout.

3   An easier, though slightly less accurate, method is to attach a stiff wire pointer to the fork slider or the swingarm and position the end a fraction of an inch from the wheel (where the wheel and tire join). If the wheel is true, the distance from the pointer to the rim will be constant as the wheel is rotated. **Note:** *If wheel runout is excessive, check the wheel bearings very carefully before replacing the wheel.*

4   The wheels should also be visually inspected for cracks, flat spots on the rim and other damage. Since tubeless tires are fitted, look very closely for dents in the area where the tire bead contacts the rim. Dents in this area may prevent complete sealing of the tire against the rim, which leads to deflation of the tire over a period of time.

5   If damage is evident, or if runout in either direction is excessive, the wheel will have to be replaced with a new one. Never attempt to repair a damaged cast aluminum wheel.

14.5 . . . and withdraw the axle from the left side

14.6 Arrow marks cast into wheel spokes show normal direction of wheel rotation - can be used to identify wheel fitting

13 Wheels - alignment check

1   Misalignment of the wheels, which may be due to a cocked rear wheel or a bent frame or triple clamps, can cause strange and possibly serious handling problems. If the frame or triple clamps are at fault, repair by a frame specialist or replacement with new parts are the only alternatives.
2   To check the alignment you will need an assistant, a length of string or a perfectly straight piece of wood and a ruler graduated in 1/64 inch increments. A plumb bob or other suitable weight will also be required.
3   Place the motorcycle on its centerstand - where no centerstand is fitted, support the machine securely in an upright position. Block the motorcycle (being careful not to damage the fairing lower panels - remove them if necessary, as described in Chapter 8) so that the front/rear wheel is clear of the ground. Measure the width of both tires at their widest points. Subtract the smaller measurement from the larger measurement, then divide the difference by two. The result is the amount of offset that should exist between the front and rear tires on both sides.
4   If a string is used, have your assistant hold one end of it about half way between the floor and the rear axle, touching the rear sidewall of the tire.
5   Run the other end of the string forward and pull it tight so that it is roughly parallel to the floor. Slowly bring the string into contact with the front sidewall of the rear tire, then turn the front wheel until it is parallel with the string. Measure the distance from the front tire sidewall to the string.
6   Repeat the procedure on the other side of the motorcycle. The distance from the front tire sidewall to the string should be equal on both sides.
7   As was previously pointed out, a perfectly straight length of wood may be substituted for the string. The procedure is the same.
8   If the distance between the string and tire is greater on one side, or if the rear wheel appears to be cocked, refer to Chapter 6, *Swingarm bearings - check*, and make sure the swingarm is tight.
9   If the front-to-back alignment is correct, the wheels still may be out of alignment vertically.
10   Using the plumb bob, or other suitable weight, and a length of string, check the rear wheel to make sure it is vertical. To do this, hold the string against the tire upper sidewall and allow the weight to settle just off the floor. When the string touches both the upper and lower tire sidewalls and is perfectly straight, the wheel is vertical. If it is not, place thin spacers under one leg of the center stand.
11   Once the rear wheel is vertical, check the front wheel in the same manner. If both wheels are not perfectly vertical, the frame and/or major suspension components are bent.

14 Front wheel - removal and installation

Removal

Refer to illustrations 14.2, 14.3a, 14.3b, 14.4, 14.5 and 14.6

1   Place the motorcycle on the centerstand, then raise the front wheel off the ground by tying down the rear of the machine. If this is not possible, remove the fairing lower panel(s) (see Chapter 8) and place a floor jack, with a wood block on the jack head, under the engine; raise the jack to lift the wheel off the ground.
2   On early models unbolt the right brake caliper, on R models unbolt both brake calipers. Unscrew its mounting bracket bolts then slide the caliper off the disc and support it with a piece of wire, taking care not to place any undue strain on the hydraulic hose **(see illustration)**. Don't disconnect the brake hose from the caliper. **Caution**: *Do not operate the front brake lever with a caliper or the wheel removed.*
3   On G through K models, undo the screw and detach the speedometer cable from its drive unit **(see illustrations)**.
4   On all models, unscrew the front axle bolt then loosen the axle clamp bolts **(see illustration)**.
5   Support the wheel, then pull out the axle and carefully lower the wheel **(see illustration)**. On early models, disengage the left brake caliper from the disc and slide the caliper out to gain the necessary clearance to withdraw the wheel from the forks.
6   Remove the spacer from the right side of the wheel and the speedometer drive (or spacer, according to model) from the left side. Note that the wheel may have arrow marks cast into the spoke roots to indicate the normal direction of wheel rotation; these, where found, can be used to identify the left and right sides of a wheel - if none can be found, make your own to be sure of installing the wheel correctly **(see illustration)**. **Caution**: *Don't lay the wheel down and allow it to rest on one of the discs - the disc could become warped. Set the wheel on wood blocks so the disc doesn't support the weight of the wheel.*
7   Roll the axle on a flat surface such as a piece of plate glass. If it's bent at all, replace it. If the axle is corroded, remove the corrosion with fine emery cloth.
8   Check the condition of the wheel bearings (see Section 16).

Installation

Refer to illustrations 14.9a, 14.9b, 14.9c, 14.13, 14.14, 14.17a and 14.17b

9   On G through K models, fit the speedometer drive to the left side of the wheel, aligning its drive gear slots with the driveplate tabs; on L models onward install the shorter spacer in this side. Install the (longer) spacer in the right side of the wheel. Apply a thin coat of grease to the seal lips before installing the spacers/drive unit and use the marks

7

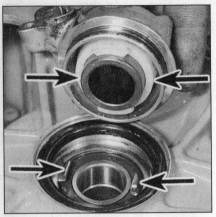

14.9a Align the speedometer drive gear slots with the driveplate tabs (arrows) when fitting the speedometer drive to the wheel left side

14.9b On L models onward, fit the shorter spacer to the wheel's left side

14.9c Do not omit the (longer) spacer from the right side of the wheel

14.13 Install the axle bolt and tighten it to the specified torque setting

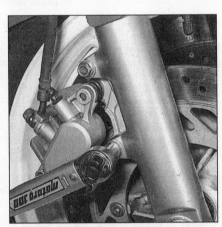

14.14 Install the caliper(s) and tighten their mounting bracket bolts to the specified torque setting

14.17a Use a feeler blade to check the caliper bracket-to-disc clearance - see text . . .

found or the notes made on removal to identify correctly the left and right sides of the wheel **(see illustrations)**.

10   Maneuver the wheel into position, engaging its brake disc between (the friction material of) the pads of the left caliper (early models only). Apply a thin coat of grease to the axle.

11   Lift the wheel into position making sure the spacer(s)/speedometer drive remains in place. On G through K models, position the speedometer drive lug against the rear of the lug on the left fork slider.

12   On all models, slide the axle into position from the left. Tighten the left axle clamp bolt to the specified torque setting.

13   Install the axle bolt and tighten it to the specified torque setting **(see illustration)**.

14   Install the right (or both, according to model) brake caliper(s) and tighten their mounting bracket bolts to the specified torque setting **(see illustration)**.

15   On G through K models, connect the speedometer cable to the drive, aligning the inner cable slot with the drive dog, and securely tighten its retaining screw.

16   On all models, remove the support from under the engine and rest the front wheel on the ground. Pump the front forks a few times to settle all components in position and tighten the right axle clamp bolt to the specified torque setting.

17   Using feeler gauges, check the clearance between each surface of each brake disc and its relevant caliper mounting bracket. There should be at least 0.7 mm (0.028 inch) clearance present. If not, slacken the axle clamp bolts and push or pull the fork slider in or out (as applicable) until the required clearance is present. With the slider

correctly positioned, tighten the clamp bolts to the specified torque **(see illustrations)**.

18   Apply the front brake, pump the forks up and down several times and check for proper brake operation.

15 Rear wheel - removal and installation

Removal

G through K models

Refer to illustrations 15.3 and 15.4

1   Place the motorcycle on its centerstand - where no centerstand is fitted, support the machine securely in an upright position. Block the motorcycle (being careful not to damage the fairing lower panels - remove them if necessary, as described in Chapter 8) so that the rear wheel is clear of the ground.

2   Brake caliper removal is not strictly necessary, but makes wheel removal/installation easier by providing increased working space. Refer to Sections 6 and 7, if required.

3   Unscrew the rear axle nut and remove it with its washer **(see illustration)**.

4   Slacken their locknuts, then fully slacken the drive chain adjuster nuts. Push the wheel forwards until the drive chain can be disengaged from the sprocket. Hang the chain over the chainguard/swingarm to keep it out of the way **(see illustration)**.

14.17b . . . when correct, tighten the right clamp bolts to the specified torque

15.3 Unscrew the rear axle nut and remove the washer, then slacken the drive chain adjuster locknuts and adjuster nuts . . .

15.4 . . . and push the wheel forwards until the drive chain can be disengaged from the sprocket, then remove the axle

15.10 On L models onward, remove the muffler (silencer) mounting bolt and move the muffler out to the right . . .

15.11 . . . to provide clearance to unscrew the nuts and remove the rear wheel

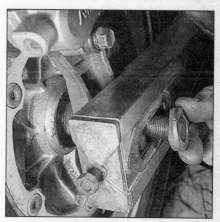
15.16 Ensure that each axle washer is installed so that its notched edge faces up

5   Support the wheel then slide out the axle and its washer and lower the wheel to the ground, being careful not to lose the spacers on each side of the hub. **Caution:** *Don't lay the wheel down and allow it to rest on the disc or the sprocket - they could become warped. Set the wheel on wood blocks so the disc or the sprocket doesn't support the weight of the wheel. Do not operate the brake pedal with the wheel removed.* Support the brake assembly by tying it loosely to the footpeg bracket.

6   Check the axle for straightness by rolling it on a flat surface such as a piece of plate glass (if the axle is corroded, first remove the corrosion with fine emery cloth). If the axle is bent at all, replace it.

7   Check the condition of the wheel bearings (see Section 16).

L models onward

Refer to illustrations 15.10 and 15.11

8   While the motorcycle's weight is on its wheels, apply the rear brake and slacken the four wheel nuts.

9   Place the motorcycle on its centerstand - where no centerstand is fitted, support the machine securely in an upright position. Block the motorcycle (being careful not to damage the fairing lower panels - remove them if necessary, as described in Chapter 8) so that the rear wheel is clear of the ground.

10   Remove the muffler (silencer) mounting bolt and rotate the muffler out to the right; on R models, slacken the muffler clamp bolts to allow this **(see illustration)**.

11   Unscrew the wheel nuts and remove the wheel **(see illustration)**.

Installation

G through K models

Refer to illustration 15.16

12   Apply a thin coat of grease to the seal lips, then slide the spacers into their proper positions on both sides of the hub.

13   Ensure both chain adjusters are correctly installed and press back the pads to ease reassembly of the caliper on the brake disc.

14   Apply a thin coat of grease to the axle and slide the axle into position in the left chain adjuster. Do not forget its washer, which must be installed with its notched edge up **(see illustration 15.16)**.

15   Lift the wheel into position ensuring both spacers remain in position and the brake disc enters correctly between the (friction material of) the rear brake pads.

16   Engage the drive chain with the sprocket and slide the axle into position. Fit the washer (notched edge up) and axle nut, but do not tighten it yet **(see illustration)**. Pull the wheel back to its original position, then hand-tighten the axle nut.

17   Ensure that the brake caliper is correctly installed, with the disc correctly positioned between the pads. Ensure the brake hose is securely retained by all its relevant retaining clips.

18   Adjust the chain slack (see Chapter 1) and tighten the adjuster locknuts to the specified torque.

19   Tighten the axle nut to the specified torque setting.

20   Operate the brake pedal several times to bring the pads into contact with the disc.

7

L models onward

Refer to illustration 15.22

21   Install the wheel and its four nuts, tightening them firmly by hand. Restore the muffler (silencer) to its correct position and tighten securely the mounting bolt (and clamp bolt, according to model) - see Chapter 4 if necessary.

22   With the motorcycle's weight back on its wheels, apply the rear brake firmly and tighten the wheel nuts to the specified torque setting **(see illustration)**.

23   On R models particularly, check that there is 25 to 35 mm (1.0 to 1.4 inches) clearance between the end of the muffler (silencer) and the edge of the rear tire. If there is significantly less clearance, check that the wheel is correctly mounted; otherwise check the muffler mounting and footpeg bracket for damage or distortion and repair/replace as necessary.

All models

24   Check carefully the operation of the brakes and the security of all disturbed components before riding the motorcycle. Check that the rear wheel rotates freely with no sign of brake drag.

---

16   Wheel bearings - removal, inspection and installation

Front wheel bearings

Refer to illustrations 16.3, 16.4, 16.6, 16.9, 16.11, 16.12a, 16.12b, 16.13 and 16.14

Note: *Always replace the front wheel bearings in pairs. Never replace the bearings individually.*

1   Remove the wheel as described in Section 14.

2   Set the wheel on blocks so as not to allow the weight of the wheel to rest on the brake discs.

3   Remove the speedometer drive (where fitted) and spacer(s) from the wheel hub **(see illustration)**.

4   Using a flat-bladed screwdriver, pry out the grease seal from the left side of the wheel, then withdraw (if fitted) the speedometer driveplate **(see illustration)**.

5   Pry out the grease seal from the right side of the wheel.

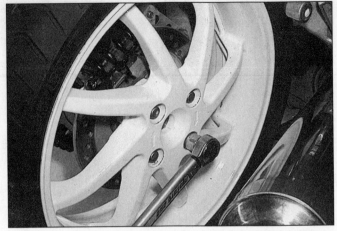

15.22 Tighten the wheel nuts to the specified torque setting

6   Using a metal rod (preferably a brass drift punch) inserted through the center of the hub bearing, tap evenly around the inner race of the left bearing to drive it from the hub **(see illustration)**. The bearing spacer will also come out.

7   Lay the wheel on its other side and remove the right bearing using the same technique.

8   If the bearings are of the unsealed type or are only sealed on one side, clean them with a high flash-point solvent (one which won't leave any residue) and blow them dry with compressed air (don't let the bearings spin as you dry them). Apply a few drops of oil to the bearing. **Note:** *If the bearing is sealed on both sides don't attempt to clean it.*

9   Hold the outer race of the bearing and rotate the inner race - if the bearing doesn't turn smoothly, has rough spots or is noisy, replace it with a new one **(see illustration)**.

10   If the bearing checks out okay and can be re-used, wash it in solvent once again and dry it, then pack the bearing with high-quality wheel bearing grease.

11   Thoroughly clean the hub area of the wheel. On installation, start

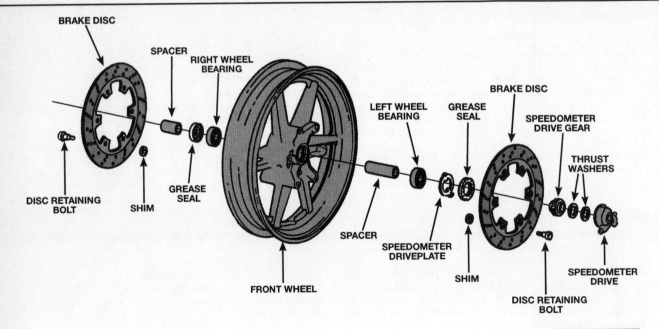

2070-7-16.3 HAYNES

16.3 Exploded view of a typical front wheel and associated components

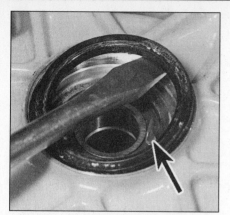

16.4 Pry out the grease seal and remove the speedometer driveplate (arrow) from the left side of the wheel

16.6 Drift the left wheel bearing out of position using a metal rod passed through from the opposite side of the wheel

16.9 Check bearing races rotate smoothly without any sign of roughness. Replace the bearing if any rough spots are felt

16.11 Drive the right bearing squarely into the hub, using a tubular spacer which bears only on the bearing's outer race . . .

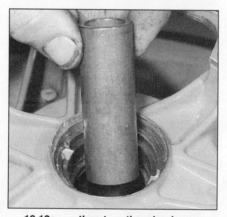

16.12a . . . then turn the wheel over, insert the spacer . . .

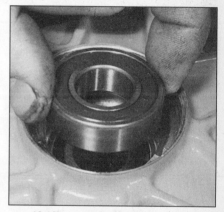

16.12b . . . and install the second (left) bearing

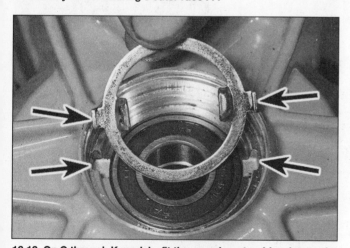

16.13 On G through K models, fit the speedometer driveplate to the left side of the wheel, making sure its tangs are correctly seated in the hub slots (arrows) . . .

16.14 . . . and press in a new grease seal

with the right side bearing; fit the bearing into the recess in the hub, with the marked or sealed side facing out. Using a bearing driver or a socket large enough to contact the outer race of the bearing, drive it in until it's completely seated **(see illustration)**.

12   Turn the wheel over and install the bearing spacer. Unless the bearings are sealed on both sides, pack the remaining space no more than 2/3 full of high-melting point wheel bearing grease. Once the grease is packed in, drive the second (left side) bearing into place as

described above **(see illustrations)**.

13   Fit the speedometer driveplate (where fitted) to the left side of the wheel ensuring its locating tangs are correctly located in the hub slots **(see illustration)**.

14   Install new grease seals, using a seal driver, large socket or a flat piece of wood to drive them into place **(see illustration)**.

15   On G through K models, fit the speedometer drive to the left side of the wheel aligning its drive gear slots with the driveplate tabs; on L

7

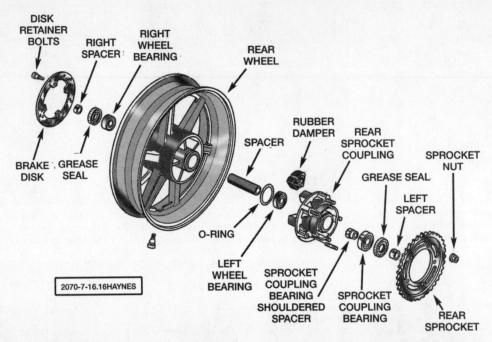

16.16 Exploded view of the rear wheel and associated components - G through K models

16.17 Remove the sprocket coupling ensuring the rubber dampers remain in position in the wheel

16.18a Remove the spacer from inside the coupling bearing . . .

16.18b . . . then pry out the grease seal from the coupling

models onward, install the shorter spacer. Install the (longer) spacer in the right side of the wheel. Clean off all grease from the brake disc(s) using acetone or brake system cleaner then install the wheel as described in Section 14.

Sprocket coupling bearing

G through K models

Refer to illustrations 16.16, 16.17, 16.18a, 16.18b, 16.19, 16.21 and 16.23

16   Remove the rear wheel as described in Section 15 and remove the spacer from the center of the sprocket coupling (see Chapter 6) **(see illustration)**.

17   Lift the sprocket coupling away from the wheel leaving the rubber dampers in position in the wheel **(see illustration)**.

18   Remove the shouldered spacer from the inside of the coupling bearing and pry out the grease seal from the outside of the coupling **(see illustrations)**.

19   Support the coupling on blocks of wood and drive out the bearing

16.19 Support the coupling and drive the bearing out from the inside using a hammer and bearing driver or socket

16.21 Drive the new coupling bearing into position using a large tubular drift which bears only on the bearing's outer race

16.23 Ensure the hub O-ring is in position on the wheel and apply a smear of oil to it to aid installation

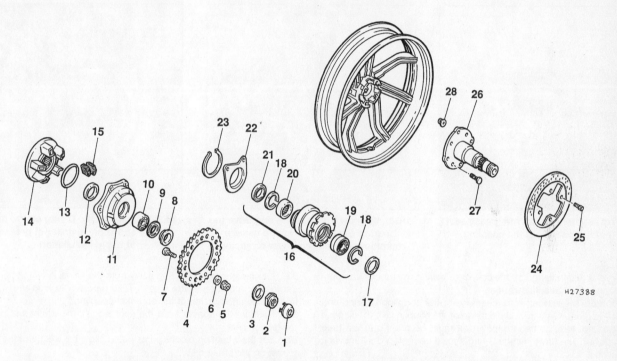

H27388

16.25 Exploded view of the rear wheel and associated components - L models onward

1	Stub axle cap	9	Grease seal
2	Stub axle nut	10	Sprocket coupling bearing
3	Conical spring washer	11	Rear sprocket coupling
4	Rear sprocket	12	Sprocket coupling bearing spacer
5	Sprocket nut	13	O-ring
6	Washer	14	Driven flange
7	Sprocket bolt	15	Rubber damper
8	Flanged collar		

16	Rear wheel bearing holder	22	Rear brake caliper stay
17	Spacer	23	Snap-ring
18	Bearing retainer	24	Brake disc
19	Wheel left side (needle roller) bearing	25	Brake disc bolt
20	Wheel right side (needle roller) bearing	26	Stub axle
21	Grease seal	27	Wheel bolt
		28	Wheel nut

with a bearing driver or socket **(see illustration)**.

20   Inspect the bearing as described above in Steps 8 through 10.

21   Thoroughly clean the bearing recess then install the bearing into the recess in the coupling, with the marked or sealed side facing out. Using a bearing driver or a socket large enough to contact the outer race of the bearing, drive it in until it's completely seated **(see illustration)**.

22   Install a new grease seal, using a seal driver, large socket or a flat piece of wood to drive it into place. Fit the shouldered spacer to the inside of the bearing.

23   Apply a smear of grease to the hub O-ring and fit the sprocket

coupling to the wheel **(see illustration)**. Grease the lip of the seal then fit the outer spacer to the coupling.

24   Clean off all grease from the brake disc using acetone or brake system cleaner then install the wheel as described in Section 15.

L models onward

Refer to illustrations 16.25, 16.26, 16.27a, 16.27b, 16.27c, 16.28, 16.32a and 16.32b

25   Remove the coupling as described in Steps 42 through 45 below **(see illustration)**.

7

16.26 Pry the driven flange off the coupling, leaving the rubber dampers in position inside

16.27a Withdraw the spacer from the inside of the coupling bearing . . .

16.27b . . . extract the flanged collar from the outside (if not already removed) . . .

16.27c . . . then pry out the grease seal from the outside of the coupling

16.28 Support the coupling and drive the bearing out from the inside using a hammer and bearing driver or socket

16.32a Install a new O-ring on the driven flange and apply a smear of grease to it to aid installation . . .

26   Pry the driven flange off the coupling, leaving the rubber dampers in position inside **(see illustration)**.

27   Remove the spacer from the inside of the coupling bearing and pry out the grease seal from the outside of the coupling - if the flanged collar has not already been removed, it must be pried out first **(see illustrations)**. The driven flange O-ring should be replaced whenever it is disturbed.

28   Support the coupling on blocks of wood and drive out the bearing with a bearing driver or socket **(see illustration)**.

29   Inspect the bearing as described above in Steps 8 through 10.

30   Thoroughly clean the bearing recess then install the bearing into the recess in the coupling, with the marked or sealed side facing out. Using a bearing driver or a socket large enough to contact the outer race of the bearing, drive it in until it's completely seated.

31   Install a new grease seal, using a seal driver, large socket or a flat piece of wood to drive it into place. Fit the spacer to the inside of the bearing.

32   Apply a smear of grease to the new driven flange O-ring when installing it and fit the flange to the coupling, taking care not to cut or damage the O-ring **(see illustrations)**. Grease the lip of the seal then fit the flanged collar to the coupling.

33   Install the coupling as described in Steps 60 through 66 below.

Rear wheel bearings

G through K models

Note: *Always replace the rear wheel bearings in pairs. Never replace the bearings individually.*

34   Remove the rear wheel as described in Section 15.

35   Lift the sprocket coupling away from the wheel leaving the rubber dampers in position in the wheel. Take care not to lose the spacers from inside and outside of the sprocket coupling.

36   Remove the spacer from the right side of the wheel and pry out the grease seal.

37   Set the wheel on blocks so as not to allow the weight of the wheel to rest on the brake disc.

38   Remove, inspect and install the bearings as described above in Steps 6 through 12.

39   Install a new grease seal to the right side of the wheel, using a seal driver, large socket or a flat piece of wood to drive them into place. Fit the spacer into the seal.

40   Apply a smear of grease to the hub O-ring and fit the sprocket coupling to the wheel, ensuring both the spacers are in position.

41   Clean off all grease from the brake disc using acetone or brake system cleaner then install the wheel as described in Section 15.

L models onward

Refer to illustrations 16.42a, 16.42b, 16.45a, 16.45b, 16.45c, 16.47, 16.48, 16.50, 16.51, 16.54, 16.55, 16.56, 16.61, 16.63a and 16.63b

42   Pry out the stub axle cap and release the staking of the stub axle nut using a hammer and a fine chisel or pin punch **(see illustrations)**. While the motorcycle's weight is on its wheels, apply the rear brake and slacken the stub axle nut and the four wheel nuts.

43   Remove the rear wheel as described in Section 15.

44   Unscrew the axle nut and withdraw the conical spring washer - note which way round it is fitted.

45   Remove the sprocket coupling from the stub axle, collecting the flanged collar from its left (outboard) side and the spacer from its right

16.32b . . . before reassembling the driven flange to the coupling

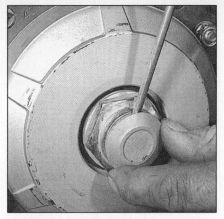

16.42a Pry out the stub axle cap and . . .

16.42b . . . release the staking of the stub axle nut using a hammer and a fine chisel or pin punch

16.45a Remove the flanged collar from the sprocket coupling . . .

16.45b . . . withdraw the sprocket coupling from the stub axle . . .

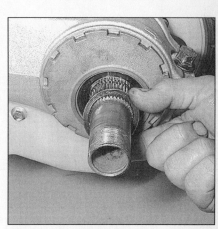

16.45c . . . and collect the spacer from its right (inboard) side

16.47 Withdrawing the rear wheel stub axle - L models onward

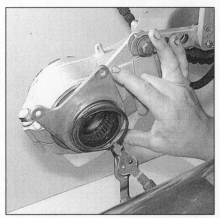

16.48 Remove the snap-ring to withdraw the rear brake caliper stay

16.50 Pry the grease seal out of each end of the bearing holder

(inboard) side and disengaging the drive chain from the sprocket **(see illustrations)**.

46 Unbolt the rear brake caliper from its stay. Either remove the caliper completely or pivot it up clear of the brake disc, unclipping the brake hose from the brake torque rod and chainguard to prevent it from being strained. Secure the caliper clear of the working area. **Caution:** *Do not operate the rear brake pedal with the caliper removed.*

47 Withdraw the stub axle **(see illustration)**.

48 Using a pair of circlip pliers, extract the large snap-ring securing the caliper stay and withdraw the stay **(see illustration)**.

49 Slacken the bearing holder clamp bolt and withdraw the bearing holder.

50 Pry the grease seal out of each end of the bearing holder **(see illustration)**.

51 Pry the bearing retainer out of each end of the bearing holder **(see illustration)**.

7

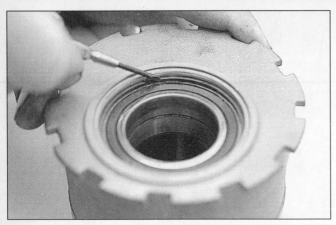

16.51 Pry the bearing retainer out of each end of the bearing holder

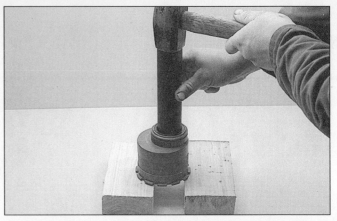

16.54 Support the bearing holder as shown if driving in new bearings using a hammer and bearing driver or socket

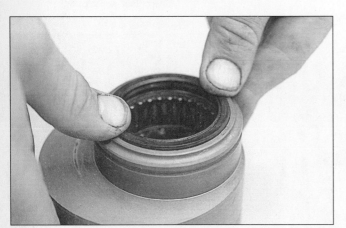

16.55 Installing a new grease seal

16.56 Grease the rear wheel bearing holder before installation

16.61 Fit the conical spring washer with its convex surface out

52   The two bearings must be removed using an internally-expanding bearing puller with suitable attachments. These are available commercially or can be hired; failing this, you must have the bearings replaced by a dealer service department or motorcycle repair specialist. **Note:** *The act of removing the bearings - especially the right (needle roller) bearing - will damage them. They must, therefore, be replaced whenever they are disturbed.*

53   Thoroughly clean and inspect all components, replacing any that are worn or damaged.

54   The two bearings - especially the right (needle roller) bearing - should be installed preferably using a hydraulic press and suitable mandrels; if you do not have such facilities, the work should be done by a dealer service department or motorcycle repair specialist. Failing this, a hammer and a bearing driver or a socket large enough to contact the outer race of the bearing can be used to drive in a bearing, but extreme care is required, especially when installing the right (needle roller) bearing **(see illustration)**. Install the bearing into the recess in the holder with the marked or sealed side facing out.

55   Install new grease seals to each side of the holder, using a seal driver, large socket or a flat piece of wood to drive them into place **(see illustration)**. Grease the lips of the seals and pack the bearings as much as possible with molybdenum disulfide grease.

56   Apply a thin coat of grease to the exterior of the bearing holder and to its recess in the swingarm, then install the bearing holder and rotate it so that the stub axle will be in the fully-forward position before hand-tightening the clamp bolt **(see illustration)**.

57   Apply a thin coat of grease to the caliper stay's contact surface with the bearing holder. Install the caliper stay and secure it with the snap-ring, which must be installed with its chamfered side facing in.

58   Apply a thin coat of grease to the stub axle's bearing journals and splines, but wipe off all surplus lubricant (to prevent any from finding its way on to the brake disc) before installing the stub axle.

59   Lower the caliper over the disc, ensuring that the disc passes correctly between the friction material of the pads, then tighten the caliper stay bolts to the specified torque setting. Ensure the brake hose is securely retained by all its relevant retaining clips.

60   Install the spacer, the sprocket coupling and, if not already in place, the flanged collar to the stub axle.

61   Install the conical spring washer (convex face out) then apply a smear of clean oil to its threads and screw on the axle nut **(see illustration)**. Tighten the nut as hard as possible by hand and check

TIRE CHANGING SEQUENCE - TUBELESS TIRES

Deflate tire. After releasing beads, push tire bead into well of rim at point opposite valve. Insert lever next to valve and work bead over edge of rim.

Use two levers to work bead over edge of rim. Note use of rim protectors.

When first bead is clear, remove tire as shown.

Before installing, ensure that tire is suitable for wheel. Take note of any sidewall markings such as direction of rotation arrows.

Work first bead over the rim flange.

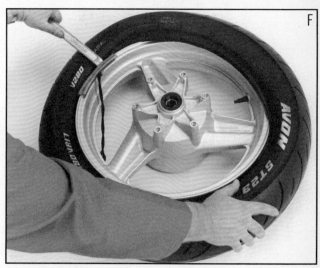

Use a tire lever to work the second bead over rim flange.

16.63a Lubricate the rear stub axle nut with clean engine oil, tighten it to the specified torque setting . . .

16.63b . . . then secure it by staking its shoulder into the stub axle groove, as shown

that the stub axle rotates easily, with no trace of drag or of freeplay. Engage the drive chain on the sprocket.

62   Clean off all grease from the brake disc using acetone or brake system cleaner then install the wheel as described in Section 15.

63   When the motorcycle's weight is back on its wheels, apply the rear brake and tighten the stub axle nut and the four wheel nuts to their specified torque settings. Use a hammer and pin punch to stake the stub axle nut's shoulder into the stub axle groove, then press in the stub axle cap **(see illustrations)**.

64   Operate the brake pedal several times to bring the pads into contact with the disc.

65   Adjust the chain slack (see Chapter 1) and tighten the bearing holder clamp bolt to the specified torque setting.

66   Check carefully the operation of the brakes and the security of all disturbed components before riding the motorcycle. Check that the rear wheel rotates freely with no sign of brake drag.

17   Tubeless tires - general information

1   Tubeless tires are used as standard equipment on this motorcycle. They are generally safer than tube-type tires but if problems do occur they require special repair techniques.

2   The force required to break the seal between the rim and the bead of the tire is substantial, and is usually beyond the capabilities of an individual working with normal tire irons.

3   Also, repair of the punctured tire and installation on the wheel rim requires special tools, skills and experience that the average do-it-yourselfer lacks.

4   For these reasons, if a puncture or flat occurs with a tubeless tire, the wheel should be removed from the motorcycle and taken to a dealer service department or a motorcycle repair shop for repair or replacement of the tire. The accompanying color illustrations can be used to replace a tubeless tire in an emergency.

Chapter 8
Fairing and bodywork

Note: *Refer to 'Identification numbers' at the beginning of this Manual to establish the model code of your motorcycle.*

Contents

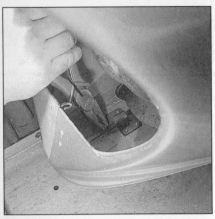

2.2 Extract the two spring clips (arrows) securing together the front fairing left and right lower panels of G and H models

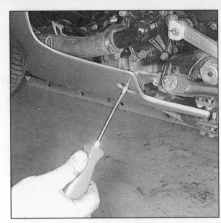

2.3 Remove the screw from the rear bottom edge . . .

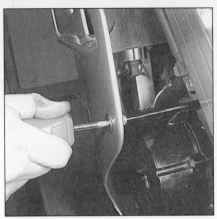

2.4 . . . from the rear edge center stay . . .

1   General information

This Chapter covers the procedures necessary to remove and install the fairing and other body parts. Since many service and repair operations on these motorcycles require the removal of the fairing and/or other body parts, the procedures are grouped here and referred to from other Chapters.

In the case of damage to the fairing or other body parts, it is usually necessary to remove the broken component and replace it with a new (or used) one. The material that the fairing and other body parts are composed of doesn't lend itself to conventional repair techniques. There are however some shops that specialize in "plastic welding", so it may be worthwhile seeking the advice of one of these specialists before consigning an expensive component to the bin.

2   Fairing panels - removal and installation

Removal

Note: *When attempting to remove any fairing panel, first study closely the panel, noting any fasteners and associated fittings, to be sure of returning everything to its correct place on installation. In most cases the aid of an assistant will be required when removing panels, to help avoid the risk of damage to paintwork. Once the evident fasteners have been removed, try to withdraw the panel as described but DO NOT FORCE the panel - if it will not release, check that all fasteners have been removed and try again. Where a panel engages another by means of tabs, be careful not to break the tab or its mating slot or to damage the paintwork. Remember that a few moments of patience at this stage will save you a lot of money in replacing broken panels!*

Several types of fairing panel fastener are used on the models covered here. Usually bolts or screws of varying sizes and head form are used, requiring straight-bladed or cross-head screwdrivers, spanners or Allen keys. Most screw into nuts, trim nuts or threads in mounting brackets (as applicable) and are released by unscrewing them counterclockwise (anti-clockwise) in the usual way. Some small (usually cross-head) screws are threaded into plastic inserts, spreading the insert apart behind the panel(s) to secure them; unscrew the screw and withdraw the insert to release it. Some types of clip, known as 'quick screws' are also used, which are released by turning them (either with a cross-head screwdriver or an Allen key, as appropriate) counterclockwise (anti-clockwise) through 90°; where their locations are known, this type are noted in the text, but otherwise their use will be self-evident on unscrewing them.

The final type of clip, known as center pin clips, is used on L models onward (particularly the R model), mostly on the fairing middle and lower center panels. These clips are released by using a pin punch

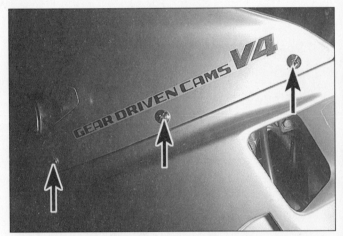

2.5 . . . then undo the screws/release the clips (arrows) securing the lower panel to the upper fairing

(or similar small pointed instrument) to press in the pin in the center of each clip - take care not to slip and scratch the paintwork - the clip insert behind the panel can then contract to allow the panel to be released.

1   Place the motorcycle on its center stand - where no center stand is fitted, support the machine securely in an upright position.

Front fairing lower panels - G and H models

Refer to illustrations 2.2, 2.3, 2.4 and 2.5

2   Using a pair of pliers, extract the spring clips securing together the fairing left and right lower panels **(see illustration)**.

3   Unscrew the single screw from the rear bottom edge of the panel **(see illustration)**.

4   Undo (where fitted) the screw securing the rear edge of the panel to the center stay **(see illustration)**.

5   Undo the screws (or release the 'quick screw' type clips, as appropriate - see the note at the beginning of this Section) along its top edge which secure the lower panel to the upper fairing **(see illustration)**.

6   Withdraw carefully the fairing lower panel.

Front fairing lower panel - J and K models

Refer to illustration 2.8

7   Remove both fairing middle panels - see Steps 32 and 33 below.

8   Unscrew the retaining screw from the rear end of each side of the panel **(see illustration)**.

9   Unscrew the retaining bolt from the front of each side of the panel, then withdraw carefully the fairing lower panel, 'springing' it apart to pass over the engine.

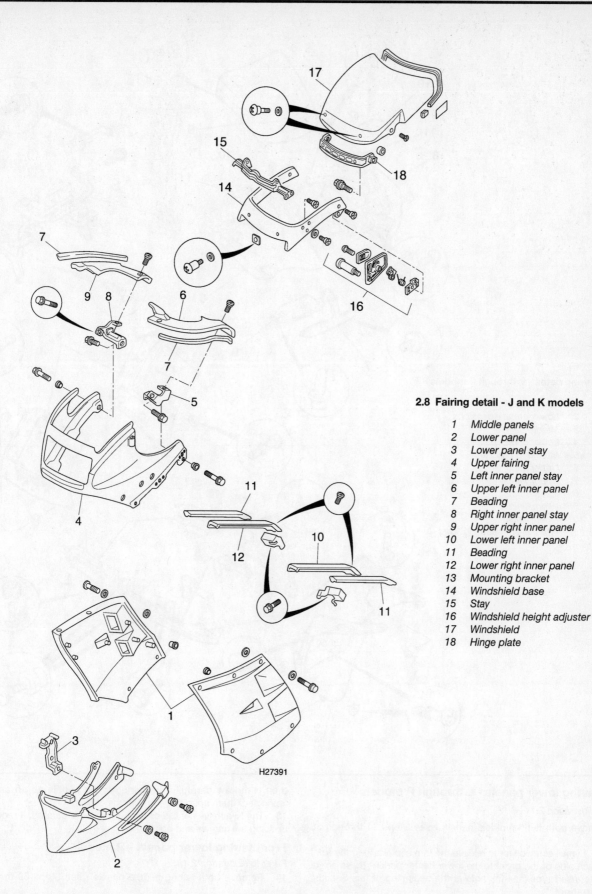

2.8 Fairing detail - J and K models

1   Middle panels
2   Lower panel
3   Lower panel stay
4   Upper fairing
5   Left inner panel stay
6   Upper left inner panel
7   Beading
8   Right inner panel stay
9   Upper right inner panel
10 Lower left inner panel
11 Beading
12 Lower right inner panel
13 Mounting bracket
14 Windshield base
15 Stay
16 Windshield height adjuster
17 Windshield
18 Hinge plate

H27391

8

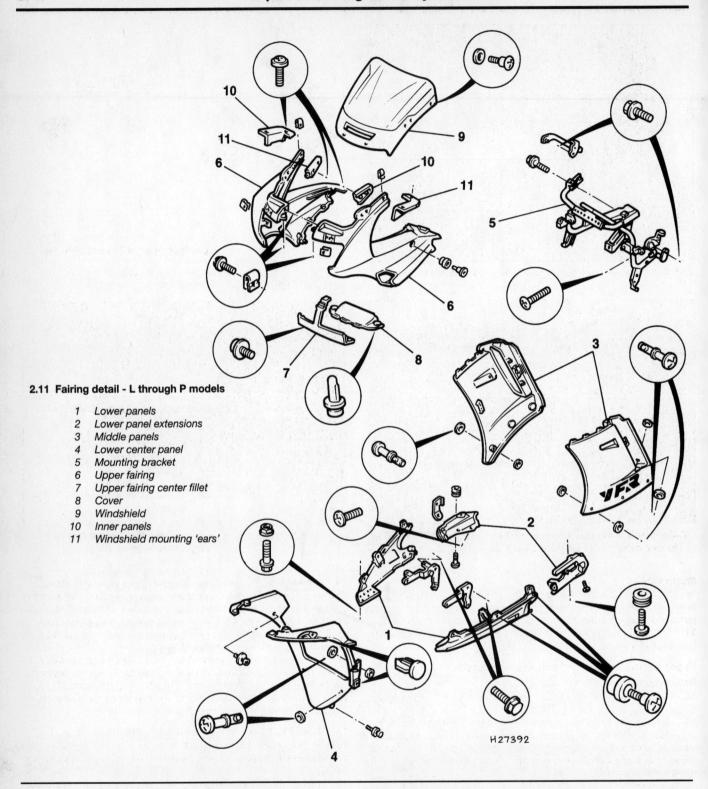

2.11 Fairing detail - L through P models

1   Lower panels
2   Lower panel extensions
3   Middle panels
4   Lower center panel
5   Mounting bracket
6   Upper fairing
7   Upper fairing center fillet
8   Cover
9   Windshield
10 Inner panels
11 Windshield mounting 'ears'

H27392

Front fairing lower panels - L through P models

Refer to illustration 2.11

10   Remove both fairing middle panels - see Steps 34 through 38 below.

11   Use a small screwdriver to release the trim clip retaining the front end of each side of the panel to the lower center panel - these are of the plastic insert type (see the note at the beginning of this Section) **(see illustration).**

12   Unscrew the three retaining bolts from each side of the panel,

then withdraw carefully the fairing lower panels as an assembly, 'springing' them apart to pass over the engine.

13   The two halves of the assembly can be separated, if required, by undoing the screws and bolts.

Front fairing lower panels - R model

Refer to illustration 2.15

14   Remove both fairing middle panels - see Steps 39 through 44 below.

15   Undo the two retaining screws from each side of the panel **(see**

2.15 Front fairing lower panel retaining screws (arrows) - R model

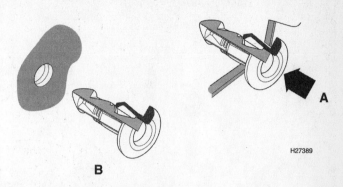

2.21 Releasing 'center pin' type of plastic insert trim clip

A   Press in center pin to unlock clip
B   Extract clip from panels

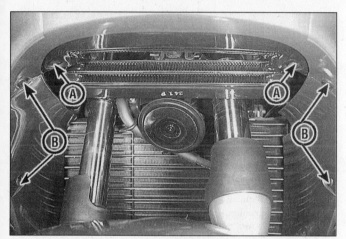

2.30a Upper fairing lower cover retaining 'center pin' trim clips
(A) and lower center panel retaining 'center pin' trim clips (B)

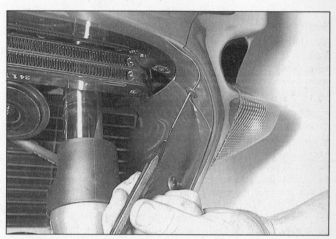

2.30b Using a pin punch to unlock 'center pin' type of
plastic insert trim clip

illustration).

16   Withdraw carefully the fairing lower panels as an assembly, lowering them at the rear to release the tabs from the lower center panel and 'springing' the lower panels apart to pass over the engine.

17   The two halves of the assembly can be separated, if required, by undoing the retaining screws.

Front fairing lower center panel - L model

Refer to illustration 2.21

18   Remove both fairing middle panels - see Steps 34 through 38 below.

19   Remove the fairing lower panels - see Steps 11 and 12 above.

20   Use an Allen key to unscrew the four bolts (two on each side) securing the panel to its upper and lower stays. Leave at least two of these bolts loosely in place to support the panel while the remaining fasteners are released.

21   Release the four trim clips retaining the top end of the lower center panel to the upper fairing (see the note at the beginning of this Section). These clips are of the 'center pin' plastic insert type that are released by pressing in the clip's center pin with a pin punch or similar **(see illustration)**.

22   Undo the supporting bolts and withdraw carefully the fairing lower center panel, disengaging it from the upper fairing.

Front fairing lower center panel - M through P models

23   Remove both fairing middle panels - see Steps 34 through 38 below.

24   Remove the fairing lower panels - see Steps 11 and 12 above.

25   Unscrew the four self-tapping screws (two on each side) securing the panel to its upper and lower stays - note the rubber grommets and the trim nuts at these locations when removing the panel. Leave at least two of these screws loosely in place to support the panel while the remaining fasteners are released.

26   Use a small screwdriver to release the four trim clips retaining the top end of the lower center panel to the upper fairing - these are of the plastic insert type (see the note at the beginning of this Section).

27   Undo the supporting screws and withdraw carefully the fairing lower center panel, disengaging it from the upper fairing.

Front fairing lower center panel - R model

Refer to illustrations 2.30a and 2.30b

28   Remove both fairing middle panels - see Steps 39 through 44 below.

29   Release the two trim clips retaining the upper fairing lower cover panel to the upper fairing - these clips are of the 'center pin' plastic insert type that are released by pressing in the clip's center pin with a pin punch or similar (see the note at the beginning of this Section and illustration 2.21).

30   Release the four 'center pin' trim clips (two on each side) securing the lower center panel to the upper fairing **(see illustrations)**.

31   Being careful to avoid damaging the paintwork, release the lower panel's top ends from the upper fairing, then disengage the lower center panel's tabs from those of the fairing lower panel and withdraw carefully the fairing lower center panel.

8

2.39 Fairing middle panel removal, R model - release two clips (arrows) from inside fairing lower center panel . . .

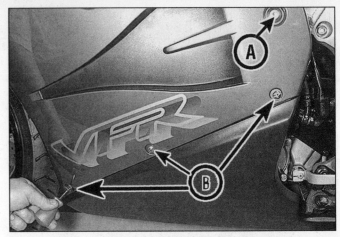

2.41 . . . unscrew retaining screw (A) and release 'quick screw' clips (B) . . .

Front fairing middle panels - J and K models

32   Undo the three screws (or release the three 'quick screw' type clips, as appropriate - see the note at the beginning of this Section) along its top and bottom edges which secure each middle panel to the upper fairing and to the lower panel (six fasteners per panel).

33   Withdraw carefully the fairing middle panel.

Front fairing middle panels - L through P models

34   Working inside the fairing lower center panel, undo the single screw and the single 'quick screw' type clip securing the middle panel to the lower center panel. Remove both these fasteners **completely**, or the middle panel will be damaged on removal.

35   Undo the screw (or release the 'quick screw' type clip, as appropriate - see the note at the beginning of this Section) inside the air vent, which secures the rear edge of the middle panel to its center stay.

36   Undo the three screws/release the three 'quick screw' type clips along its bottom edge which secure the middle panel to the lower panel.

37   Move the middle panel out at its bottom edge, then down until the four tabs (three at the front, one at the rear edge) can be disengaged which secure the middle panel to the upper fairing - note carefully how the middle panel's projecting air vent engages with the recess in the upper fairing. **Caution:** *Exercise great care, or you will break one or both of the panels!*

38   Withdraw carefully the fairing middle panel.

Front fairing middle panels - R model

Refer to illustrations 2.39, 2.41 and 2.43

39   Working inside the fairing lower center panel, undo the two 'quick screw' type clips securing the middle panel to the lower center panel **(see illustration)**. Remove both clips **completely**, or the middle panel will be damaged on removal.

40   Use an Allen key to undo the screw securing the rear edge of the middle panel to its center stay.

41   Release the three "quick screw" type clips along its bottom edge which secure the middle panel to the lower panel **(see illustration)**.

42   Release the front bottom edge of the middle panel from the lower panel and release the tab at the rear end of the middle fairing's top edge from the upper fairing's groove.

43   Move the middle panel out at its bottom edge, then down, until the two tabs can be disengaged which secure the middle panel to the upper fairing **(see illustration)**. **Caution:** *Exercise great care, or you will break one or both of the panels!*

44   Withdraw carefully the fairing middle panel.

Front fairing inner panels - G through P models

45   The upper inner panel is secured by two screws on G through K models and a single screw on later models.

46   The lower inner panel is secured by a single screw at its

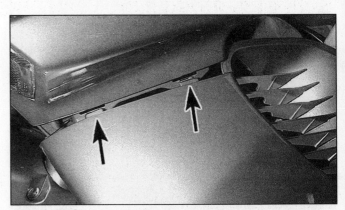

2.43 . . . then maneuver middle panel out and down until front tabs (arrows) can be disengaged from upper fairing

bottom end.

47   Either of these panels can be removed independently of the other.

Upper fairing assembly - G through K models

Refer to illustration 2.52

48   Remove the fairing inner panels - see Step 45 (and 46, where applicable) above.

49   Remove both fairing lower (or middle, according to model) panels - see the relevant Steps above.

50   Disconnect the wiring plug from the rear of the headlight unit.

51   Disconnect the wiring connectors or unplug the sidelight bulb holder from the headlight unit, as required (UK models only).

52   On G and H models, disconnect their wiring connectors and unbolt both turn signal assemblies **(see illustration)**.

53   Remove the rear view mirrors as described in Section 4. **Caution:** *Have an assistant support the upper fairing as soon as the mirrors are unbolted.*

54   With an assistant supporting and guiding the opposite side, withdraw carefully the upper fairing, 'springing' it apart to clear the frame and front forks. Examine the fairing rubber mounts for signs of damage and replace if necessary.

Upper fairing assembly - L through P models

55   Remove the fairing middle, lower and lower center panels - see the relevant Steps above.

56   Remove the fairing inner panel - see Step 45 above.

57   On UK models only, unbolt the fuel tap stay bolt (where fitted) and secure the tap clear of the upper fairing.

58   Remove the rear view mirrors as described in Section 4.

59   Use an Allen key to unscrew the two retaining screws securing

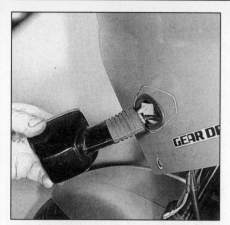

2.52 Removing upper fairing, G through K models - unbolt both front turn signal assemblies

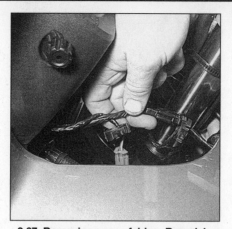

2.67 Removing upper fairing, R model - disconnect wiring and release from clips inside left fairing panel . . .

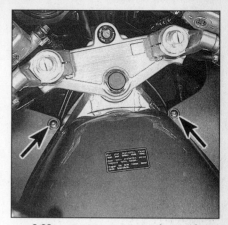

2.68a . . . remove screws (arrows) securing upper fairing to center . . .

2.68b . . . and rear stays (arrowed) to release upper fairing

2.76 Rear fairing removal, L through P models - unscrew grab rail mounting bolts . . .

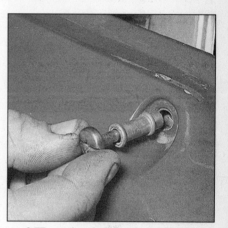

2.77 . . . then bolts and shouldered spacers at rear fairing middle mountings . . .

the rear ends of the upper fairing to the stay. **Caution:** *Have an assistant support the upper fairing as soon as these are unfastened.*

60 Support the fairing, then trace the wiring back from each turn signal assembly and the sidelight (UK models only) and disconnect each wiring connector, or unplug the bulb holders, as required.

61 Disconnect the wiring plugs from the rear of the headlight unit.

62 With an assistant supporting and guiding the opposite side, withdraw carefully the upper fairing from the motorcycle, 'springing' it apart to clear the frame and front forks. Examine the fairing rubber mounts for signs of damage and replace if necessary.

Upper fairing assembly - R model

Refer to illustrations 2.67, 2.68a and 2.68b

63 Remove the fairing middle panels - see Steps 39 through 44 above.

64 Remove the fairing lower center panel - see Steps 28 through 31 above.

65 Remove the rear view mirrors as described in Section 4.

66 It is useful, but not absolutely necessary, to remove the windshield. Refer to Section 3.

67 Disconnect the wiring plugs from the rear of the headlight unit. Trace the wiring back from each turn signal assembly and the sidelight (UK models only) and disconnect each wiring connector, or unplug the bulb holders, as required. Free the wiring from its clips on the inside of the left fairing panel, just inside the air intake duct **(see illustration)**.

68 Use an Allen key to unscrew the four retaining screws (two each side) securing the rear ends of the upper fairing to their stays **(see illustrations)**. **Caution:** *Have an assistant support the upper fairing as soon as these are unfastened.*

69 With an assistant supporting and guiding the opposite side, withdraw carefully the upper fairing from the motorcycle, 'springing' it apart to clear the frame and front forks. Examine the fairing rubber mounts for signs of damage and replace if necessary.

Rear fairing panel - G through K models

70 Remove the seat as described in Section 9.

71 Remove the grab rail as described in Section 10.

72 Trace the wiring back from each taillight assembly and disconnect each wiring connector, or unplug the bulb holders, as required.

73 Unscrew the two remaining mounting bolts (one each side, at the front ends of the panel) and withdraw the rear fairing from the motorcycle, 'springing' it apart to clear the subframe and other components.

Rear fairing panel - L through P models

Refer to illustrations 2.76, 2.77 and 2.78

74 Remove the seat as described in Section 9.

75 Trace the wiring back from each taillight and turn signal assembly and disconnect each wiring connector, or unplug the bulb holders, as required.

76 Unscrew the grab rail (where fitted) mounting bolts and swing both grab rails into their retracted position - if no grab rails are fitted, unscrew the two bolts at these locations **(see illustration)**.

77 Unscrew the two mounting bolts (one each side, with a shouldered spacer) from the rear fairing middle mounting points - if a single seat cowl was removed, these will already be unscrewed **(see illustration)**.

8

2.78 . . . and screws at front mountings

2.82 Rear fairing removal, R models -
unscrew grab rail mounting bolts (arrows),
followed by bolt at middle mountings . . .

2.84 . . . then screws at front
mountings . . .

2.85 . . . and pull each front end of rear fairing squarely away from
fuel tank to release retaining pegs from rubber grommets
(arrows) - lubricate to aid installation

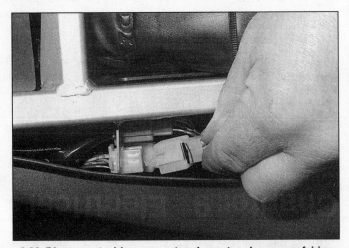

2.86 Disconnect wiring connector shown to release rear fairing

78   Use an Allen key to unscrew the remaining bolt from each front end of the rear fairing **(see illustration)**.
79   Pull each front end of the rear fairing squarely away from the machine to release both its retaining pegs from their rubber grommets and withdraw the rear fairing as an assembly from the motorcycle, 'springing' it apart to clear the subframe and other components.
80   The two halves of the assembly can be separated, if required, by undoing the screws and brackets.

Rear fairing panel - R model

Refer to illustrations 2.82, 2.84, 2.85 and 2.86

81   Remove the seat as described in Section 9.
82   Unscrew the grab rail (where fitted) mounting bolts and remove both grab rails - if no grab rails are fitted, unscrew the two bolts at these locations **(see illustration)**.
83   Unscrew the two mounting bolts (one each side, with a shouldered spacer) from the rear fairing middle mounting points (see illustration 2.77). Note that if a single seat cowl was removed, these will already be unscrewed.
84   Use an Allen key to unscrew the remaining bolt from each front end of the rear fairing **(see illustration)**.
85   Pull each front end of the rear fairing squarely away from the machine to release both its retaining pegs from their rubber grommets in the fuel tank **(see illustration)**.
86   Trace the taillight and turn signal wiring forwards from each assembly to the wiring connector inside the left rear fairing panel, next to the tool kit. Unplug the wiring connector and release the wiring from

any clamps or ties so that it will not prevent fairing removal **(see illustration)**.
87   Withdraw the rear fairing as an assembly from the motorcycle, 'springing' it apart to clear the subframe and other components.
88   The two halves of the assembly can be separated, if required, by undoing the screws and brackets.

Installation

Note: *When installing a fairing panel, first study closely the panel, noting any fasteners and associated fittings removed with it, to be sure of returning everything to its correct place. Check that all fasteners are in good condition, including all trim nuts or clips and damping/ rubber mounts; any of these must be replaced if faulty, before the panel is reassembled. Check also that all mounting brackets are straight and repair/replace them if necessary before attempting to install the panel. Where assistance was required to remove a panel, ensure that your assistant is on hand for installation.*

When installing a panel, a small amount of lubricant (liquid soap or similar) applied to mounting rubbers will assist panel retaining pegs to engage without the need for undue pressure. Carefully settle the panel in place, following the specific instructions provided, and check that the panel engages correctly with its partners (where applicable) before tightening any of the fasteners. Where a panel engages another by means of tabs, be careful not to break the tab or its mating slot or to damage the paintwork.

Tighten the fasteners securely, but be careful not to overtighten any of them or the panel may break (not always immediately) due to the uneven stress.

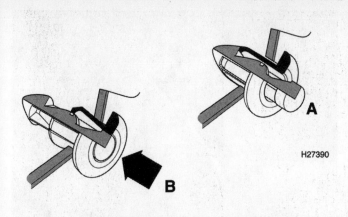

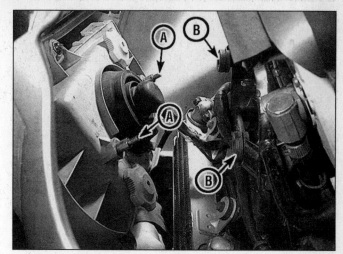

2.92 Securing 'center pin' type of plastic insert trim clip

A   Insert clip into panels
B   Press in center pin until flush to lock clip

**2.98a Installing upper fairing, G through K models shown -
engage pegs (A) on headlight with rubber grommets (B)
on fairing stay**

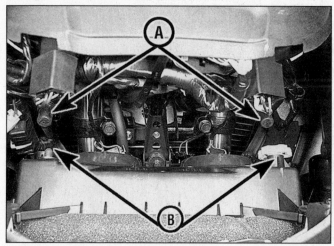

**2.98b Installing upper fairing, R model shown - engage pegs (A)
on fairing stay in headlight locations (B)**

Front fairing lower panel(s)

89   Installation is the reverse of removal, with reference to the comments in the note above and ensuring that the fairing lower panels are correctly hooked together and secured in position by all the relevant screws and fasteners.
90   On R models, ensure that the tabs at the front of the lower panel engage correctly with the lower center panel and take care not to bend the fairing brackets when tightening the screws.

Front fairing lower center panel

Refer to illustration 2.92

91   Installation is the reverse of removal, with reference to the comments in the note above and ensuring that the panel is correctly hooked into the upper fairing. Locate the panel loosely in place using the larger bolts/screws or the fairing lower panel's tabs (according to model) while the trim clips are secured; then check that the panel is correctly in position before tightening all the relevant fasteners.
92   Where the 'center pin' type of trim clip is used, locate the panel in place, install the clip and lock it by pressing in the center pin until it is flush **(see illustration)**.
93   On R models, ensure that the tabs at the front of the lower center panel engage correctly with those of the lower panel.

Front fairing middle panels

94   On J and K models, installation of these panels is the reverse of removal, with reference to the comments in the note above and

ensuring that all panels are correctly hooked together and secured in position by all the relevant screws/fasteners.
95   On L through P models, proceed as follows:
a)   Offer up the middle panel so that the front of its projecting air vent enters the cutout in the bottom edge of the upper fairing and the front three of the tabs along its top edge engage with the slots in the upper fairing.
b)   Carefully move ins the bottom edge of the middle panel, ensuring that the rear of its projecting air vent enters the cutout in the bottom edge of the upper fairing. **Caution:** *Failure to ensure that the middle panel's projecting air vent mates exactly with the upper fairing recess will lead to subsequent cracking of the upper fairing.*
c)   With an assistant supporting the bottom edge of the middle fairing, press down on the upper fairing immediately above the slot in its rear end which engages with the rear tab of the middle panel. Engage the tab in the slot and settle the middle panel on the lower and lower center panels.
d)   Be **very careful** to check that the panel is correctly engaged with its partners before installing and securing the six fasteners.
96   On R models, proceed as follows:
a)   Offer up the middle panel so that the two tabs along its top edge engage with the slots in the upper fairing and so that the tab at the rear end of its top edge enters correctly into the upper fairing's groove.
b)   Carefully move ins the bottom edge of the middle panel, ensuring that the front two tabs and its bottom edge engage correctly with the upper fairing and fairing lower/lower center panels, respectively.
c)   Be **very careful** to check that the panel is correctly engaged with its partners before installing and securing the six fasteners.

Front fairing inner panels - G through K models

97   Installation is the reverse of removal.

Upper fairing assembly

Refer to illustrations 2.98a and 2.98b

98   Installation is the reverse of removal ensuring the pegs on the headlight are correctly engaged with the rubbers on the fairing stay **(see illustrations)**. On R models, ensure that the four rubber windshield seats are in place on the fairing stay mounting bosses. On completion check the headlight aim as described in Chapter 9.

Rear fairing panel

99   Installation is the reverse of removal. On L models onward, lubricate the rubber grommets to assist the front retaining pegs to engage without undue pressure. Tighten the grab rail mounting bolts to the torque setting given in Chapter 6 Specifications.

3.11 Removing the windshield - R model

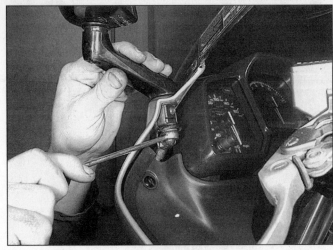

**4.1a Rear view mirror removal, G through K models -
unscrew retaining nut . . .**

4.1b . . . withdraw mirror . . .

4.1c . . . and collect spacer

**4.2 Rear view mirror removal, L models
onward - peel back rubber cover to
reach two retaining bolts**

3   Windshield - removal and installation

Removal

G and H models

1   Unscrew the six windshield retaining screws.
2   Carefully lift the windshield away from the upper fairing and recover the rubber mounts and nuts.

J and K models

3   Unscrew their retaining screws and withdraw the windshield height adjuster knobs and the trim plates beneath.
4   Unscrew their retaining screws and withdraw the trim plates covering the height adjuster mechanism.
5   Unbolt and withdraw the windshield assembly from the upper fairing. The assembly can now be disassembled by unscrewing the various fasteners and the shield itself can be replaced.

L through P models

6   Remove the rear view mirrors as described in Section 4.
7   Use an Allen key to unscrew the two retaining screws securing each of the trim panels to the rear ends of the upper fairing windshield mounting 'ears'. Withdraw both trim panels.
8   Unscrew the windshield fasteners and carefully lift the windshield away from the upper fairing.

R model

Refer to illustration 3.11

9   Remove the rear view mirrors as described in Section 4.
10   Unscrew the two retaining screws securing each of the trim panels to the rear ends of the upper fairing windshield mounting 'ears.' Withdraw both trim panels and unscrew the larger screw beneath each.
11   Carefully spread the upper fairing's windshield mounting 'ears' while an assistant lifts the windshield away from the upper fairing assembly **(see illustration)**.

Installation

12   Installation is the reverse of removal. On R models, ensure that the windshield's front end aligns with the grooves in the upper fairing and that the four rubber seats are in place on the fairing stay mounting bosses.

4   Rear view mirrors - removal and installation

Removal

G through K models

Refer to illustrations 4.1a, 4.1b and 4.1c

1   Unscrew the nut at the base of each mirror and withdraw the mirror, collecting the spring and plain washers and spacer **(see illustrations)**.

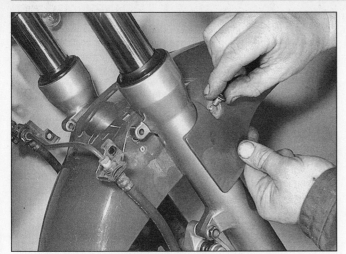

7.2 Undo the mounting bolts on each side and remove the front fender/mudguard

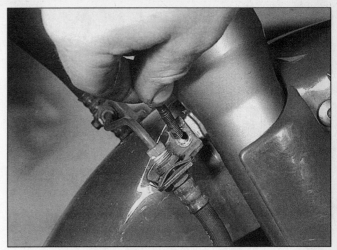

7.3 On installation, ensure that the brake pipe retainers are positioned behind the rear bolts

L models onward

Refer to illustration 4.2

2   Peel back the rubber cover, then undo the two bolts and remove the rear view mirror with its mounting plate and rubber **(see illustration)**.

Installation

G through K models

3   Installation is the reverse of removal. On completion check the mirror positioning.

L models onward

4   Install the mounting plate to the mirror. On the left mirror the plate must be fitted with its marked side facing the mirror and the arrows stamped on the plate pointing ups and forwards. On the right mirror the plate must be fitted with its marked side facing the fairing and the arrows stamped on the plate pointing ups and forwards.

5   Install the mounting rubber to the mirror. On the left mirror the rubber should be fitted so that the 'L' marking is facing the mirror. On the right mirror the rubber must be fitted so that the 'R' marking is facing the fairing.

6   Install the mirror on the fairing and securely tighten its bolts. Slide the rubber cover back into position over the mounting plate.

5   Fairing stay - removal and installation

Removal

1   Remove the upper fairing assembly as described in Section 2.
2   Remove the instrument cluster as described in Chapter 9.
3   Carefully note the correct routing of the wiring harness around the stay. Disconnect the relevant wiring connectors, then release the clips and detach the harness from the stay.
4   Undo the stay nuts and bolts and take the fairing stay off the motorcycle. Depending on model, there may be further sub-stays which also retain other components.

Installation

5   Installation is the reverse of removal.

6   Side covers - removal and installation

Removal

Note: *Refer to the general notes made in Section 2 before starting work.*

1   Undo the side cover retaining screw. Pull the front upper end of the cover squarely away from the machine to release both its retaining pegs from their rubber grommets.
2   Slide the side cover forwards to release it from the rear fairing and withdraw it.

Installation

Note: *Refer to the general notes made in Section 2 before commencing installation.*
3   Offer up the side cover and engage it with the rear fairing.
4   Align the cover retaining pegs with their rubbers and clip the cover into position.
5   Secure the cover in position by tightening its screw securely.

7   Front fender/mudguard - removal and installation

Removal

Note: *Refer to the general notes made in Section 2 before starting work. Refer to illustration 7.2*
1   Place the motorcycle on its center stand - where no center stand is fitted, support the machine securely in an upright position.
2   Undo the four bolts and remove the fender/mudguard, taking care not to damage its painted finish **(see illustration)**.

Installation

Note: *Refer to the general notes made in Section 2 before commencing installation.*
Refer to illustration 7.3
3   Installation is the reverse of removal not forgetting to position the brake pipe retainers behind the rear bolts **(see illustration)**.

8   Rear fender/mudguard - removal and installation

Removal

Note: *Refer to the general notes made in Section 2 before starting work.*
1   Place the motorcycle on its center stand - where no center stand is fitted, support the machine securely in an upright position. Block the motorcycle (being careful not to damage the fairing lower panels - remove them if necessary, as described in Section 2) so that the rear wheel is clear of the ground.
2   Remove the seat as described in Section 9.
3   Remove the rear fairing as described in Section 2.
4   On G through K models, disconnect the wiring connectors from the rear turn signal assemblies and unbolt the turn signal assembly

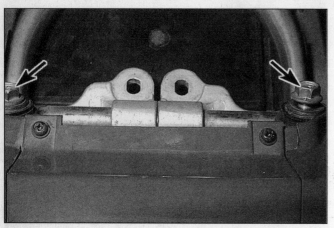

10.2 Grab rail mounting bolts - L model shown

stays from the subframe/seat rail.
5   Remove the battery. Refer to Chapter 9.
6   On G through K models, remove the coolant reservoir as described in Chapter 3.
7   Depending on model and circumstances, unbolt or unclip and move aside all ancillary components such as the fuel pump and the various electrical components attached to the rear fender/mudguard (Chapter 9), the rear brake fluid reservoir (Chapter 7) and the ignition system spark unit (Chapter 5).
8   Unbolt the fender/mudguard (two pieces on G through K models) and remove it from the motorcycle. Examine the fender/mudguard rubber mounts for signs of damage and replace if necessary.

Installation

Note: *Refer to the general notes made in Section 2 before commencing installation.*
9   Installation is the reverse of removal. On completion check the operation of the turn signals and all other disturbed electrical components before taking the machine on the road.

---

9   Seat - removal and installation

Removal

1   Remove the single seat cowl (where fitted) as described in Section 11.
2   Unlock the seat. On G models turn the ignition key counter-clockwise (anti-clockwise) in the seat/helmet lock. On all other models turn the ignition key clockwise in the seat/helmet lock and pull down the locking lever.
3   Lift the seat at the back, sliding it to the rear to disengage it from the fuel tank and remove it from the motorcycle.

Installation

4   Installation is the reverse of removal, noting the following:
 a) *On G through K and R models the seat is located at the front by one projecting tongue which slots **under** the fuel tank rear mounting, and by two further prongs which hook under the frame crossmember.*

 b) *On L through P models the seat is located at the front by one projecting tongue which slots **under** the fuel tank rear mounting, with two further tongues, one each inside the seat front ends, which engage with hooks in the fuel tank sides. Ensure these tongues are straight and unbroken - if they are damaged or distorted, repair them before attempting to install the seat.*
 c) *On all models, **always** lubricate the seat lock, catches and locating tongues with a smear of grease to prevent stiffness and to assist installation. **Always** ensure that the seat's front locating tongue fits **under** the fuel tank mounting - this ensures that the seat is correctly secured and is centered on the motorcycle, thus preventing excessive stress from being placed on the side tongues. With the front of the seat located, engage the remaining tongues/prongs and press the seat down at the back until the lock is securely fastened.*

---

10   Grab rail(s) - removal and installation

Removal

Refer to illustration 10.2
1   Remove the seat as described in Section 9.
2   Unbolt and remove the grab rail(s) from the motorcycle - on L through P models, unscrew the two small bolts securing each end of the grab rail support tube to release the assembly **(see illustration)**.

Installation

3   Installation is the reverse of removal. On L models onward, tighten the grab rail mounting bolts to the torque setting given in Chapter 6 Specifications.

---

11   Single seat cowl - removal and installation

Removal

Note: *Refer to the general notes made in Section 2 before starting work.*

G through K models

1   Unscrew the two mounting screws (one each side).
2   Lift the cowl carefully at the **front** and slide it gently forwards to release its rear retaining tab from the rear fairing groove. Withdraw the cowl from the motorcycle.

L models onward

3   Unscrew the two mounting bolts (one each side, with a shouldered spacer) from the rear fairing middle mounting points **(see illustration 2.77)**.
4   To avoid the risk of breaking the hooks, press gently down on the cowl and slide it forwards to ensure that its two rear mounting hooks are in the correct position for removal. Lift the cowl carefully at the **front** and withdraw it from the motorcycle.

Installation

Note: *Refer to the general notes made in Section 2 before commencing installation.*
5   Installation is the reverse of removal. Tighten securely the cowl/rear fairing mounting bolts.

Chapter 9 Electrical system

Note: *Refer to 'Identification numbers' at the beginning of this Manual to establish the model code of your motorcycle.*

Contents

Specifications

Battery
Capacity
G through K models ... 12V, 12Ah
L models onward ... 12V, 10Ah
Specific gravity ... See Chapter 1

Alternator
Type ... Three-phase AC
Nominal output - at 5000 rpm
G and H models ... 350 watts
J models onward ... 335 watts
Regulated charging voltage (approx.) - at 5000 rpm:
G through K models ... 13.7 to 15.3 volts
L models onward ... 13.5 to 16.0 volts
Charging current (approx.) - at 5000 rpm
G through K models ... Not specified
L models onward ... 5 to 9 amperes
Stator coil resistance - at 20°C (68°F)
G and H models ... 0.2 to 0.5 ohms
J and K models ... 1.0 to 2.0 ohms
L models onward ... 0.1 to 1.0 ohms

9

Starter motor
Brush length
   New .... 12 to 13 mm (0.472 to 0.512 inch)
   Service limit .... 6.5 mm (0.260 inch)

Fuses
Main fuse (on starter relay) 30A
All other fuses (in fuse box)* .... 6 x 10A and 1 x 15A or 20A
*See fuse box lid and/or wiring diagrams at the back of this manual for details of fuses and of circuits protected.

Bulbs

	US models	UK models
Headlight		
G and H models	12V 60/55W	12V 60/55W
L models onward	12V 45/45W	12V 60/55W
Sidelight		
G through K models	-	12V 4W
L models onward	-	12V 5W
Brake and taillight:		
G through P models	12V 27/8W	12V 21/5W
R models	12V 32/2cp	12V 21/5W
Turn signals/running lights		
Front	12V 23/8W	12V 21W
Rear	12V 23W	12V 21W
License plate light		
G and H models	12V 8W	-
L through P models	12V 4cp	-
R models	12V 8W	-
Instrument illuminating lights - including clock		
G through K models	12V 3.4W*	12V 3.4W
L models onward	12V 1.7W	12V 1.7W
Warning lights		
R models		
Fuel reserve warning light	12V 5W	12V 5W
All other warning lights	12V 1.7W	12V 1.7W
All other models	12V 3.4W	12V 3.4W

*US VFR700F-G and VFR750F-G models have an additional 12V 3W instrument illuminating bulb.

Torque settings

	Nm	ft-lbs
Ignition (main) switch bolts		
G through K models		
Shear-head bolts	Tighten until head shears off	
Standard bolts	Not specified	
L models onward	25	18
Neutral switch	12	9
Sidestand switch bolt	9	7
Alternator stator coil bolts	12	9
Speed sensor bolts - R models	10	7
Oil pressure switch*	12	9

*Apply sealant to the switch threads, except for the 3 to 4 mm (0.1 to 0.2 inch) next to its tip.

1 General information

Refer to illustration 1.3

    The machines covered by this manual are equipped with a 12-volt electrical system. The components include a three-phase alternator and a regulator/rectifier unit.

    The regulator/rectifier unit maintains the charging system output within the specified range to prevent overcharging and converts the AC (alternating current) output of the alternator to DC (direct current) to power the lights and other components and to charge the battery.

    An electric starter is mounted on the engine below and in front of the cylinders. The starting system includes the motor, the battery, the relay and the various wires and switches. If the engine stop switch and the ignition (main) switch are both in the RUN or ON positions respectively, the circuit relay allows the starter motor to operate only if the transmission is in Neutral (neutral switch on) or the clutch lever is pulled to the handlebar (clutch switch on) and (on L models onward) the sidestand is up (sidestand switch on) **(see illustration)**. Several of these are also elements of the ignition cut-out safety system which cuts the ignition if the engine is running with the transmission in gear and the sidestand down.

Note: *Keep in mind that electrical parts, once purchased, can't be returned. To avoid unnecessary expense, make very sure the faulty component has been positively identified before buying a replacement part.*

1.3 Typical starter circuit wiring diagram - refer to the wiring diagrams at the end of this book for full details and wire color codes specific to your motorcycle

2 Electrical troubleshooting

Warning: *To prevent the risk of short circuits, the battery negative (-) cable should be disconnected before any of the motorcycle's other electrical components are disturbed. Don't forget to reconnect the cable securely once work is finished.*
Refer to illustration 2.5

A typical electrical circuit consists of an electrical component, the switches, relays, etc. related to that component and the wiring and connectors that hook the component to both the battery and the frame. To aid in locating a problem in any electrical circuit, refer to the *wiring diagrams* at the end of this book.

Before tackling any troublesome electrical circuit, first study the appropriate diagrams thoroughly to get a complete picture of what makes up that individual circuit. Trouble spots, for instance, can often be narrowed down by noting if other components related to that circuit are operating properly or not. If several components or circuits fail at one time, chances are the fault lies in the fuse or ground (earth) connection, as several circuits often are routed through the same fuse and ground (earth) connections.

Electrical problems often stem from simple causes, such as loose or corroded connections or a blown fuse. Prior to any electrical troubleshooting, always visually check the condition of the fuse, wires and connections in the problem circuit. Intermittent failures can be especially frustrating, since you can't always duplicate the failure when it's convenient to test. In such situations, a good practice is to clean all connections in the affected circuit, whether or not they appear to be good. All of the connections and wires should also be wiggled to check for looseness which can cause intermittent failure.

If testing instruments are going to be utilized, use the diagrams to plan where you will make the necessary connections in order to accurately pinpoint the trouble spot.

The basic tools needed for electrical troubleshooting include a test light or voltmeter, a continuity tester (which includes a bulb, a

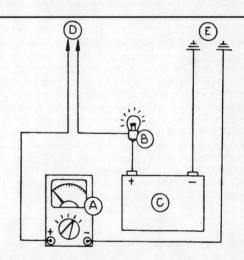

2.5 Simple testing equipment for checking the wiring

A	Multimeter	D	Positive probe (+)
B	Bulb	E	Negative probe (-)
C	Battery		

battery and a set of test leads) and a jumper wire, preferably with a circuit breaker incorporated, which can be used to bypass electrical components **(see illustration)**. Specific checks described later in this Chapter may also require an ohmmeter. Ideally a multimeter with resistance, current and voltage measuring facilities should be available.

Voltage checks should be performed if a circuit is not functioning properly. Connect one lead of a test light or voltmeter to either the negative (-) battery terminal or a known good ground (earth). Connect the other lead to a connector in the circuit being tested, preferably

9

3.2a Battery removal, G through K models - remove right side cover, then first screw (A) securing battery negative (-) cable, next screw (B) securing positive (+) cable, undo clamp bolt (C) and remove battery

Note: *Location of clutch switch diode (D) (Section 23)*

A continuity check is performed to see if a circuit, section of circuit or individual component is capable of passing electricity through it. Disconnect the battery and connect one lead of a self-powered test light (continuity tester) to one end of the circuit being tested and the other lead to the other end of the circuit. If the bulb lights, there is continuity, which means the circuit is passing electricity through it properly. Switches can be checked in the same way.

Remember that all electrical circuits are designed to conduct electricity from the battery, through the wires, switches, relays, etc. to the electrical component (light bulb, motor, etc.). From there it is directed to the frame (ground/earth) where it is passed back to the battery. Electrical problems are basically an interruption in the flow of electricity from the battery or back to it.

3 Battery - inspection and maintenance

Refer to illustrations 3.2a, 3.2b, 3.2c and 3.2d

1   The battery fitted to the early models covered in this manual is of the conventional lead/acid type, requiring regular checks of the electrolyte level, as described in Chapter 1, as well as the checks detailed below. On L models onward however, the battery is of the maintenance-free (sealed) type and therefore requires no maintenance as such. However, the following checks should still be regularly performed.

2   To remove the battery, proceed as follows:

a) *On G through K models, remove the right side cover (see Chapter 8, if necessary),* then remove the screws securing the battery cables to the battery terminals (remove the negative (-) cable first, positive (+) cable last), undo the battery clamp bolt and remove the battery from its box, removing the upper cover (where fitted) and disconnecting the vent tube **(see illustration)**.

b) *On L models onward, remove the seat (see Chapter 8)* then unclip its retaining band and lift off the battery cover. Remove the screws securing the battery cables to the battery terminals (remove the negative (-) cable first, positive (+) cable last) and remove the battery from its box **(see illustrations)**.

nearest to the battery or fuse. If the bulb lights, voltage is reaching that point, which means the part of the circuit between that connector and the battery is problem-free. Continue checking the remainder of the circuit in the same manner. When you reach a point where no voltage is present, the problem lies between there and the last good test point. Most of the time the problem is due to a loose connection. Keep in mind that some circuits only receive voltage when the ignition key is in the ON position.

One method of finding short circuits is to remove the fuse and connect a test light or voltmeter in its place to the fuse terminals. There should be no load in the circuit (it should be switched off). Move the wiring harness from side-to-side while watching the test light. If the bulb lights, there is a short to ground (earth) somewhere in that area, probably where insulation has rubbed off a wire. The same test can be performed on other components in the circuit, including the switch.

A ground (earth) check should be done to see if a component is grounded (earthed) properly. Disconnect the battery and connect one lead of a self-powered test light (continuity tester) to a known good ground (earth). Connect the other lead to the wire or ground (earth) connection being tested. If the bulb lights, the ground (earth) is good. If the bulb does not light, the ground (earth) is not good.

3   Check the battery terminals and cables for tightness and corrosion. If corrosion is evident, disconnect the cables from the battery, disconnecting the negative (-) terminal first, and clean the terminals and cable ends with a wire brush or knife and emery paper. Reconnect the cables, connecting the negative (-) terminal last, and apply a thin coat of petroleum jelly to the connections to slow further corrosion.

4   The battery case should be kept clean to prevent current leakage, which can discharge the battery over a period of time (especially when it sits unused). Wash the outside of the case with a solution of baking soda and water. Rinse the battery thoroughly, then dry it.

5   Look for cracks in the case and replace the battery if these are

3.2b Battery removal, L models onward - remove seat, then unclip retaining band and remove the cover . . .

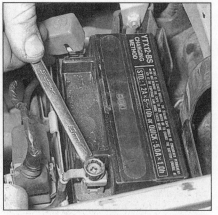

3.2c . . . always disconnect the battery negative (-) cable first (and reconnect it last) . . .

3.2d . . . then remove the battery - sealed type shown has no vent tube

found. If acid has been spilled on the frame or battery box, neutralize it with a baking soda and water solution, dry it thoroughly, then touch up any damaged paint. Make sure the battery vent tube (if equipped) is directed away from the frame and is not kinked or pinched.

6   If the motorcycle sits unused for long periods of time, disconnect the cables from the battery terminals. Refer to Section 4 and charge the battery approximately once every month.

7   The condition of the battery can be assessed by measuring the voltage present at the battery terminals; voltmeter positive (+) probe to the battery positive (+) terminal and negative (-) probe to battery negative (-) terminal. When fully charged there should be approximately 13 volts present. If the voltage falls below 12.3 volts the battery must be removed, disconnecting the negative (-) terminal first, and recharged as described below in Section 4.

4   Battery - charging

Refer to illustration 4.2

1   To charge the battery, first remove it from the motorcycle as described in Step 2 of the previous Section.

2   The manufacturer recommends that the conventional type of battery (G through K models) be charged at a rate of no more than 1.2 amps for as long as is necessary to restore the electrolyte's specific gravity to the specified value (see Chapter 1 Specifications and *Battery - check*). The recommendation for a maintenance-free (sealed) type of battery is to charge it at a rate of 1.2 amps for between 5 and 10 hours. Exceeding these figures can cause the battery to overheat, buckling the plates and rendering it useless. Few owners will have access to an expensive current controlled charger, so if a normal domestic charger is used check that after a possible initial peak, the charge rate falls to a safe level **(see illustration)**. If the battery becomes hot during charging **stop**. Further charging will cause damage. **Note:** *In emergencies the manufacturer states that the maintenance-free (sealed) type of battery can be charged at a rate of 5 amps for a period of 1 hour. However, this is an emergency measure only and the low amp charge is by far the safer method of charging the battery in normal use.*

3   If the recharged battery discharges rapidly when left disconnected it is likely that an internal short caused by physical damage or sulfation has occurred. A new battery will be required. A sound item will tend to lose its charge at about 1% per day.

4   On installation, clean the battery terminals and cable ends with a wire brush or knife and emery paper. Reconnect the cables, connecting the negative (-) terminal last, and apply a thin coat of petroleum jelly to the connections to slow further corrosion. Secure the battery with its clamp or cover, ensure the battery vent tube (G through K models only) is routed correctly, directed away from the frame and is not kinked or pinched. Install the seat or side cover as described in Chapter 8.

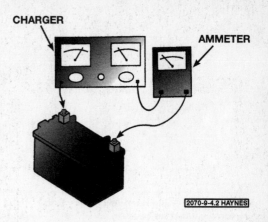

4.2 If the charger doesn't have an ammeter built in, connect one in series as shown; DO NOT connect the ammeter between the battery terminals or it will be ruined

5   Fuses - check and replacement

Main fuse

Refer to illustrations 5.1, 5.2a and 5.2b

1   Apart from the starter motor and starter relay switch themselves, all electrical equipment is protected by the main fuse fitted to the top of the starter relay switch. On G through K models, the relay switch is located behind the right side cover, next to the battery; on L models onward, the relay switch is underneath the seat, in front of the battery **(see illustration)**.

2   To reach the main fuse remove the side cover or seat as required (see Chapter 8, if necessary). Unclip the starter relay switch wiring connector to expose the fuse **(see illustrations)**. A spare main fuse is clipped to the base of the starter relay switch.

Fuse box fuses

Refer to illustrations 5.3a, 5.3b, 5.4a, 5.4b and 5.4c

3   Most individual circuits are additionally protected by fuses of different ratings - refer to the *wiring diagrams* at the end of this book for details. All these fuses are located in the fuse box which is situated at the base of the instrument panel on G and H models, and on the right side of the upper fairing on all other models **(see illustrations)**.

5.1 Unclip the starter relay switch wiring (G through K models shown) to reach the main fuse (A) - note spare main fuse (B)

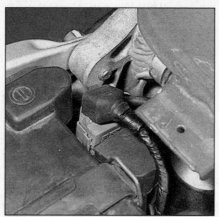

5.2a On L models onward, remove seat to reach starter relay switch between fuel tank mounting and battery . . .

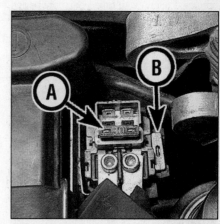

5.2b . . . relay switch wiring unclipped to reveal main fuse (A) and spare (B)

9

5.3a Fuse inspection, G and H models -
remove screws (other arrowed) to
release fuse box cover . . .

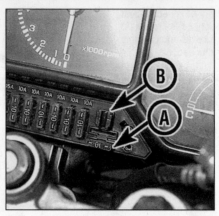

5.3b . . . and reveal fuses; note spare fuse
locations (A) and fuse-removing
tweezers (B)

5.4a Fuse inspection, R models - undo
the screw and lift off the fuse box
upper cover . . .

4   To reach the fuses, proceed as follows:
a) *G and H models - undo the two screws and remove the fuse box
cover.*
b) *J through P models - undo the screw(s) and remove the fairing
upper inner panel, then unclip the fuse box lid.*
c) *R models - undo the screw and remove the fuse box upper cover,
then unclip the fuse box lid (see illustrations).*

5   All fuse box fuses are labelled for easy identification. Spare fuses
of each rating are located in the fuse box.

All fuses

6   The fuses can be removed and checked visually. If there isn't a
pair of fuse-removing tweezers supplied and you can't pull the fuse out
with your fingertips, use a pair of needle-nose pliers. A blown fuse is
easily identified by a break in the element. Each is clearly marked with
its rating and must only be replaced by a fuse of the correct rating.
Caution: *Never put in a fuse of a higher rating or bridge the terminals
with any other substitute, however temporary it may be. Serious
damage may be done to the circuit, or a fire may start.*

7   If the spare fuses are used, always replace them so that a spare
fuse of each rating is carried on the machine at all times.

8   If a fuse blows, be sure to check the wiring circuit very carefully
for evidence of a short-circuit. Look for bare wires and chafed, melted
or burned insulation. If a fuse is replaced before the cause is located,
the new fuse will blow immediately.

9   Occasionally a fuse will blow or cause an open-circuit for no
obvious reason. Corrosion of the fuse ends and fuse box terminals
may occur and cause poor fuse contact. If this happens, remove the
corrosion with a wire brush or emery paper, then spray the fuse end
and terminals with electrical contact cleaner.

6   Lighting system - check

Warning: *To prevent the risk of short circuits, the battery negative (-)
cable should be disconnected before any of the motorcycle's other
electrical components are disturbed. Don't forget to reconnect the
cable securely once work is finished.*

1   The battery provides power for operation of the headlight,
taillight, brake light, license plate light and instrument panel lights. If
none of the lights operate, always check battery voltage before
proceeding. Low battery voltage indicates either a faulty battery or a
defective charging system. Refer to Section 3 for battery checks and
Sections 29 and 30 for charging system tests. Also, check the
condition of the fuses and replace any blown fuses with new ones.

Headlight

Refer to illustrations 6.3a and 6.3b

2   On G through K models, if the headlight is out when the engine is
running (US models) or it won't switch on (UK models), check the fuse
first with the ignition ON (see Section 5), then check the bulb (see
Section 7). If everything checks out okay so far unplug the headlight
wiring connector and use jumper wires to connect the bulb directly to
the battery terminals. If the light comes on, the problem lies in the
wiring or one of the switches in the circuit. Refer to Section 19 for the
switch testing procedures, and also to the *wiring diagrams* at the end
of this book.

3   On L models onward, the headlights are operated through relays;
one for high beam and another for low. The relays are mounted on the
fairing stay; while the relays can be detached by reaching behind the
instrument panel when the fairing is still in place, for adequate access

5.4b . . . to reveal the fuse box lid; fuse
locations are marked on the lid . . .

5.4c . . . unclip the fuse box lid to
remove the fuses

6.3a Headlight high beam relay (A), low
beam relay (B) - L through P models

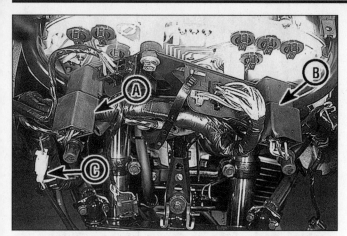

6.3b Headlight high beam relay (A), low beam relay (B) - R models

Note: *Location of clutch switch diode (C) (Section 23)*

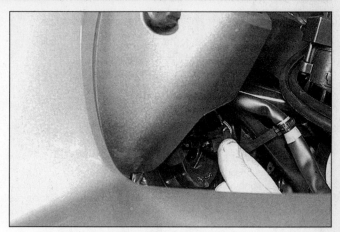

7.2 On R models, headlight wiring connector can be unplugged from above . . .

when tracing wiring faults, remove first the upper fairing assembly as described in Chapter 8 **(see illustrations)**. Proceed as follows:

 a) *If the headlight won't switch off (UK models only), first make the preliminary checks outlined in Step 2, then check the switches (Section 19) and the relay itself (see Steps (d) and (e) below); finally check the wiring harness for evidence of shorts.*

 b) *If the headlight won't come on, first check the fuses, (Section 5) then the bulb itself. Next check the switches (Section 19).*

 c) *If everything checks out okay so far the relay itself should be suspected, especially if the fault is confined to one beam only. Remember that the relay should be felt or heard to click as its circuit is switched on; if nothing is heard or felt the relay is either faulty or is not being energized correctly.*

 d) *The first check of either relay is to look for loose or corroded connections, physical damage, etc., and rectify as necessary. Check for continuity between the relay's green terminal and ground (earth); if there is no continuity, trace and rectify the fault as outlined in Section 2. Check for full battery voltage at the relay's black/red and blue (low beam) or white (high beam) terminals with the ignition (and lighting) switch(es) ON and the dimmer switch on 'Lo' or 'Hi' as applicable. If there is no battery voltage, there is an open-circuit between the relay and the fuse - trace and rectify the fault as outlined in Section 2; refer to the wiring diagrams at the end of this book. If battery voltage is measured, the relay must be checked.*

 e) *If a relay is thought to be faulty, the simplest way of checking it is to substitute a relay that is known to be sound; both headlight relays are the same and can be swapped if only one circuit is functional, to check the relay of the inoperative circuit. If you wish to be certain of a relay's condition before having to purchase a new one, check it as follows: Set a multimeter to the ohms x 1 scale and connect it across the relay's black/red and white/black (low beam) or blue/black (high beam) terminals. Using a fully-charged 12 volt battery and two insulated jumper wires, connect the positive (+) terminal of the battery to the relay's blue (low beam) or white (high beam) terminal and its negative (-) terminal to the relay's green terminal; the relay should click and the multimeter read 0 ohms (continuity). If this is the case the relay is serviceable; if the relay does not click when battery voltage is applied and indicates no continuity across its terminals, it is faulty and must be replaced.*

 f) *If the relay is found to be okay, there must be an open-circuit in the wiring between the switch(es) and the relay or between the relay and the headlight. Trace and rectify the fault as outlined in Section 2.*

Taillight/license plate light

4   If the taillight fails to work, check the bulbs and the bulb terminals first, then check for battery voltage at the taillight electrical connector. If voltage is present, check the ground (earth) circuit for an open or poor connection. If no voltage is indicated, check the wiring between the taillight and the ignition switch, then check the switch. On UK models, check the lighting switch as well.

Brake light

5   See Section 13 for the brake light switch checking procedure.

Neutral indicator light

6   If the neutral light fails to operate when the transmission is in Neutral, check the fuses and the bulb (see Sections 5 and 16). If the bulb and fuses are in good condition, check for battery voltage at the switch's connector on the right of the engine. If battery voltage is present, refer to Section 21 for neutral switch check and replacement procedures.

7   If no voltage is indicated, check the wiring between the switch and the bulb for open-circuits and poor connections.

Oil pressure warning light

8   See Section 17 for the oil pressure switch check.

Sidestand switch warning light

9   If the sidestand light fails to operate when the stand is down, check the fuses and the bulb (see Sections 5 and 16). If the bulb and fuses are in good condition, refer to Section 22 for sidestand switch check and replacement procedures.

10   If the switch is functioning correctly check for voltage at the switch wiring connector. If no voltage is indicated, check the wiring between the switch and the bulb for open-circuits and poor connections.

---

7   Headlight bulb and sidelight (UK models only) bulb - replacement

---

Note: *The headlight bulb is of the quartz-halogen type. Do not touch the bulb glass as skin acids will shorten the bulb's service life. If the bulb is accidentally touched, it should be wiped carefully when cold with a rag soaked in stoddard solvent (methylated spirit) and dried before fitting. Allow the bulb time to cool before removing it if the headlight has been used.*

Headlight

Refer to illustrations 7.2, 7.3a and 7.3b

1   Where fitted, undo the two screws or release the two trim clips (according to model - see Chapter 8, Section 2 if necessary) and remove the lower cover panel from the base of the upper fairing assembly. Take care not to break the panel's retaining tabs when releasing it from the fairing.

2   Reaching up from beneath or in from above, whichever is easiest, unplug the wiring connector from the headlight bulb and remove the rubber dust cover **(see illustration)**.

9

3   Release the retaining clip and swing it away, then remove the bulb **(see illustrations)**.

4   Fit the new bulb, locating its three tangs in the back of the headlight unit and bearing in mind the information in the note at the start of this Section, then secure it in position with the retaining clip.

5   Install the dust cover, making sure it's correctly seated (TOP mark upwards) and plug in the wiring connector.

6   Check the operation of the headlight then install the lower cover panel (where fitted).

Sidelight (UK models only)

Refer to illustrations 7.8a and 7.8b

7   Proceed as described in Step 1, where necessary.

8   Pull the bulbholder out of the base of the headlight. On G through K models, push the bulb into the holder and twist it counterclockwise (anti-clockwise) to remove it. On L models onward, pull the bulb out of its holder **(see illustrations)**. If the socket contacts are dirty or corroded, they should be scraped clean and sprayed with electrical contact cleaner before new bulb is installed.

9   Carefully install the new bulb, then push the bulbholder back into the headlight.

10   Check the operation of the sidelight then install the lower cover panel (where fitted).

---

8   Headlight assembly - removal and installation

Removal

Refer to illustration 8.2

1   Remove the upper fairing assembly as described in Chapter 8.

2   Undo the screws and washers (three on G through K models, four on L models onward) and remove the headlight assembly from the fairing **(see illustration)**.

Installation

3   Ensure the headlight assembly is correctly seated and fit the screws and washers, tightening them securely.

4   Install the upper fairing as described in Chapter 8.

---

9   Headlight aim - check and adjustment

Refer to illustration 9.4

1   An improperly adjusted headlight may cause problems for oncoming traffic or provide poor, unsafe illumination of the road ahead. Before adjusting the headlight, be sure to consult with local traffic laws and regulations.

2   The headlight beam(s) can be adjusted both vertically and

7.3a . . . then remove rubber cover and unhook retaining clip . . .

horizontally. Before performing the adjustment, check that the suspension settings and tire pressures are correct, make sure the fuel tank is at least half full, and have an assistant of your weight sit on the seat - two if you are adjusting the headlight before carrying a passenger.

3   On all models except R, remove the retaining screw(s) and withdraw the upper fairing's (upper) inner panels. On L through P models, undo also the two screws or release the two trim clips (according to model - see Chapter 8, Section 2 if necessary) and remove the lower cover panel from the base of the upper fairing assembly. Take care not to break the panel's retaining tabs when releasing it from the fairing.

4   The headlight aim is altered using the adjusters on the rear of the headlight unit **(see illustration)**. Proceed as follows:

a) On G models the knob on the top right corner of the assembly adjusts the vertical aim of the beam (rotate the knob clockwise to raise the beam) and the knob on the bottom left corner of the assembly alters its horizontal aim (rotate the knob clockwise to move the beam to the left).

b) On H through K models the knob on the top right corner of the assembly adjusts the horizontal aim of the beam (rotate the knob clockwise to move the beam to the right) and the knob on the bottom left corner of the assembly alters its vertical aim (rotate the knob clockwise to lower the beam).

c) On L through P models the knobs on the top corners of the assembly adjust the vertical aim of the beam and the knobs at the bottom of the assembly alter each beam's horizontal aim.

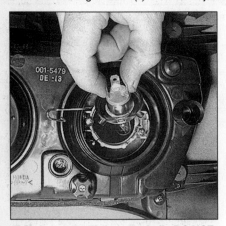

7.3b . . . and withdraw the bulb. DO NOT touch the bulb glass (illustrations shown with fairing removed for clarity)

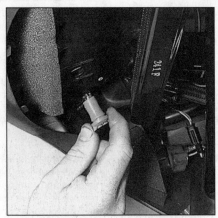

7.8a On UK models, pull the sidelight bulbholder out from the base of the headlight unit . . .

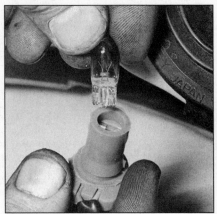

7.8b . . . and (L models onward only) pull the bulb from the holder

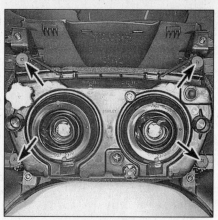

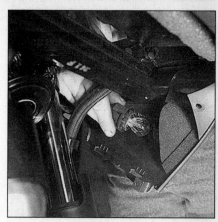

8.2 Headlight unit is retained by four screws (arrows) on L models onward

9.4 Adjusting headlight beam vertical aim - R models. Horizontal adjuster (A) is reached from above (illustration shown with fairing removed for clarity)

10.2 On L models onward, fairing panels must be removed to reach the front turn signal bulbholders

d) On R models the large white knob on the top left corner of the assembly adjusts the horizontal aim of the beam and the knob at the bottom of the assembly alters its vertical aim.

5   Rotate the adjusters as required until the headlight beam is correctly aimed, then install the fairing panel(s) removed.

---

10   Turn signal, taillight and license plate bulbs - replacement

Turn signal bulbs

Front

Refer to illustration 10.2

1   On G through K models, undo the screw from the base of the turn signal and withdraw the turn signal lens. Twist the bulbholder counter-clockwise (anti-clockwise) to release it from the lens.

2   On L models onward, remove the fairing lower center panel as described in Chapter 8. Twist the bulbholder counterclockwise (anti-clockwise) to release it from the back of the turn signal **(see illustration)**.

3   On all models, push the bulb into the holder and twist it counter-clockwise (anti-clockwise) to remove it. Check the socket terminals for corrosion and clean them if necessary. Line up the pins of the new bulb with the slots in the socket, push in and turn the bulb clockwise until it locks into place. **Note:** *On US models the pins on the bulbs are*

offset so it can only be installed one way. It is a good idea to use a paper towel or dry cloth when handling the new bulb to prevent injury if the bulb should break and to increase bulb life.

4   Fit the bulbholder to the lens/turn signal (according to model) and twist the bulbholder clockwise until it is locked into place. Install the fairing panels removed for access.

5   On G through K models, install the turn signal lens and securely tighten its screw.

Rear

Refer to illustrations 10.8a, 10.8b and 10.8c

6   On G and H models, remove the bulbholder as described in Step 1 above.

7   On J and K models, unscrew the screw from behind (the front of the unit) the turn signal assembly and remove the lens.

8   On L models onward, remove the bulbholder as described in Step 1 above **(see illustrations)**.

9   On all models, replace the bulb as described above in Step 3 - note that all rear bulbs can be installed either way round. Check the lens seal and replace if damaged.

10   Installation is the reverse of the removal procedure. Be careful not to overtighten the screw as the lens is easily cracked.

Taillight bulbs

Refer to illustrations 10.12 and 10.13

11   Remove the seat as described in Chapter 8.

12   Twist the relevant bulbholder counterclockwise (anti-clockwise) to

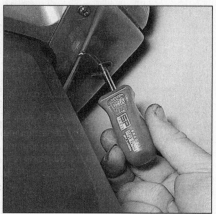

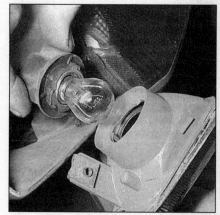

10.8a Rear turn signal bulb replacement, L models onward - undo screw from base of turn signal . . .

10.8b . . . withdraw turn signal lens from rear fairing . . .

10.8c . . . and release bulbholder from lens

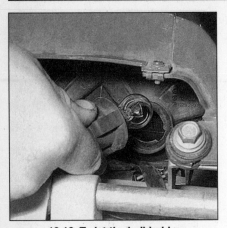

10.12 Twist the bulbholder counterclockwise (anti-clockwise) to release it from the taillight unit

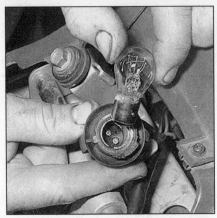

10.13 Note the pins of the taillight bulb are offset - ensure they are correctly aligned on installation

11.2 On L models onward, front turn signals are secured inside upper fairing by a single screw (arrow)

release it from the light unit **(see illustration)**.
13   Push the bulb into the holder and twist it counterclockwise (anti-clockwise) to remove it. Check the socket terminals for corrosion and clean them if necessary. Line up the pins of the new bulb with the slots in the socket, push in and turn the bulb clockwise until it locks into place **(see illustration)**. **Note:** *The pins on the bulb are offset so it can only be installed one way. It is a good idea to use a paper towel or dry cloth when handling the new bulb to prevent injury if the bulb should break and to increase bulb life.*
14   Install the bulbholder and twist it clockwise until it is locked into place.
15   Install the seat as described in Chapter 8.

License plate bulb - US models

16   Unscrew the two securing nuts and withdraw the lens and its cover.
17   Replace the bulb as described above in Step 3. Check the lens seal and replace it if damaged.
18   Fit the lens and cover, then install the nuts. Be careful not to overtighten the nuts as the lens is easily cracked.

11 Turn signal assemblies - removal and installation

Warning: *To prevent the risk of short circuits, the battery negative (-) cable should be disconnected before any of the motorcycle's other electrical components are disturbed. Don't forget to reconnect the cable securely once work is finished.*

Removal

Front

Refer to illustration 11.2
1   On G through K models, remove as required the fairing inner panels (see Chapter 8 if necessary). Trace the wiring back from the turn signal and disconnect its wiring connectors. Unscrew the nut(s) securing the turn signal assembly and withdraw it.
2   On L models onward, remove the bulb as described in Section 10. Unscrew the retaining screw and withdraw the turn signal lens from the fairing **(see illustration)**.

Rear

3   Remove the seat as described in Chapter 8.
4   Trace the wiring back from the turn signal and disconnect its wiring connectors.
5   On all G and H models, and on US L through P models, unscrew the nut securing the assembly to its stay, then withdraw the assembly.
6   On J and K models, undo the two bolts securing the assembly to its stay, then withdraw the assembly with the mounting rubber, and the collar fitted to each bolt.

7   On UK L through P models and all R models, remove the unit as described in Section 10.

Installation

8   Installation is the reverse of the removal procedure.

12 Turn signal circuit - check

Warning: *To prevent the risk of short circuits, the battery negative (-) cable should be disconnected before any of the motorcycle's other electrical components are disturbed. Don't forget to reconnect the cable securely once work is finished.*
Refer to illustrations 12.3a and 12.3b
1   The battery provides power for operation of the turn signal lights, so if they do not operate, always check the battery voltage first. Low battery voltage indicates either a faulty battery or a defective charging system. Refer to Section 3 for battery checks and Sections 29 and 30 for charging system tests. Also, check the fuses (see Section 5) and the switch (see Section 19).
2   Most turn signal problems are the result of a burned out bulb or corroded socket. This is especially true when the turn signals function properly in one direction, but fail to flash in the other direction. Check the bulbs and the sockets (see Section 10).
3   If the bulbs and sockets check out okay, check for power at the turn signal relay with the ignition ON. On G through K models the relay is mounted on the fairing stay; while it may be possible to reach the relay from underneath or by removing the fairing (upper) inner panel, for best access during trouble-shooting remove the upper fairing assembly as described in Chapter 8 **(see illustration)**. On L models onward the relay is mounted on the subframe/seat rail left side; to reach the relay, remove the seat and the rear fairing - refer to Chapter 8 if necessary **(see illustration)**. Refer to the *wiring diagrams* at the end of this book to identify the power source terminal.
4   If power is present, check the wiring between the relay and the turn signals (see the *wiring diagrams* at the end of this book).
5   If the wiring checks out okay, replace the turn signal relay.

13 Brake light switches - check and replacement

Warning: *To prevent the risk of short circuits, the battery negative (-) cable should be disconnected before any of the motorcycle's other electrical components are disturbed. Don't forget to reconnect the cable securely once work is finished.*

Circuit check

1   Before checking any electrical circuit, check the bulb (see Section 10) and fuses (see Section 5).

12.3a Turn signal relay is mounted on fairing stay on
G through K models . . .

12.3b . . . and on left side of subframe seat rail (arrow)
on L models onward

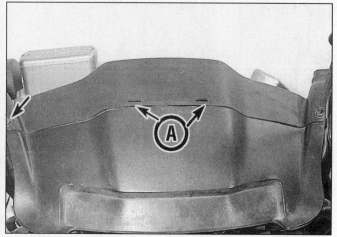

14.2a On L models onward, remove retaining screws on top
surface (other arrowed) and disengage tabs (A) to remove
instrument panel front cover . . .

14.2b . . . then undo screws in bottom corners to remove
instrument panel cover

2   Using a test light connected to a good ground (earth), check for
voltage at the brake light switch wiring connector (see Steps 8 and 9
for the rear brake light switch). If there's no voltage present, check the
wire between the switch and the fuse box (see the *wiring diagrams* at
the end of this book).
3   If voltage is available, touch the probe of the test light to the other
terminal of the switch, then pull the brake lever or depress the brake
pedal. **Note:** *The wiring connectors must be joined for this test and the
probes inserted in the back of each connector.* If the test light doesn't
light up, replace the switch.
4   If the test light does light, check the wiring between the switch
and the brake lights (see the *wiring diagrams* at the end of this book).

Switch replacement

Front brake lever switch

5   Remove the mounting screw and unplug the wiring connectors
from the switch.
6   Detach the switch from the master cylinder.
7   Installation is the reverse of the removal procedure. The switch
isn't adjustable.

Rear brake pedal switch

8   Remove the seat and either the right side cover or the rear fairing,
according to model, as described in Chapter 8.
9   Trace the wiring back from the switch and disconnect it at its

wiring connector. Work back along the wiring releasing it from any
relevant retaining clips and ties.
10   Unhook the spring from the switch and brake pedal and remove
it.
11   Free the switch from the right footpeg bracket and remove it.
12   Install the switch by reversing the removal procedure, then adjust
it by following the procedure described in Chapter 1.

14   Instrument panel and speedometer cable - removal and installation

Warning: *To prevent the risk of short circuits, the battery negative (-)
cable should be disconnected before any of the motorcycle's other
electrical components are disturbed. Don't forget to reconnect the
cable securely once work is finished.*

Removal

Instrument panel

Refer to illustrations 14.2a, 14.2b, 14.4, 14.5a, 14.5b and 14.5c
1   Remove the upper fairing assembly as described in Chapter 8.
2   On L models onward, unscrew the two screws on the top surface
and withdraw the front cover (noting the two tabs locating it to the
panel cover) then unscrew the two screws at the bottom corners and
withdraw the instrument panel cover (see illustrations).

9

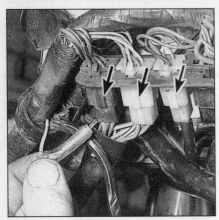

14.4 Disconnect instrument panel wiring at multi-pin connectors (arrows), L through P models

14.5a Unscrew the three instrument panel mounting nuts (arrows) - G through K models . . .

14.5b . . . L through P models . . .

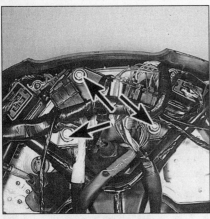

14.5c . . . and R model, to lift instrument panel assembly away from motorcycle

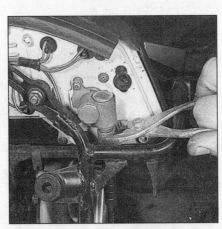

14.9 Unscrew the retaining ring to detach the speedometer cable from the instrument panel

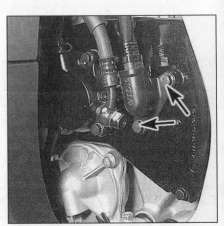

14.15 Unscrew bolts (arrows) to remove speed sensor unit, R models

3   Where fitted, disconnect the speedometer cable (see Step 9 below).

4   Trace all the wiring back from the panel, releasing it from any clips, and disconnect it at the wiring connectors clipped to the front of the fairing stay/instrument panel **(see illustration)**.

5   Unscrew the instrument panel mounting nuts **(see illustrations)**.

6   Carefully maneuver the instrument panel assembly out of position.

7   Inspect the mounting rubbers for signs of damage and replace if necessary.

Speedometer cable - G through P models

Refer to illustration 14.9

8   Remove the upper fairing assembly as described in Chapter 8.

9   Unscrew the retaining ring and detach the speedometer cable from the instrument panel **(see illustration)**.

10   Undo the screw and detach the speedometer cable from its drive unit.

11   Free the cable from any clips or ties securing it and remove it from the motorcycle, noting its correct routing.

Speedometer drive unit - G through K models

12   Refer to Section 14 of Chapter 7.

Speedometer drive unit - L through P models

13   Undo the screw and detach the speedometer cable from its drive unit.

14   Unscrew the two bolts and withdraw the speedometer drive unit from the front sprocket cover. Note the presence of the speedometer drive hexagon.

Speedometer drive unit (speed sensor) - R models

Refer to illustration 14.15

15   Unscrew the two bolts and withdraw the speedometer drive/speed sensor from the front sprocket cover **(see illustration)**. Note the presence of the speedometer drive hexagon.

16   Remove the seat and rear fairing as described in Chapter 8 and trace the sensor wiring from the unit back up to its connector, releasing the wiring from any clips or ties securing it. The speed sensor connector is the white 3-pin wiring connector situated immediately above the fuel pump.

17   Withdraw the speed sensor from the motorcycle.

Installation

Instrument panel

18   Maneuver the instrument panel into position. Connect the panel wiring connectors and seat the panel on the fairing stay.

19   Install the mounting nuts and tighten them securely.

20   Where fitted, connect the speedometer cable to the panel (see Step 23 below).

21   On L models onward, install the instrument panel covers; tighten the screws securely.

22   Install the upper fairing assembly as described in Chapter 8.

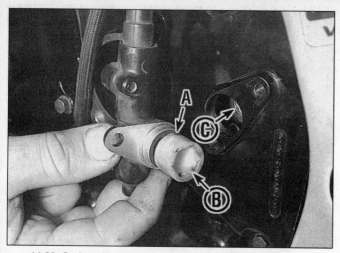

14.28 On installing speedometer drive unit (A), L through P models, engage drive hexagon (B) on front sprocket bolt's head (C)

Speedometer cable - G through P models

23   Attach the speedometer cable to the instrument panel and securely tighten its retaining ring.
24   Ensure the cable is correctly routed and secured by any clips or ties provided.
25   Make sure that the O-ring is fitted to the cable's lower end, then connect the cable to the drive unit, aligning the inner cable slot with the drive dog, and securely tighten its retaining screw.
26   On completion check that the cable doesn't cause the steering to bind or interfere with any other components.

Speedometer drive unit - G through K models

27   Refer to Section 14 of Chapter 7.

Speedometer drive unit - L through P models

Refer to illustration 14.28

28   Install the speedometer drive hexagon on the drive unit and fit the assembly to the front sprocket cover, engaging the drive hexagon on the front sprocket bolt's head **(see illustration)**. Tighten the two bolts securely.
29   Make sure that the O-ring is fitted to the speedometer cable's lower end, then connect the cable to the drive unit, aligning the inner cable slot with the drive dog, and securely tighten its retaining screw.

Speedometer drive unit (speed sensor) - R models

30   Install the speedometer drive hexagon on the speed sensor and fit the assembly to the front sprocket cover, engaging the drive hexagon on the front sprocket bolt's head. Tighten the two bolts to the specified torque setting.
31   Ensure the wiring is correctly routed up to the connector and retained by the clips and ties.
32   Securely reconnect the wiring connector and check the operation of the speedometer.
33   Install the rear fairing and seat as described in Chapter 8.

15   Meters and gauges - check and replacement

Warning: *To prevent the risk of short circuits, the battery negative (-) cable should be disconnected before any of the motorcycle's other electrical components are disturbed. Don't forget to reconnect the cable securely once work is finished.*

Check

Temperature gauge

1   The temperature gauge check is described in Chapter 3.

Speedometer

2   Special instruments are required properly to check the operation of these meters. Take the machine to a Honda dealer service department or other qualified repair shop for diagnosis.

Tachometer

3   Remove the upper fairing assembly as described in Chapter 8.
4   Trace the wiring from the back of the tachometer to the instrument panel connector and use a voltmeter to check for battery voltage (when the ignition is switched ON) across the tachometer wire terminals. On G through K models check between the black/brown and green wires; on L models onward, check between the yellow/green and green (see the *wiring diagrams* at the end of this book). If there's no voltage present, check the wire between the instrument panel and fuse box.
5   If the supply checks out okay, check the yellow/green wire to the spark unit for continuity, open circuits etc. **Caution:** *Disconnect the spark unit connector(s) before making this test, otherwise you may damage the unit if improper test equipment is used.*
6   If the wiring is okay, the tachometer is faulty and must be replaced.

Fuel reserve warning light - G and H models

7   The circuit consists of the sensor unit mounted in the bottom of the fuel tank and the warning light mounted in the instrument panel. If the system malfunctions check first that the bulb is sound, that the battery is fully charged and that all fuses are in good condition.
8   Disconnect the sensor unit's wiring; if necessary drain and remove the fuel tank as described in Chapter 4.
9   Using a length of insulated jumper wire, bridge the terminals of the main harness side of the sensor unit's wiring connector, then switch the ignition ON; the warning light should come on.
10   If the light fails to come on, remove the upper fairing assembly as described in Chapter 8 and use a voltmeter to check for battery voltage (when the ignition is switched ON) at the light's black/brown wire. If there's no voltage present, check the wire between the instrument panel and fuse box.
11   If the supply checks out okay, check the gray/black wire to the sensor unit for continuity, open circuits, etc. and the green/black wire from the unit for a good ground (earth).
12   If the bulb and wiring are okay, the sensor unit is faulty and must be replaced.

Fuel gauge - UK J through P models

13   The circuit consists of the sensor unit mounted in the bottom of the fuel tank and the gauge assembly mounted in the instrument panel. If the system malfunctions check first that the battery is fully charged and that all fuses are in good condition.
14   Disconnect the sensor unit's wiring; if necessary drain and remove the fuel tank as described in Chapter 4.
15   Using a length of insulated jumper wire, bridge the terminals of the main harness side of the sensor unit's wiring connector, then switch the ignition ON; the gauge needle should immediately move across to the 'F' position.
16   If the gauge fails to respond, remove the upper fairing assembly as described in Chapter 8 and use a voltmeter to check for battery voltage (when the ignition is switched ON) at the black/brown wire. If there's no voltage present, check the wire between the instrument panel and fuse box.
17   If the supply checks out okay, check the gray/black wire to the sensor unit for continuity, open circuits, etc. and the green/black wire from the unit for a good ground (earth).
18   If the wiring seems okay, the gauge or sensor unit is faulty; the sensor unit can be eliminated by removing it (see Steps 46 and 47 below) and using an ohmmeter to measure its resistance with the float fully raised (a resistance of 4 to 10 ohms should be measured) and then with the float fully lowered (a resistance of 90 to 100 ohms should be measured); the resistance values should increase smoothly as the float is moved from one position to the other. If the resistances recorded are significantly different, the sensor unit is faulty and must

9

15.42 View of underside of instrument panel, L through P models

A   Wiring clamp screw
B   Speedometer mounting screws
C   Tachometer terminal screws
D   Tachometer mounting screws
E   Fuel gauge terminal screws
F   Temperature gauge terminal screws

be replaced.
19   If the wiring and sensor unit are sound, the gauge is be faulty and must be replaced.

Fuel gauge and fuel reserve warning light - US L to P models, all R models

20   The circuit consists of the sensor unit mounted in the bottom of the fuel tank and the gauge assembly and warning light mounted in the instrument panel. Note that the bulb is controlled by the indicator light check unit so that it comes on (as a check of its function) for a few seconds and then goes out (unless, of course the fuel level is very low) whenever the ignition is switched ON. If the system malfunctions check first that the bulb is sound, that the battery is fully charged and that all fuses are in good condition.
21   To check the operation of the fuel gauge, remove the sensor unit (see Steps 46 and 47 below), reconnect its wiring and switch the ignition ON; the gauge needle should move in response to the movement of the sensor unit's float arm.
22   If the gauge fails to respond, use an ohmmeter to measure the sensor unit's resistance with the float fully raised (a resistance of 4 to 10 ohms should be measured) and then with the float fully lowered (a resistance of 90 to 100 ohms should be measured); the resistance values should increase smoothly as the float is moved from one position to the other. If the resistances recorded are significantly different, the sensor unit is faulty and must be replaced.
23   If the sensor unit seems okay, remove the upper fairing assembly as described in Chapter 8 and use a voltmeter to check for battery voltage (when the ignition is switched ON) at the black/brown wire. If there's no voltage present, check the wire between the instrument panel and fuse box.
24   If the supply checks out okay, check the gray/black wire to the sensor unit for continuity, open circuits, etc. and the green/black wire from the gauge and sensor unit for a good ground (earth).
25   If the sensor unit and wiring seem okay, the gauge is faulty and must be replaced.
26   To check the fuel reserve warning light circuit, if the light does not go out, first ensure that there is sufficient fuel (4.5 liters/1.2 US gal on L through P models, 3.3 liters/0.87 US gal/0.73 Imp gal on R models) in the tank to cover the reserve sensor. Next disconnect the sensor unit's wiring; if necessary drain and remove the fuel tank as described in Chapter 4. Use a voltmeter to check for battery voltage across the terminals of the reserve sensor's wires (see the *wiring diagrams* at the

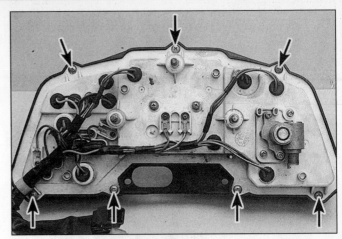

15.43 Undo the screws (arrows) to remove the front of the instrument panel

end of this book). If there's no voltage present, check the wire between the instrument panel, sensor unit and fuse box; if voltage is present, the sensor unit is faulty and must be replaced.
27   If the fuel reserve warning light does not come on and the bulb is okay, disconnect the sensor unit's wiring; if necessary drain and remove the fuel tank as described in Chapter 4. Use a voltmeter to check for battery voltage across the terminals of the reserve sensor's wires (see the *wiring diagrams* at the end of this book); if voltage is present, the sensor unit is faulty and must be replaced, although it is worth checking first that all connections are good. If there's no voltage present, check the wire between the instrument panel, sensor unit and fuse box until the fault is found and corrected.

Speedometer drive (speed sensor) - R models

28   Remove the seat and rear fairing as described in Chapter 8 and trace the sensor wiring from the unit back up to its connector, the white 3-pin wiring connector situated immediately above the fuel pump.
29   The circuit consists of the sensor unit mounted on the front sprocket cover and the speedometer mounted in the instrument panel. If the system malfunctions check first that the battery is fully charged and that the wiring (particularly the connections) and all fuses are in good condition.
30   To check the circuit, use a voltmeter to check for battery voltage across the terminals of the black and green wires at the sensor's connector, making the check with the connector remaining connected and with the ignition switched ON; if there's no voltage present, check carefully the condition of the connector's pins (looking for signs of loose fit or poor contact). If that does not reveal the fault, check carefully for open circuits in the black, black/brown or green/black wires (see the *wiring diagrams* at the end of this book).
31   If voltage is present, remove the upper fairing assembly as described in Chapter 8, then unscrew the instrument panel mounting nuts and lift the assembly without disconnecting its wires until you can see the printed circuit on the back of the panel. Trace each printed circuit track from the black/brown and green/black wires (in the panel's green 10-pin connector) to their respective terminal screws on the back of the speedometer; check for battery voltage between the screws when the ignition is switched ON. If there's no voltage present, check carefully the condition of the green 10-pin connector's pins (looking for signs of loose fit or poor contact). If that does not reveal the fault, check carefully for open circuits in the black/brown or green/black wires or for a fault in the printed circuit itself.
32   If voltage is present, check for continuity in the pink wire between the speed sensor and the speedometer, tracing the wire through both connectors and along its printed circuit track to the terminal screw on the back of the speedometer. If continuity is not found at any point, trace and rectify the fault, bearing in mind the possibilities of an open

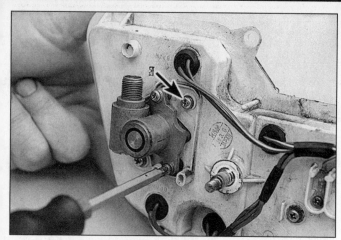

15.44a Speedometer right-angle drive is retained by two screws (other arrowed) . . .

15.44b . . . withdraw O-ring beneath . . .

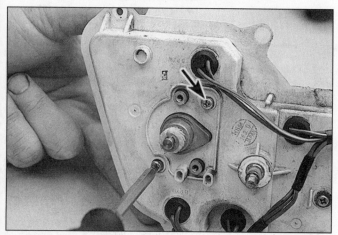

15.44c . . . and unscrew meter retaining screws (other arrowed) . .

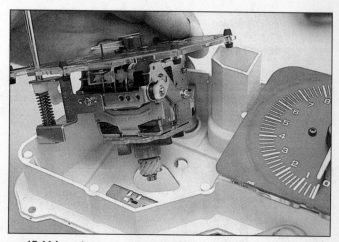

15.44d . . . to remove speedometer assembly - L through P models shown

circuit in the pink wire or of a fault in the printed circuit itself.

33   If the pink wire is sound, connect a voltmeter between the terminals of the green/black and pink wires in the back of the instrument panel's green 10-pin connector, making the check with the connector remaining connected and with the ignition switched ON. Check for an output signal from the speed sensor while the rear wheel is turned (fairly fast) by hand. If the sensor is operating correctly a fluctuating (ON/OFF, from 0 to 4.5 - 5.3 volts) voltage should be measured, the rate of repetition corresponding to the rate at which the wheel is turned.

34   If the output signal is correct, the speedometer is faulty; if it is incorrect, the speed sensor is faulty. If either unit is faulty, it must be replaced.

Clock

35   To check the clock's circuit, first remove the fairing's left upper inner panel (J and K models) or the upper fairing assembly (all later models) as described in Chapter 8.

36   On J through P models, disconnect the clock's white 4-pin wiring connector, then use a voltmeter to check for battery voltage on the main harness side between the brown/white and green wires (ignition and lighting switches ON), between the black and green wires (ignition switch ON or lighting switch OFF) and between the red (or red/green) and green wires (ignition switch ON). Specific details are not available for R models, but a similar test sequence can be followed, referring to the *wiring diagrams* at the end of this book.

37   If battery voltage is not found at any point, check for short circuits or poor connections on the wire(s) affected.

38   If battery voltage is found in spite of a non-functioning clock, check the connector for poor or loose contacts; if the clock still does not work, it is faulty and must be replaced.

39   If the clock is unable to reset, even though the ignition is switched ON, check the black wire for short circuits or a blown fuse; if the clock still does not work, it is faulty and must be replaced.

Replacement

Instrument panel meters and gauges

Refer to illustrations 15.42, 15.43, 15.44a, 15.44b, 15.44c and 15.44d

40   Remove the panel from the motorcycle as described in Section 14.

41   Invert the panel onto a layer of clean cloth (to avoid damaging its surface).

42   Make written notes of the location of all components such as wiring clamps, wire terminal screws, bulb holders, etc.; note that the location of each bulbholder is indicated by the wire colors of that bulb being molded into the instrument panel casing **(see illustration)**.

43   Note also the number and type of screw or nut securing each component. To remove a component (all are fragile) undo its terminal screws (note the correct fitted positions of the wires) and any mounting fasteners before removing the retaining screws and separating the panel pieces **(see illustration)**.

44   Undo the screws and lift the meters and gauges out of the casing as required. The accompanying photographic sequence shows speedometer removal on L through P models - a similar procedure applies to the instrument panel components for all other models **(see illustrations)**.

9

15.51a **Invert the instrument panel and undo the two screws (other arrowed) . . .**

15.51b **. . . to release the clock from the panel**

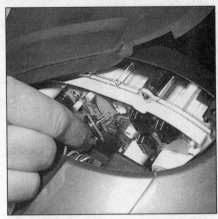

16.1 **Some bulbs may be removed from the instrument panel without disturbing the upper fairing - here (R model) high beam indicator bulb has been reached by removing windshield and folding back rubber cover . . .**

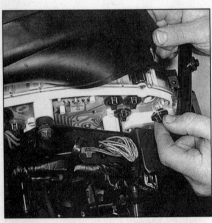

16.2 **. . . if this is not possible, upper fairing must be removed to allow access to back of panel - note bayonet-fixing bulbholders used with printed circuit . . .**

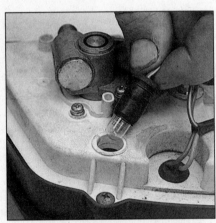

16.3a **. . . and rubber plug fixing bulbholders used on earlier type - with relevant bulbholder removed from panel . . .**

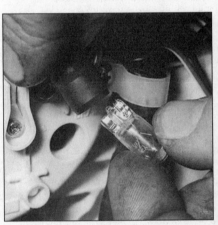

16.3b **. . . pull the bulb out of its holder**

45   Install the components by reversing the removal sequence. Use the notes made on disassembly to ensure that all are correctly installed and all wires correctly reconnected. Take care not to overtighten the screws or nuts as the components are very fragile and can be easily damaged.

Fuel level sensor unit - all models

46   Drain and remove the fuel tank as described in Chapter 4.

47   Unscrew the four retaining nuts and withdraw the sensor unit from the tank's underside. Note the sealing O-ring; to prevent fuel leakage onto the engine, this must be replaced if there is the slightest doubt about its condition.

48   Installation is the reverse of the removal procedure; be careful not to bend the float arm, install a new O-ring and tighten securely and evenly the retaining nuts. Check carefully that there are no fuel leaks when the tank is refilled.

Speedometer drive (speed sensor) - R models

49   Refer to Section 14.

Clock

Refer to illustrations 15.51a and 15.51b

50   Remove the panel from the motorcycle as described in Section 14.

51   On J through P models, invert the panel on to a layer of clean cloth (to avoid damaging its surface), then undo the two screws and

withdraw the clock from the panel **(see illustrations)**.

52   On R models, the instrument panel must be disassembled as outlined above to allow the two parts of the clock assembly to be withdrawn; to not attempt to separate the two parts, which are available only as a single replacement part.

53   Installation is the reverse of the removal procedure.

16   Instrument and warning light bulbs - replacement

Refer to illustrations 16.1, 16.2, 16.3a, 16.3b and 16.4

1   Depending on the size of your hands and the actual location of the bulb to be replaced, it may be possible to reach the bulbholder by reaching up to the back of the instrument panel from underneath or in from above **(see illustration)**. Remove the fairing lower cover, its (upper) inner panel(s) or the windshield, according to model and circumstances - see Chapter 8, if necessary.

2   If you cannot reach the bulbholder concerned by these means, remove the upper fairing as described in Chapter 8 **(see illustration)**.

3   To remove the bulb, if it is held in a large black rubber bulbholder, pull the relevant bulbholder out of the back of the panel; if the bulbholder is a smaller black plastic unit (usually used where a printed circuit is evident on the back of the panel), turn it counterclockwise

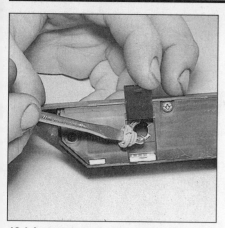

16.4 Instrument panel must be removed to reach back of clock for access to (bayonet-fixing) bulbholder through small flap

17.3 Oil pressure switch (arrow) is screwed into the top of the crankcase on the right side

18.7 Unscrewing ignition (main) switch Torx screws

(anti-clockwise) to release it and withdraw it. Pull the bulb out of its holder **(see illustrations)**. If the socket contacts are dirty or corroded, they should be scraped clean and sprayed with electrical contact cleaner before a new bulb is installed.

4 If replacing the clock's bulb on L through P models, remove the instrument panel (see Section 14) and open the flap in the back of the clock for access to the bulbholder **(see illustration)**.

5 Carefully push the new bulb into position, then install the bulbholder into the rear of the panel. Note that the location of each bulbholder is indicated by the wire colors of that bulb being molded into the instrument panel casing.

6 Installation is the reverse of the removal procedure.

17 Oil pressure switch - check and replacement

Warning: *To prevent the risk of short circuits, the battery negative (-) cable should be disconnected before any of the motorcycle's other electrical components are disturbed. Don't forget to reconnect the cable securely once work is finished.*

Check

Refer to illustration 17.3

1 Before checking the electrical circuit, check the bulb (see Section 16) and fuses (see Section 5).

2 Remove the right lower (or middle, according to model) fairing panel as described in Chapter 8 to reach the oil pressure switch, which is screwed into the top of the crankcase.

3 Peel back the rubber cover then undo the screw and detach the wiring connector from the switch **(see illustration)**.

4 With the wire detached and the ignition switched ON the light should be out. If it is illuminated, the wire between the switch and instrument panel must be grounded (earthed) at some point.

5 Ground (earth) the wire on the crankcase and check that the warning light comes on. If the light does come on, either the switch is defective or the engine oil pressure is low. Perform an oil pressure check as described in Chapter 2. If the oil pressure checks out okay the switch is defective and must be replaced.

6 If the light does not come on when the wire is grounded (earthed), check for voltage at the wire terminal using a test light. If there's no voltage present, check the wire between the switch, the instrument panel and fuse box for continuity (see the *wiring diagrams* at the end of this book).

Replacement

7 Detach the wire from the switch as described above in Steps 2 and 3.

8 Unscrew the switch from the top of the crankcase.

9 Ensure the switch threads are clean and dry and apply a thin coat of suitable sealant to the threads, leaving clear the end 3 to 4 mm (0.1 to 0.2 inch) next to the switch's tip.

10 Screw the switch into the top of the crankcase and tighten it to the specified torque setting.

11 Attach the wire, tightening its screw securely, then seat the rubber cover correctly over the switch.

12 Check the operation of the oil pressure warning light then install the fairing panel(s) as described in Chapter 8.

18 Ignition (main) switch - check, removal and installation

Warning: *To prevent the risk of short circuits, the battery negative (-) cable should be disconnected before any of the motorcycle's other electrical components are disturbed. Don't forget to reconnect the cable securely once work is finished.*

Check

1 Disconnect the switch wiring connector as described in Step 4 or 5, according to model.

2 Using an ohmmeter, check the continuity of the terminal pairs (see the *wiring diagrams* at the end of this book). Continuity should exist between the terminals connected by a solid line when the switch is in the indicated position.

3 If the switch fails any of the tests, replace it.

Removal

Refer to illustration 18.7

4 On G through K models, remove the fairing (upper) inner panel (see Chapter 8 if necessary). Trace the wiring back from the base of the switch, releasing it from any clips, and disconnect it at the wiring connector clipped in the bracket inside the fairing.

5 On L models onward, remove the upper fairing (see Chapter 8 if necessary). Trace the wiring back from the base of the switch, releasing it from any clips, and disconnect it at the wiring connector clipped to the front of the fairing stay/instrument panel.

6 Remove the top triple clamp as described in Chapter 1, Section 23.

7 Undo the two bolts securing the switch to the underside of the top triple clamp and remove the switch. These bolts may be of the shear-head type which must be drilled out (preferably, mount the triple clamp upside down in a pillar drill, drill off the remains of the bolt heads until the switch can be withdrawn, then extract the remains of each bolt by unscrewing it with a pair of self-locking pliers or similar) or they will have Torx-type heads (requiring a Torx key of suitable size to unscrew them); finally, they may be conventional hexagon-headed bolts which can be unscrewed with a spanner **(see illustration)**. If

9

shear-head bolts are encountered, obtain new replacements for reassembly.

8   For some models, it is possible to obtain the switch's contact base as a separate item. If this is the case, insert the key and turn it to between the ON and OFF positions, unscrew the three screws securing the contact base to the lock cylinder and press in the lugs in their slots to release the contact base from the lock cylinder.

Installation

9   If removed, install the contact base to the switch following the reverse of the removal procedure.

10   Thoroughly clean the switch bolts and apply a few drops of suitable locking compound to them. Install the bolts and tighten them securely, to the specified torque setting (where applicable). If the bolts are of the shear-head type, tighten each until its head shears off.

11   Install the top triple clamp as described in Chapter 1. For full details of the procedures involved, refer to Chapter 6; tighten all bolts and nuts to the specified torque settings.

12   Secure the switch wiring in position with any relevant clips or ties. Pass the connector through the bracket or fairing stay and reconnect it.

13   Install the fairing or inner panel as described in Chapter 8.

20.3 Each handlebar switch is retained by two screws

19   Handlebar switches - check

Warning: *To prevent the risk of short circuits, the battery negative (-) cable should be disconnected before any of the motorcycle's other electrical components are disturbed. Don't forget to reconnect the cable securely once work is finished.*

1   Generally speaking, the switches are reliable and trouble-free. Most troubles, when they do occur, are caused by dirty or corroded contacts, but wear and breakage of internal parts is a possibility that should not be overlooked. If breakage does occur, the entire switch and related wiring harness will have to be replaced with a new one, since individual parts are not usually available.

2   The switches can be checked for continuity with a multimeter set to the resistance function (ohmmeter) or a continuity test light. Always disconnect the battery negative (-) cable, which will prevent the possibility of a short circuit, before making the checks.

3   On G through K models, remove the fairing (upper) inner panel (see Chapter 8 if necessary). Trace the wiring back from the switch, releasing it from any clips, and disconnect it at the wiring connector clipped in the bracket inside the fairing.

4   On L models onward, remove the upper fairing (see Chapter 8 if necessary). Trace the wiring back from the switch, releasing it from any clips, and disconnect it at the wiring connector clipped to the front of the fairing stay/instrument panel.

5   Using the multimeter or test light, check for continuity between the terminals of the switch harness with the switch in the various positions (see the *wiring diagrams* at the end of this book).

6   If the continuity check indicates a problem exists, refer to Section 20, remove the switch and spray the switch contacts with electrical contact cleaner. If they are accessible, the contacts can be scraped clean with a knife or polished with crocus cloth. If switch components are damaged or broken, it will be obvious when the switch is disassembled.

20   Handlebar switches - removal and installation

Warning: *To prevent the risk of short circuits, the battery negative (-) cable should be disconnected before any of the motorcycle's other electrical components are disturbed. Don't forget to reconnect the cable securely once work is finished.*

Removal

Refer to illustration 20.3

1   On G through K models, remove the fairing (upper) inner panel (see Chapter 8 if necessary). Trace the wiring back from the base of

the switch, releasing it from any clips, and disconnect it at the wiring connector clipped in the bracket inside the fairing.

2   On L models onward, remove the upper fairing (see Chapter 8 if necessary). Trace the wiring back from the base of the switch, releasing it from any clips, and disconnect it at the wiring connector clipped to the front of the fairing stay/instrument panel.

3   Unscrew the two handlebar switch screws and free the switch from the handlebar **(see illustration)**.

4   On the left handlebar, disconnect the choke cable from its lever, then unscrew the choke cable from the lower half of the switch and remove the switch.

5   On the right handlebar, disconnect the throttle cables from the carburetors then free the cables from the switch as described in Section 10 of Chapter 4.

6   Remove the switch.

Installation

7   Installation is a reversal of the removal procedure, noting the following points:

a) *Reconnect the throttle cables to the twistgrip or the choke cable to the lever, as appropriate.*

b) *Fit the switch lower half to the handlebar, locating its peg in the handlebar hole. Fit the upper half of the switch and securely tighten the screws - always tighten the front screw first, until the switch halves mate properly, then the rear screw. Don't overtighten the rear screw in an attempt to close the gap between the switch halves at the rear; you will only break the switch.*

c) *Adjust the throttle cables as described in Chapter 1.*

d) *Check the choke cable operation and, if necessary, adjust as described in Chapter 1.*

e) *Ensure that the switch wiring is correctly routed and secured as noted on removal.*

f) *Install the fairing or inner panel as described in Chapter 8.*

21   Neutral switch - check and replacement

Warning: *To prevent the risk of short circuits, the battery negative (-) cable should be disconnected before any of the motorcycle's other electrical components are disturbed. Don't forget to reconnect the cable securely once work is finished.*

Check

Refer to illustration 21.2

1   In addition to operating the warning light in the instrument panel, this switch is part of the starter safety circuit **(see illustration 1.3)**

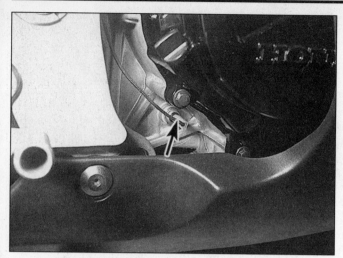

21.2 Neutral switch (arrow) is screwed into right side of crankcase, immediately beneath engine oil filler

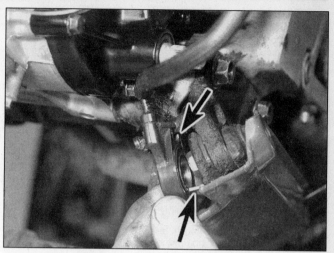

22.11 On installation ensure the sidestand switch lug engages the stand hole and the switch recess engages the retaining pin (arrows)

which prevents the starter motor operating whilst the transmission is in gear unless the clutch lever is pulled in. It is also part of the ignition cut-out safety system which cuts the ignition if the engine is running with the transmission in gear and the sidestand down. Before checking the electrical circuit, check the bulb (see Section 16) and fuses (see Section 5).

2   The switch is screwed into the right side of the crankcase, immediately beneath the engine oil filler **(see illustration)**. If necessary, remove the (right) lower fairing panel(s), as described in Chapter 8, to reach the switch. It may be necessary (if not already done) to remove also the fairing middle panel when tracing wiring faults. On G through K models, the switch's wiring connector is accessible only once the right side cover has been removed.

3   Disconnect the wiring connector from the switch and shift the transmission into neutral.

4   With the wire detached and the ignition switched ON, the neutral light should be out. If not, the wire between the switch and instrument panel must be grounded (earthed) at some point.

5   Ground (earth) the wire on the crankcase and check that the neutral light comes on. If the light does come on, the switch is defective.

6   If the light does not come on when the wire is grounded (earthed), check for voltage at the wire terminal using a test light. If there's no voltage present, check the wire between the switch, the instrument panel and fuse box (see the *wiring diagrams* at the end of this book).

Replacement

7   If necessary, remove the (right) lower fairing panel(s), as described in Chapter 8, to reach the switch.

8   Disconnect the wiring connector from the switch.

9   Unscrew the switch from the crankcase. Recover the sealing washer and plug the switch opening to minimize oil loss whilst the switch is removed.

10   Clean the threads of the switch and fit a new sealing washer to it.

11   Remove the plug from the crankcase and install the switch. Tighten the switch to the specified torque setting then reconnect the wiring connector.

12   Check the operation of the neutral light.

13   Check the oil level as described in Chapter 1 and top up if necessary.

22 Sidestand switch - check and replacement

Warning: *To prevent the risk of short circuits, the battery negative (-) cable should be disconnected before any of the motorcycle's other*

electrical components are disturbed. Don't forget to reconnect the cable securely once work is finished.

Check

1   In addition to operating the warning light (J models onward) in the instrument panel, this switch is part of the starter safety circuit **(see illustration 1.3)** which prevents the starter motor operating whilst the transmission is in gear unless the sidestand is up. It is also part of the ignition cut-out safety system which cuts the ignition if the engine is running with the transmission in gear and the sidestand down. Before checking any electrical circuit, check the bulb (see Section 16) and fuses (see Section 5).

2   To reach the switch wiring connector remove the seat and either the left side cover or the rear fairing, according to model, as described in Chapter 8. The sidestand switch connector is the green 3-pin wiring connector situated immediately above the fuel pump.

3   Disconnect the wiring connector and check the operation of the switch using an ohmmeter or continuity test light.

4   Set the meter to the ohms x 1 scale and connect the meter between the yellow/black and green wires on the switch side of the wiring connector. With the sidestand down (extended) there should be continuity between the terminals, and with the stand up there should be no continuity (infinite resistance).

5   Connect the meter between the green/white and green wires on the switch side of the connector. With the sidestand up there should be continuity between the terminals, and with the stand down there should be no continuity (infinite resistance).

6   If the switch does not perform as expected, it is defective and must be replaced.

7   If the switch checks out okay, check the wiring between the wiring connector, instrument panel and fuse box (see the *wiring diagrams* at the end of this book).

Replacement

Refer to illustration 22.11

8   Disconnect the switch wiring connector as described above in Step 2.

9   Work back along the switch wiring, freeing it from any clips and ties, and noting its correct routing. Access to the wiring can be improved by removing the left lower or middle fairing panel(s) as described in Chapter 8.

10   Unscrew the bolt securing the switch to the sidestand mounting bracket, then remove the switch.

11   Fit the new switch to the rear of the sidestand bracket making sure the switch lug engages the hole in the sidestand, and the switch recess engages with the retaining pin **(see illustration)**. Install the

9

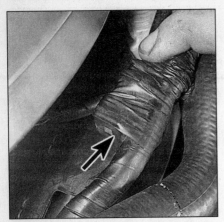

23.2 Clutch switch diode is plugged into main wiring harness, on right side - L through P models shown here

24.2 Clutch switch (arrow) is mounted on the underside of the master cylinder

25.4 Horn mounting bolts (one arrowed, other hidden) on bottom triple clamp

switch bolt and tighten it to the specified torque setting.

12 Ensure the wiring is correctly routed up to the connector and retained by the clips and ties.

13 Securely reconnect the wiring connector and check the operation of the warning light.

14 Install the rear fairing, side cover, seat and, if necessary, the fairing panel as described in Chapter 8.

23 Clutch switch diode - check and replacement

Warning: *To prevent the risk of short circuits, the battery negative (-) cable should be disconnected before any of the motorcycle's other electrical components are disturbed. Don't forget to reconnect the cable securely once work is finished.*

Refer to illustration 23.2

1 The diode is part of the starter safety circuit **(see illustration 1.3)** which prevents the starter motor operating whilst the transmission is in gear unless the clutch lever is pulled in. It is also part of the ignition cut-out safety system which cuts the ignition if the engine is running with the transmission in gear and the sidestand down. If either circuit is faulty, first check the fuses (see Section 5).

2 The diode is plugged into the main wiring harness clipped on the right of the frame. To reach the diode **(see also illustrations 3.2a and 6.3b)** remove the right side cover, the right lower (or middle) fairing panel or the upper fairing assembly, according to model, as described in Chapter 8 **(see illustration).**

3 Unplug the diode from the wiring harness and using a multimeter set to the resistance scale (ohmmeter) or a continuity test light, check for continuity between the terminals of the diode. Transpose the meter probes and check for continuity in the opposite direction. If the diode is serviceable there should be continuity in one direction (indicated by the arrow on the diode) and no continuity (infinite resistance) in the other. If not, the diode must be replaced.

4 If the clutch switch diode checks out okay, check the other components in the starter safety circuit (clutch switch, sidestand switch, neutral switch and starter relay switch) as described in the relevant sections of this Chapter. If all components check out fine, check the wiring between the various components (see the *wiring diagrams* at the end of this book).

5 Plug the clutch switch diode back into position and install the removed fairing panel(s) as described in Chapter 8.

24 Clutch switch - check and replacement

Warning: *To prevent the risk of short circuits, the battery negative (-) cable should be disconnected before any of the motorcycle's other*

electrical components are disturbed. Don't forget to reconnect the cable securely once work is finished.

Check

Refer to illustration 24.2

1 The switch is part of the starter safety circuit (see Section 1) which prevents the starter motor operating whilst the transmission is in gear unless the clutch lever is pulled in. It is also part of the ignition cut-out safety system which cuts the ignition if the engine is running with the transmission in gear and the sidestand down. If either circuit is faulty, first check the fuses (see Section 5).

2 The switch is mounted under the clutch master cylinder. To check it, disconnect the wiring connectors **(see illustration).** Using a multimeter set to the resistance scale (ohmmeter) or a continuity test light, check for continuity between the terminals of the switch with the lever pulled into the handlebar and no continuity (infinite resistance) with the lever released. If this is not the case, the switch is faulty and must be replaced.

3 If the switch checks out okay, check the other components in the starter safety circuit (clutch switch diode, neutral switch, sidestand switch and starter relay switch) as described in the relevant sections of this Chapter. If all components check out fine, check the wiring between the various components (see the *wiring diagrams* at the end of this book).

Replacement

4 Remove the mounting screw and unplug the wiring connectors from the switch.

5 Detach the switch from the master cylinder.

6 Installation is the reverse of the removal procedure.

25 Horn - check and replacement

Warning: *To prevent the risk of short circuits, the battery negative (-) cable should be disconnected before any of the motorcycle's other electrical components are disturbed. Don't forget to reconnect the cable securely once work is finished.*

Check

1 The horn is mounted on the bottom triple clamp. Remove the fairing lower center panel (where fitted) to reach the horn - see Chapter 8 if necessary.

2 Unplug the wiring connectors from the horn. Using two jumper wires, apply battery voltage directly to the horn's terminals. If the horn sounds, check the switch (see Section 19) and the wiring between the switch and the horn (see the *wiring diagrams* at the end of this book).

3 If the horn doesn't sound, replace it.

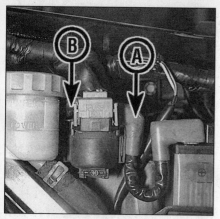

26.1 The starter relay switch is located behind the right side cover on G through K models - note battery cable connection (A) and starter motor lead connection (B)

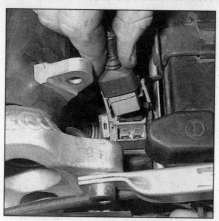

26.8a Disconnect relay switch's wiring connector by squeezing together plastic clips and pulling connector away . . .

26.8b . . . remove screws (arrows) to disconnect starter motor lead and battery cable . . .

26.9 . . . then withdraw starter relay switch from motorcycle - L models onward shown

Replacement

Refer to illustration 25.4

4   Unplug the wiring connectors from the horn then unbolt the horn from its mounting bracket and remove it **(see illustration)**.
5   Connect the wiring connectors to the new horn and securely tighten its mounting bolt(s).

26 Starter relay switch - check and replacement

Warning: *To prevent the risk of short circuits, the battery negative (-) cable should be disconnected before any of the motorcycle's other electrical components are disturbed. Don't forget to reconnect the cable securely once work is finished.*

Check

Refer to illustration 26.1

1   If the starter circuit is faulty, first check the fuses (see Section 5). The starter relay switch is located behind the right side cover next to the battery on G through K models, and under the seat in front of the battery on L models onward (see Chapter 8, if necessary) **(see illustration)**.
2   With the ignition switch ON, the engine kill switch in RUN and the transmission in neutral, press the starter button. The relay switch

should click.
3   If the relay switch doesn't click, switch the ignition OFF, then remove the relay, as described below, and test it as follows:
4   Set a multimeter to the ohms x 1 scale and connect it across the relay switch's starter motor lead and battery cable terminals. Using a fully-charged 12 volt battery and two insulated jumper wires, connect the positive (+) terminal of the battery to the yellow/red terminal of the relay, and the negative (-) terminal to the green/red terminal of the relay. At this point the relay switch should click and the multimeter read 0 ohms (continuity). If this is the case the relay switch is serviceable and the fault lies in the starter safety circuit (check the clutch switch diode, clutch switch, sidestand switch and neutral switch as described elsewhere in this Chapter), if the relay switch does not click when battery voltage is applied and indicates no continuity across its terminals, it is faulty and must be replaced.

Replacement

Refer to illustrations 26.8a, 26.8b and 26.9

5   On G through K models, remove the right side cover (see Chapter 8, if necessary).
6   On L models onward, remove the seat (see Chapter 8).
7   On all models, disconnect the battery terminals, remembering to disconnect the negative (-) terminal first.
8   Disconnect the relay switch's wiring connector by squeezing together the plastic clips and pulling the connector away. Peel back the rubber cover(s) then undo the two nuts or screws and disconnect the starter motor lead and battery cable from the relay switch **(see illustrations)**.
9   Remove the relay switch from the motorcycle **(see illustration)**.
10   Installation is the reverse of removal, ensuring that the terminal nuts or screws (according to model) are securely tightened. Connect the negative (-) terminal last when reconnecting the battery.

27 Starter motor - removal and installation

Warning: *To prevent the risk of short circuits, the battery negative (-) cable should be disconnected before any of the motorcycle's other electrical components are disturbed. Don't forget to reconnect the cable securely once work is finished.*

Removal

Refer to illustrations 27.3, 27.4 and 27.5

1   Drain the engine oil and unscrew the oil filter as described in Chapter 1. On early models, it may prove necessary to disconnect the oil cooler return line (undo its two bolts) from the front of the crankcase to provide sufficient clearance for the motor to be removed; refer to

9

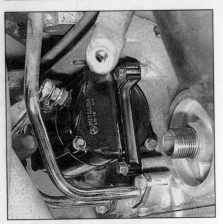

27.3 Peel back the rubber cover then undo the nut and disconnect the starter cable from the motor

27.4 Undo the starter motor bolts . . .

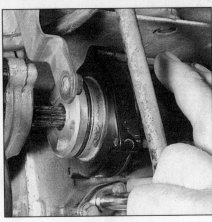

27.5 . . . and maneuver the motor out of the engine

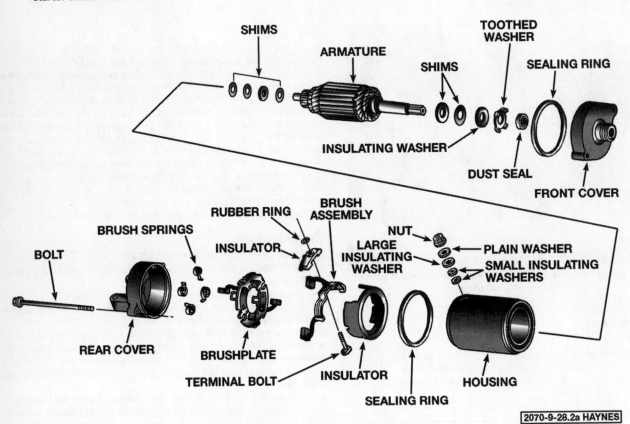

28.2a Exploded view of the starter motor

Chapter 2 if necessary.

2   On G through K models, remove the right side cover. On L models onward, remove the seat, unclip its retaining band and lift off the battery cover. On all models, disconnect the battery terminals, remembering to disconnect the negative (-) terminal first.

3   Peel back the rubber cover and unscrew the nut securing the lead to the motor (see illustration).

4   Unscrew the starter motor bolts (see illustration).

5   Slide the starter motor out from the crankcase and remove it from the machine (see illustration).

6   Inspect the O-ring on the end of the starter motor and replace it if necessary.

Installation

7   Make sure the O-ring is correctly seated in its groove and apply a smear of engine oil to it to aid installation.

8   Maneuver the motor into position and slide it into the crankcase.

9   Fit the bolts and tighten them securely.

10   Connect the lead and securely tighten the nut. Make sure the rubber cover is correctly seated over the terminal.

11   If it was disconnected, fit the oil cooler line to the union on the front of the crankcase, with a new O-ring to prevent oil leaks, and tighten the bolts as described in Chapter 2.

12   Install a new oil filter and refill the engine with clean oil as described in Chapter 1. Don't forget to recheck the oil level once the

28.2b Make alignment marks between the housing and end covers before disassembly

28.6 Unscrew the nut and remove the washers from the terminal bolt noting their correct fitted order

28.7 Lift the brush springs and slide the brushes out from their holders

28.8 Measuring brush length. Replace brushes if they are worn to less than the service limit

28.10a Inspect commutator segments for wear and test as described in text, checking for continuity between the commutator bars . . .

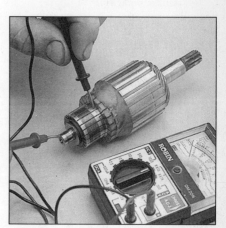

28.10b . . . and for no continuity (infinite resistance) between each commutator bar and the armature shaft

engine has been restarted and allowed to warm up to normal operating temperature.
13 Connect the battery; install the battery cover (L models onward).
14 Install the seat and/or side cover (as appropriate) and fairing panel(s) as described in Chapter 8.

28 Starter motor - disassembly, inspection and reassembly

Disassembly

Refer to illustrations 28.2a, 28.2b, 28.6 and 28.7
1 Remove the starter motor as described in Section 27.
2 Make alignment marks between the housing and end covers **(see illustrations)**.
3 Unscrew the two long bolts then remove the rear cover with its sealing ring from the motor. Remove the shim(s) from the rear end of the armature, noting their correct fitted locations.
4 Remove the front cover with its sealing ring from the motor. Recover the toothed washer from the cover and slide off the insulating washer and shim(s) from the front end of the armature, noting their correct fitted locations.
5 Withdraw the armature from the housing.
6 Noting the correct fitted location of each washer, unscrew the nut from the terminal bolt and remove the plain washer, the various

insulating washers and the rubber ring **(see illustration)**. Withdraw the terminal bolt and brushplate assembly from the housing and recover the insulator.
7 Lift the brush springs and slide the brushes out from their holders **(see illustration)**.

Inspection

Note: *Check carefully what component parts are available as replacements before starting overhaul procedures.*
Refer to illustrations 28.8, 28.10a and 28.10b
8 The parts of the motor that are most likely to require attention are the brushes. Measure the length of the brushes and compare the results to the brush length listed in this Chapter's Specifications **(see illustration)**. If any of the brushes are worn beyond the service limit, replace the brushplate assembly with a new one. If the brushes are not worn excessively, nor cracked, chipped, or otherwise damaged, they may be re-used.
9 Inspect the commutator for scoring, scratches and discoloration. The commutator can be cleaned and polished with crocus cloth, but do not use sandpaper or emery paper. After cleaning, wipe away any residue with a cloth soaked in electrical system cleaner or denatured alcohol.
10 Using an ohmmeter or a continuity test light, check for continuity between the commutator bars. Continuity should exist between each bar and all of the others **(see illustration)**. Also, check for continuity between the commutator bars and the armature shaft. There should be

9

28.14 Install the brushplate assembly and terminal bolt

28.15 Fit the terminal bolt nut and tighten it securely

28.17a Install shims on armature, then insert armature . . .

28.17b . . . and locate brushes on commutator

28.18 Fit toothed washer to front cover so that its teeth engage with cover ribs

28.19 Install shims and washers on armature making sure they are fitted in correct order

no continuity between the commutator and the shaft **(see illustration)**. If the checks indicate otherwise, the armature is defective.

11   Check the starter pinion gear for worn, cracked, chipped and broken teeth. If the gear is damaged or worn, replace the starter motor.

12   Inspect the insulating washers and front cover dust seal for signs of damage and replace if necessary.

Reassembly

Refer to illustrations 28.14, 28.15, 28.17a, 28.17b, 28.18, 28.19, 28.20, 28.21 and 28.22

13   Lift the brush springs and slide all the brushes back into position in their holders.

14   Fit the insulator to the housing and install the brushplate. Insert the terminal bolt through the brushplate and housing **(see illustration)**.

15   Slide the rubber ring and small insulating washer(s) onto the bolt, followed by the large insulating washer(s) and the plain washer. Fit the nut to the terminal bolt and tighten it securely **(see illustration)**.

16   Locate the brushplate assembly in the housing making sure its tab is correctly located in the housing slot.

17   Fit the shims to the armature shaft and insert the armature in the housing, locating the brushes on the commutator bars. Check that each brush is securely pressed against the commutator by its spring and is free to move easily in its holder **(see illustrations)**.

18   Fit the toothed washer to the front cover so that its teeth are correctly located with the cover ribs **(see illustration)**. Apply a smear of grease to the cover dust seal lip.

19   Slide the shim(s) onto the front end of the armature shaft then fit the insulating washer **(see illustration)**. Fit the sealing ring to the

housing and carefully slide the front cover into position, aligning the marks made on removal.

20   Ensure the brushplate inner tab is correctly located in the housing slot and fit the sealing ring to the housing **(see illustration)**.

21   Align the rear cover groove with the brushplate outer tab and install the cover **(see illustration)**.

22   Check the marks made on removal are correctly aligned then fit the long bolts and tighten them securely **(see illustration)**.

23   Install the starter motor as described in Section 27.

29   Charging system testing - general information and precautions

Warning: *To prevent the risk of short circuits, the battery negative (-) cable should be disconnected before any of the motorcycle's other electrical components are disturbed. Don't forget to reconnect the cable securely once work is finished.*

1   If the performance of the charging system is suspect, the system as a whole should be checked first, followed by testing of the individual components (the alternator stator coils and the voltage regulator/rectifier). **Note:** *Before beginning the checks, make sure the battery is fully charged and that all system connections are clean and tight.*

2   Checking the output of the charging system and the performance of the various components within the charging system requires the use of a multimeter (with voltage, current and resistance checking facilities).

3   When making the checks, follow the procedures carefully to

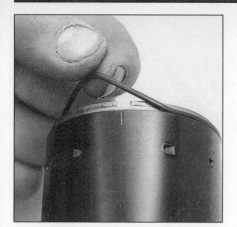

28.20 Fit the sealing ring . . .

28.21 . . . and install the rear cover aligning its groove with the brushplate outer tab

28.22 Align the marks made on removal and install the starter motor bolts

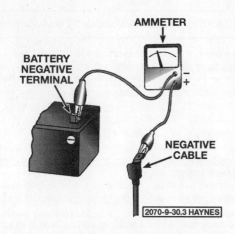

30.3 Checking the charging system leakage rate; connect meter as shown

prevent incorrect connections or short circuits, as irreparable damage to electrical system components may result if short circuits occur.

4　If a multimeter is not available, the job of checking the charging system be left to a dealer service department or a reputable motorcycle repair shop.

30　Charging system - leakage and output test

1　If the charging system of the machine is thought to be faulty, perform the following checks. First access the battery by removing the right side cover (see Chapter 8) on G through K models, or by removing the seat (see Chapter 8) then unclipping its retaining band and lifting off the battery cover on L models onward.

Leakage test

Refer to illustration 30.3

2　Turn the ignition switch OFF and disconnect the cable from the battery negative (-) terminal.

3　Set the multimeter to the mA (milli Amps) function and connect its negative (-) probe to the battery negative (-) terminal, and positive (+) probe to the disconnected negative (-) cable **(see illustration)**. With the meter connected like this the reading should not exceed 1.2 mA.

4　If the reading exceeds the specified amount it is likely that there is a short circuit in the wiring. Thoroughly check the wiring between the various components (see the *wiring diagrams* at the end of this book).

5　If the reading is below the specified amount, the leakage rate is satisfactory. Disconnect the meter and connect the negative (-) cable to the battery, tightening it securely, Check the alternator output as described below.

Output test

6　Start the engine and warm it up to normal operating temperature.

7　Allow the engine to idle and connect a multimeter set to the 0 to 20 volts scale (voltmeter) across the terminals of the battery (positive (+) cable to battery positive (+) terminal, negative (-) cable to battery negative (-) terminal). Slowly increase the engine speed to 5000 rpm and note the reading obtained. At this speed the voltage should be within the specified range (see the Specifications at the beginning of this Chapter). If the voltage is below this, check the alternator and regulator as described in the following Sections. **Note:** *Occasionally the condition may arise where the charging voltage is excessive. This condition is almost certainly due to a faulty regulator/rectifier which should be tested as described in Section 32.*

31　Alternator stator coils - check and replacement

Warning: *To prevent the risk of short circuits, the battery negative (-) cable should be disconnected before any of the motorcycle's other electrical components are disturbed. Don't forget to reconnect the cable securely once work is finished.*

Check

1　On G through K models, remove the left side cover; on L models onward, remove the fairing right middle panel - see Chapter 8 if necessary.

2　Disconnect the 3-pin block connector containing the yellow wires. Using a multimeter set to the ohms x 1 (ohmmeter) scale measure the resistance between each of the yellow wires on the alternator side of the connector, taking a total of three readings, then check for continuity between each terminal and ground (earth). If the stator coil windings are in good condition there should be no continuity (infinite resistance) between any of the terminals and ground (earth) and the three readings should be within the range shown in the Specifications at the beginning of this Chapter. If not, the alternator stator coil assembly is at fault and should be replaced. **Note:** *Before condemning the stator coils as trash, check the fault is not due to damaged wiring between the connector and coils.*

Replacement

Refer to illustration 31.4

3　Remove the left crankcase end cover as described in Chapter 2. On G through K models, remove also the alternator rotor.

9

31.4 Alternator stator coil bolts (A) and wiring clip bolt (B) - L models onward shown

32.1a The regulator/rectifier unit (mounting bolts arrowed) is mounted behind the left side cover on G through K models . . .

32.1b . . . and on the right, behind the rear fairing, on L models onward

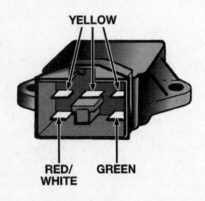

UNIT: KΩ

− +	RED/ WHITE	YELLOW 1	YELLOW 2	YELLOW 3	GREEN
RED/WHITE		∞	∞	∞	∞
YELLOW 1	0.5-10		30-500	30-500	10-200
YELLOW 2	0.5-10	30-500		30-500	10-200
YELLOW 3	0.5-10	30-500	30-500		10-200
GREEN	1-20	0.5-10	0.5-10	0.5-10	

2070-9-32.6 HAYNES

32.6 Regulator/rectifier unit terminal identification and resistance readings

4 Unscrew the bolt and remove the wiring clip **(see illustration)**.
5 Undo the four bolts and withdraw the stator coil assembly.
6 Remove all trace of sealant from the wiring grommet and apply a smear of fresh sealant to the grommet.
7 Clean the crankcase and bolt threads and apply a few drops of suitable locking compound to the stator bolts. Fit the stator coil assembly and tighten the bolts to the specified torque.
8 Ensure the grommet is correctly seated in the casing then install the clip and securely tighten its retaining screw.
9 Install the rotor (G through K models) and the cover as described in Section 23 of Chapter 2.

32 Regulator/rectifier unit - check and replacement

Warning: *To prevent the risk of short circuits, the battery negative (-) cable should be disconnected before any of the motorcycle's other electrical components are disturbed. Don't forget to reconnect the cable securely once work is finished.*

Check

Refer to illustrations 32.1a, 32.1b and 32.6
1 To reach the regulator/rectifier unit remove the seat and either the left side cover or the rear fairing, according to model, as described in Chapter 8 **(see illustrations)**.
2 Connect the negative (-) probe of a multimeter to a suitable ground (earth) point then switch the ignition switch ON and carry out the following checks.
3 Set the multimeter to the 0 to 20 dc volts setting then connect the meter positive (+) probe to the red/white terminal of the wiring connector and check for voltage. Full battery voltage should be present. Switch the ignition switch OFF.
4 Switch the multimeter to the resistance (ohms) scale. Disconnect the wire connector from the regulator/rectifier unit and make the following test on the wire harness side of the connector. Check for continuity between the green terminal of the wiring connector and ground (earth) then check the resistance between the yellow terminals of the wiring connector. There should be continuity between the green terminal and ground (earth) and a resistance reading of 0.1 to 2.0 ohms should be obtained between each pair of the yellow terminals of the wiring connector.
5 If the above checks do not provide the expected results check the wiring between the battery, regulator/rectifier and alternator (see the *wiring diagrams* at the end of this book).
6 If the wiring checks out, the regulator/rectifier unit is probably faulty. To check the unit, unplug its wire connector and remove it from the machine. Using a multimeter set to the appropriate resistance scale check the resistance between the various terminals of the regulator/rectifier **(see illustration)**. If the readings do not compare closely with those shown in the accompanying table the regulator/rectifier unit can be considered faulty. **Note:** *The use of certain multimeters could lead to false readings being obtained. Therefore, if the above check shows the regulator/rectifier unit to be faulty take the unit to a Honda dealer for confirmation of its condition before replacing it.*

Replacement

7 Remove the seat and either the left side cover or the rear fairing, according to model, as described in Chapter 8.
8 Disconnect the wiring connector from the rectifier/regulator unit

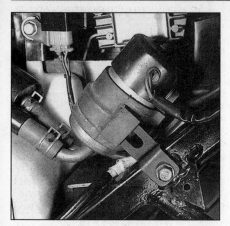

33.2a Fuel pump and fittings - G through K models

33.2b Fuel pump and fittings - L models onward

33.3a Fuel cut relay (A) - G through K models. Note regulator/rectifier unit mounting nuts (B)

then unbolt the unit.

9   On installation, tighten the bolts securely and connect the wiring connector. Install the side cover or rear fairing and seat (see Chapter 8, if necessary).

33 Fuel pump - check and replacement

Warning: *To prevent the risk of short circuits, the battery negative (-) cable should be disconnected before any of the motorcycle's other electrical components are disturbed. Don't forget to reconnect the cable securely once work is finished.*

Check

General

Refer to illustrations 33.2a, 33.2b, 33.3a and 33.3b

1   The fuel pump is controlled through the fuel cut relay so that it runs whenever the ignition is switched ON and the ignition is operative (i.e., only when the engine is turning over). As soon as the ignition is killed, the relay will cut out the fuel pump's electrical supply (so that there is no risk of fuel being sprayed out under pressure in the event of an accident).

2   The fuel pump is mounted on the subframe/seat rail left side, with the relay adjacent **(see illustrations)**.

3   To reach the fuel pump and the relay, remove the seat and either the left side cover or the rear fairing, according to model - refer to Chapter 8 if necessary **(see illustrations)**.

Circuit check

4   It should be possible to hear the pump running whenever the engine is turning over; either place your ear close beside the pump or feel it with your fingertips. If you can't feel or hear anything, check the circuit fuse (see Section 5). If this checks out okay, check the pump and relay (looking for loose or corroded connections, physical damage, etc.), and rectify as necessary; if the fault is intermittent, wiggle the wires and connectors to see whether the cause is due to loose connections or damaged wires - refer to Section 2.

5   If the circuit seems to be fine so far, switch the ignition OFF, unplug the relay's wiring connector and bridge the relay's black and black/blue terminals with a short length of insulated jumper wire. Switch the ignition ON; the pump should operate.

6   If the pump now works, the relay is probably at fault and should be eliminated by testing the wiring as described in the following Step.

7   Check for full battery voltage at the relay's black terminal with the ignition switch ON. If there is no battery voltage, there is a fault in the circuit between the relay and the fuse - trace and rectify the fault as outlined in Section 2; refer to the wiring diagrams at the end of this book. Next, test for continuity on the yellow/green wire (G through K

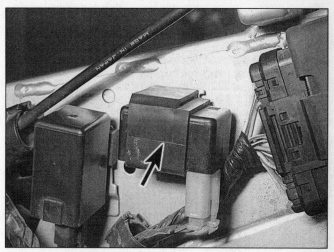

33.3b Fuel cut relay (arrow) - L models onward

models) or the red/yellow wire (L models onward) between the relay and the ignition system spark unit, then on the black/blue wire between the relay and the pump; if there is no continuity, trace and rectify the fault as outlined in Section 2.

8   If these wiring checks reveal no faults, replace the relay and try the circuit again.

9   If the relay and wiring check out okay so far and the pump still does not work, disconnect its wires. Using a fully-charged 12 volt battery and two insulated jumper wires, connect the positive (+) terminal of the battery to the pump's black/blue terminal and its negative (-) terminal to the pump's green terminal; the pump should operate. If the pump still shows no sign of life it must be replaced.

10   If both the relay and pump check out okay but the fault still exists, the wiring between the various components must be examined closely and tested for faults (see Section 2, and also Step 7 above); refer to the *wiring diagrams* at the end of this book. If no fault can be found, bear in mind the possibility of a defective ignition system spark unit (see Chapter 5); on G through K models, this may be confirmed by the presence of a tachometer fault.

Fuel cut relay

11   With the preliminary checks made that are outlined in Steps 4 through 6 above, the only definitive test of the relay is to substitute one that is known to be good. If you want to be more certain of the relay's condition before a replacement is purchased, make sure that all other possible faults have been eliminated first by testing the wiring as described in Step 9.

9

Fuel pump

Warning: *Gasoline (petrol) is extremely flammable, so take extra precautions when you work on any part of the fuel system. Don't smoke or allow open flames or bare light bulbs near the work area, and don't work in a garage where a natural gas-type appliance (such as a water heater or clothes dryer) is present. If you spill any fuel on your skin, rinse it off immediately with soap and water. When you perform any kind of work on the fuel system, wear safety glasses and have a fire extinguisher suitable for a Class B type fire (flammable liquids) on hand. Refer also to the warnings given in Section 1 of Chapter 4 before starting work.*

12   If the pump operates, but is thought to be supplying insufficient fuel, check first the fuel tank breather and the condition and routing of the lines between the tank, the pump and the filter (see Chapter 4). Check carefully for signs of kinked, trapped, pinched or blocked lines, and especially on models with the Evaporative emissions control system (EVAP), for defective tank breathing. Replace or clean the filter(s) as condition dictates (see Chapter 1).

13   The pump's output can be checked, if required, as follows: With the seat and the left side cover or the rear fairing, as applicable, removed (see Step 3 above), switch the ignition OFF and unplug the relay's wiring connector, then bridge the relay's black and black/blue terminals with a short length of insulated jumper wire. Wrapping a shop towel around the pump to soak up any spilt fuel, use a pair of pliers to slacken the clamp securing the pump's outlet hose (the one without the filter), disconnect the hose from the pump's stub and plug it to prevent the entry of dirt into the carburetors. Now connect a spare length of hose to the pump's outlet stub, directing it into a finely-graduated measuring vessel. Switch the ignition ON for exactly five seconds, then switch OFF. Measure the amount of fuel in the vessel and multiply by twelve to give the pump's fuel flow per minute; this should be 900 cc (30.43 US fl oz, 31.68 Imp fl oz).

14   If the pump's output is significantly less than the specified value, and the tank breather, fuel tap and filter(s) are known to be clear, then the pump must be replaced.

15   If the pump does not work at all, or if it has an intermittent fault (see above), it must be replaced.

Replacement

Fuel cut relay

16   With the seat and the left side cover or the rear fairing, as applicable, removed (see Step 3 above), switch the ignition OFF and unplug the relay's wiring connector, then slip the relay out of its rubber sleeve and withdraw it.

17   Installation is the reverse of removal.

Fuel pump

Warning: *Gasoline (petrol) is extremely flammable, so take extra precautions when you work on any part of the fuel system. Don't smoke or allow open flames or bare light bulbs near the work area, and don't work in a garage where a natural gas-type appliance (such as a water heater or clothes dryer) is present. If you spill any fuel on your skin, rinse it off immediately with soap and water. When you perform any kind of work on the fuel system, wear safety glasses and have a fire extinguisher suitable for a Class B type fire (flammable liquids) on hand. Refer also to the warnings given in Section 1 of Chapter 4 before starting work.*

18   With the seat and the left side cover or the rear fairing, as applicable, removed (see Step 3 above), ensure that the ignition is switched OFF, then switch OFF the fuel tap.

19   Disconnect the battery negative (-) terminal to prevent the risk of sparks due to short-circuits, then disconnect the pump's wires and release the wiring from any clamps or ties securing it to the subframe/seat rail.

20   Either label the pump's inlet and outlet hoses or make written notes to identify them and the pump stub to which they are connected before disconnecting them. Wrapping a shop towel around the pump to soak up any spilt fuel, use a pair of pliers to slacken the securing clamps, then disconnect each hose from the pump and plug it immediately to minimize the loss of fuel and to prevent the entry of dirt into the carburetors or filter.

21   Unbolt and remove the fuel pump.

22   Installation is the reverse of removal; ensure that the pump's hoses and wiring are correctly reconnected and securely fastened. Reconnect the battery, start the engine and check the pump's hose connections very carefully, looking for any signs of fuel leaks. When you are sure that there are no leaks, install the rear fairing or side cover and seat.

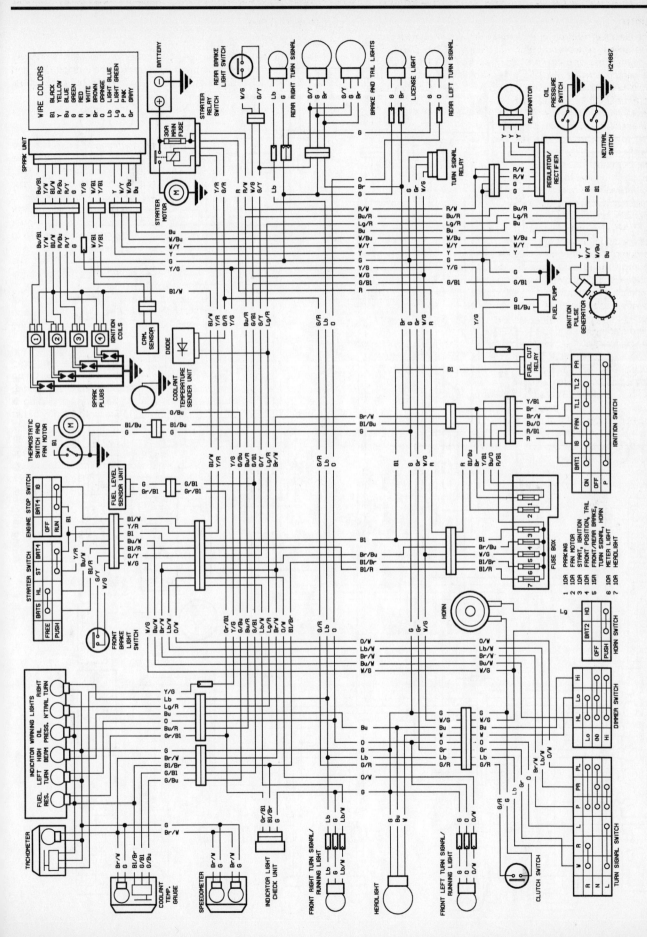

Wiring diagram - US 1986 VFR700F and VFR750F

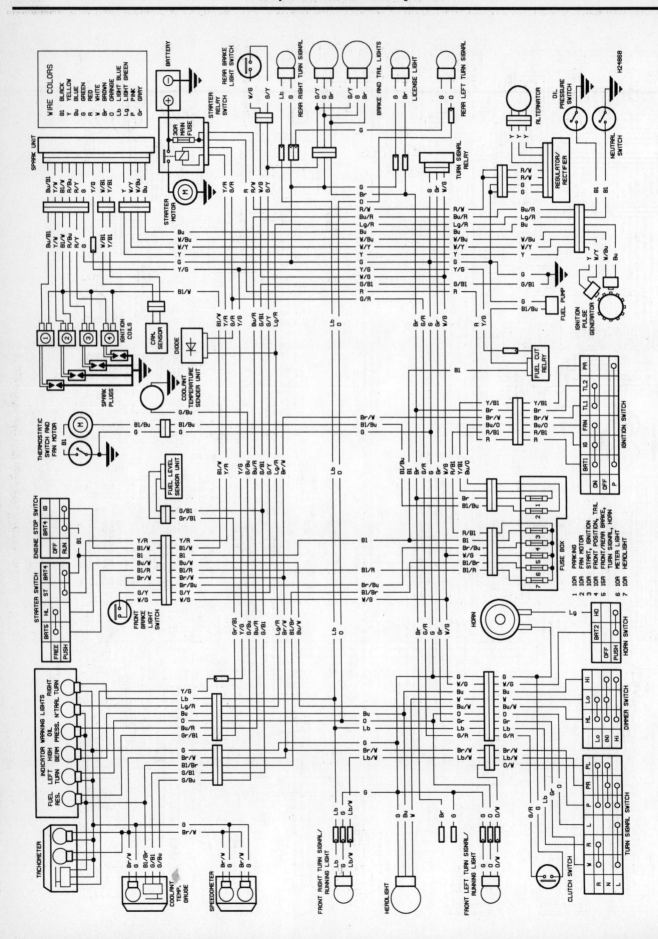

Wiring diagram - US 1986 VFR700F-II

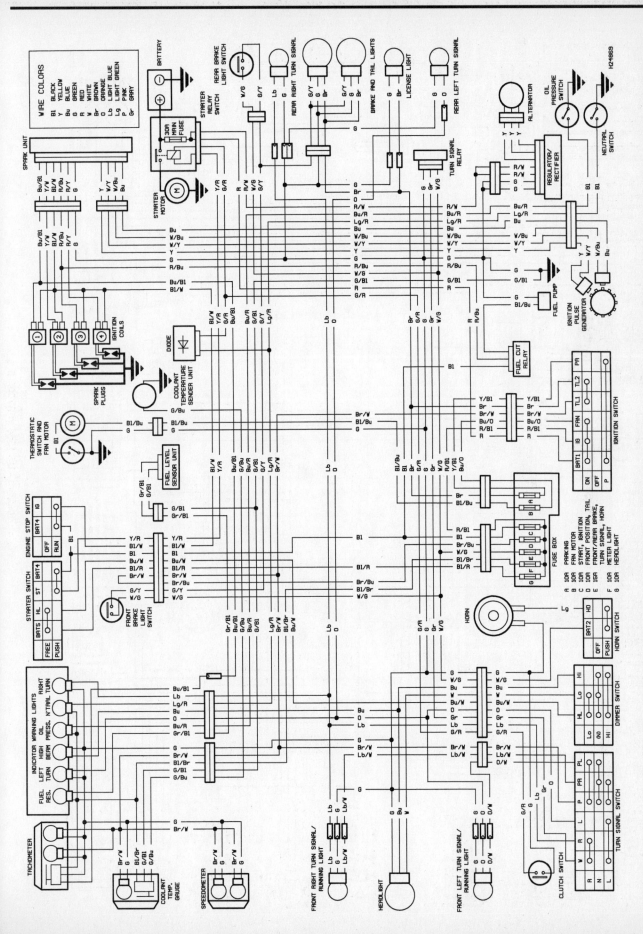

Wiring diagram - US 1987 VFR700F-II

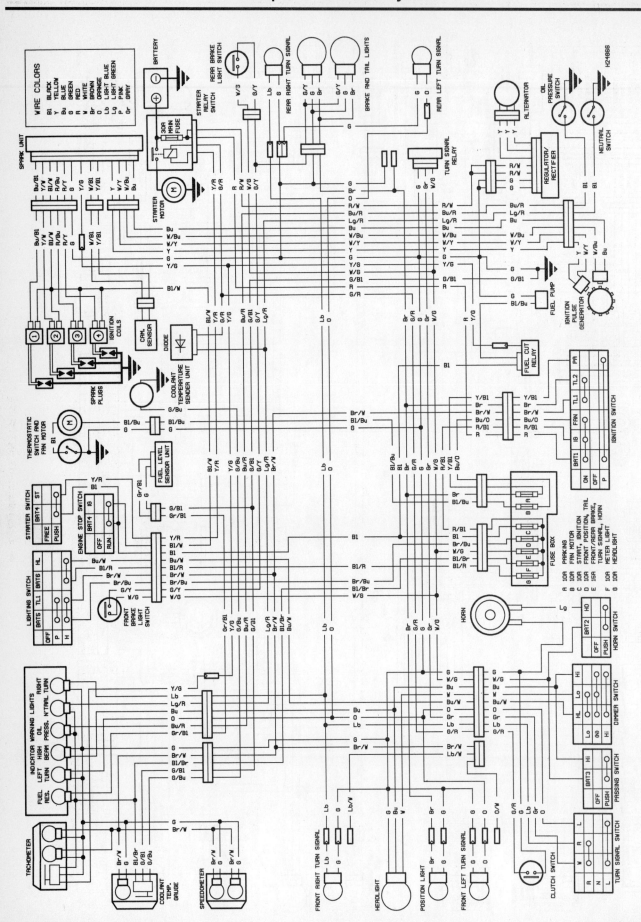

Wiring diagram - UK VFR750F-G

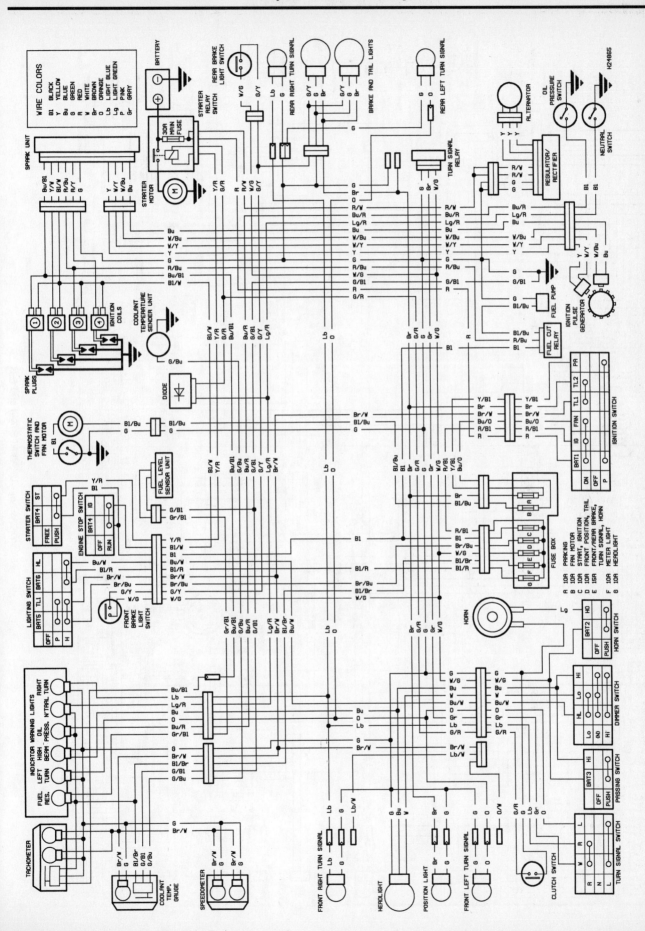

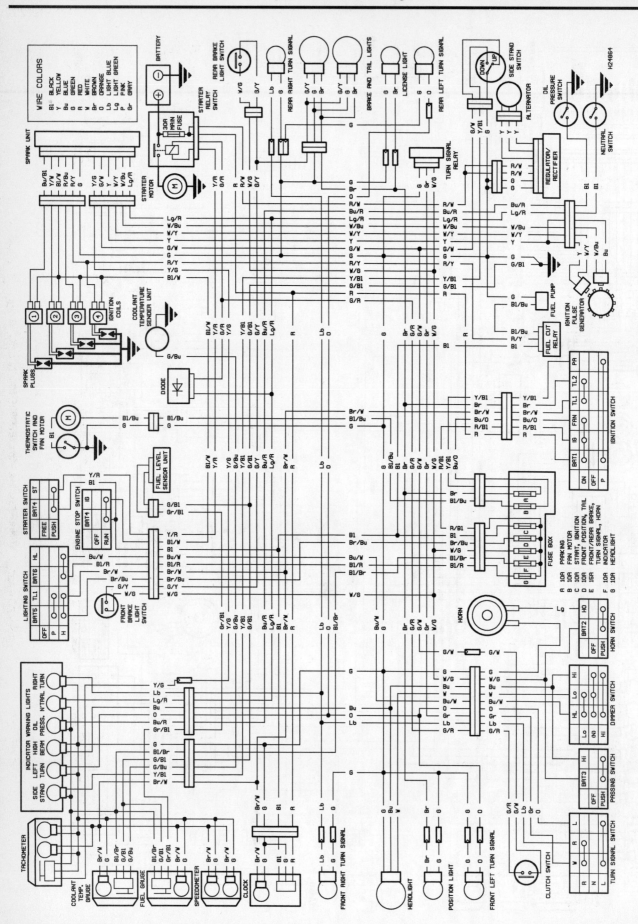

Wiring diagram - UK VFR750F-J and F-K

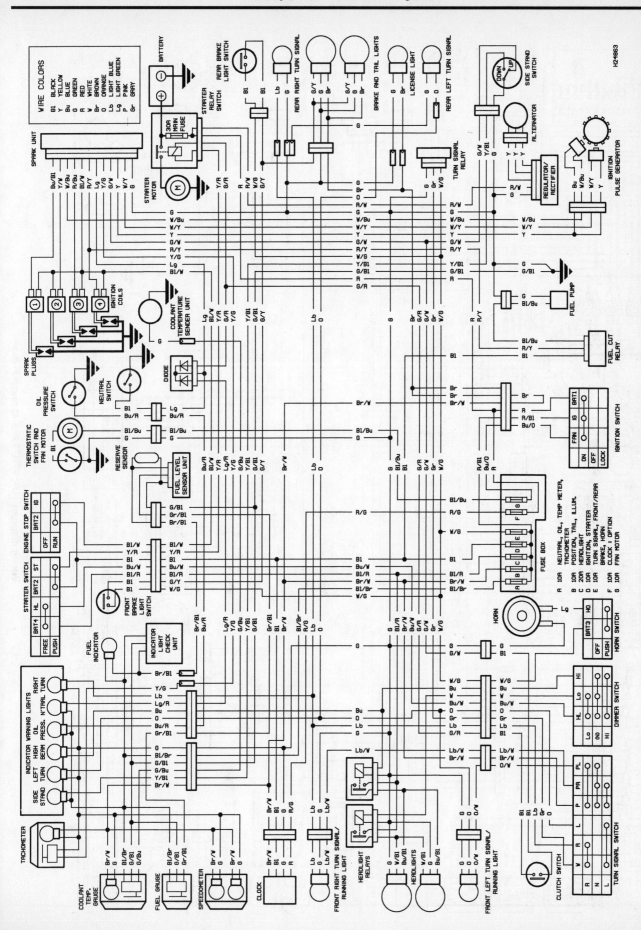

Wiring diagram - US VFR750F-L through F-P (1990 through 1993)

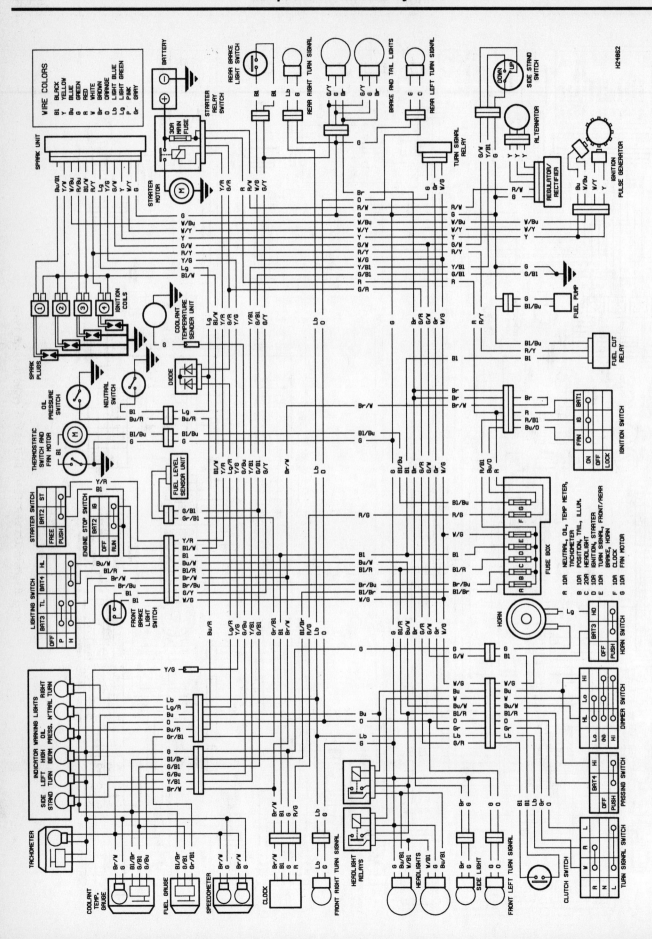

Wiring diagram - UK VFR750F-L through F-P

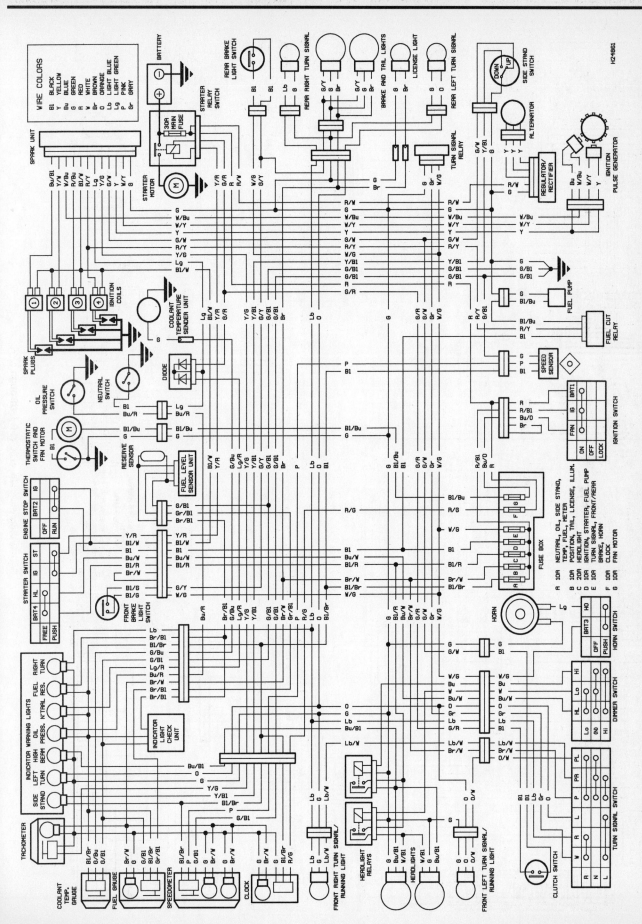

Wiring diagram - US VFR750F-R (1994)

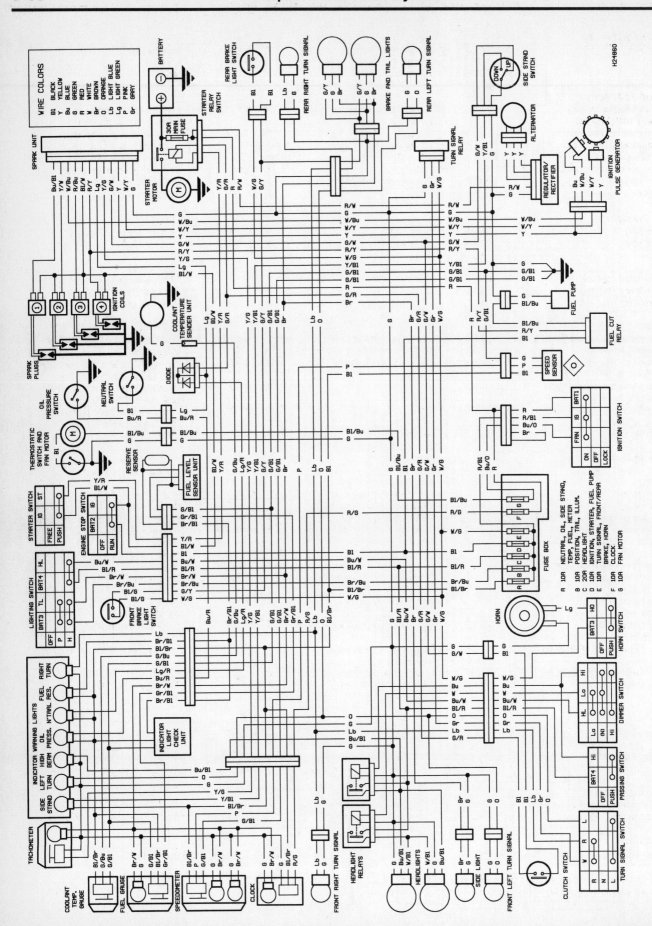

Wiring diagram - UK VFR750F-R

Conversion factors

Length (distance)
	X		=		X		=	
Inches (in)	X	25.4	=	Millimetres (mm)	X	0.0394	=	Inches (in)
Feet (ft)	X	0.305	=	Metres (m)	X	3.281	=	Feet (ft)
Miles	X	1.609	=	Kilometres (km)	X	0.621	=	Miles

Volume (capacity)
	X		=		X		=	
Cubic inches (cu in; in³)	X	16.387	=	Cubic centimetres (cc; cm³)	X	0.061	=	Cubic inches (cu in; in³)
Imperial pints (Imp pt)	X	0.568	=	Litres (l)	X	1.76	=	Imperial pints (Imp pt)
Imperial quarts (Imp qt)	X	1.137	=	Litres (l)	X	0.88	=	Imperial quarts (Imp qt)
Imperial quarts (Imp qt)	X	1.201	=	US quarts (US qt)	X	0.833	=	Imperial quarts (Imp qt)
US quarts (US qt)	X	0.946	=	Litres (l)	X	1.057	=	US quarts (US qt)
Imperial gallons (Imp gal)	X	4.546	=	Litres (l)	X	0.22	=	Imperial gallons (Imp gal)
Imperial gallons (Imp gal)	X	1.201	=	US gallons (US gal)	X	0.833	=	Imperial gallons (Imp gal)
US gallons (US gal)	X	3.785	=	Litres (l)	X	0.264	=	US gallons (US gal)

Mass (weight)
	X		=		X		=	
Ounces (oz)	X	28.35	=	Grams (g)	X	0.035	=	Ounces (oz)
Pounds (lb)	X	0.454	=	Kilograms (kg)	X	2.205	=	Pounds (lb)

Force
	X		=		X		=	
Ounces-force (ozf; oz)	X	0.278	=	Newtons (N)	X	3.6	=	Ounces-force (ozf; oz)
Pounds-force (lbf; lb)	X	4.448	=	Newtons (N)	X	0.225	=	Pounds-force (lbf; lb)
Newtons (N)	X	0.1	=	Kilograms-force (kgf; kg)	X	9.81	=	Newtons (N)

Pressure
	X		=		X		=	
Pounds-force per square inch (psi; lbf/in²; lb/in²)	X	0.070	=	Kilograms-force per square centimetre (kgf/cm²; kg/cm²)	X	14.223	=	Pounds-force per square inch (psi; lbf/in²; lb/in²)
Pounds-force per square inch (psi; lbf/in²; lb/in²)	X	0.068	=	Atmospheres (atm)	X	14.696	=	Pounds-force per square inch (psi; lbf/in²; lb/in²)
Pounds-force per square inch (psi; lbf/in²; lb/in²)	X	0.069	=	Bars	X	14.5	=	Pounds-force per square inch (psi; lbf/in²; lb/in²)
Pounds-force per square inch (psi; lbf/in²; lb/in²)	X	6.895	=	Kilopascals (kPa)	X	0.145	=	Pounds-force per square inch (psi; lbf/in²; lb/in²)
Kilopascals (kPa)	X	0.01	=	Kilograms-force per square centimetre (kgf/cm²; kg/cm²)	X	98.1	=	Kilopascals (kPa)
Millibar (mbar)	X	100	=	Pascals (Pa)	X	0.01	=	Millibar (mbar)
Millibar (mbar)	X	0.0145	=	Pounds-force per square inch (psi; lbf/in²; lb/in²)	X	68.947	=	Millibar (mbar)
Millibar (mbar)	X	0.75	=	Millimetres of mercury (mmHg)	X	1.333	=	Millibar (mbar)
Millibar (mbar)	X	0.401	=	Inches of water (inH₂O)	X	2.491	=	Millibar (mbar)
Millimetres of mercury (mmHg)	X	0.535	=	Inches of water (inH₂O)	X	1.868	=	Millimetres of mercury (mmHg)
Inches of water (inH₂O)	X	0.036	=	Pounds-force per square inch (psi; lbf/in²; lb/in²)	X	27.68	=	Inches of water (inH₂O)

Torque (moment of force)
	X		=		X		=	
Pounds-force inches (lbf in; lb in)	X	1.152	=	Kilograms-force centimetre (kgf cm; kg cm)	X	0.868	=	Pounds-force inches (lbf in; lb in)
Pounds-force inches (lbf in; lb in)	X	0.113	=	Newton metres (Nm)	X	8.85	=	Pounds-force inches (lbf in; lb in)
Pounds-force inches (lbf in; lb in)	X	0.083	=	Pounds-force feet (lbf ft; lb ft)	X	12	=	Pounds-force inches (lbf in; lb in)
Pounds-force feet (lbf ft; lb ft)	X	0.138	=	Kilograms-force metres (kgf m; kg m)	X	7.233	=	Pounds-force feet (lbf ft; lb ft)
Pounds-force feet (lbf ft; lb ft)	X	1.356	=	Newton metres (Nm)	X	0.738	=	Pounds-force feet (lbf ft; lb ft)
Newton metres (Nm)	X	0.102	=	Kilograms-force metres (kgf m; kg m)	X	9.804	=	Newton metres (Nm)

Power
	X		=		X		=	
Horsepower (hp)	X	745.7	=	Watts (W)	X	0.0013	=	Horsepower (hp)

Velocity (speed)
	X		=		X		=	
Miles per hour (miles/hr; mph)	X	1.609	=	Kilometres per hour (km/hr; kph)	X	0.621	=	Miles per hour (miles/hr; mph)

Fuel consumption*
	X		=		X		=	
Miles per gallon, Imperial (mpg)	X	0.354	=	Kilometres per litre (km/l)	X	2.825	=	Miles per gallon, Imperial (mpg)
Miles per gallon, US (mpg)	X	0.425	=	Kilometres per litre (km/l)	X	2.352	=	Miles per gallon, US (mpg)

Temperature

Degrees Fahrenheit = (°C x 1.8) + 32

Degrees Celsius (Degrees Centigrade; °C) = (°F - 32) x 0.56

*It is common practice to convert from miles per gallon (mpg) to litres/100 kilometres (l/100km), where mpg (Imperial) x l/100 km = 282 and mpg (US) x l/100 km = 235

Index